Y0-AAI-945

PARALLEL PROCESSING AND ARTIFICIAL INTELLIGENCE

COMMUNICATING PROCESS ARCHITECTURE

Series Editor: David May, INMOS Ltd, UK

Parallel Processing and Artificial Intelligence
Mike Reeve and Steven Ericsson Zenith (eds)

PARALLEL PROCESSING AND ARTIFICIAL INTELLIGENCE

Edited by
Mike Reeve,
Imperial College of Science and Technology, London, UK
Steven Ericsson Zenith,
INMOS Ltd, Bristol, UK

COMMUNICATING PROCESS ARCHITECTURE

JOHN WILEY & SONS
Chichester · New York · Brisbane · Toronto · Singapore

Other Wiley Editorial Offices

John Wiley & Sons, Inc., 605 Third Avenue,
New York, NY 10158-0012, USA

Jacaranda Wiley Ltd, G.P.O. Box 859, Brisbane,
Queensland 4001, Australia

John Wiley & Sons (Canada) Ltd, 22 Worcester Road,
Rexdale, Ontario M9W 1L1, Canada

John Wiley & Sons (SEA) Pte Ltd, 37 Jalan Pemimpin 05-04,
Block B, Union Industrial Building, Singapore 2057

British Library Cataloguing in Publication Data available:

ISBN 0 471 92497 0

Printed and bound in Great Britain by Courier International,
Tiptree, Essex

Preface

Parallel Processing and Artificial Intelligence

Parallel Processing and Artificial Intelligence are two key themes which have risen to the fore of technology in the past decade. This carefully selected collection of invited and submitted papers brings together the very best researchers currently working in the field.

This book arises from an international conference held at Imperial College, London on the 17th and 18th of July 1989 entitled *Communicating Process Architecture and Artificial Intelligence*. The objective of the conference was to bring together the two communities of parallel processing and artificial intelligence. Indeed, as the papers for the conference came in and the interests of the editors combined, it became clear that the conference would more appropriately have been titled *Parallel Processing and Artificial Intelligence*, and that is how we chose to entitle this book.

The topics covered span much of the spectrum in the field of artificial intelligence, with new contributions made to the field of parallel processing. Artificial intelligence topics covered include: neural networks, robotics, image understanding, parallel implementations of logic languages, parallel implementation of Lisp.

Many of the papers here detail use of the INMOS transputer. However, it is parallelism in its broader sense that is the issue here, and not just the Communicating Process Architecture on which the INMOS transputer was founded. Even so, it is clear from this collection of papers that the transputer has been a major stimulant in many areas of Artificial Intelligence.

In the course of developing next generation components for parallel machines, it is events such as this conference which have a profound influence. This is what INMOS gains by promoting such an event; contact with the experience of a community which seeks to apply parallelism to the most demanding applications. For many, Communicating Process Architecture is just the starting point.

Communicating Process Architecture is one of the most successful models for exploiting the potential power of parallel processing machines. Artificial Intelligence is perhaps the most challenging applications for such machines. This book explores the interaction between these two technologies, and seeks to further the parallel architecture debate.

The invited papers

The following list provides brief biographic details of the authors of the invited papers.

Prof. Igor Aleksander *Myths and Realities about Neural Computing Architectures.*

Professor Igor Aleksander is Head of the Electrical Engineering Department at Imperial College, where he is also Professor of Neural Systems Engineering. He is one of the worlds leading researchers in Neural Computing Architectures and has been developing usable systems since 1965.

He was responsible for the design and transfer into industry of WISARD; the worlds first general purpose neural system directed at vision problems. He has written 14 books and over 100 papers in the area. He was Chairman of the British Pattern Recognition Association, Kelvin Lecturer of IEE and has held several distinguished visiting posts all over the world.

Prof. Colin Besant *Application of Artificial Intelligence to the Programming of Robots.*

Colin Besant is Professor of Computer-Aided Manufacture in the Department of Mechanical Engineering at Imperial College. His interests are predominantly in the field of flexible Manufacturing Systems including Robotics. His research concentrates on the programming of manufacturing systems in order to achieve a high degree of flexibility in terms of manufacturing batch size and past variety. Artificial Intelligence plays an increasing role in this research in the scheduling of manufacturing systems and in robotics, where problems of collision avoidance, path planning and grasping require a solution.

Professor Besant is also a director of RD Projects Ltd, which is a spin off company from Imperial College specialising in control of machine tools, robots and manufacturing systems.

Prof. David Gelernter *Information Management in Linda.*

David Gelernter is an associate professor of computer science at Yale. He works on parallelism, on heuristic programming (particularly medical applications) and on the overlap between the two. As a graduate student at SUNY Stony Brook he designed a parallel programming system called Linda; several years ago he and his colleagues built the first working version at Yale. The system is now seeing increasingly widespread use, and has been advertised by the heads of two independent parallel-machine startups as an "emerging industry standard" (which it isn't – yet).

David Gelernter continues to develop Linda, and is working also on "symmetric languages", a class of languages which make no distinction between program structures and data objects. His work in heuristic programming centers on intelligent monitoring systems and on expert inferencing from databases.

He has published widely in the usual technical places, and has written for general audiences (e.g. Scientific American, Byte) as well. He was editor of IEEE Computer's 1986 special issue on parallel programming languages, program committee chairman for ACM's first symposium on Parallel Programming (1988), is the author of forthcoming books on programming language design (with Suresh Jagannathan) and parallel programming (with Nicholas Carriero), and continues to be involved in the growth of parallelism as a field within computer science.

Dr. Atsuhiro Goto *Research and Development of the Parallel Inference Machine in the FGCS Project.*

Dr Goto is a Senior Researcher at the Institute for New Computer Technology (ICOT) Tokyo, which he joined in August 1985. He is conducting research and development of parallel inference machine architecture. His current research interests include parallel architectures for parallel logic programming languages, garbage collection, memory architectures and parallel programming.

Atsuhiro Goto recieved the B.S. degree in electrical engineering from the University of Tokyo, Japan in 1979, and the M.S. and Ph.D degrees in information engineering from the University of Tokyo in 1981 and in 1984. His dissertation work was concerned with the goal-rewriting model for the highly parallel inference engine and its architecture.

Prof. Tosiyasu Kunii *A Communicating Process Architecture Model of Primitive Image Understanding - A Case Study.*

Tosiyasu L. Kunii is currently Professor of Information and Computer Science, at the University of Tokyo. He began his work in raster computer graphics at the University in 1968, which led to the Tokyo Raster Technology Project. His particular research interest is in the elements of artificial intelligence to recognize and create images. He has authored and edited more than 25 computer science books, and published more than 100 refereed papers and articles in computer science and applications.

Professor Kunii is former President and Founder of the Computer Graphics Society, Editor-in-Chief of *The Visual Computer: An International Journal of Computer Graphics* and on the Editorial Board of *IEEE Computer Graphics and Applications.* He is a member of the IFIP Data Base Working Group, and the IFIP Computer Graphics Working Group. He organized and chaired the Technical Committee on Software Engineering of the Information Processing Society of Japan from 1976 to 1981. He also organised and was President of the Japan Computer Graphics Association (JCGA) from 1981 to 1983. He served as General Chairman of the 3rd International Conference on Very Large Data Bases (VLDB) in 1977, Program Chairman of InterGraphics '83, Organising Committee Chairman and Programme Chairman of Computer Graphics Tokyo in 1984, Programme Chairman of Computer Graphics Tokyo in 1985 and 1986, Organising Committee Chairperson and Programme Chairperson of CG International '87, Programme Co-Chairman of COMPSAC '87, and Honorary Committe Chairman of CG International '88. He is serving as Organising Committee Chairman of IFIP TC-2 Working Conference on Visual Database Systems to be held in 1989.

Professor Kunii is also chairman of the Occam User Group in Japan.

Dr. Rajiv Trehan *Concurrent Logic Languages for the design and implementation of Parallel AI Systems.*

Rajiv Trehan has been working for the last four year in the area of parallel declarative systems within the Department of Artificial Intelligence, Edinburgh. His research activities include: hardware support for large knowledge bases; concurrent logic languages, like PARLOG, GHC and Concurrent Prolog; distributed Artificial Intelligence and parallel architectures. This work has formed the basis of his PhD, which is an investigation of the concurrent logic languages and how they support Artificial Intelligence programming techniques and applications. Much of his work has been adopted by the Parallel Architectures Laboratory, Artificial Intelligence Applications Institute (AIAI), Edinburgh. This has produced demonstrators, the AIAI parallel logic languages starter package, and a course on parallel logic languages and Artificial Intelligence.

Rajiv Trehan obtained his first degree from King's College London in Mathematics and Physics, and worked for a period for Marconi in real time computer simulation. Prior to his PhD he obtained an MSc in Computer Systems from Edinburgh.

Prof. Les Valiant *Bulk-synchronous Parallel Computing.*

Professor Leslie G. Valiant is currently Gordon McKay Professor of Computer Science and Applied Mathemmatics at Harvard University. His current research interests are computational complexity, machine learning and the theory of parallel algorithms and architectures. In 1986 he received the Navanlinna prize for theory of information processing from the International Mathematical Union.

Professor Valiant holds a BA degree in mathematics from Kingsd College, Cambridge, a Diploma in Computing Science from Imperial College, London, and a Ph.D. in Computer Science from Warwick University. He has taught at Carnegie Mellon, Leeds, and Edinburgh University.

Sadly, not all the invited speakers were able to provide us with copy of their papers before the publication of this book. We understand their busy schedule and forgive them. These speakers were

Prof. Iann Barron of INMOS/SGS-THOMPSON.

John Bridle of RSRE, Cheltenham, UK.

Prof. Alan Robinson of Syracuse University, USA.

Acknowledgements

First thanks are due to Bobby Palmer, a secretary in the Micro-Computer Division of INMOS for her untiring efforts, and to Colin Clark, a technical author at INMOS who managed to find the time amongst his heavy work load to convert all the papers to a common form and to improve the layout and diagrams.

Thanks also to the conference organising committee who diligently reviewed all the papers we received. They were

J.T Amenyo	*Ctr. Telecoms Research, Columbia University.*
Jean-Jacques Codani	*INRIA, France.*
Dr. Atsuhiro Goto	*Institute for New Generation Computer Technology (ICOT), Japan.*
Dr.med.Ulrich Jobst	*Ostertal - Klinik fur Neurologie und Klinische Neurophysiologie*
Dr. Peter Kacsuk	*Multilogic Computing, Budapest, Hungary.*
Pasi Koikkalainen	*Lappeenranta University of Technology, Finland.*
Prof. T. L. Kunii	*The University of Tokyo, Japan.*
Dr. Heather Liddell	*Queen Mary College, London.*
Prof. Y. Paker	*Polytechnic of Central London*
Prof. L. F. Pau	*Technical University of Denmark.*
Prof. Bernd Radig	*Institut Fur Informatik, Munchen.*
Prof. Alan Robinson	*Syracuse University, USA.*
Kai Ming Shea	*University of Hong Kong.*
Prof. David Warren	*Bristol University, UK.*
Chung Zhang	*Brighton Polytechnic. UK.*

Steven Ericsson Zenith
INMOS Limited, Bristol, UK.
June 1, 1989

Contents

Chapter 1

Myths and realities about neural computing architectures

Igor Aleksander
Professor of Neural Systems Engineering
and Head, Department of Electrical Engineering
Imperial College of Science Technology and Medicine,
London.

Abstract The late 1980s will be remembered among computer scientists as the time when something called CONNECTIONISM or NEURAL NETWORKS or PARALLEL DISTRIBUTED PROCESSING really took off.

It turns out that this is not a new field: it is one with a past stretching back further than the invention of the conventional computer. Yet it is only recently that the field has been properly analysed and understood. All the above names are synonyms; they refer to a concern with machines that are like brains even at the structural level, unlike conventional computers. In the late 1960s this neural type of machine design gave way completely to Artificial Intelligence programs running on ordinary computers. These AI programs only simulate limited brain-like behavior, but they take no notice of the mechanisms involved.

In this paper we comment on some of the history of the connectionist way of doing things, give reasons for the revival of interest. Ultimately this has to do with the fact that mechanisms DO matter and, in order to design machines that work well, mechanisms need to be understood. The second half of the paper relates to the author's contributions to architectural studies.

1.1 Why the fuss?

In 1987 the American Institute of Electrical and Electronic Engineering called the first conference on Neural Nets. It took place at San Diego, California. It was described as 'the dawn of a new era'. Two hundred authors presented their papers and 2000 delegates heard them out. These scientists were talking of a kind of computing that is inspired by the cellular networks of living brains. The following year saw even bigger events: more papers and more delegates. So, as far as most computer scientists were concerned, something new was going on.

The feeling was underlined as many computer experts still had a memory of a highly influential book written by Marvin Minsky and Seymour Papert in the late 1960s. This book made major criticisms of what can and cannot be done with neural nets, and effectively put paid to work on this type of brainlike computing. This reminiscence is significant in two ways, first it stresses that there had been work prior to this criticism which then became dormant for about fifteen years, and second, it indicates that something must have been discovered that went beyond the limitations perceived by these two researchers. Indeed, on the first of these counts, the history of neural computing is known to go back further than that of conventional computing and, on the second, John Hopfield had suggested a powerful, new analysis that applied to systems that were neural net-like [Hopfield, 1982]. It was this analysis that led Hinton, Sejnowski & Ackley to solve, in 1984, the major difficulty identified in 1969 by Minsky and Papert. This was done by equating training to gradient-descent optimization.

The 1987 conference had an interdisciplinary flavour not normally known in computer science. Papers were contributed from physicists, biologists, neuropsychologists and statisticians in numbers that equalled the computer scientists. That, indeed, is the character of this science: it defines an interdisciplinary culture which is based on brainlike learning as opposed to traditional computing which is based on programming. The fuss is about the discovery of a computing culture which is distinct from the traditional variety, and which seems likely to open up a realm of new possibilities.

1.2 The conventional computing culture: algorithms

Computers have become so much part of our our lives that we forget that their strucutre is based on just one person's view of the way in which a computational process can be organised. We are referring to John von Neumann's incredibly far-sighted view of the way a computer might work: an arithmetic/logic unit that operates on data held in memory.

Artificial Intelligence makes use of the highest levels of a hierarchy of packaging, to get a computer to do things which if done by humans would be said to require intelligence.

For example, a computer that plays chess merely executes a massive series of instructions such as "if the board state is A, then find all the possible next moves which can be made from state A...". The rules for doing this are arranged in an ordered series of levels. For example, the above instruction is at a "high" level, and needs to be broken up into simpler steps at lower levels. The rules which test a given move, to see whether it is applicable to that particular board state or not, are at a lower level. At an even lower level there are rules that determine the legality of the applicable rules within the conventions of the game of chess, and so on.

The concept that is used at *each* of these levels is the *algorithm*. An algorithm is "a series of steps that achieves a desired aim". Multiplying A by B may require the algorithm: "To achieve A $\times$ B add A to itself B times". Similarly, to make a chess-playing program work, the computer needs algorithms such as "For board state A, test for all applicable rules" and "For each applicable rule and for each board piece to which it applies, apply the rule and store the resulting board state". To win the game, the program must also be given a way of evaluating the listed board states: this too is a series of algorithms.

The central question here is where these algorithms come from. The answer is simple: they are representations of human knowledge. The humble repetition of additions to achieve multiplication is a representation of early knowledge of arithmetic that we learn as children at school. The algorithms that go into an AI chess playing or problem solving program are representations of human knowledge of the rules and strategies of chess or of solving problems. The art of the programmer is that of turning algorithms into code that the computer can understand through a suitable computer language, while the art of the AI scientist is to find algorithms for the forms of computer behavior he is trying to achieve. Complicated hierarchies and interactions between algorithms are what make a computer work, whether it is number-crunching or playing chess. All of these algorithms must be invented and implemented by a human being to give a computer a semblance of intelligence.

The sober implication of this is that the range of what can be done with a conventional computer is limited to those tasks for which a human can find algorithms. This simple fact puts processing in conventional computers apart from the way that human beings process information: the human is capable of developing his behavior through "learning" while the computer has to wait for some human to feed it the steps required to accomplish the desired task.

1.3 The neural computing culture: experience acquisition

Living creatures have no means of being programmed. They are endowed with some predispositions when they are born, but they mostly become viable through a process of gathering 'experience' about the environment they live in through a process of exploration or interaction with other living creatures. Humans have developed sophisticated languages whereby they can interchange experience and this may seem a form of programming. But the difference between this and the discourse one can have with a computer is quite enormous.

A computer is programmed by spelling out to it every step of a process. A human being relates its conversations to experience. When a child is told "be gentle with the new kitten" whether the child obeys this command or not will depend on a whole variety of previous events that the child may have experienced. She may not know what the word 'gentle' means; she may have been scratched by a cat and not wish to approach the kitten at all or she may have previously been rough with a cat which then hissed and ran away. So, stored experience is the basis from which the interaction with the world is interpreted by living creatures.

In many ways, if one's aim is to build machines that work well, doing it by conventional programming seems a more direct and controlled way of doing things. Experience seems to be too closely related to the makeup of an individual and, if this mode were to exist in machines, it might lead to individualistic and enigmatic devices. Their control might become expensive and unreliable. But neural computing is *not* about building humanoid machines: it is about discovering *how* machines might store and use experience, should this be necessary to the design devices with skills that cannot be achieved by programmming. Are there such skills?

1.4 Where experience scores over programming

The years between the mid 1960s and the mid 1980s was a time of great euphoria and confidence among those working in artificial intelligence laboratories. The programming style seemed set to conquer a vast variety of tasks which "if done by humans would be said to require intelligence" (as defined earlier). Programming rules were being discovered that could look for *good* moves at chess rather than exhaustively looking at all possible moves; general methods of solving clearly stated problems were being developed; robot planning programs were shown to be feasible and algorithms were being developed that would extract meaning from sentences input into the computer in something that resembles natural language.

The first warning signs were sounded in 1973 in a review by Sir James Lighthill in the UK. He pointed out that most of these methods relied on getting the computer to sift through vast amounts of data and that the techniques were being tested on highly restricted "toy-like" problems. He foresaw that applying the methods to real problems would require a growth rate for computer power and speed which was greater than that which was conceivable: he called it the "combinatorial explosion". It is this graphic notion of the computer having slavishly to search through myriads of possibilities that begins to point to the limitations of the programming approach. When a person sees an old friend she does not search a database of stored images of all the people she knows. The recognition, if it happens at all, is almost instantaneous. So the brain does not succumb to the combinatorial explosion. The suggested search through stored images too is a totally fruitless algorithm. The face may be older, distorted by a grimace or partly obscured by hair — how then does one effect a match with similar faces stored in memory?

In recent years, much work in artificial intelligence has been tidied up under the heading of "expert systems". An expert system is an algorithmic method for trying to capture experience by having two standard components: a memorised list of rules and ways of inferring conclusions from these rules and some supplied facts in order to answer a questioner's questions.

Going back to vision tasks such as face recognition, the key point is that there are no obvious rule sets that can equal the performance of the brain in important tasks such as recognizing a friend, or reacting rapidly to a dangerous situation while driving. A typical example of a task that has unfortunately proved the stumbling block for the application of expert systems is the provision of guidance to unmanned vehicles from the image "seen" by a computer through a television camera. Such vehicles might be important in the exploration of dangerous or remote areas. Is the image in figure 1.1a a road or a tree? Notice how once little clues are added in figures 1.1b and 1.1c, it is easier to decide that 1.1b is a tree, and 1.1c is a road. Of course, rules could be developed to distinguish between these images, but the occurrence of each slightly different distinguishing clue would require the addition of yet another rule.

Thus a seemingly endless explosion of rules seems to be inevitable whenever the algorithmic approach is applied to this type of input, making the understanding of images and speech the veritable Achilles' heels of algorithmic, rule-based methods.

Human beings find these tasks easy, and all they have to go on is their experience stored in a mass of interconnected brain cells (neurons). The "computing" that these devices muster is clearly different in kind from the algorithmic, rule-based method. So the quest for investigators of neural nets is to identify how it is that these networks are capable of storing and using experience.

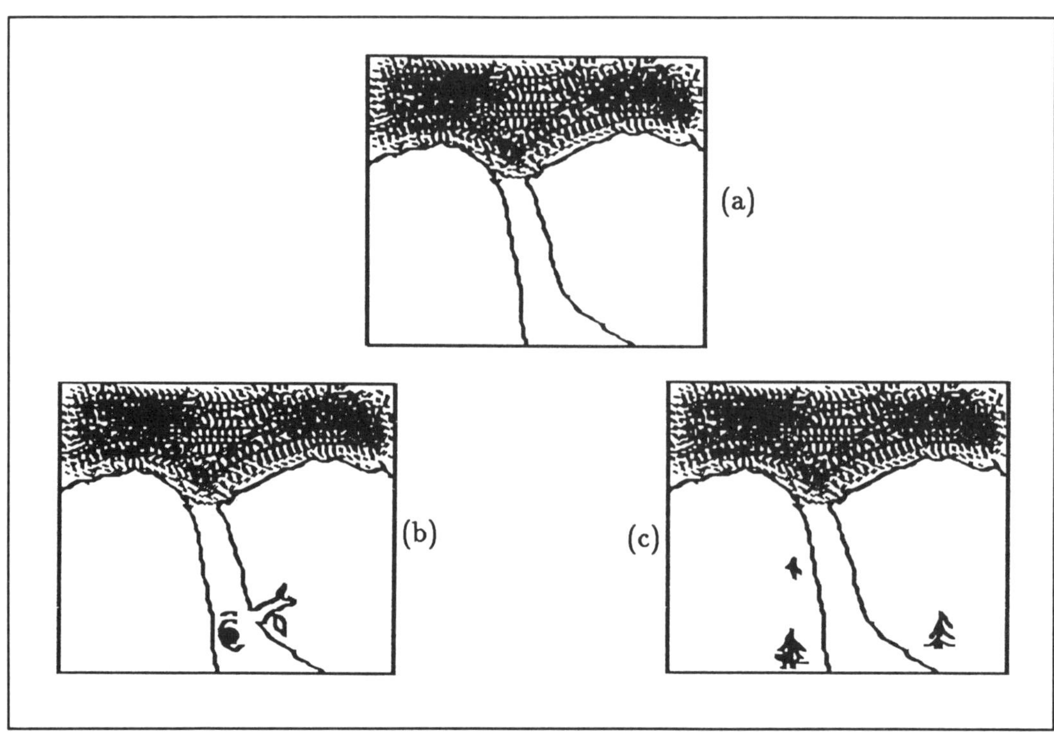

Figure 1.1:

1.5 Turing, others and brains

Many will be aware of the fact that in 1936 Alan Turing laid down the principles for defining what is and what is not computable. But not so many will be aware of the fact that Turing was highly conscious of the fact that brains do their computations in ways that do not depend on algorithms [Turing, 1936]. He wrote of the way in which the brain did its computations through cycles of activity in neural nets. He rejected this as a way of thinking about computing machines solely because it did not help with theorizing about computable numbers, which was the subject that motivated his personal interest in theoretical computing machines.

Indeed John von Neumann, also talked of neural nets, seeing them as providing a way of doing computations that emerge from the structure of the net itself. Notable is his concept of 'Self-reproducing automata' [Burks/von Neumann, 1966] where neural structures are analysed for their ability to transfer a behavior that takes place in one part of a net to another part of the net. Norbert Wiener, whose name is associated with the definition of Cybernetics (a study of communication and control in man and machine), saw the interplay of logic and network structure as being fundamental to a mathematical understanding of computation in both brains and machines [Wiener, 1946].

So it seems that the algorithmic method has always been seen as the well-behaved, predictable end of mathematical descriptions of computing, while the neural mode has always been seen as the less predictable but nonetheless powerful way of carrying out computations. Indeed, it has always been recognised that the latter has properties that emerge from the structure of the net, a topic that is only now being properly discussed.

So how is it that the algorithmic methodology has shot ahead so fast, and neural work lain largely dormant for so long? The answer (puting the Minsky and Papert objection aside) lies in the stress put on the technique by Hopfield: the timeliness of achieving content addressable, experience storage in silicon. In what follows we describe in some detail a particular approach to this: the logic approach.

1.6 The role of hardware

There is no doubt that the future promise of neural systems can only be exploited by the hardware implementation of such sytems. Emulations and simulations are too slow and only marginally compete with conventional computing. Most current effort on hardware implementation is based on McCulloch and Pitts (MCP) model which carries a major problem of implementing what are essentially analog weight memories. This can be done with clever circuit tricks often based on charge retention on capacitors and the use of operational amplifiers. This hardly follows in the wake of the opportunities created by VLSI. Were the weights to be made digitally, the line of argument taken by the author and his team goes back over more than 20 years and develops as follows.

Rather than modelling the MCP function it uses the variable function properties of a Random Access Memory to make the RAM the node of a net. In this paper this argument is explained in some detail, as the philosophy has already led to the world's first neural machine containing 250,000 nodes: the WISARD. The prototype was built in 1981, and a commercial version appeared in 1984. This gives the industry/university team involved an important perspective on the future based on real, industrial experiance.

1.7 What is the WISARD?

WISARD stands for **WI**lkie, **S**tonham and **A**leksander's **R**ecognition **D**evice. It is an adaptive pattern recognition machine which is based on neural principles. The prototype was completed in 1981 at Brunel University in London by a team under the direction of the author (IA). Subsequently the machine was patented, and produced commercially in 1984. The object of this paper is to examine the principles on which these machines are based. The history of these principles goes back to 1965, when IA suggested that a simple memory device (which, nowdays would be called a RAM: random-access memory) has neural-like properties.

Broadly, the difference between an MCP node and a RAM node is that the RAM can perform all the functions of the inputs and does not generalise. This makes it appear to be a less interesting device than the MCP. However ***networks of RAM nodes*** do generalise and this makes them as interesting as networks of MCP nodes, if not more. The main advantage of the RAM node, is that systems may be built using conventional digital circuitry, without the need to develop special VLSI devices. It can also be shown that learning in such systems is much faster than in the MCP variety.

1.8 The RAM node

The random-access memory is the silicon building brick of the local memory of any modern computer. It is the component which in conjunction with the silicon processing chip has been responsible for the microprocessor revolution. Prior to the early 1970s the salient way of achieving local memory in a computer was by means of intricately threaded ferrite rings. Such systems were bulky, expensive and limited in capacity. The advent of the silicon RAM transformed the computer industry. The cost and capacity of such chips has been improving spectacularly, where the cost of an armchair would buy one chip containing about 100 bits of memory in 1970, the same cost in 1989 buys about 10,000,000 bits of memory distributed over a handful of chips. Designing neurocomputers which exploit this development is therefore more promising for the achievement of usable machines of significant capacity than relying on node designs that still require VLSI development. Figure 1.2 is a simplified diagram of the way in which a RAM operates. This is not the description of any particular circuit, it is merely intended to clarify an explanation of what a RAM does. For a typical, commercially available RAM chip, M is 8 (making the chip "byte-oriented" — a byte being eight bits) and N could be 18. Normally this would be called a 256 Kilobyte RAM, as 2^{18} is 262,144, but it is conventional to name these devices with the first three digits of the nearest power of 2 which, in this case, is 256.

In order to relate the RAM to the neuron, two steps need to be taken. First, it is noted that, taking one column of the memory registers at a time, the values of this column can be set independently, and represent precisely the truth table of a logic device with one output. Therefore a RAM with M bits in the memory register, can be thought of as M RAMs each with one bit per memory register, connected to the same N input variables. This notion is shown in figure 1.3a. The second step is to concentrate only on one of these one-bit-per-word RAMs as shown in figure 1.3b. Clearly, the data-in memory has not been shown, and the data out memory of one bit is assumed to be resident inside the boundary of the RAM.

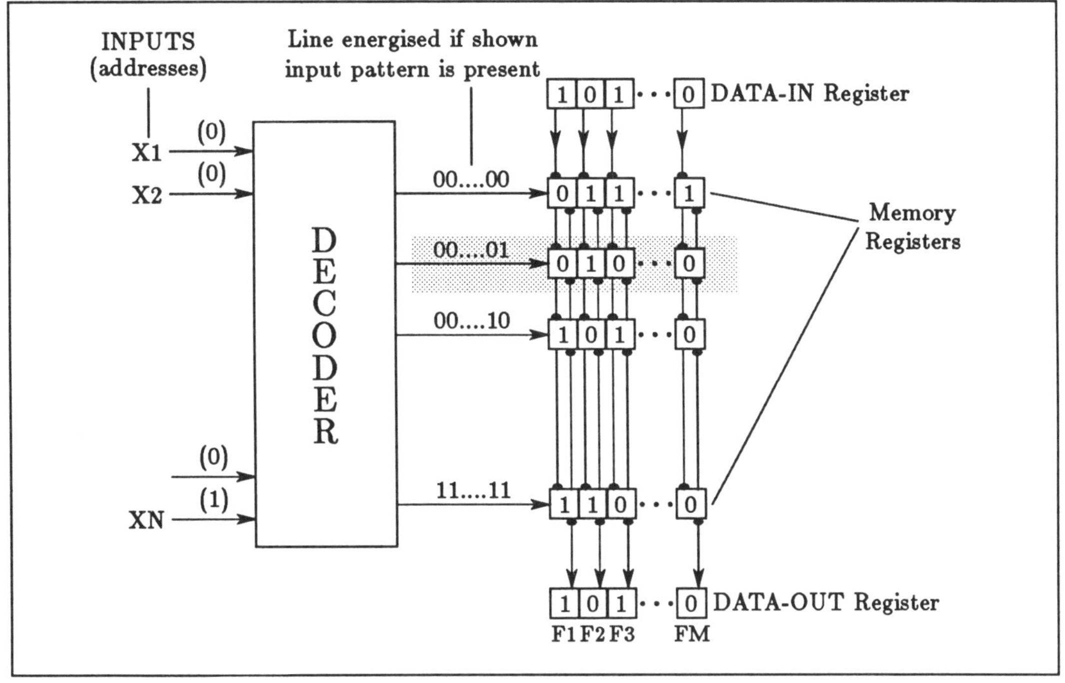

Figure 1.2:

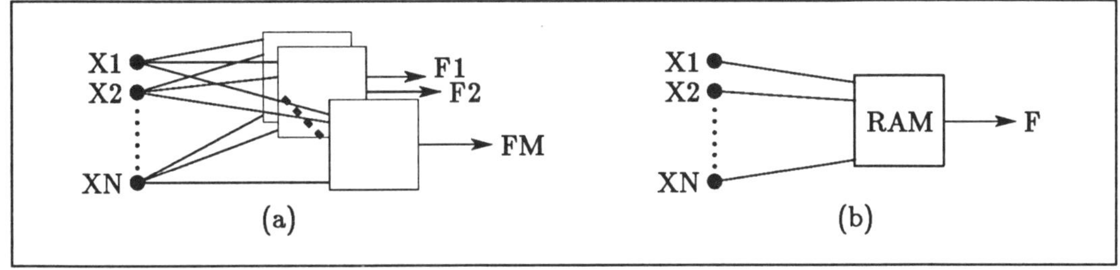

Figure 1.3:

So, the sense in which figure 1.3b **is like a neuron**, is that given an input at X1 to XN, and a desired output at the data-in terminal, setting the RAM into the reading mode will cause it to "learn" this desired response. This can be overwritten by a subsequent training step.

The sense in which figure 1.3b **is not like a neuron**, is that there is no need for a sophisticated training algorithm, as the setting for one input does not affect another, therefore, what has been described in the last paragraph IS the training algorithm. Also, there is no generalisation in the RAM itself. This is mistakenly seen as a disadvantage. It is shown from here on that *networks* of RAMs have generalisation which is similar to networks of neurons.

1.9 The RAM discriminator

The simplest RAM network with properties of generalisation is called a discriminator and is shown in figure 1.4. This consists of K RAMs with N inputs each. This single layer receives a binary pattern of KN bits. It is assumed that before any training takes place, all the memory cells in the RAMs are set to 0. Training consists of placing a pattern of 0s and 1s at the input terminals (as an example of a pattern in a class to be learnt by the discriminator) and placing a 1 into the memory location of each RAM addressed by the input pattern. This is done for other patterns of the same class. When an unknown pattern is later presented at the input, the summing device designated $\sum$, produces a number which is equal to the number of RAMs that output a 1.

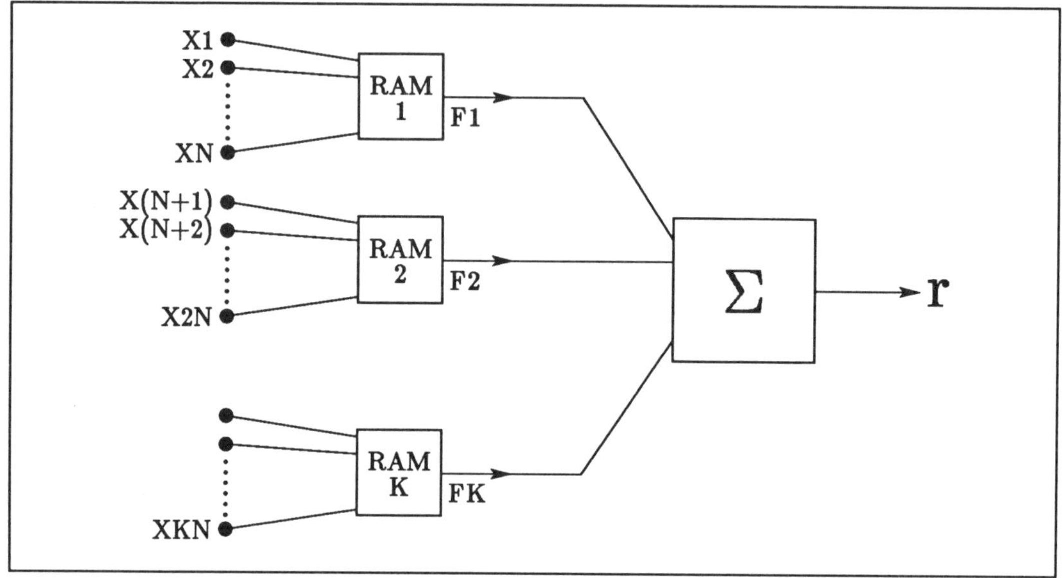

Figure 1.4:

This number is said to be the ***response*** of the discriminator and given the symbol **r**. Clearly, if one of the training patterns were to be entered at the input of the net, it would find storage locations that contain a 1 in each of the RAMs and therefore **r** would have a value of K. Whereas if the unknown input pattern were to be totally different from any of the training patterns, in the sense that no RAM would receive an individual input on which it had been trained, then the value of **r** becomes 0. Therefore, **r** is, in some way, a measure the similarity of an unknown pattern to each of the patterns in the training set. It is quite possible, but beyond the scope of this paper to predict this response if the geometry of the patterns concerned is known. Basically this shows that high values of N give high discrimination and low generalisation.

1.10 Multi-discriminator systems: the WISARD

A multi-discriminator system has each of its discriminators trained to a different class of object. If the task is one of recognising the hand-printed letters of the alphabet, say, then the scheme would contain 26 discriminators, one for each letter. The notion of a multi-discriminator system is quite general and takes the form shown in figure 1.5. The WISARD is a hardware implementation of this scheme directed towards the recognition of images. We asume that there are G discriminators, each of which covers a binary "image" with K RAMs of N address inputs each.

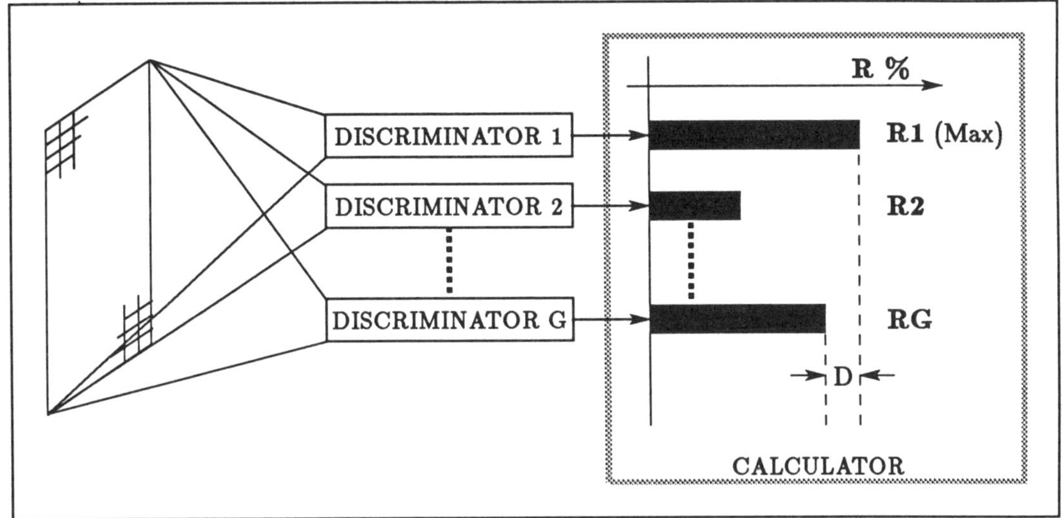

Figure 1.5:

It is assumed that at the start of any training regime, all the RAMs of all the discriminators are set to 0. The training consists of making the discriminator appropriate to the desired class output all 1s. Say that a 26-discriminator system is being trained to recognise hand-printed characters, that the system is currently being trained to recognise a hand-printed letter A, and that discriminator 1 is designated to recognise As. Then discriminator 1 is trained to respond with a 1 at all the RAMs it possesses. This is repeated for many other slightly different As and many examples of each of the other letters, taking care that the appropriate discriminator only is trained.

After training is complete, a response **Rj** (% of K RAMs that output a 1) will occur at the jth discriminator for the presentation of an unknown pattern to the entire system. The system *recognises* the unknown pattern as belonging to the class for which **Rj** is highest. This comparison and selection is performed by the calculator section of the system shown in figure 1.5. Two more tasks performed by the calculator need to be described. The first is a measure of *absolute confidence*. This is merely the actual value of the highest **Rj**.

Should this be close to 100%, the system is saying: "not only is this a member of class **j**, but also it is very much like one of the training patterns in that class". Should the highest **Rj** be low, however, this can be interpreted as the system saying: "this pattern is not much like any that have been used in training, but, if pushed, I will say that it is a member of class **j**". The second additional task done by the calculator is to provide a measure of ***relative confidence*** **C**. This is calculated by looking at the difference D between the highest **Rj** and the second highest. **C** is then given by:

$$\mathbf{C} = \mathrm{D}/\mathbf{Rj}$$

An example of this system at work is given in figure 1.6. The object of the exercise is to recognise an intruder in a normally empty room and figure 1.6 is a stylised representation of real data on which the system was tested. One discriminator is trained on T1, the empty room, and the other is trained on the scene with the intruder wondering around it (I1-I3). With 8-input RAMs the presence of the intruder was noted even in the presence of 40% noise (U1 and U2).

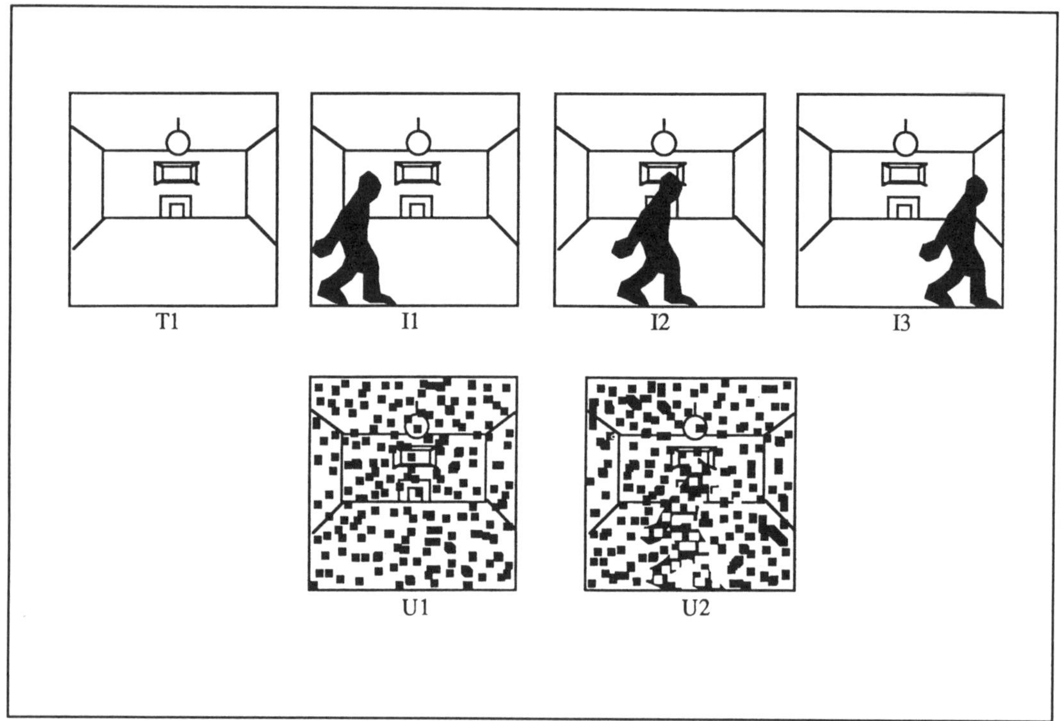

Figure 1.6:

1.11 Current work

We have described the principles of a general-purpose neural machine which not only exists but is currently being applied to problems in industry: quality control, positioning control of robot-held objects, security of buildings and fields, face, speech and signature verification and so on. But this, in terms of general promises of the neural net paradigm is only a simplified net: it has no feedback, nor does it have the probabilistic character that it needs for associative information retrieval which is the emergent property of systems with feedback.

So feedback and probabilistic behavior are the current concerns of the Neural Systems Engineering laboratory at Imperial College and its industrial partners. A commercial WISARD has been software-modified to act as a 1000-node Hopfield-like net (but faster and with a higher capacity than such a net). A major Department of Trade and Industry grant has just been announced to allow the industry/university group to finalise WISARD II which will contain the feedback and the probabilistic character and make one million nodes available to the user, with a response time still within the order of 1/25th of a second! The moral of the story? The direct path to the placement of the advantages offered by neural nets into industry is to use available RAM silicon technology while exploiting the broad properties offered by the neural net paradigm.

1.12 References

Detailed references have specifically not been given. Two general works have been produced that not only survey the complete European contribution to Neural Nets [1] but also provide full details of the subject of this paper in relatively advanced form [1] or directed at the novice [2].

[1] Aleksander I. (Editor): Neural Computing Architectures, North Oxford Academic Press, 1989.

[2] Aleksander I. and Morton H.: An Introduction to Neural Computing, North Oxford Academic Press (available October,1989).

Chapter 2

Bulk-synchronous parallel computers[1]

Leslie G. Valiant
Aiken Computation Laboratory
Harvard University
Cambridge, MA 02138, USA

Abstract We attribute the success of the von Neumann model of sequential computation to the fact that it is an efficient bridge between software and hardware. On the one hand high level languages can be efficiently compiled on to this model. On the other, it can be efficiently implemented in hardware in current technology. We argue that an analogous bridge between software and hardware is required for parallel computation if that is to become as widely used. We introduce the bulk-synchronous parallel (BSP) model as a candidate for this role. We justify this suggestion by giving a number of results that quantify its efficiency both in implementing some high level language features, as well as in being implemented in hardware.

2.1 Why a new parallel model?

In a conventional sequential computer processing is channelled through one physical location. In a parallel machine processing can occur simultaneously at many locations and consequently many more computational operations per second should be achievable. Because of the rapidly decreasing cost of processing, memory, and communication it has

[1]This research was supported in part by the National Science Foundation under grant DCR-86-00379.

appeared inevitable for at least two decades that parallel machines will eventually displace sequential ones in computationally intensive domains. This, however, has not yet happened. Consequently we need to identify what is missing in our understanding of parallel computation that in the sequential case is present and makes possible a huge and diverse industry.

We take the view that the enabling ingredient in sequential computation is a central unifying model, namely the von Neumann computer. Even with rapidly changing technology and architectural ideas hardware designers can still share the common goal of realizing efficient von Neumann machines, without the need for too much concern about the software that is going to be executed. Similarly, the software industry in all its diversity can aim to write programs that can be executed efficiently on this model, without explicit consideration of the hardware. Thus the von Neumann model is the connecting bridge that enables programs from the diverse and chaotic world of software to run efficiently on machines from the diverse and chaotic world of hardware.

We introduce a model of computation that we call the bulk-synchronous parallel (BSP) model. Its aim is to capture in the parallel setting the advantages had by the von Neumann model in the sequential case. Most important among these are conceptual simplicity, universality or general purpose functionality, efficiency in executing high level language features such as automatic storage allocation, and efficiency of realization in foreseeable technologies. Success in capturing these advantages would help isolate the problems of software and hardware from each other, and hence make possible both general purpose machines and transportable software.

The BSP model makes no assumptions about technology or about the degree of parallelism, whether it is two or a million. The main area where a restriction is implied is in that of programming style. We argue, however, that these restrictions are the least that one can hope for in this context. The main advantage of the programming style required is that storage allocation and interprocessor communication can be efficiently hidden from the programmer. For this to be possible, the program has to contain parallel *slackness*. In other words for a p-processor machine the program needs to be written for v virtual processors with v rather larger than p. Efficient automation of storage allocation and communication does not appear possible if $p = v$, for example, or if the degree of parallelism v is not explicitly controlled by the programmer. The prospects for parallelizing sequential code (i.e. $v = 1$) seem even worse.

The justification of the BSP model is based on a number of efficient universality results [1,4–7,11–14] of which a more complete review can be found in [14]. The BSP model can be viewed as an attempt at a pragmatic embodiment of these results, much as the von Neumann model is a pragmatic embodiment of the Turing machine.

2.2 The BSP model

2.2.1 The basic characterization

The BSP model is a combination of three attributes:

a) A number of components that each perform processing and/or memory functions.

b) A communication medium that enables messages to be sent point to point from one component to another, and

c) Facilities for synchronizing all or a subset of the components at regular intervals of time, say L time units. Within this time each processor can execute several instructions locally independent of the other components, and the components can exchange messages among themselves in arbitrary permutations. The intention is that L should be large enough to make efficient throughput in computation and communication possible, but not so large that the required degree of parallelization is unavailable in the program run.

The working of a BSP computer can be thought of as follows. The compiled program assigns to each processor a task or superstep. At each multiple of L time the machine checks whether all the processors have completed their current task. If so then they are allocated new tasks. Otherwise further periods of L are given until completion is achieved by all the processors. Completion of a superstep may require certain computation steps to be performed and certain messages to be sent and received. No synchronization among the components is assumed within each interval of L.

A formalization of this model with a particular choice of parameters is defined and analysed in [14] and is there called an XPRAM.

2.2.2 Some implementation options

In the simplest case each processor can be regarded as a von Neumann computer, but more generally, parallelism may be allowed in each component. At a higher level, multiple instruction streams across the components give the most flexibility but we do not exclude single instruction stream machines.

An attractive combination is to have each component consisting of a processor and a memory unit. This enables the programmer to exploit ***strict locality***, i.e. assigning tasks to processors to take advantage of accessibility of data without use of the communication medium. (Locality, in the sense of proximity in a communication network, we do not exploit since it does not fit well with our general purpose viewpoint here.)

The basic simplicity of the communication medium is that each message has a single destination address to which it is to be delivered. We do not assume any other functionality (such as combining networks), or computational capabilities other than message routing. Clearly, for pragmatic reasons, it may be worthwhile to provide actual machines with hardware implementations of other functions such as broadcasting or the parallel prefix.

Synchronization can be an extremely onerous task if controlled entirely be the programmer. Barrier synchronization at regular intervals L of time is a pragmatic way of achieving efficiently much of what needs to be achieved in executing computationally intensive synchronized algorithms. Such algorithms occur frequently, for example, in scientific computation and also in combinatorial algorithms. Additional synchronization primitives, however, are not excluded.

2.2.3 Programming for the BSP model

For some computational problems efficient parallel algorithms can be found that require little interprocessor communication. These can be programmed on existing parallel machines with little difficulty. The purpose of the BSP model is to cater for the large class of other problems that can be efficiently parallelized also, but only with the use of substantial amounts of interprocessor communication.

When programming a parallel machine numerous directions of optimization are possible, (such as minimizing communication, load balancing, and exploiting locality), if the programmer is willing to program it at a low enough level. The main advantage of the BSP model is that it makes possible near-optimal implementations of unoptimized programs, as long as the latter have sufficient parallel slackness. In other words the degree v of parallelism explicit in the program needs to be sufficiently larger than the physical parallelism p of the machine.

The high-level parallel languages we envisage are therefore those where the degree of parallelism is explicit, but the programmer has the option of relinquishing all control of memory allocation or communication management. PRAM models formalize this idea and are reviewed in [3]. PRAMs of many varieties have been studied. One distinction among them is whether we view the memory space as totally undivided, or share it among the processors so as to allow strict locality to be exploited [14]. The PRAM models in general have proved to be a good framework for developing efficient parallel algorithms and a large literature on these is now available [2,3].

2.3 Arguments for bulk-synchrony

In this section we shall review four aspects of parallel computation and argue that quantitative analysis in all four cases points to the BSP model as a good one. We shall consider throughout that the programs to be executed are parallel and synchronized. It is then natural to have a machine model synchronized at regular intervals. If the regular interval L is too large then the burden on the programmer to write programs decomposable into such large independent tasks may be too great. The question, therefore, is how large should L be?

First we note that there is a clear superficial argument for bulk-synchrony, which is that of overcoming latency. If communication between two processors is much slower than processing then synchronization at every processing step causes gross inefficiencies in processing throughput. The four arguments for bulk-synchrony that we consider below, are all somewhat deeper. The first two concern implementation of high-level language features. The last two concern implementation in hardware.

2.3.1 Smoothing out memory-accesses

Any high-level language has to automate the allocation of storage so that the programmer is free from the responsibility of assigning physical locations to the variables. Conventional compiler techniques work efficiently if there is just one processor. In the parallel case, where there are many memory units and many accesses simultaneously, a new problem arises of how to allocate storage so as to avoid overloading any individual unit.

The most promising method known for smoothing out memory accesses in parallel machines is hashing and this has been analysed in detail by Mehlhorn and Vishkin [6]. The intention of hashing is that for any program run the memory accesses at each step should be distributed randomly independent of the program. Since true random functions require too many bits to be specified, the practical approach is to use pseudo-random hash functions. If p processors issue one memory request each simultaneously to words in a global memory of m words partitioned into, say, p units the intention is that the number of accesses should be small for every unit, since the worst case will produce a bottleneck in a synchronized parallel algorithm. Unfortunately even with a truly random hash function, with large probability some unit will receive $\log p / \log \log p$ accesses, and an inefficiency of this order would ensue.

Suppose that we bulk-synchronize at intervals of $\log p$ accesses (i.e. each processor is allowed $\log p$ read or write operations in a superstep). Then it can be shown [14] using a hash function of Mehlhorn and Vishkin [6] that with high probability no more than

$3\log p$ accesses will be made to any processor if $m > p\log p$. This means that only a small constant fraction loss of efficiency is achieved compared with the best possible.

2.3.2 Simulating concurrent reads and writes

In parallel algorithms we may wish to allow several processors to access (read or write) a single word in memory in a single parallel step. A direct way of achieving this is to give the communication medium combining capabilities (e.g. Schwartz [10], Ranade [8]) that allow the several requests to the same location to combine together in the course of being routed there. The disadvantage of this approach is the apparent expense and complexity of combining networks. Bulk-synchrony and parallel slackness can be used, however, in this context also to give efficient implementations on a hypercube network of Ranade's scheme.

In this section we will emphasize the alternative approach of simulating concurrent reads and writes using a pure message passing communication medium without combining capabilities. A useful subroutine is a parallel algorithm for computing the parallel prefix operation. This is the problem of computing the n values $y_i = x_1 \circ x_2 \circ \cdots \circ x_i$ for $i = 1, \cdots, n$ where $\circ$ is an arbitrary associative operation on elements of a set of which $x_1, \cdots, x_n$ are members. An algorithm of Ladner and Fischer [5] allows this to be implemented efficiently on several models of parallel computation. One application is to define the operation $\circ$ as $s \circ t = s$. Then the parallel prefix defines the operation of broadcasting the value of x_1 to n distinct places.

In general we may wish our high level language to allow arbitrary patterns of simultaneous reads and writes, rather than just simple broadcasts. In [14] it is shown, by combining ideas from [4] and [7] as well as using hashing and the parallel prefix, that this can be achieved with a BSP machine with only a constant factor slowdown for any memory size as long as the number of virtual processors v exceeds $p^{1+\epsilon}$, for some constant $\epsilon > 0$. We expect that for any specific values of v, p and m much better constants can be achieved than implied by the above proof. Also there may exist suitable hash functions that are easier to compute than the one used there, which involves evaluating a polynomial of degree logarithmic in p.

2.3.3 Implementation on packet switching networks

If we turn to the question of implementing a parallel machine using a packet switching network as the communication medium, then bulk-synchrony again contributes substantially to efficiency. Consider a hypercube network with p nodes each one containing a processor and a memory unit. It takes up to $\log p$ edge traversals for a single packet transmission. If p packets are to be transmitted simultaneously, one from each node and one to each node, $O(\log p)$ suffice [12]. It turns out that if instead $p \log p$ are to be transmitted, $\log p$ of them from and to each node, the $O(\log p)$ bound still holds [11] and with small constant multipilers. The problem of simulating a BSP computer with L large enough that $\log p$ packet transmissions can be made between neighbors, is essentially this problem. Overloading any memory unit by more than $\log p$ accesses will slow the simulation down by the same factor as we have to charge the BSP computer.

We note that networks other than the hypercube suffice also. One example is the butterfly where there are $\log p$ levels of p switching nodes and one level of p processor/memory components.

We also note that the analysis is for store and forward message passing. Since it demonstrates essentially optimal information throughput we do not expect that analysis of alternative schemes will change the conclusion.

2.3.4 Smoothing out irregularities in communication

An alternative model of communication is suggested by the possibilities of optical crossbar technology. Here each of p components communicates a message by directing a beam of light to a chosen other component. If a component receives just one message it acknowledges it and transmission is considered successful. On the other hand if more than one beam is directed at a node then none of the messages is received at that node, and the absence of correct acknowledgements informs the senders of this failure. Such a model has been suggested by [1,9].

The instructive case is that of a superstep requiring at most $\log p$ messages to be sent from or received by any processor. Adapting an algorithm of Anderson and Miller [1] it is observed in [14] that $O(\log p)$ parallel steps suffice, which is optimal to within a constant factor.

2.4 References

[1] R.J. Anderson and G.L. Miller. Optical communication for pointer based algorithms. Tech. Rep. CRI 88-14, Comp. Sci. Dept., Univ. of Southern California (1988).

[2] D. Eppstein and Z. Galil. Parallel Algorithmic Techniques for Combinatorial Computation. Ann. Rev. Comput. Sc. (1988) 3:233-83.

[3] R.M. Karp and V. Ramachandran. A survey of parallel algorithms for shared-memory machines. In Handbook of Theoretical Computer Science, (ed. J. van Leeuwen), North Holland, Amsterdam (1989).

[4] C.P. Kruskal, L. Rudolph and M. Snir. A complexity theory of efficient parallel algorithms. Report RC13572, IBM T.J. Watson Research Center, Yorktown Heights, NY (1988).

[5] R.E. Ladner and M.J. Fischer. Parallel prefix computation. JACM 27 (1980) 831-838.

[6] K. Mehlhorn and U. Vishkin. Randomized and deterministic simulations of PRAMs by parallel machines with restricted granularity of parallel memories. Acta Informatica 21 (1984) 339-374.

[7] S. Rajasekaran and J.H. Reif. Optimal and sublogarithmic time randomized parallel sorting algorithms. Manuscript (1988).

[8] A.G. Ranade. How to emulate shared memory. Proc. 28th IEEE Symp. on Foundations of Comp. Sci. (1987) 185-194.

[9] J.H. Reif and K. Johnson. Constant time holographic message routing using O(n log n) switches. Manuscript (1989).

[10] J.T. Schwartz. Ultracomputers. ACM TOPLAS 2 (1980) 484-521.

[11] E. Upfal. Efficient schemes for parallel communication. JACM 31:3 (1984) 507-517.

[12] L.G. Valiant. A scheme for fast parallel communication. SIAM J. on Computing, 11 (1982) 350-361.

[13] L.G. Valiant. Optimally universal parallel computers. Phil. Trans. R. Soc. Lond. A326 (1988) 373-376.

[14] L.G. Valiant. General purpose parallel architectures. In Handbook of Theoretical Computer Science, (ed. J. van Leeuwen), North Holland, Amsterdam (1989).

Chapter 3

Information management in Linda

David Gelernter
Yale University
Department of Computer Science
New Haven, Connecticut

Abstract We describe three information management projects: the "parallel process trellis" architecture and the intensive care unit monitor that is serving as a test case; parallel database searchers that allow geneticists to search sequence databases for a nearest match against some target sequence; and the "FGP machine", which uses fuzzy retrieval and "simulated speculation" to convert pools of data directly into quasi-expert advice. Each project involves specific domain goals, but some general points emerge as well. A language for applications of this sort should comfortably accomodate the powerful idea of program-as-machine, rather than forcing on programmers an ostensibly higher-level mathematical model; Linda, with its shared, associative object memory, is proving itself a good vehicle for (among other things) applications conceived as loosely-coupled process ensembles.

3.1 Introduction

Linda is a parallel programming model based on a shared, associative object memory. A Linda program consists of a collection of objects occupying a region called "tuple space". Some of the objects are data tuples and some are processes, which eventually turn into data tuples indistinguishable from the others. We provide operations to generate data tuples (`out`) and processes (`eval`), to read data tuples (`rd`) and to remove them (`in`). Data tuples form an associative memory, accessible not via name or pointer but in terms of any combination of the values of their fields.

A series of implementations and programming experiments, mainly in our own group but increasingly in others as well, has demonstrated that Linda is a simple, powerful and efficient programming tool [e.g. CG89b]. Our research effort has expanded accordingly: good tools are in hand; now we need to investigate program structures for parallellism and a methodology for parallel programming (while continuing, of course, to refine the tools). We've based much of this structures-and-methodology work on information management problems.

Information management software comes in two flavors. Programs can be installed directly in the path of oncoming data, or they can be focussed on existing databases. In both categories, the need to handle large volumes of data quickly and (often) to build programs structured as complex aggregates ("communicating experts", for example) have been complicating factors. Parallelism can advance the state of information management software by contributing two important commodities: computational horsepower and conceptual clarity. This paper describes research software in both information management flavors. First, the "parallel process trellis" architecture and the intensive care unit monitor that is serving as a test case. This program structure is designed for monitoring problems in which streams of low-level data are to be converted, using a hierachical, heteregeneous collection of decision procedures, into usable information. Second, parallel database searchers: we describe several programs that are designed to allow geneticists to search sequence databases for a nearest match against some target sequence. Finally the "FGP machine", which uses fuzzy retrieval and "simulated speculation" to convert pools of data directly into quasi-expert advice.

Each of the experiments we describe — two are parallel programs, and one is a serial prototype that soon will be — involves a separate program architecture and some highly-specific domain goals. Independent of software engineering and parallelism, we hope to learn something about monitors, database searchers and case-driven expert systems. But several common threads emerge as well. We outline each project in turn, and then summarize the general points.

This paper draws extensively on research by several members of our group: the process trellis is mainly the work of Michael Factor, the DNA database searchers of Dr. Nicholas Carriero and Robert Bjornson, and the FGP machine of Scott Fertig.

3.2 Process trellises

The process trellis is a software architecture for systems intended to filter, analyze, and find patterns in a collection of incoming data streams. We refer to the class of such applications as "monitor problems." One example is is a hemodynamic monitor for a post-operative intensive care unit (ICU). This monitor[1], which is intended ultimately for clinical trial, is still a basic research project. But it is a sizable and growing application built with the new software architecture, and a useful test case.

Consider a series of separate, sequential decision procedures. The procedures are hierarchical; for example, the lowest level interfaces directly to external data sources, the next-higher levels perform initial data filtering, trending and baseline calculations, levels above this recognize fairly narrow patterns, still higher levels recognize broader or more complex patterns, and top level procedures perform "meta" services, evaluating the reliability of certain aspects of the system, the applicability of the existing decision structure and so on. Each procedure runs continuously as a separate process, concurrently with all other processes. It is an essential attribute of the architecture that these procedures are logical black boxes with respect to the trellis; as long as they obey the information-flow protocol, they can incorporate any kind of logic that seems appropriate.

Each node in the trellis (where a node is simply a decision process) continuously attempts to calculate a state based upon the states of inferior nodes. When sufficient information is available from a node's inferiors — each decision procedure defines for itself what "sufficient information" means — it generates a new state. As a result, nodes one level up may recalculate their own states, and so on. Values in this sense flow upward through the trellis. Besides passively waiting for inferior nodes to change state, nodes may send queries downward through the trellis, forcing their inferiors to generate updated state values. Queries in this sense filter downward. (If we equip bottom-rank nodes with warning lights, a flashing warning light means "enter data".)

We supply two types of "logic probe" with the system, an "inject value" probe and a "read value" probe. We can touch any node with an "inject value" probe, thereby setting the state of the node we touch to any value we choose. In the default configuration described above, each node in the bottom rank has a null decision procedure; each bottom-rank node has a permanently-attached inject-value probe through which we pump new values into the system. We can read any node's current state by touching it with a "read-value" probe. If the node has insufficient information to have a currently defined state, touching it with a read-probe causes queries to propagate down to each of the its inferiors. Eventually new data values arrive and a response is produced.

[1]joint research with Drs. Perry Miller, Aaron Cohen, Dean Sittig and Stanley Rosenbaum of the Anesthesiology Department and Medical Informatics Program at Yale.

The ICU monitor experiment is described in [CG88] and [FacG88]. The current prototype encompasses about sixty nodes, ranging from bottom-level data filtering nodes (Kalman filtering applied to blood pressure readings, for example), through patterns that might occur in the context of several diagnoses (for example intravascular depletion, hypotension) through the diagnoses themselves (hypovolemia, sepsis) and an upper level that evaluates general questions (is an infectious disease workup called for at this point?).

3.2.1 Evaluating the trellis machine

What makes the trellis a good design for an information filter machine? There are a number of other possible approaches; blackboard architectures are the most prominent. The trellis is distinguished from other possiblities mainly by two characteristics: its structure is ***transparent*** and ***locally comprehensible.*** Transparency refers to the fact that it's easy to figure out exactly what each part of the trellis does, because the structure of the machine reflects the structure of the problem-situation it is designed to monitor. This in turn makes it relatively easy for users to understand what the trellis can do, what it can't, and how to use it effectively — important (and often neglected) criteria in the design of any machine, but vital where a particularly complex machine and a high-pressure situation are combined. Imagine a master contol panel on which a schematic representation of the trellis appears: a user can easily ascertain that the machine has notions about two forms of congestive heart failure (but knows nothing about — let's say — kidney failure); the machine's judgements about congestive heart failure will clearly depend on its information about ischemia, cardiac output and other nodes directly dominated by the "congestive heart failure" node, and so on.

"Local comprehensibility" means that, if we need to change or add modules, we need only understand the new module's "neighborhood" — the modules connected to it directly above and below. We don't need to understand the program as a whole. This makes it possible to envision enormous trellises incorporating thousands, even tens of thousands of modules. A trellis with ten thousand modules is a machine of staggering complexity. No one programmer could understand such a program in its entirety. "Local comprensibility" means that, notwithstanding, we can imagine such a machine being methodically assembled, tested and put into service.

3.2.2 Future trellises

The completed intensive care unit monitor will probably incorporate several hundred nodes, making it a complex program in itself. It's possible to envision much bigger trellises as well. Any active system is a candidate for this kind of monitoring — a factory, the stock market, an aircraft carrier, a national economy. In every case, a trellis machine tries to answer the same basic question: what's going on here? What does this mass of small, individually-inscrutable detail add up to?

Consider, for example, a "transportation watcher" trellis: it gathers up the millions of small facts that describe a regional (or national) transportation system at some particular moment, and converts them into usable information, tailored to the specific needs of any traveller or the local authorities. (This would be merely a more ambitious, sophisticated and generally-available version of the traffic congestion monitors already installed in several large cities.) The system is designed to answer the obvious questions: what's the best route this morning to work, or across the country? Where should a tow-truck be dispatched? Which bridge is most likely to collapse next? If we start at the lowest levels with nodes dedicated to local conditions on particular roads, runways or rail segments, building to top-level nodes that integrate the complicated pieces and respond to sophisticated questions, we may be envisioning a million-node trellis. Within this huge and intricate machine, data values stream constantly upwards as (perhaps) thousands of data-requests filter downwards simultaneously, and a complex blur of data comes into focus.

3.3 DNA database searching

Suppose users need to examine every element in a database, and a substantial amount of computing is required for each element. The example we will discuss involves DNA sequences: when a new sequence is discovered, geneticists may need to know which previously-known sequences the new one resembles, and to do so they may need to examine a large database of existing sequences. Obviously, the time necessary to examine the database increases with the size of the database. As the database grows, examination time may go from seconds to minutes to hours, crossing a series of cost and inconvenience thresholds along the way.

We've discussed earlier stages of our work on this problem elsewhere; here we summarize the current state of the project, and then discuss some general conclusions respecting the use of programs of this sort.

Comparing two long sequences can be expensive, and this operation can be effectively parallelized using Linda [BjCG89]. But geneticists usually require not a single comparison, but an extensive series of comparisons in which the target is compared against all or a major portion of a large database. It's clear, then, that we should consider parallelizing not the sequence-to-sequence comparison, but the database search — have our program perform many sequential comparisons simultaneously. Such an approach is attractive because, since it involves coarser-grained parallelism, we expect a highly efficient program to result.

This approach does work well ([CG88]) — except when we need to search a database partition that includes very-long sequences, in which case the work required to perform a single comparison can dominate the (parallelized) search time for the entire remaining database. The parallel sequence-to-sequence comparison handles long sequences efficiently, but otherwise becomes too fine-grained to perform well. We can combine the virtues of both programs in a new and different approch that works as follows: the sequence-comparison algorithm we are using requires the contruction of an $n \times m$ comparison matrix, when comparing a length-n to a length-m sequence; the dependencies within the matrix allow all elements along a counter-diagonal to be computed simultaneously as soon as the previous counter-diagonal is known. Equivalently, we can compute the matrix in blocks (rather than single elements), and compute all blocks along a counter-diagonal simultaneously. We define as a task the computation of of an $i \times j$ sub-block of the comparison matrix. When comparing a target whose length is $\leq i$ to a database sequence whose length is $\leq j$, the entire comparison matrix fits inside an $i \times j$ block, and therefore constitutes a single task by itself. When dealing with larger comparands, the comparison is partitioned into a series of sub-block computations, which may be pursued by many processes simultaneously.

We have implemented several versions of this approach. All take as their starting point the simple parallel database searcher referred to above, which works as follows. We create one master process and many workers (as many workers as we can accomodate on our machine; since each worker will in effect be busy continuously, it doesn't pay to create more than one per available processor). The master hands each worker a copy of the search target (the new DNA sequence, in this case), by outing a tuple that each worker rds. Then the master reads through the database, grabbing each sequence and releasing it into tuple space. Each worker reaches into tuple space, grabs a sequence, compares it to the target, releases the result back into tuple space, and repeats. The master gathers up the results, and reports back to the user when the search is complete.

In one of several hybrid versions, we modify the procedure as follows. A task tuple may specify a complete (short) sequence, or the first part of a long sequence. When a worker picks up a complete sequence, it performs the entire comparison against the target. When it picks up an initial segment, it computes all blocks along the first horizontal band of the comparson matrix. As soon as it completes the first block, it generates a task-descriptor tuple specifying computation of the next band (the one immediately beneath this one) as an available task; as it completes each block, it generates a tuple describing that sub-block's bottom row.

On a typical task, a search though the Primate sub-section (roughly 2 Mbytes) of the standard sequence database GenBank against a median-length sequence (about 500 bases), this C-Linda program achieved a speedup of roughly 55 times running on the 64 nodes of an Intel iPSC-2 hypercube, relative to a serial C program on one node.

Implications The capacity to search large databases fast offers, in some domains, a qualitative improvement in their usefulness. Running the DNA searcher on all 64 nodes of the iPSC-2 reduces the search time for the task described from slightly under four hours on an 80386 processor (one node of the iPSC-2) to slightly over four minutes. Dramatic improvements of this sort promise a new spontaneity in the use of this kind of database. Our experience so far is limited to DNA comparison, but we suspect that there are many related problems. For example: we might wish to identify images by comparison against a large library of paradigm samples; chemists search large reaction libraries, using graph-comparison algorithms, against a target reaction. Sophisticated text-retrieval systems might possibly fall into this category; database-driven inferencing systems (like the one described below) almost certainly will.

This problem domain is also a promising test case for "low-end parallelism" — parallel applications potentially of interest to a broad range of users, and capable of performing well on cheap parallel workstations. The adjustable granularity of programs like the hybrid DNA searcher (we can vary the size of the matrix sub-blocks) makes them potentially good applications for networked conventional machines as well. We discuss elsewhere [CG89] an application that is similar in character to the DNA searcher, and shows comparable performance on the Intel machine, and on shared-memory multiprocesors; increasing the grain size by a factor of 10 (a change to one line of the code) gives us a very coarse-grained application that runs well on eight Ethernet-connected Unix workstations. (See also [WL88], for discussion of a Linda application that run faster on fourteen networked VAXes than on a Cray.) Parallel database searching may not even require a parallel computer.

3.4 The FGP machine

Does expertise require knowledge? Traditional expert systems assume it does, and they supply knowledge in the form of rules, frames, domain-specific problem-solving strategies and so on. On the other hand, consider an expert system whose goal is to identify or to "comment intelligently about" objects, cases or events in some category x; if we could use a large database of previously identified x-type objects to power the system, we could dispense with "knowledge" and various desirable consequences would follow. We could skip the rule-compilation stage; the system's performance should improve steadily as the database grows; the system should be able to cite relevant precedents specifically, rather than relying on general principles. Various of these observations underlie several current research topics, including Waltz and Stanfill's memory-based reasoning [WS86], Lebowitz's generalization-based memory [Leb88], vague and fuzzy databases [e.g. Mot88], and the growing body of work on connectionist and neural-net expert systems [e.g. Gal88].

Our own goals are related but not identical to the goals of these projects [FG88]. The FGP machine's goal is to use the cases themselves (not a network compiled on the basis of training examples) to drive the system. The system should "reason" on the basis of specific cases and groups of cases, and should therefore be able to cite specific precedents (including precedents that are themselves incompletely understood), to modify its behavior on the basis of every new information-providing transaction, and to subsume the functions of a conventional information-retrieval system. Unlike the Waltz and Stanfill system and some connectionist approaches, it should be designed to interact with a user as a case is described incrementally, or to generate line-by-line commentary on new cases. Most important, and in a sense distinguishing it from all of the projects mentioned above, it should attempt to display not only "quantitative" but "qualitative" expertise. According to our experimental definition, qualitative expertise requires (particularly on hard cases, but these are the whole point) pursuing possibly premature hypotheses, offering (occasionally brash) guesses and citing interesting precedents on the basis of a small but evocative degree of feature overlap. We believe that such behavior will be potentially thought-provoking and helpful. We are developing "simulated speculation" in an effort to approximate it.

Consider a large database of related cases, where a "case" describes some interesting object or event. An x-ray film, for example: the database with which we've worked most extensively to date stores descriptions of mammograms in standard medical terminology. Give such a database, we should be able to hand the system an incomplete description of a case, and have it fill in the blanks. We may have a full description of the image of a mass on the film, for example, but may not know whether the mass is benign or malignant, or what the diagnosis is. We'd like the system to fill in these blanks — to guess the diagnosis — based on patterns in similar cases. A related problem, actually a logically antecedent one, is to program the database in such a way that it can respond to vague inquiries of the form "get me all cases that resemble this one".

Second, our database must attempt to mimic (albeit crudely) an important characteristic of human experts. Real experts don't merely stick to what is statistically solid and unquestionable; they make guesses, form hypotheses and jump to conclusions. Our system should attempt something similar. It should alert users to interesting possibilities even when, statistically speaking, they can't be established firmly.

Finally, we want a database that grows every time it is used. Whenever a user presents a query to the database — "fill in the blanks, and tell me about related cases" — the database can save the query as if it were merely another case. When new data (in the form of new case descriptions) are added to the system, the system might be reminded of earlier inquiries. The system might say, in effect, "the new case you've just entered recalls a query entered by XYZ six months ago — perhaps sheds new light on it."

(AGE 58)	
(MASS_DENSITY ISO_DENSE)	
(MASS_BORDER_COMPLETE? NO)	
(MASS_TYPE_BORDER IRREGULAR)	
(MASS_BORDER_DEFINED? NO)	*Speculating: MASS_DENSITY_CHANGED?...* *Guessing INCREASED - e.g.* *case ((id 14) (age 46) (diagnosis CA_INF_DUCTAL))* *case ((id 50) (age 70) (diagnosis CA_INF_DUCTAL))* *Speculating: MASS_COMET?...* *Guessing YES - e.g.* *case 14* *case ((id 40) (age 69) (diagnosis CA_INF_DUCTAL))*
(MASS_LOCATION UIL)	
(MASS_SIZE_CHANGED? YES)	
(MASS_DENSITY_CHANGED? NO)	
(MASS_COMET? NO)	*Speculating: BACKGROUND_DENSITY...* *Guessing DENSE - e.g.* *case ((id 21) (age 61) (diagnosis cyst))* *case ((id 47) (age 45) (diagnosis fcd))*
(MASS_HALO? NO)	
(BACKGROUND_DENSITY MODERATE)	*Concluding* *(ARCHITECTURAL_DISTORTION? NO)* *Speculating: MALIGNANT?...* *Guessing YES - e.g. cases (2 6 8)* *Speculating: SKIN_CHANGES...* *Guessing RETRACTION - e.g. cases (2 8 28)*
...	
(SKIN_CHANGES NO)	
(NIPPLE_INVERSION? NO)	
(ADENOPATHY? NO)	
(FAMILY_HISTORY_CANCER SISTER)	
(PERSONAL_HISTORY_CANCER NO)	*Closest known cases:* *(19) (YES) (CA_INF_DUCTAL)* *(33) (YES) (CA_INF_DUCTAL)* *(26) (YES) (CA_INF_DUCTAL)* *(28) (YES) (CA_INF_DUCTAL)* *(18) (YES) (CA)* *YES has been concluded or guessed for MALIGNANT?* *Speculating: DIAGNOSIS...* *CA?* *CA_INF_DUCTAL?*

Figure: An FGP transcript, type-set and slightly reformatted *post facto*. The user's case description is in the left column, the system's commentary on the right. The system can operate interactively, but here it is working in "commentary" mode: the user presents an entire case; the system scans it element-by-element, offering comments. This case initially seems malignant (note the early mention of related cases with diagnoses of infiltrating ductal carcinoma); the fact that the mass has not changed in density and has no comet (contradicting the system's guesses, which in the nature of guesses will often be wrong) points in the other direction ("cyst" and "fcd" refer to benign diagnoses); but further data, particularly the absence of a halo, tips the balance, and the system guesses that this is a malignant mass. This guess is correct, and the diagnosis was in fact infiltrating ductal carcinoma. This transcript is driven by a small collection of roughly 70 cases. For a discussion of the system's accuracy, and a comparison of these transcripts to similar ones produced by a radiologist as he examined the same cases, see [FerG89].

3.4.1 The prototype

The program we've built in an initial attempt to realize these properties is the FGP machine, after its basic operations — fetch, generalize and project. We imagine the FGP machine's database as a collection of regions in space (*cf.* the standard vector space text-retrieval model). Each element of the database corresponds to some region. Nearby regions correspond to nearby cases. When presented with an inquiry, the machine's basic task is to add to the database a new region corresponding to the inquiry. Stationing itself on top of this new region (so to speak), the machine then looks around and reports the identities of the nearby regions — these will correspond to elements of the database that are nearby to, in other words closely related to, the subject of the inquiry. We can then inspect this list of nearby regions and "generalize" — determine which attributes tend to be shared in common by all or by most of them. We can guess that these common attributes are likely to hold true for the case being described in the inquiry as well.

Having reached whatever conclusions seem reasonable, the machine may now indulge in a bit of simulated speculation. Temporarily turning aside from the inquiry in hand, it focusses on any "evocative possiblities" that may have suggested themselves during the examination of nearby regions. An "evocative possibility" is a datum that *might* be true, and that would be significant if it were. The machine's interaction with the user (see figure) represents a combination of fairly safe conclusions, speculation experiments and the subsequent investigation of resulting guesses.

The FGP machine is a working prototype, but its current status reflects on the preceding discussion in a significant way, because we haven't yet turned it into a parallel program. Although it is built to be reasonably efficient, the current FGP machine is slow even with small numbers of case records, and the technique is intended specifically for use with large databases — the larger the better. Generating transcripts like the one in the figure requires repeated computations against many or all elements in the database. Standard indexing strategies are useful to some extent, but in this problem (unlike the keyword-based text retrieval problem, for example), the database is intended to be fairly homogeneous, with most features present in most cases. It's clear that if this program is to perform well, we must be able to execute operations involving large portions of large databases quickly. Techniques related to ones used by the DNA searcher seem promising.

3.5 Conclusions

All the projects discussed here remain under active development. Research on the trellis architecture focusses on a realtime version (the prototype is a "realtime" program but only in an informal sense), and on the user interface; a parallel version of the FGP machine will be under construction shortly. New information management projects will soon be under way as well. One such project centers on a model in which Linda distributed data structures are accessed by (in effect) people instead of processes: it appears to be simple to specify a powerful distributed office-management package to handle mail, messages and tasking on this basis.

Several general points emerge from the work outlined above.

1. Each of the applications discussed was conceived as a virtual machine. In the design of parallel systems generally, and particularly within the information management domain, the idea of "software machinery" has served us well as a basic thought-tool. It is accepted as obvious and natural that "hardware" machines are built out of simultaneously active elements, with some kind of coordinating framework linking them together. Software machines can be conceived in the same way. From this point of view it becomes clear that, although parallel programs may be simpler or more complicated than serial ones in particular instances, they are no less "natural"; on the contrary, insisting that a program (or any machine) do *only one thing at a time* is unnatural, an arbitrary restriction that no longer need be enforced. Parallelizing compilers, and functional or logic languages that suppress the "machine building" aspect of programming in favor of ostensibly higher-level mathematical models, are for our purposes conceptually inept. If a high-level language is one that accomodates the programmer's way of thinking, rather than forcing him to accomodate the language's, then a high-level language for these purposes must be an explicitly parallel one, and *should* be one that comfortably accomodates the powerful idea of program-as-machine.

2. Linda, with its global, associative object memory, is proving itself a good tool for applications of this sort. Broadly speaking, the loosely-coupled process ensemble is a promising architecture for many information management and heuristic applications, and Linda seems like the ideal programming vehicle for loosely coupled ensembles. Linda's global, associative object memory supports a highly "uncoupled" programming style in which processes remain mutually anonymous. Mutual anonymity makes it easy (we have found) to develop and debug parallel applications, and to support programs in which the number and character of constituent processes can be set at run time and may change dy-

namically. It simplifies the construction of applications that may be monitored in flexible, non-predetermined ways by control modules. Linda also appears to be a strong basis for heterogeneous computing, in which modules may run on different types of machines and may be written in different languages. Invoking a service by adding an object to tuple space (rather than sending a message or calling a procedure) makes it possible for any currently-appropriate process to pick up the tuple and perform the sevice. Tuple space automatically and implicitly buffers communication between computations taking place at different rates, in different places or during disjoint lifetimes. Supporting heterogeneous computations in Linda is a main focus of our current research.

It's fair to note that for applications with a symbolic or heuristic flavor, Lisp-Linda would probably be a better vehicle than C-Linda — the Linda dialect that's most advanced at present, and the language used for the parallel applications discussed above. Other groups are working on Scheme-Linda and on Common Lisp-Linda; we plan to begin work on Lisp-Linda ourselves in the near future.

3.6 References

[BjCG89] R.Bjornson, N.Carriero and D.Gelernter, "The implementation and performance of hypercube Linda," Yale Univ. Dept. Comp. Sci. RR-690 (March 1989).

[CG88] N. Carriero and D. Gelernter, "Applications Experience with Linda," in Proc. ACM Symp. Parallel Programming, July 1988.

[CG89] N. Carriero and D. Gelernter, "How to write parallel programs: A guide to the perplexed." *ACM Comp. Surveys* (to appear).

[CG89b] N. Carriero and D. Gelernter, "Linda in Context." *Comm. ACM* (to appear).

[FacG88] M. Factor and D. Gelernter, "Experiments with the process-trellis architecture for expert monitors." Yale Univ. Dept Comp. Sci RR (Dec. 1988).

[FerG89] S. Fertig and D. Gelernter, "Does expertise require knowledge? Experiments with a database-driven expert system." Yale Univ. Dept. Comp. Sci. RR (April 1989).

[FG88] S. Fertig and D. Gelernter, "Musing in an expert database," in L. Kershberg, *ed.*, *Expert Database Systems* (Cummings: 1989): 605-620.

[Gal88] S.I. Gallant, "Connectionist expert systems," *Comm. ACM* 31,2 (Feb. 1988):152-169.

[Leb86] M. Lebowitz, "Using memory in text understanding," in J.L. Kolodner and C.K. Riesbeck, *eds.*, "Experience, memory and reasoning." (Erlbaum: 1986):181-194.

[Mot88] A. Motro, "VAGUE: A user interface to relational databases that permits vague queries." *ACM Trans. Off. Info. Sys.* 6,3(1988):187-214.

[SF86] C. Stanfill and D. Waltz, "Toward memory-based reasoning," *Comm. ACM* 29,12 (Dec. 1986):1213-1228.

[WL88] R.A. Whiteside and J.S. Leichter, "Using Linda for supercomputing on a local area network." in *Proc. Supercomputing '88* (Nov. 1988).

Chapter 4

Information-driven parallel pattern recognition through communicating processes – a case study on classification of wallpaper groups

Tosiyasu L. Kunii
Satoshi Asami
Kaoru Maeda
Department of Information Science
Faculty of Science, University of Tokyo

Abstract The application of transformation geometry to processing of repetitive patterns has recently become a subject of great interest in the research area of computer graphics and pattern recognition. This paper presents a method to accelerate the process of classifying the wallpaper group of a given pattern. It utilizes cross-correlation and autocorrelation as similarity measures. An approach to parallelization of classification procedures using communicating processes is also outlined.

4.1 Introduction

This paper proposes a method to accelerate the process of classifying the wallpaper group of a given pattern. It is based on cross-correlation and autocorrelation as similarity measures [1]. To further improve the processing speed, an approach to parallelization of classification procedures are outlined. This section gives a brief overview on the problem. Automatic recognition of an object by a machine eye has been one entire goal for scientists and engineers involved in computer studies. Feature extraction of a given picture is one useful tool for recognition. There are two major approaches to feature extraction: the statistical approach and the structural approach [6][10].

The method described in this paper is a combination of the two approaches. It utilizes autocorrelation to detect the repetitions, and cross-correlation to detect the centers of rotations and lines of symmetries in the given pattern. Instead of calculating autocorrelation or cross-correlation of the entire plane, this method calculates them only at the points necessary to find the relative maximums. It utilizes communicating processes to parallelize the search.

This method can be applied to the structural analysis of a material. For example, a picture by an electron microscope of a material showing high-temperature superconductivity can be analyzed by this method to find out the structural repetitions in the material, and the data can be utilized to detect the irregularity residing in the repetition, which might be the reason for superconductivity.

Section 4.2 introduces transformation geometry related to repetitive patterns. Section 4.3 describes how cross-correlation and autocorrelation can be utilized to classify the wallpaper group of a given pattern. Section 4.4 explains roughly the procedure of classification. Section 4.5 shows how detection of relative maximums can be accomplished by parallel searching.

4.2 Transformation geometry

This section offers an introduction to transformation geometry [3][8], and explains its relationship with repetitive patterns.

An isometry is a transformation by which the distance between two points remains unchanged. An Isometry on the plane is exactly one of the following: *translation, rotation, reflection,* and *glide reflection*. Translations, rotations, and glide reflections are products of reflections. Translations and rotations are called *even isometries* because they are combinations of two reflections.

If a point A is moved to point B by a translation, the vector $\overrightarrow{AB}$ is called the vector *indicating* the translation, and the translation is denoted by $\tau_{A,B}$. Let M be the midpoint of $\overline{AB}$, a and m be the lines perpendicular to $\overline{AB}$ and through A and M, respectively. σ_l denotes the reflection in line l. Then $\tau_{A,B} = \sigma_m\sigma_a$. ($\sigma_m\sigma_a$ is the products of the reflections σ_a and σ_m.) See Figure 4.1.

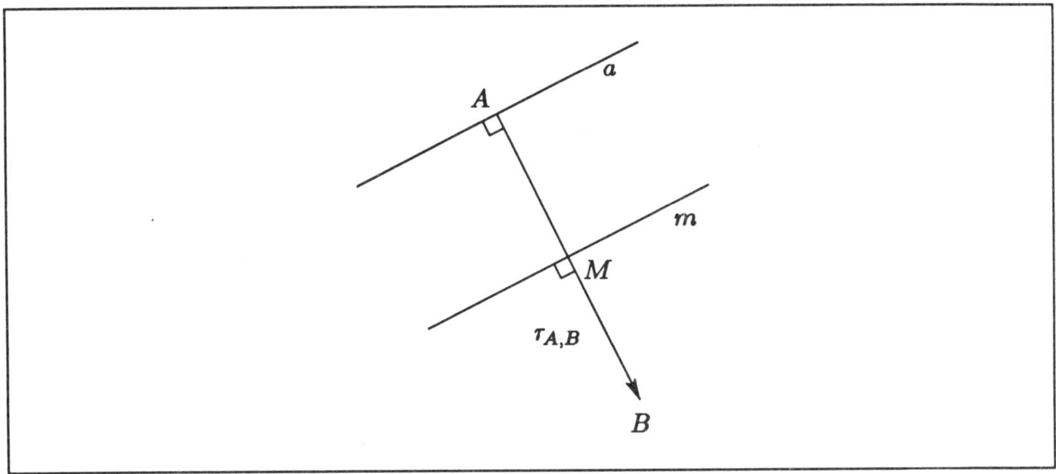

Figure 4.1: Translation as a product of two reflections.

A rotation with center C and directed angle θ is denoted by $\rho_{C,\theta}$. If $\rho_{C,\theta}$ takes a point A to point B, then $\angle ACB = \theta$. Let M be the midpoint of $\overline{AB}$, and a and m be the lines through A, C and M, C, respectively. Then $\rho_{C,\theta} = \sigma_m\sigma_a$. This is shown in Figure 4.2.

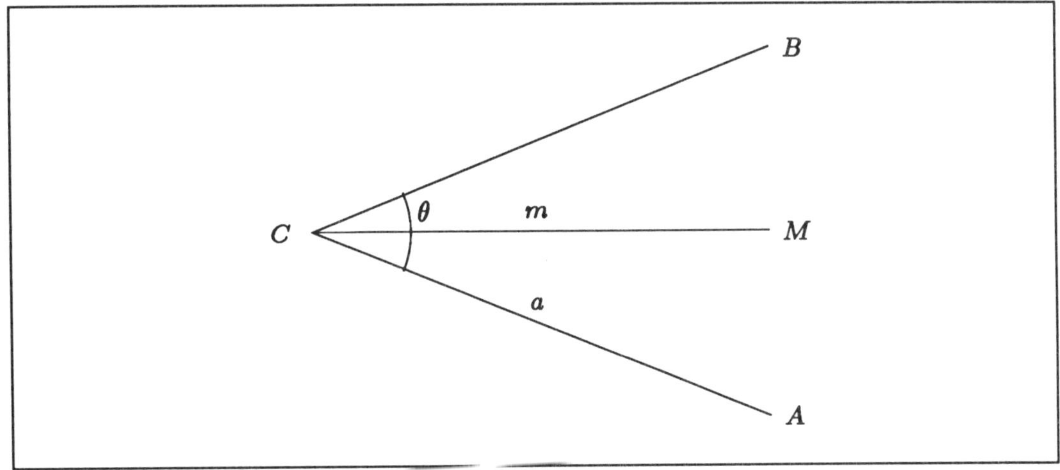

Figure 4.2: Rotation as a product of two reflections.

A rotation of 180° is called a *halfturn*. A center of a halfturn is called a *point of symmetry*, and a center of a rotation of $360°/n$ is called an *n-center*.

Glide reflections are combinations of three reflections (this is obvious from the fact that a glide reflection is a combination of a translation and a reflection, and a translation is a product of two reflections), and they are called *odd isometries* as well as reflections.

The groups of isometries on the plane are called the *ornamental groups.* They are classified into three sets.

4.2.1 Rosette groups

The first set of ornamental groups is composed of finite groups. They contain no translations. By Leonardo's theorem, they are the groups C_n and D_n. C_n is called a *cyclic group,* and is a group of order n of rotations. This is the definition of C_n:

$$C_n = \left\langle \rho_{C,360°/n} \right\rangle = \left\{ \rho^i_{C,360°/n} \mid 1 \leq i \leq n \right\}.$$

C is the center of rotation. D_n is called a *dihedral group,* and its order is $2n$. The subgroup of rotations of D_n is equal to C_n, and the rest is equal to the group

$$\left\{ \sigma_l \rho^i_{C,360°/n} \mid 1 \leq i \leq n \right\}.$$

σ_l is a reflection in a line l through C.

$$\begin{aligned} D_n &= \left\langle \sigma_l, \rho_{C,360°/n} \right\rangle \\ &= \left\{ \sigma^j_l \rho^i_{C,360°/n} \mid 1 \leq i \leq n, 0 \leq j \leq 1 \right\} \end{aligned}$$

is the formal definition of D_n.

4.2.2 Frieze groups

The elements of the second set of ornamental groups are the *frieze groups.* They are the groups of isometries whose subgroups of translations are generated by a single translation. Let c be a line fixed by the elements of a frieze group $\mathcal{F}$. Then an isometry in $\mathcal{F}$ is one of the following:

a translation

a halfturn with center on c

a reflection in c

a reflection in a line perpendicular to c

a glide reflection with center c

By the existences of these symmetries, frieze groups are classified into seven sets.

4.2.3 Wallpaper groups

The third set of ornamental groups contain *wallpaper groups*. In a wallpaper group, the elements of the subgroup of translations are those in the group $\langle \tau_1, \tau_2 \rangle$ where τ_1 and τ_2 are nonidentity translations and the vectors indicating τ_1 and τ_2 are not parallel. The translations τ_1 and τ_2 are called the *generating translations*.

If a point is an n-center for a wallpaper group, then n is one of 2, 3, 4, or 6. This is called the *crystallographic restriction*. By the combinations of n-centers, lines of symmetry, and axes of glide reflections, the wallpaper groups are classified into seventeen sets.

At first, groups without n-centers are considered. They have a common subscript 1. The groups without odd isometries are called $\mathcal{W}_1$. Those without lines of symmetry but with axes of glide reflections are called $\mathcal{W}_1^3$. Groups with both lines of symmetry and axes of glide reflections are left. When the two are coincident, the group is called $\mathcal{W}_1^2$; when there are some axes of glide reflection which are not lines of symmetry, the group is called $\mathcal{W}_1^1$.

Next comes the group with only 2-centers as n-centers. Their common subscript is 2. If it doesn't contain odd isometries, it is called $\mathcal{W}_2$. When they do not contain lines of symmetry but axes of glide reflection, they are called $\mathcal{W}_2^4$. If all lines of symmetry are parallel, the group is called $\mathcal{W}_2^3$. The groups with non-parallel lines of symmetry are left. When the 2-centers are always on the lines of symmetry, it is called $\mathcal{W}_2^2$; when there are 2-centers off the lines of symmetry, the group is called $\mathcal{W}_2^1$.

A group with 4-centers cannot contain a 3-center or a 6-center. They have the common subscript 4. If the group doesn't contain odd isometries, they are called $\mathcal{W}_4$. When the lines of symmetry are on 4-centers, the group is called $\mathcal{W}_4^1$; when the lines of symmetry are off 4-centers it is called $\mathcal{W}_4^2$.

A group with only 3-center as an n-center has a subscript 3. If it contains no odd isometries, it is called $\mathcal{W}_3$. When all the 3-centers are on the lines of symmetry, it is called $\mathcal{W}_3^1$; when there are some 3-centers off the lines of symmetry, it is called $\mathcal{W}_3^2$.

The groups with 6-centers are left. When it contains no odd isometries, the group is called $\mathcal{W}_6$. The groups with lines of symmetry are called $\mathcal{W}_6^1$.

4.3 Autocorrelation and cross-correlation

This section introduces the notion of similarity measures. Autocorrelation and cross-correlation as similarity measures are also introduced.

A *similarity measure* of two intensity functions f and g which have two variables is another function with two variables defined over the entire plane.

The metric based on the L^2 norm, or the standard Euclidean distance between two vectors, is defined by

$$E(m,n) = \left\{ \sum_i \sum_j [f(i,j) - g(i-m, j-n)]^2 \right\}^{1/2}.$$

Cross-correlation, which is stated below, can be derived by squaring it and discarding terms whose sums are constant.

$$R(m,n) = \sum_i \sum_j f(i,j) g(i-m, j-n)$$

4.3.1 Translations

To compare the image to itself translated along a vector (m,n), the function g should be set equal to f. In this case,

$$R(m,n) = \sum_i \sum_j f(i,j) f(i-m, j-n)$$

is called *autocorrelation*. The relative maximums of R indicate the translations by which the original picture f is preserved.

4.3.2 Rotations

Let $g_{C,\theta}(i,j)$ be the image of f rotated by $\rho_{C,\theta}$. Then

$$R(m,n) = \sum_i \sum_j f(i,j) g_{C,\theta}(i,j) \quad \left((m,n) = \overrightarrow{OC}\right)$$

indicates the similarity of f and $g_{C,\theta}$. The relative maximums of R under a fixed θ shows the centers of rotations with directed angle θ.

The previous section stated that $\rho_{C,\theta}$ can be expressed as a product of two reflections σ_p and σ_q, where p and q are lines which intersect at C by the angle $\theta/2$. It is possible to take p and q so that p passes through the coordinate origin. Let r be the line through O and parallel to q. Then

$$\rho_{C,\theta} = \sigma_q \sigma_p = \sigma_q \sigma_r \sigma_r \sigma_p = \tau_{O,A} \rho_{O,\theta}$$

where A is the image of O by the translation $\tau_{O,A} = \sigma_q \sigma_r$. (See Figure 4.3.)

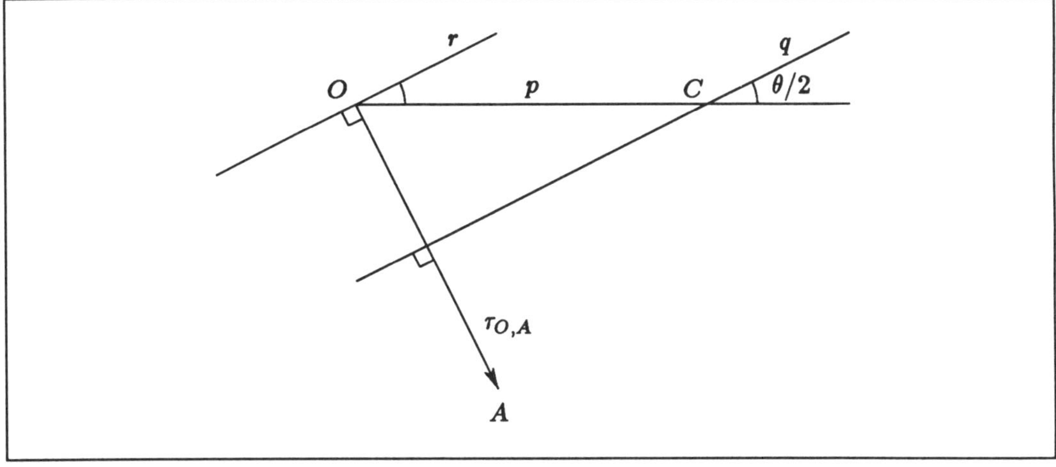

Figure 4.3: The product of a translation and a rotation.

Thus,

$$R(m,n) = \sum_i \sum_j f(i,j) g_{O,\theta}(i-a, j-b)$$

where

$$\begin{aligned}
&(a,b) \\
&= \overrightarrow{OA} \\
&= 2\sin(\theta/2) \cdot \overrightarrow{OC} \cdot \Phi\left(-(90^\circ - \theta/2)\right) \\
&= 2\sin(\theta/2) \cdot (m,n) \cdot \Phi\left(-(90^\circ - \theta/2)\right)
\end{aligned}$$

$\Phi\left(-(90^\circ - \theta/2)\right)$ is a matrix for a rotation of $-(90^\circ - \theta/2)$ around the coordinate origin.

$$\begin{aligned}
&\Phi\left(-(90^\circ - \theta/2)\right) \\
&= \begin{pmatrix} \cos(90^\circ - \theta/2) & -\sin(90^\circ - \theta/2) \\ \sin(90^\circ - \theta/2) & \cos(90^\circ - \theta/2) \end{pmatrix} \\
&= \begin{pmatrix} \sin(\theta/2) & -\cos(\theta/2) \\ \cos(\theta/2) & \sin(\theta/2) \end{pmatrix}
\end{aligned}$$

By this method, centers of rotations can be detected as relative maximums of the cross-correlation of the original picture and itself rotated with center O and angle θ.

4.3.3 Comparison with Fourier transform

Currently, our method utilizes autocorrelation and cross-correlation to evaluate the similarity of the input picture and itself transformed by an isometry. They can be calculated more effectively by using Fast Fourier transform [2][4][7] and its inverse counterpart, but our method has some advantages.

By the parallelization method described in Section 4.5, it is possible to accelerate the classification by calculating the autocorrelation or cross-correlation only at points necessary to find the relative maximums. By using FFT, it is necessary to process the entire data area.

It is impossible to utilize more complex similarity measures by FFT. For example, suppose the input picture is colored. In this case, the distance on the CIE chromacity diagram [9] is more suitable than conventional differences.

4.4 Classification method

The classification of the group is based on the existence of rotations, reflections, and glide reflections.

The actual classification proceeds in the following steps:

Find translations from the autocorrelation of the pattern.

Find rotations and reflections based on the translations.

Compute the generating translations.

Construct unit cell of the repeating pattern.

Classify wallpaper patterns based on the information obtained.

This section introduces methods to find translations and rotations utilizing autocorrelation and cross-correlation. The information obtained during the process is used immediately in the successive operations.

4.4.1 Translation

In the classification, finding generating translations τ_1, τ_2 is important. However, images similar to the original image may be obtained by the translations which do not belong to the symmetry, for example, by $\frac{1}{2}\tau_1$. Therefore the classification method first tries to find two smallest translations indicated by the relative maximums. At this time, these translations may not belong to the symmetry. After the rotations and reflections are detected, it examines the translation again to compute the generating translations as the products of the previous findings.

4.4.2 Find relative maximums

Translations appear as relative maximums in the autocorrelation of the pattern. The problem is reduced into finding relative maximums in the image.

Autocorrelation $R(m,n)$ always has the maximum value $R(0,0)$, because it represents the similarity measure between two identical images. Other relative maximums $R(m,n)$ informs that the image has self-similarity with a translation indicated by the vector (m,n). The value $R(m,n)$ represents how the two images are similar, a higher value means a stronger similarity.

However, not all of the relative maximums represent translations. One way to exclude relative maximums not corresponding to translations is to filter them according to its value in comparison with $R(0,0)$. A relative maximum with the similar magnitude with $R(0,0)$ can be considered as a translation. The comparison must take care that correlations are taken over the limited area, i.e., $R(m,n)$ becomes lower when (m,n) gets far from $(0,0)$. To normalize R by dividing the overlapping area between f and g avoids this problem. *Correlation coefficient* [5] is a possible alternative, though it is computationally expensive.

The method searches for a nearest relative maximum around the origin by conventional hill-climbing techniques, e.g., by maximum gradient method. On finding one at (m_1,n_1), it checks whether that is a translation, by searching relative maximums by the same method starting at (km_1,kn_1), with non-zero integer k. If all the relative maximums found by this are recognized as translations, (m_1,n_1) is qualified to be a candidate for the generating translations. If this check fails, multiples of (m_1,n_1) is used instead, until one candidate or none is found. Then the method searches another candidate, with the different direction.

4.4.3 Rotations and reflections

Rotations and reflections appear as relative maximums in cross-correlations between the image and the image rotated or reflected. The process to find them is similar to the case of translation.

If none of relative maximums in the cross-correlation is at similar magnitude as the translation with $(0,0)$, the method insists that there is no rotations (or reflections).

If one rotation or reflection is found, a similar procedure as in the case of translation is repeated, to search ones which are translated from the first by the multiples of translation previously found. not all of the translated ones may be always an actual rotation or reflection, for the reason described in 4.4.1. The generating translations is now determined by the existence of rotations or reflections. If none exists, the candidate translations are the generating translations.

4.4.4 Unit cell

The parallelogrammatical region bounded by τ_1 and τ_2 is called *unit cell,* because the entire image is the repetition of the unit cell. After the generating translations have been determined, the average over the images translated by all τ in $\langle \tau_1, \tau_2 \rangle$ results the unit cell, with perturbation removed.

If rotations or reflections are contained in the wallpaper groups, the unit cell should be located in the image to have them at the fixed point, for example, on the edges. Otherwise, the unit cell can be cut out from anywhere.

4.4.5 Classification

According to the information obtained, a given wallpaper group is classified into one of seventeen classes, as described in section 4.2.3. In some classes, the unit cell is divided into smaller regions, based on rotations and reflections.

Once the group is classified, the entire image can be reproduced from the unit cell and the generating translations. The reproduced image has less noise because the unit cell is taken from the average of repeated patterns.

4.5 Communicating processes

The method to find translations and rotations can be parallelized by communicating processes. Some processes do the hill-climbing simultaneously. A process computes the correlation only at the needed point. This allows to adapt more complex formula instead of the correlation, as described in 4.3.3.

This section presents a brief outline to the parallelization of the method.

4.5.1 Parallel search for translations

There is two phase in finding translations, as explained in 4.4.2: (1) find a peak. (2) make sure it is a translation. Each of them is essentially a general hill-climbing problem. This paper assumes to adapt maximum-gradient method to solve it, but the discussion below generally applies to other methods.

Search for peaks is done by several processes, starting from different points. Each process computes the gradient of the correlation at the point, computing the value of the correlation. If it decide that this point is not a peak, the next point to be checked is computed from the gradient value. At this time, it marks that this point has been checked, allowing other processes to avoid checking the same point again. The search proceeds from the next point, unless that is marked. Otherwise, the process determines the next searching point radomly, at a bit distant. Figure 4.4 illustrates the trajectories of six processes. The process b and e show the examples of random teleportations.

On reaching a peak, the process signals other processes that it found a candidate for a translation. The signalled processes suspend the searching, then all the processes check if the candidate is a translation. Each process searches for the peaks corresponding to a multiple of the translation. If almost all multiples are recognized as translations, the candidate is qualified as a translation in the wallpaper group. Otherwise, the result is gathered to determine whether the twice of the candidate is a translation, or the thrice, ..., or the candidate was actually a noise. In the last case, the suspended search continues on each process. Figure 4.5 illustrates the communication among the processes.

The generating translations can be searched simultaniously by dividing hill-climbing processes into two teams with different orientations. After one team has found a translation, two teams are merged into one, searching for another translation. The checking phase might check peaks on each products of the two translations for gettig more reliability.

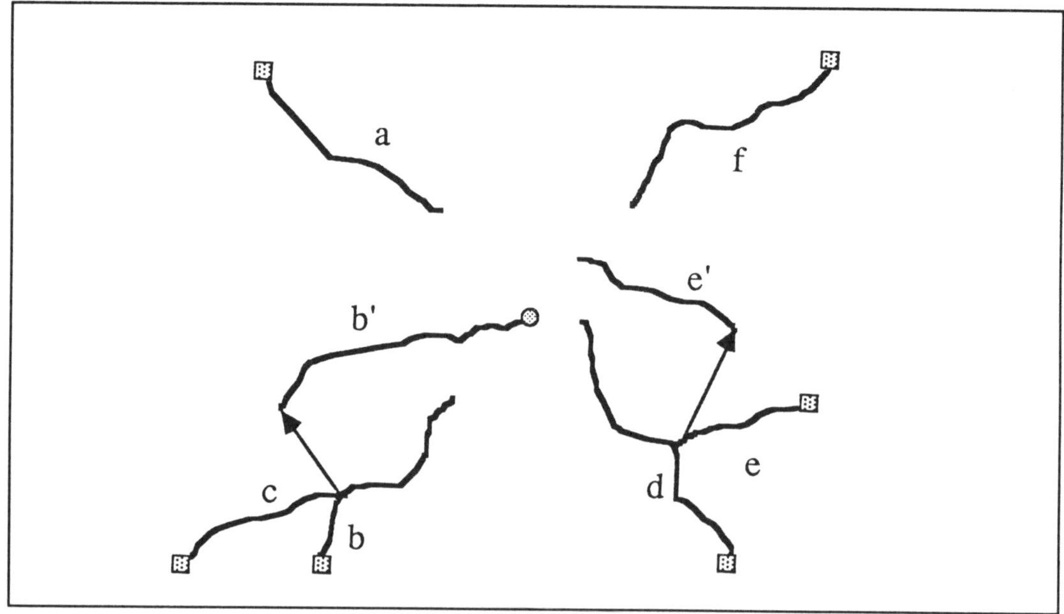

Figure 4.4: Trajectories of searching processes

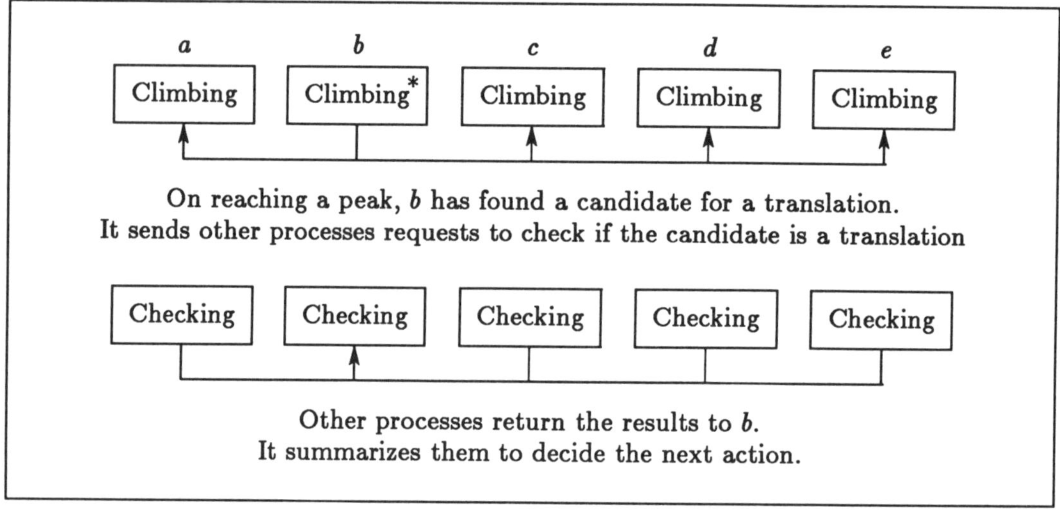

Figure 4.5: Communication among processes

4.5.2 Parallel search for rotations and other symmetries

Searching n-centers, axes of reflections and glide reflections is parallelized in a similar way. The check is done for the translated points by all translations.

2-, 3-, and 4-centers may be searched simultaneously by one team for each. Since 3- and 4-centers do not coexist, if one of either is found, the search for the other is stopped.

4.6 Conclusions

A method to classify the wallpaper group of a given pattern was presented. Also an infomation-driven approach to accelerate the classification process was explained. The method utilized autocorrelation to find translation-symmetry and cross-correlation to find rotation-symmetry. An approach to parallelization using communicating processes was outlined.

4.7 References

[1] Duda, Richard O., and Peter E. Hart, *Pattern Classification and Scene Analysis,* (John Wiley & Sons, Inc., 1973).

[2] Duff, M. J. B., and S. Levialdi, *Languages and Architectures for Image Processing,* (Academic Press Inc., 1981).

[3] Durbin, John R., *Modern Algebra: an Introduction,* 2nd ed., (John Wiley & Sons, Inc., 1985).

[4] Eckmiller, Rolf, and Christoph v. d. Malsburg., *Neural Computers,* (Springer-Verlag, 1988).

[5] Gonzalez, R. C., and P. Wintz, *Digital Image Processing,* 2nd Ed., (Addison-Wesley, 1987).

[6] Gool, L. V., P. Dewaele, and A. Oosterlinck, "Texture Analysis Anno 1983," *Comput. Vision Graphics Image Process.,* 29(1985), 336–357.

[7] Hockney, R. W., and C. R. Jesshope, *Parallel Computers 2: Architecture, Programming and Algorithms,* (Adam Hilger, 1988).

[8] Martin, George E., *Transformation Geometry: An Introduction to Symmetry,* (Springer-Verlag New York Inc., 1982).

[9] Murch, G. M., "Human Factors of Colour Displays," in *Advances in Computer Graphics II* (F. R. A. Hopgood, R. J. Hubbold and D. A. Duce. eds), (Springer-Verlag, 1986).

[10] Young, Tzay Y., and King-sun Fu, *Handbook of Pattern Recognition and Image Processing,* (Academic Press, Inc., 1986).

Chapter 5

Fault tolerant transputer network for image processing

S. Pfleger, G. Kasch
Technical University
Computer Science
8000 Munich 80, Orleansstr. 34
West Germany

Abstract This paper presents a novel network architecture for parallel and pipelined image processing, which allows execution continuation in the presence of faults. The fault tolerance capability is based on process migration and scheduling self-reorganisation.

A task consisting of several parallel and sequential processes is distributed among the nodes. Parallel and pipelining execution techniques are used with the aim of improving the system efficiency.

A ring network has been used for message passing between the processing nodes and the controller. The nodes are connected additionally to a communication panel, with the aim of providing direct communication links between them.

This architecture is very suitable for image processing since it allows the exchange of large data without decreasing the response time performance. The implemented network, consisting of a set of 16 processing nodes (Transputer T800), a controller node (T800) and a communication panel (Link multiplexer C004) shows a substantial improvement of the availability performance in the presence of execution faults.

There is a trade-off between the degree of parallelism and the respose time performance, due to communication and process management overhead, and additional research effort is therefore needed.

Finally, it is the authors' believe, that heterogenerous networks, consisting of Transputers and signal processors, could drastically improve the efficiency of the image processing system, since they allow a flexible distribution of processes to the most suitable processor.

KEYWORDS: artificial intelligence, parallel processes, image processing, Transputer networks, availability.

5.1 Introduction

Several network architectures have been proposed for image processing. Three main architectures for image processing machines can be distinguished [Hwan 83]:

- SIMD array processor [Bat 80] [Duff 82] [Hord 82] [Rohr 77]
- pipelined vector processor [Gran 81] [Loug 80] [Yen 81]
- MIMD multiprocessor [Anto 81] [Brig 82] [Brig 81] [Kush 81] [Leut 80] [Mori 78] [Rieg 81]

Several image processing machines have been presented and some have been implemented, based on multi-microprocessor systems [Kido 78].

Special template controlled image processors [Temm 80] can achieve concurrent operations by using a pipeline technique through the data flow operational graph representation. This processor type is suitable for image processing computations , such as the two-dimensional fast Fourier transform, affine transformation, two-dimensional convolution, and arithmetic and logical operators between images [Kido 83].

The Transputer is specially suitable for building large networks [Bau 89] due to its communication channels facilities [Arch 86] and due to the communication constructs of the OCCAM programming language [Bur 88] [Occam 88] [Trans 88].

The programmable link switch IMS-C004 [Link 87] provides full duplex communication between members of the INMOS Transputer family, according to the INMOS serial link protocol. It can be cascaded to any depth without loss of signal integrity and can be used to construct reconfigurable networks of different size. This simple switch provides a full crossbar connection between 32 link inputs and 32 link outputs, and therefore it is especially suitable for building image processing networks, since it allows non-sophisticated and direct connections between the communicating Transputers.

Several Transputer network architectures can be used for image processing.

5.2 Network architecture

Flexible network structures are useful for image processing applications, since they allow an easy net reconfiguration for different classes of algorithms [Harp 88]. The architecture presented in [Harp 88] has been tested for different algorithms which are used in low-level image processing. The processing speed has been increased by reconfigurating the net to a SIMD machine. Several combinations of SIMD and MIMD systems have been developed for image processing [Sieg 84]. The ring communication architecture has been suggested and implemented in [Rieg 81] for general AI applications.

The model of execution which has been used, plays an important role in the capability of a system to allow parallel image processing. Several computation models have been developed with the aim of allowing an automatic parallelism of the processes belonging to a user task [Trel 86]:

- Control Flow model [Trel 84]
- Data Flow model [Gurd 85] [Trel 82]
- Reduction concept [Trel 82] [Vegd 84]
- Actor model [Hewi 80] [Wiln 80]
- Knowledge representation model [Higu 85] [Stol 84]
- Predicate logic model [Hert 84] [Mura 84]

Our execution Model combines the Data Flow model [Gurd 85] [Trel 82] with the Actor model [Bake 78] [Hewi 80]. We start procedures containing several communication processes, which transform the input data to output data, at several levels of execution. In our data flow model we allow an overlapped execution of the procedures (pipelining). Since the usual low-level image processing algorithms work sequentially on image data, we improve in this way the respose time performance. The overlapped procedure execution, known as pipelining ensures a substantial improvement of the processing speed.

For synchronising the system we use the Actor model [Bake 78] [Hewi 80], where objects communicate by sending messages and the arrival of messages starts the execution of the next instruction.

Our network combines the ring topology with the star topology (see figure 5.1).

The message ring connects the nodes and is used only for synchronising the process execution on different nodes. The ring is implemented with a switchable controller which

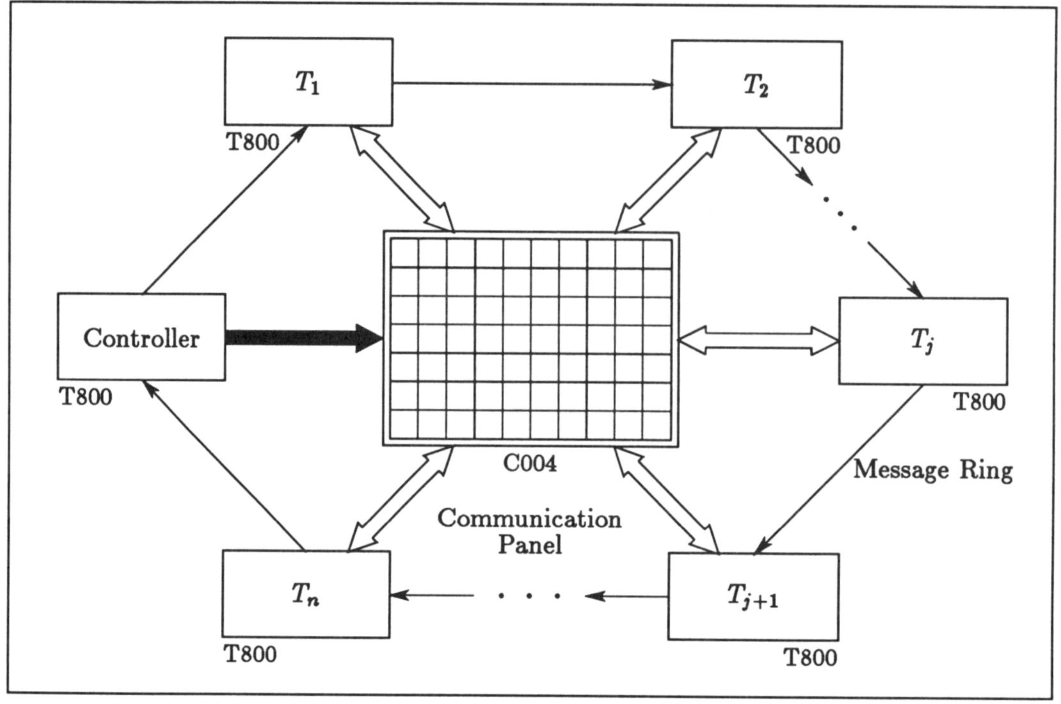

Figure 5.1: Network architecture

allows to disconnect the faulty nodes during execution, and also to add additional nodes to the network, if it is needed.

The star topology has been used for allowing data communication between the nodes. A communication panel (see figure 5.1) allows the direct connection between the nodes and permits to improve in this way the performance of the data transfer between two processes residing on different nodes. This data communication topology maintains the data transfer performance by an increasing number of nodes.

Each node contains three different types of processes, which are executed parallely (see figure 5.2):

- the message handler,
- the process handler, and
- the data handler.

The message handler is connected to the message ring and it controls the message communication between the nodes. Additionally it controls the process handler and the data handler (i.e. it starts these processes and receives their execution state messages,

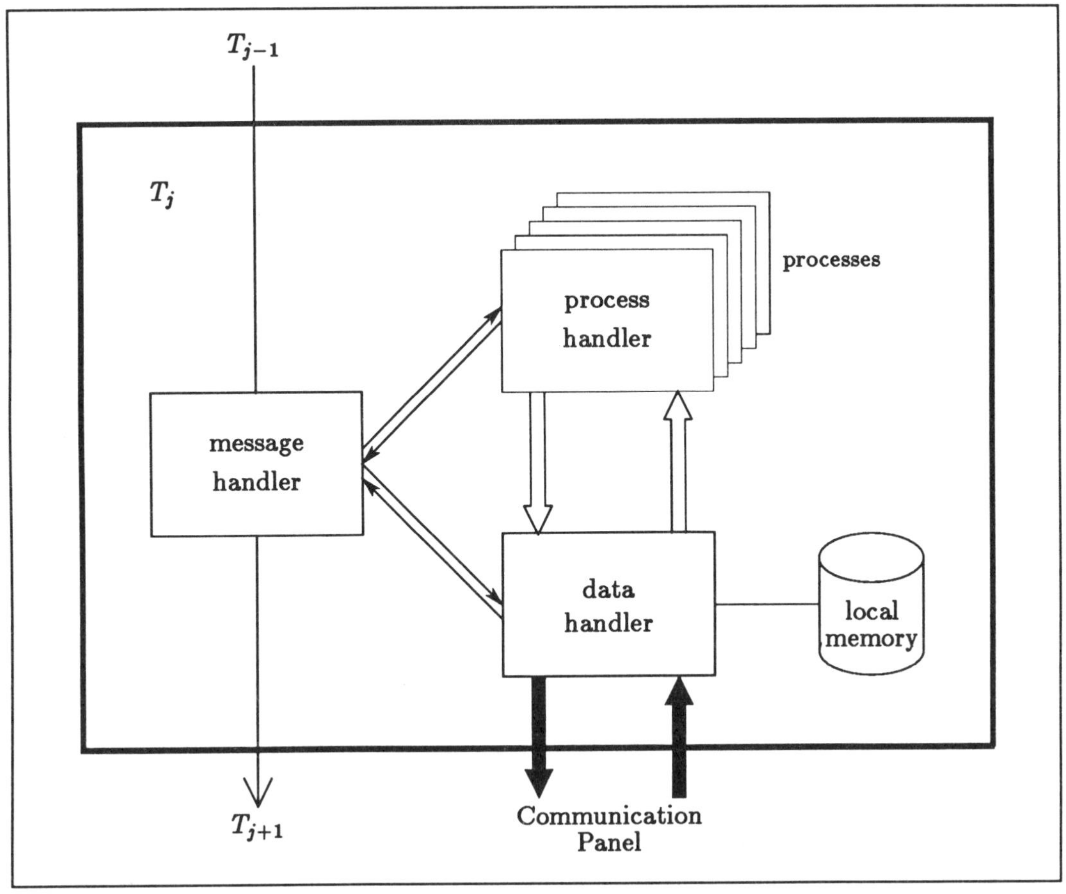

Figure 5.2: Node architecture

and also their termination messages).

The process handler is concerned with the process creation and its execution.

The data handler performs the data transfer between processes and the local memory, and also the data transfer between processes through the communication panel. The local memory is used as a FIFO queue for the processes of a pipeline, and as a buffer for storing duplicated data. In this way we ensure that the restart of a procedure in the pipeline can be performed in the presence of execution faults (faulty nodes or communication line failures).

Each node (processing or controlling) consists of a IMS-T800 Processor [Trans88] which runs at 20MHz with an size of 8 MByte of local memory. We use the line switching technique for the switchboard and the message ring. The communication panel has been implemented by using an IMS-C004 programmable link switch [Link87].

The first experimental implementation of the system contains 8 processing nodes (T800), one controlling node (T800) and a communication panel (C004). Four Transputers are used for usual execution, and four additional stand-by Transputers can be activated for performing fault tolerance functions.

We intend to evolve the system by expanding the switchboard of the communication panel and by adding more processing nodes. Our second experimental implementation will contain 16 processing nodes and a pool of 3 stand-by node for fault tolerance reasons. We also intend to experiment the suitability of this architecture for heterogeneous networks. This type of network will contain signal processors additionally to the Transputers. A procedure will be preferentially sheduled to the node with the highest processing speed. This response time optimisation criterion will facilitate the integration of Transputers in existing networks for image processing.

5.3 Availability

An execution task can be represented as a serial - parallel structure of communicating processes. The processes which are distributed to different Transputers are executed parallely and build a parallel construct, called "Par" e.g. Par (processes p1, p2, p5, p7) in figure 5.3.

The sequantial processes build a processing sequence, called sequence construct "Seq". The processes belonging to the same sequence are executed on the same Transputer, e.g. Seq (p2, p3, p4) in figure 5.3.

Let's assume that an execution task is executed on the network of (m) Transputers. Let (nj) be the number of the processes Pr_{ji}, (for $i = 1, 2, \ldots\ nj$) which are sequentially executed on the Transputer T_j. The total number of processes of a task is N:

$$N = \sum_{j=i}^{j=m} \sum_{i-1}^{i=nj} ji$$

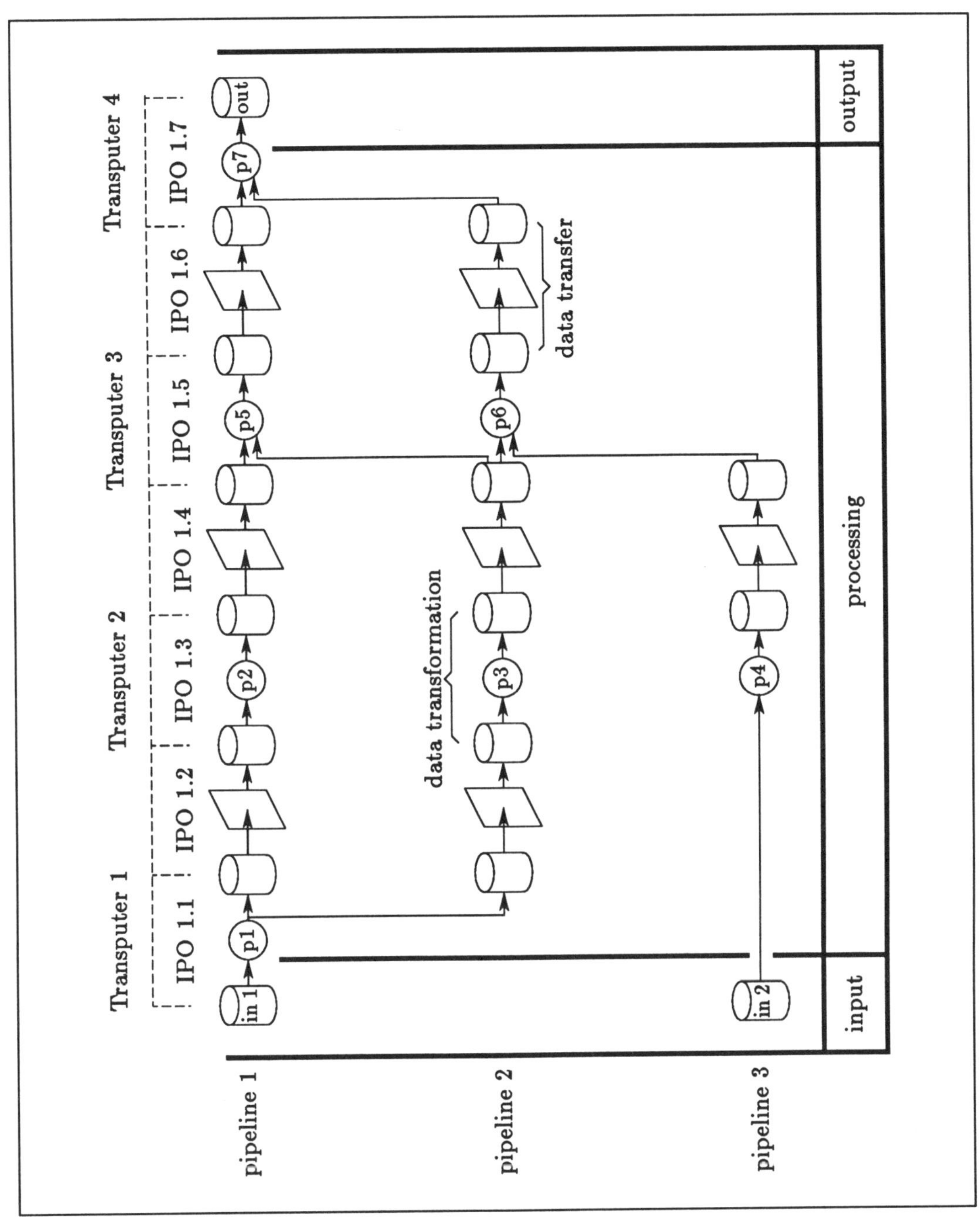

Figure 5.3: Data flow diagram in the IPO (input/processing/output) form

The set of sequences which can be executed on the network (one on each Transputer) at a given time can be represented by:

$$\begin{cases} \mathsf{Seq}_1(Pr_{11}, Pr_{12}, \ldots Pr_{1i}, \ldots Pr_{1.n1}) \text{ on } T_1 \\ \mathsf{Seq}_2(Pr_{21}, Pr_{22}, \ldots Pr_{2i}, \ldots Pr_{2.n2}) \text{ on } T_2 \\ \ldots\ldots\ldots \\ \mathsf{Seq}_j(Pr_{j1}, Pr_{j2}, \ldots Pr_{ji}, \ldots Pr_{j.nj}) \text{ on } T_j \\ \ldots\ldots\ldots \\ \mathsf{Seq}_m(Pr_{m1}, Pr_{m2}, \ldots Pr_{mi}, \ldots Pr_{m.nm}) \text{ on } T_m \end{cases}$$

An execution task containing a number of (m) sequences is executed parallely on the network:

$\mathsf{Par}\ (\mathsf{Seq}_1, \mathsf{Seq}_2, \ldots \mathsf{Seq}_j \ldots \mathsf{Seq}_m)$ on $(T_1, T_2, \ldots T_m)$

A task containing less then (m) sequences does not use efficiently the parallel execution facilities. If the number of sequences is higher then (m), a segmentation in blocks with maximal (m) sequences is performed by the controller. In this last case, several execution "epochs" (as many as resulting blocks) are requiered in order to execute completly the task:

$$\begin{aligned} \mathsf{Seq}_{task}\ \ (\ \ & \mathsf{Par}_1(\mathsf{Seq}_1, \mathsf{Seq}_2, \ldots \mathsf{Seq}_m), \\ & \mathsf{Par}_2(\mathsf{Seq}_{m+1}, \mathsf{Seq}_{m+2}, \ldots \mathsf{Seq}_{2m}), \\ & \ldots\ldots\ldots\ldots\ldots\ldots\ldots\ldots\ldots\ldots \\ & \mathsf{Par}_x(\mathsf{Seq}_{(x-1)m+1}, \ldots \mathsf{Seq}_{xm}) \\ ). & \end{aligned}$$

A given task is correctly processed with a probability which is a function of the availability of the parallel and serial processes, and of the Transputer availability.

Availability is defined here as the probability that a unit (process, Transputer) is operational at a given time. The unit may have only one of the following states at a given time:

- "operational state", if it performs correctly (i.e. it is available), or

- "faulty state" if it performs incorrect execution (it is non-available). We assume here a stationary state and constant down-time ratio in time. Two classes of process and Transputer failures may occur during execution:

- non-catastrophic failures, due to activated transient faults, and

- catastrophic failures, due to permanent execution faults.

Notation:

p, P	- availability
q, Q	- non-availability ($q = 1 - p$)
Q_{Tj}	- Transputer non-availability for non-catastrophal failures
$\hat{Q}_{Tj}$	- Transputer non-availability for catastrophal failures
Q_{Mj}	- non-availability of the process migration procedure M_j
q_{ji}	- process non-availability for non-catastrophal failures
$\hat{q}_{ji}$	- process non-availability for catastrophal failures
T	- total number of Transputers
r	- number of redundant Transputers
n	- number of the processes belonging to a sequence
m	- the degree of parallelism (max $m = T$ for $r = 0$)
N	- the number of processes of a task ($N = m.n$ for uniform process distribution)

The availability of a sequence of processes

$$\mathbf{Seq}_j(p_{j1}, p_{j2}, \dots p_{j.nj})$$

is a function of the processes belonging to the sequence, and also a function of the Transputer on which this sequence is executed:

$$A_{Seq_j} = \exp - \left[\sum_{i=1}^{i=nj} (q_{ji} + \hat{q}_{ji}) + Q_{T_j} + \hat{Q}_{T_j} \right] \tag{5.1}$$

The availability of a task which contains a set of (m) sequences becomes:

$$A_{task} = \prod_{j=1}^{j=m} \exp - \left[\sum_{i=1}^{i=nj} (q_{ji} + \hat{q}_{ji}) + Q_{T_j} + \hat{Q}_{T_j} \right] \tag{5.2}$$

for $m <= T$

5.4 Fault tolerance

The fault tolerance is defined here as the capability of the image processing to continue its correct execution in the presence of execution faults. The fault tolerance to transient execution faults (non-catastrophic Transputer and process faults) is ensured by resuming execution from its beginning. The restart procedure is very simple, since no state preservation and restoration is needed:

`do`	process Pr_{jx} on Transputer T_j
`signal`	fault
`stop`	process Pr_{jx}
`reset`	process Pr_{jx}
`restart`	process Pr_{jx} on Transputer T_j

The tolerance of the permanent Transputer faults is ensured by migrating the actual sequence of processes running on this Transputer to a stand-by Transputer, and resuming execution.

`do`	Seqj on Transputer T_j
`signal`	fault
`stop`	process $Pr_{jx} \in Seq_j$
`migrate`	processes $(Pr_{jx}, Pr_{j(x+1)}, \ldots Pr_{j.nj})$ on Transputer T_r
`restart`	process Pr_{jx} on Transputer T_r

The duplicated execution is a simple form of replication, and allows a substantial increase of availability of the sequence of processes:

$$\overset{*}{A}_{Seq_j} = \exp - \left\{ \left[1 - \exp - \left[\sum_{i=1}^{i=nj} (q_{ji} + \hat{q}_{ji}) + Q_{ji} + \hat{Q}_{ji} \right] \right] \cdot \right.$$
$$\left. \cdot \left[1 - \exp - \left[Q_{M_j} + \left[\sum_{i=1}^{i=nj} (q_{ji} + \hat{q}_{ji}) + Q_{ji} + \hat{Q}_{ji} \right] \right] \right] \right\} \quad (5.3)$$

The improvement of the sequence availability due to Transputer redundancy is visualised in figure 5.4. The availability expression of a task executed on Transputer network containing a number of (t) processing Transputers and additionally a pool of (r) redundant Transputers in stand-by state becomes:

$$\overset{*}{A}_{task} = \prod_{j=r+1}^{j=T} A_{Seq_j} \cdot \prod_{j=1}^{j=r} \overset{*}{A}_{Seq_j} \quad (5.4)$$

where A_{Seq_j} and $\overset{*}{A}_{Seq_j}$ can be obtained from (5.2) and (5.3)

REMARKS: The tolerance of the permanent process faults is not intended to be covered here, since it is an application problem. The fault masking and/or fault preventing capabilities for process protection against permanent design faults should be implemented on the application layers.

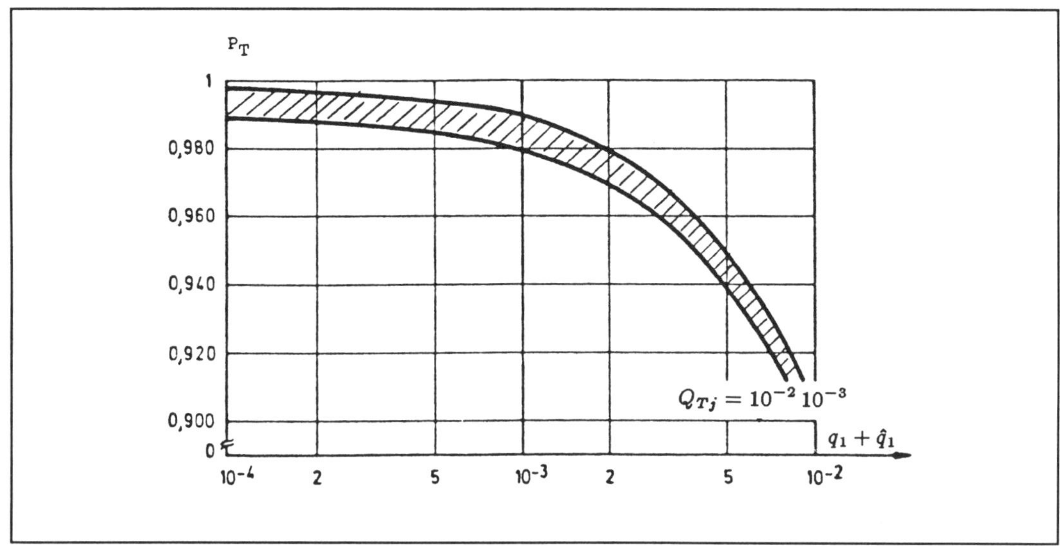

Figure 5.4: Availabilty increasement of a sequence of processes due to transputer redundancy

5.5 Conclusions

We presented here a fault tolerant architecture which allows parallel process execution and pipelining. This architecture has been implemented on a Transputer network for image processing, consisting of 8 nodes (T800), a communication panel (C004) and a network controller (T800). The parallelism degree is here restricted by a number of four Transputer, the other four Transputers (stand-by) are used for fault masking reasons. This restriction applies only to the optional fault tolerant execution mode. In the fault intolerant mode all 8 Transputers are used for process execution. The fault intolerant execution mode is more efficient in comparison with the fault tolerant mode, provided that no Transputer errors occur. The price therefore is a graceful performance degradation of processing availability and a drastical decrease of the parallelism degree, in the presence of Transputer execution faults.

We intend to extend the network up to 16 Transputers, and to reserve a pool of 3

Transputers for the fault masking reasons. Additionally we intend to investigate the limits imposed by the Amdahl's law (for the task parallelism and pipelining) in our Transputer network for image processing.

Acknowledgement The authors are very grateful to Karin Kasch and Professor Bernd Radig for their assistance.

5.6 References

[Anto 81] D. Antonsson et al., 'PICAP-A System Approach to Image Processing' Proc. Workshop Computer Architecture for PAIDM, 1981.

[Arch 86] INMOS, 'Transputer Architecture' Reference Manual, INMOS Limited, 1986.

[Bake 78] H. G. Baker, 'Actor Systems for Real-Time Computation', Tech. Rep., MIT lab for Computer Science, 1978.

[Bat 80] K. E. Batcher, 'Design of a Massively Parallel Processor', IEEE Trans. Computers, Vol. C-29, No. 9, 1980.

[Bau 88] F. Baude, 'Topologies for Large Transputer Networks : Theoretical Aspect and Experimental Approach', Occam User Group 10 Conference, 1988.

[Brig 81] F. A. Briggs, M. Dubois, K. Hwang, 'Throughput Analysis and Configuration Design of a Shared-Resource Multiprocessor System: PUMPS', Proc. Eight Annual Symp. Computer Architecture, 1981.

[Brig 82] F. A. Briggs et al., 'PUMPS Architecture for Pattern Analysis and Image Database Management', IEEE Trans. Computers, Vol. C-31, No. 10, 1982.

[Bur 88] A. Burns, 'Programming in OCCAM 2', Addison Wesley Publishing Company, 1988.

[Duff 82] M. J. Duff, 'CLIP 4', Special Computer Architecture for Pattern Recognition, CRC Press, 1982.

[Gran 81] G. H. Grandlung et al., 'The GOP Image Processor', Proc. Workshop Computer Architecture for PAIDM, 1981.

[Gurd 85] J. Gurd et al, 'The Manchester Prototype Data-Flow Computer', Comms, ACM, Vol. 28, No. 1, 1985.

[Harp 88] J. G. Harp, K. J. Palmer, H. C. Webber, 'Image Processing On The Reconfigurable Transputer Processor', Parallel Programming of Transputer Based Machines, IOS, Amsterdam, 1988.

[Hert 84] L. O. Hertzberger, 'The Architecture of Fifth Generation Inference Computers', Future Generation Computer Systems, Vol. 1, No. 1, 1984.

[Hewi 80] C. E. Hewitt, 'The APIARY Network architecture for Knowledge Systems', Proc. LISP Conf, Stanford, 1980.

[Higu 85] T. Higuchi et al, 'A Semantic Network Language Machine', Microcomputers Usage and Design, Elsevier Science Publishers, North-Holland, 1985.

[Hord 82] R. M. Hord, D. K. Stevenson, 'The Illiac IV Architecture and Its Suitability for Image Processing', Special Computer Architecture for Pattern Recognition, CRC Press, Boca Raton, 1982.

[Hwan 83] K. Hwang, K. Fu, 'Integrated Computer Architectures for Image Processing and Database Management', Computer Vol. 16, No. 1, p. 51-60, 1983.

[Kido 78] M. Kidode, et al, 'Design of Local Parallel Processor for Image Processing', AFIPS Conf. Proc., Vol. 47, No. 17, 1978.

[Kido 83] M. Kidode, 'Image Processing Machines in Japan', Computer Vol. 16, No. 1, 1983.

[Kush 81] T. Kushner, A. Y. Wu, A. Rosenfeld, 'Image Processing on ZMOB' Proc. Workshop Computer Architecture for PAIDM, 1981.

[Leut 80] K. Leutjen, 'FLIP: A Flexible Multiprocessor System for Image Processing', Proc. Fifth Int'l Conf. Pattern Recognition, 1980.

[Link 87] INMOS, 'IMS C004 Programmable link switch' Preliminary Data, INMOS Limited, 1987.

[Loug 80] R. M. Lougheed, D. L. Mc Cubbrey, S. R. Sternberg, 'Cytocomputers: Architectures for Parallel Image Processing', Proc. Workshop Picture Data Description and Management, 1980.

[Mori 78] K. I. Mori et al., 'Design of Local Parallel Pattern Processor for Image Processing', AFIPS Conf. Proc.m Vol. 47, 1978.

[Mura 84] K. Murakami et al, 'Architectures and Hardware Systems: Parallel Inference Machine and Knowledge Base Machine', Proc. Int. Conf. on Fifth Generation Computer Systems, Tokyo, 1984.

[Occam 88] INMOS, 'OCCAM 2 Reference Manual', Prentice Hall, New York, 1988.

[Pott 83] J. L. Potter, 'Image Processing on the Massively Parallel Processor', Computer, Vol. 16, No. 1, 1983.

[Rieg 81] C. Rieger, 'ZMOB: Doing It in Parallel', Proc. Workshop Computer Architecture for PAIDM, 1981.

[Rohr 77] D. Rohrbacher, 'Image processing with STARAN Parallel Computer', Computer, Vol. 10, No. 8

[Stol 84] S. J. Stolfo, D. P. Miranker, 'DADO: A Parallel Processor for Expert Systems', Proc. of the 1984 Int. Conf. on Parallel Processing, 1984.

[Sieg 84] H. J. Siegel, T. Schwederski, N. J. Davis, J. T. Kuehn 'PASM: A Reconfigurable Parallel System For Image Processing', Computer Architecture News, Vol. 12, No. 4, 1984.

[Temm 80] T. Temma, S. Hasegawa, S. Hanaki, 'Dataflow Processor for Image Processing', Proc. Mini and Microcomputers Symp., Vol. 5, No. 3, Feb. 1980.

[Trel 86] P. C. Treleaven, A. N. Refenes, 'Computer Architectures for Artificial Intelligence', Lecture Notes in Computer Science, No. 272, Springer, Berlin, 1986.

[Trel 84] P. C. Treleaven, I. G. Lima, 'Future Computers: logic, data flow, ..., control flow?', IEEE Computer, Vol. 17, No. 3, 1984.

[Trel 82] P. C. Treleaven et al, 'Data Driven and Demand Driven Computer Architecture', ACM Computing Surveys, Vol. 14, No. 1, 1982.

[Trans88] INMOS, 'Transputer Development System' Prentice Hall, New York, 1988.

[Vegd 84] S. R. Vegdahl, 'A Survey of Proposed Architectures for Execution of Functional Languages', IEEE Trans. Computers, Vol. C-33, No. 12, 1984.

[Wiln80] Winston W.T. 'Recursive Machines' Palo Alto Research Center, Internal Report, 1980.

[Yen 81] D. W. L. Yen, A. V. Kulkami, 'The ESL Systolic Processor for Signal and Image Processing', Proc. Workshop Computer Architecture for PAIDM, 1981.

Chapter 6

Research and development of the parallel inference machine in the FGCS project

Atsuhiro Goto
Institute for New Generation Computer Technology (ICOT)
21F, Mitakokusai Building,
1-4-28, Mita, Minato-ku,
Tokyo, 108, JAPAN
CSNET: goto%icot.jp@relay.cs.net,
UUCP: ihnp4!kddlab!icot!goto

Abstract As part of the FGCS project, we are developing parallel inference machine (PIM) systems based on a logic programming framework. The research and development of PIM includes the PIM hardware architectures and the parallel implementation of KL1.

KL1 has been designed as the PIM kernel language, so that both PIM applications and the parallel operating system (PIMOS) can be written in KL1. The characteristics of KL1 are used to solve KL1 parallel implementation problems, such as distributed resource management, goal scheduling and distribution, memory management, and distributed unification. They have been condensed into the abstract machine instruction set, KL1-B.

In designing the hardware architecture of the PIM pilot machine, a hierarchical configuration has been introduced to connect more than 100 processing elements. A new instruction architecture for KL1 is provided for the processing elements. A coherent cache protocol has been designed to make high-performance clusters, each of which includes eight processing elements connected with shared memory. These clusters will be connected by a multiple hyper-cube network.

6.1 Introduction

The research and development (R&D) of the parallel inference machine (PIM) is one of the most important targets in the FGCS project. The PIM will be the pioneer of parallel processing in knowledge information processing system (KIPS) application fields.

The principal aim of parallel processing is to increase the execution performance so that users will be able to solve big application programs. The PIM should have many more features than conventional general-purpose machines. For example, pattern matching operations are important in many KIPS applications. However, it is insufficient to increase the efficiency of only limited functions in KIPS applications. In other words, development of the PIM should strive to develop more general and powerful machines than conventional ones. The PIM should also cover the functions of conventional computers, because AI machines are not simply game tree searching machines.

During the initial stage (1982 to 1984) of the FGCS project, the elementary mechanisms of the PIM were studied from various standpoints [12]. One of our most important policies in the R&D of the PIM system is to build up a total system based on logic programming, so that the system designers of the PIM can easily look through all levels of the system in a logic programming framework. This is an important way to solve the *semantic gap* argument: application and implementation are closer, therefore execution is faster. Therefore, the R&D of the current PIM, started in 1985 [13,11], is being conducted with the design and implementation of the kernel language (KL1) and the PIM operating system (PIMOS) [6], which is written in KL1 as a *self-contained* operating system.

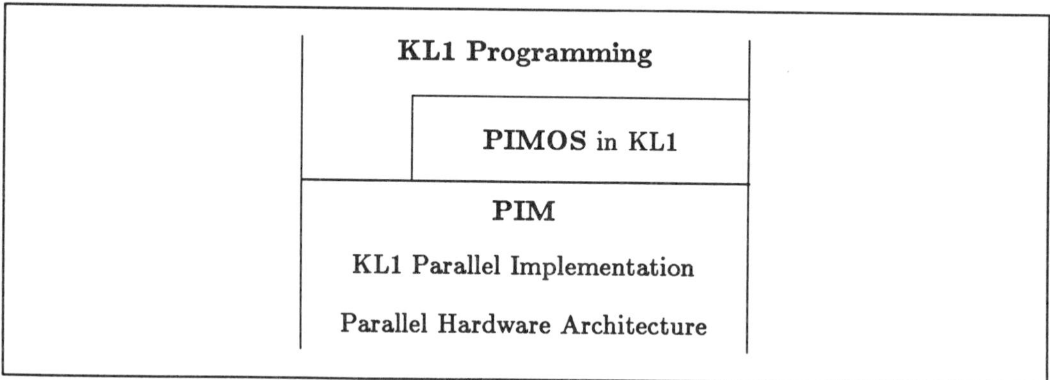

Figure 6.1: Parallel inference machine system overview

We set the following goals aiming at the PIM system shown in Figure 6.1.

First, we hope to realize a very high execution performance for logic programming in KL1. We believe that more than 100 times the performance of current machines will be necessary to enhance logic programming application research. Next, we aim to build practical systems that will be available as research tools in the final stage of the project. This is essential for application research. In addition, the development of total and practical systems stresses the importance of memory management and program control in parallel processing systems, and it also reveals the hidden problems in parallel processing. Finally we are trying to build the PIM system using KL1. The language features of KL1 are used to the full in the parallel architecture design.

This report describes the KL1 parallel implementation and the hardware architecture of the PIM pilot machine. Section 6.2 introduces KL1 with its meta-programming capability using shōen. Section 6.3 describes scheduling of KL1 goals within a cluster. Section 6.4 describes inter-cluster distribution of goals and their management using the shōen facility. Section 6.5 discusses how to reduce the communication cost in inter-cluster distributed unifications. Section 6.6 describes the incremental garbage collection mechanism embedded in the parallel KL1 implementation. The above schemes for the KL1 parallel implementation are condensed into an abstract instruction set called KL1-B [16]. KL1-B interfaces PIMs and KL1, just as WAM [29] interfaces Prolog and sequential machines. Section 6.7 overviews the KL1-B features.

The hardware architecture of the PIM pilot machine is described in section 6.8. We introduced a hierarchical configuration into the PIM hardware architecture (shown in Figure 6.2), which is assumed in the discussions about KL1 parallel implementation. Several PEs form a *cluster* with a shared memory. These clusters are interconnected by a communication network.

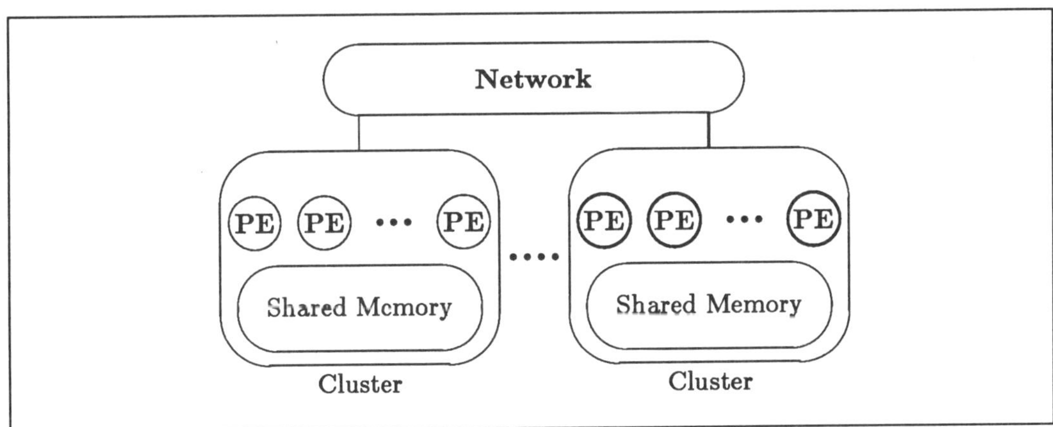

Figure 6.2: Abstract PIM configuration

The Multi-PSI [28] system has been built to enhance the research for the KL1 parallel implementation and the PIMOS design. The Multi-PSI is a collection of the PSI machines [18] connected by fast mesh network [27]. Most of the KL1 implementation issues in distributed environments have been studied through the design of the Multi-PSI system [17].

6.2 The kernel language KL1

6.2.1 FGHC: base of KL1

KL1 was initially specified as Flat Guarded Horn Clauses (FGHC) [23], taking efficient implementation into consideration. The major reasons for choosing FGHC as the basis for KL1 are as follows. GHC has clear and simple semantics as a concurrent logic programming language, by which programmers can express important concepts in parallel programming, such as inter-process communication and synchronization. In addition, FGHC is an efficient language, in the sense that we can specify the machine level language.

FGHC is a language based on Horn clauses of the form: H :- $G_1, ...G_m | B_1, ..., B_n$. where H is the head of the clause, G_i are guards, "|" is the commit, and B_j are the body goals. In FGHC, as in Prolog, procedures are composed of sets of clauses with the same name and arity. Unlike Prolog, there are no nondeterminate procedures. Execution proceeds by attempting unification between a goal (the caller) and a clause head (the callee). If unification succeeds, execution of the guard goals is attempted. These goals can only be system-defined built-in procedures, e.g. arithmetic comparison. If the guard succeeds, the procedure call "commits" to that clause, i.e. any other possibly good candidate clauses are dismissed. If the head or guard fails, another candidate clause in the procedure is attempted (if all clauses fail, the program fails). There is a third possibility however: that the call *suspends*.

FGHC restricts unification in the head and guard (the "passive part" of the clause) to be input unification only, i.e. bindings are not exported. Output unification can be performed only in the body part (the "active part"). These restrictions allow AND-parallel execution of body goals and even OR-parallel execution of passive parts during a procedure call (the implementation discussed here executes passive parts sequentially and executes body goals in a depth-first). Synchronization between processes is inherently performed by the requirement that no output bindings can be made in the passive part. If a binding is attempted, the call *potentially* suspends. If none of the clauses succeeds, and one or more potentially suspend, then the procedure call suspends (possibly on multiple variables).

When any of the variables to which an export binding was attempted are in fact bound (by another process), the suspended call is resumed. These semantics permit stream AND-parallel execution of the program, i.e. incomplete lists of data can be streamed from one parallel process to another in a producer-consumer relationship. For example, when a stream runs dry, the consumer receives the unbound tail of a list and suspends. When the producer generates more data, the consumer is resumed and continues processing the transmitted data.

6.2.2 Meta-programming capability using shōen

Starting from FGHC, KL1 has been extended so that it has become a practical language with the features required for the PIMOS design[1].

In GHC and FGHC, all goals compose a logical conjunction, so that the failure of a certain goal causes a global failure. However, the relation between the operating system and user programs must be that of a meta-level program and object-level programs, where the meta-level program controls or monitors the object-level programs. Therefore, it is necessary to introduce a meta-programming capability into KL1.

The meta-programming capability of KL1 is realized by the shōen facility. While tail-recursively executed goals look like small-grain threads of control (*processes*), a shōen defines a larger-grain computational unit, i.e. the concept of a *job* or a *task*. It deals with execution control of programs, resource management and exception handling.

A shōen may include child shōens, so that we can see KL1 goals form a tree-like structure (shōen tree) whose nodes are shōens and whose leaves are KL1 goals. In this case, when the execution in an outside (or parent) shōen stops, all execution in an inside (child) shōen stops automatically. When the outside execution is restarted, inside execution is also restarted.

Computing resources can be managed in each shōen to avoid, for example, infinite execution of user programs. The management of computing resources is roughly implemented as how many goal reductions can be performed within a shōen. The inside shōen can consume the computing resources within the amount of the resources that the outside shōen has.

A shōen is created by a call to the built-in predicate *execute/6*:

execute(Goal,Control,Report,Min,Max,Mask)

Goal specifies the initial goal, that is, the predicate name and its arguments, to execute in the shōen. All forked goals from the given *Goal* belong to the same shōen. *Min* and *Max* are the minimum and maximum possible priorities of goal scheduling allowed in the

[1]Chikayama et al. [6] describe the system programming features in KL1.

shōen. (See section 6.3.2.)

Control and *Report* are the control and the report streams. The control stream is used to start, stop or abort the shōen from outside. The monitoring process can be informed of events within a shōen such as the end of execution and exceptions through the report stream. Exceptions that have occurred in the shōen or are delegated from one of the child shōens are reported as a message to the report stream. *Mask* is a bit pattern for determining which exceptions should be handled in this shōen. The monitoring process can substitute a new goal for the goal that has given rise to the exception. An important thing to note is that there is no failure in a shōen. Any kind of failure is treated as an exception. The logical conjunction between KL1 goals is maintained within each shōen. In other words, goals in a shōen do not form a conjunction with goals outside the shōen. With the above meta-programming capability, we can describe not only the PIM applications but also the PIMOS, which controls parallel processes.

6.3 Goal scheduling

6.3.1 Goal reduction by register machines

While any unification of KL1 can be done in parallel under the semantics of GHC [23], we did not adopt this fine-grained parallelism, but, instead, the parallelism between goal reductions. This is because (1) unifications are granules that are too small to implement in parallel, and (2) we can extract enough parallelism between goal reductions.

A set of candidate clauses for the same predicate is compiled to KL1-B code as shown in section 6.7, executed by a single thread of control from guard to body. No parallelism is expected within each goal reduction. Each passive and active unification can be done by discrete KL1-B instructions as register-memory or register-register operations, so that we can expect optimization by the compiler such as in register allocation.

6.3.2 Goal scheduling on the processor

A goal can be a ***ready goal*** (RG), a ***suspended goal*** (SG) or a ***current goal*** (CG), as shown in Figure 6.3. The ***ready*** goals are linked into a list forming a ***ready-goal-stack***. In principle, a current goal is popped from the ready-goal-stack, then the goal reduction is performed by the KL1-B code corresponding to the goal predicate.

When any unification suspends, the goal is linked as a suspended goal from the variable which caused the suspension [14,22]. Here, the ***non-busy waiting*** method has been adopted.

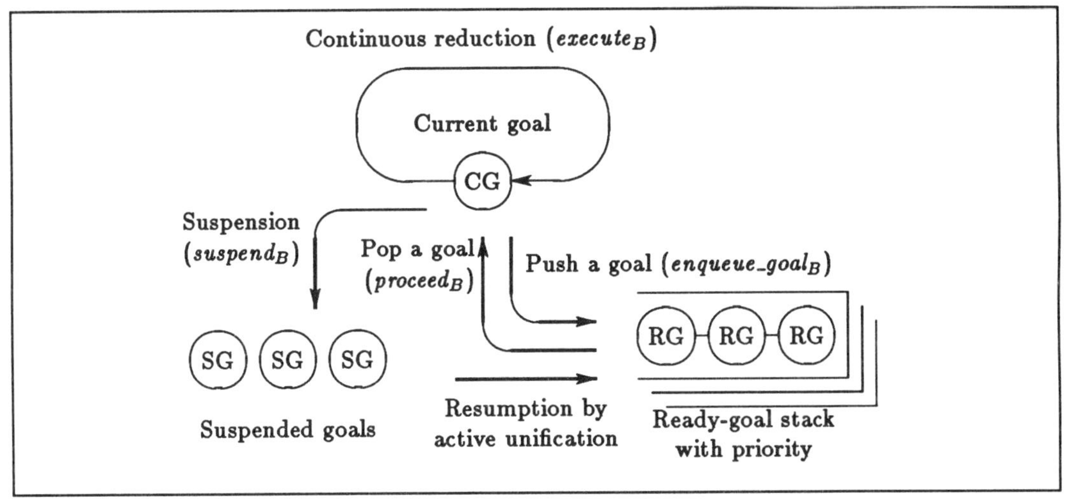

Figure 6.3: Goal state transition and KL1-B instructions

That is, the suspended goal is not scheduled until the variable will be instantiated. When a suspended goal is resumed, it is linked to the ready-goal-stack again.

Depth-first scheduling is, in principle, adopted for body goals. A left-most body goal can be executed without pushing it to the ready-goal-stack (see figure 6.3), while other body goals are linked to the ready-goal-stack.

The priority of goal scheduling can be controlled by specifying pragmas [25]. While each shōen is created with the maximum and minimum priority (see section 6.2.2), the pragmas can specify the relative priority within the range allowed for the shōen. The ready-goal-stack is managed with the priority of goals. The forked goal specified with priority is linked to the specified position. Otherwise, the same priority as with the current goal is adopted.

6.3.3 Goal distribution within a cluster

How to keep the processing load well-balanced is a key issue in making the best use of parallel processing resources. Currently, the following strategies are provided in the KL1 implementation on PIM.

In a cluster, we provided an individual ready-goal-stack with priority to avoid conflicts of access to the common goal-stack [22]. New ready goals with higher priority than the current highest priority are possibly born in a cluster, or sent from other clusters. These higher priority goals are distributed gradually to keep the processor loads in good balance. We found *on-demand* distribution to be an effective way to realize a good balance within a cluster while reducing the amount of wasteful communication among processors [21]. In the on-demand scheme, an idle processor, or a processor executing low priority goals, sends a request to a busy processor executing higher priority goals. On receiving the request, the busy processor sends the goal from its ready-goal-stack to the idle processor. This communication should be done efficiently within a cluster, so we designed a coherent cache and an inter-processor signaling by *slit-checking* for the PIM pilot machines. (See section 6.8.2.)

6.4 Distributed goal management

6.4.1 Inter-cluster goal distribution

The load among clusters should be distributed carefully because the communication cost is more expensive than within a cluster. Therefore, we provided pragmas by which users can indicate load distribution while we plan to implement a dynamic load-balancing mechanism.

The pragmas for load distribution are of the form *goal@node*(CL), attached to body goals as suffixes, and throw KL1 goals to a certain cluster. A body goal *goal@node*(CL) is thrown by a message *%throw* to a cluster CL when the clause containing the body goal is committed to. The semantics of programs with pragmas is the same as that without them. The node (more precisely, a certain processing element in the cluster CL) that received the *%throw* message links the goal to its ready-goal-stack as well as to the foster-parent [2] as described in the next section.

6.4.2 Shōen and foster-parent scheme

The main role of a shōen is to control the execution under the shōen, i.e. the shōen status is checked in each goal reduction. Within a cluster, processing elements can share the shōen status, so that the hardware mechanism (a coherent cache, see section 6.8.4) can reduce the cost of checking the shōen status in every goal reduction. In inter-cluster parallel processing, the shōen tree crosses memory space boundaries of clusters. If we simply represented a link of a shōen tree using an external reference link, the rate of inter-cluster operations would be very high and the synchronization would be very complicated. We provided a ***shōen and foster-parent scheme*** to avoid this [14].

In the shōen and foster-parent scheme, a foster-parent for a certain shōen is created, if necessary, in a cluster. The foster-parent works as a branch of the shōen within the

[2] If there is no foster-parent, one will be created on the spot.

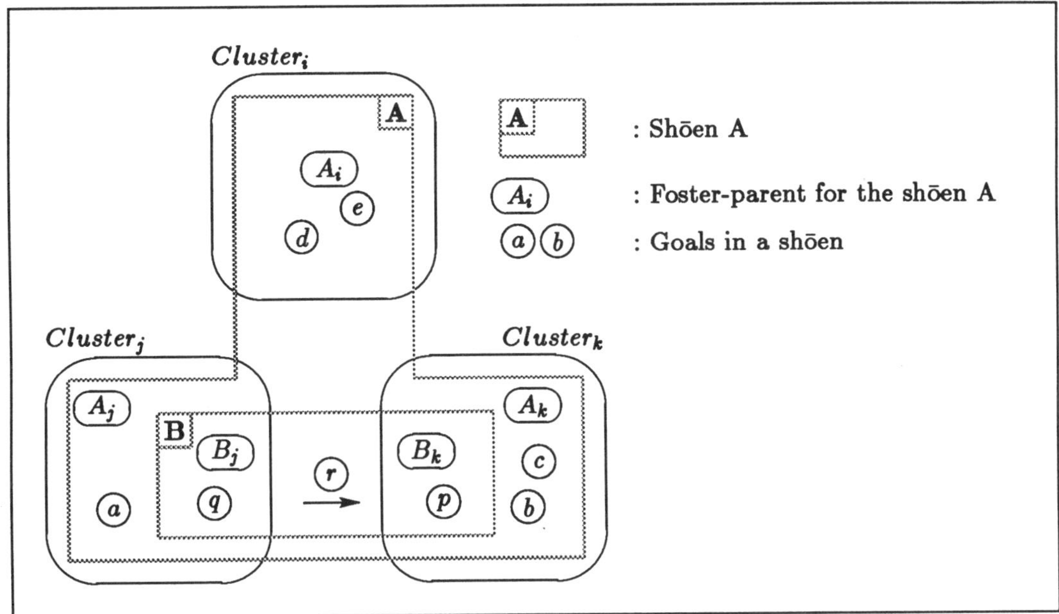

Figure 6.4: Shōen and foster-parents

cluster. The foster-parent manages the child shōens or goals belonging to the shōen in that cluster, i.e. it may start, stop and abort its children. By this scheme, most communication between the child shōens or goals and the parent shōen can be performed by the communication between the children and the foster-parent within a cluster, so that the inter-cluster communication traffic can be reduced.

Figure 6.4 shows the following situation. A shōen A has a child shōen B and several child goals in clusters, $Cluster_i$, $Cluster_j$ and $Cluster_k$. Therefore, each cluster includes a foster-parent (A_i,A_j or A_k). Shōen B has its child goals, p, q and r. They were created at $Cluster_j$ and were linked to the foster-parent B_j. When one goal p is thrown to another cluster, $Cluster_k$, a new foster-parent, B_k, is created, and the goal p is linked to it.

6.4.3 Weighted throw count

Termination detection of some or all processes is one of the principal functions in any system. The end of a KL1 program execution corresponds to the end of the shōen. When all goals in a shōen or descendant shōens are reduced to null, the execution of the shōen finishes.

When all goals under a foster-parent have been reduced to null, the foster-parent sends a termination message to the shōen and disappears. The shōen seems to be able to detect the termination when it receives termination messages from all foster-parents. However, there may be goals in transit as the goal r in Figure 6.4.

The weighted throw count (WTC) method was provided to solve this problem [20], where a certain weight is assigned for the shōen, its foster-parents, and messages. The WTC can be seen as an application of weighted reference counting [2,30].

In the WTC scheme, a shōen has a certain weight of negative value, and all its foster-parents and messages have a positive weight. The following condition is maintained during their execution:

$$W_{shoen} + \sum (W_{fosterparent}) + \sum (W_{message}) = 0$$

For example, when a foster-parent sends a goal to another foster-parent, the sender assigns a certain weight from its own to the goal, then sends the goal with the weight. The receiver adds the weight sent with the goal into its own weight. When a foster-parent disappears, it sends a termination message to the shōen with its weight. When the weight of the shōen becomes zero by adding the weight of the message, the termination of all goals in the shōen is detectable.

6.5 Distributed unification

6.5.1 Export and import tables

A goal is thrown by the *%throw* message between the clusters. The *%throw* message includes the following encoded information: the code of the predicate of the goal, the arguments of the goal, and the shōen to which the goal belongs. The encoding of arguments (or any KL1 data) is called *export*; decoding is called *import*.

In the KL1 parallel implementation, an external reference, i.e. a reference to non-local data, is identified by the pair $\langle node, ent \rangle$, where *node* is the cluster number in which the referenced data resides, and *ent* is the unique data identifier in that cluster. We did not choose to take the memory location directly as the identifier, *ent*, because that would make it very difficult to perform garbage collection locally within one cluster. If the locations of data have moved as the result of marking or moving garbage collection (see section 6.6.2), it must be announced to all clusters that may reference the data. Instead, each cluster maintains an *export table* to register all locations that are referenced from other clusters [14]. Each externally referenced cell is pointed to by an entry in the table, and the entry number is used as the unique identification number. When externally referenced cells are moved as the result of a local garbage collection, the pointers from the export table entries are updated to reflect the movements.

Also, each cluster maintains an *import table* to register all imported external references.

All references in a cluster to the same external reference are represented by internal references to the same *external reference cell*. The external reference cell points to the import table entry and vice versa. Export and import tables are shown in Figure 6.5, where an external reference cell is indicated by the EX cell[3].

6.5.2 Avoiding duplicated export/import

Data objects in a cluster may be exported more than once. In such cases, each export tends to use export table entries. In addition, if a cluster imports the same data structure more than once, the cluster must allocate its memory for the same data structure. To avoid the duplicated exports and imports, a hash table is attached to the export table. If a data object is exported more than once, the same export table entry can be retrieved from the object address and used in the second and later export. There is also a hashing mechanism for retrieving an import table entry from an external reference, so that even if a cluster imports the same external reference more than once, only one external reference cell is allocated.

The introduction of export and import tables help reduce the number of inter-cluster read requests as follows. Suppose that $Cluster_n$ exports the same data X twice to $Cluster_m$ as an argument to goals p and q. Since X is exported with the same external reference in the two exports (using the export table mechanism with hashing), $Cluster_m$ allocates only one external reference cell to X (using the import table mechanism with hashing). Even if both p and q attempt to read X, only one read request message is sent to $Cluster_n$, because the first read attempt is remembered by the external reference cell and the second attempt only waits for the return of the value. This mechanism also prevents $Cluster_m$ from making duplicate copies of the same external data.

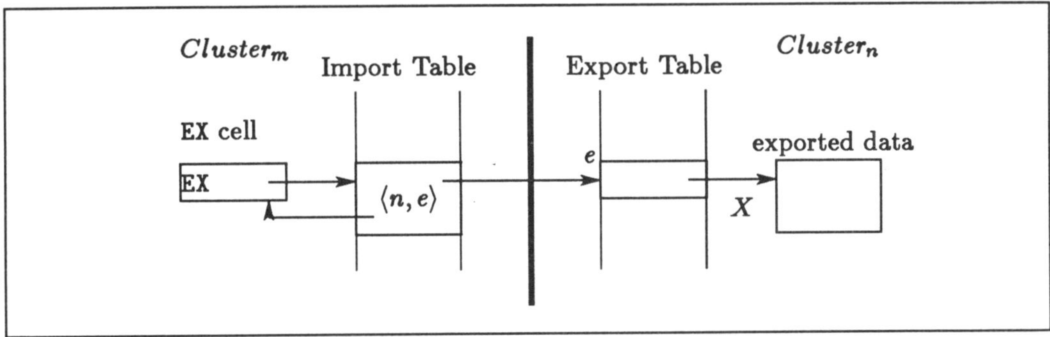

Figure 6.5: Export table and import table

[3]EX cell is either an EXREF cell or an EXVAL cell. The data referenced by an EXVAL cell is known to have a concrete value.

6.5.3 Unification messages

In passive unification, the two terms to be unified are read and compared. To read an external reference (EX) cell to X, a read request is made by sending a message:

%read(X, ReturnAddress)

to the referenced cluster, where X is the external reference $\langle n, e\rangle$ in figure 6.5, and *ReturnAddress* is new export table entry $\langle m, i\rangle$ for returning the value[4].

If the referenced cell has a concrete value V, it is returned by the *%answer_value* message:

%answer_value(ReturnAddress, V)

If the referenced cell is an unbound variable, the read request is suspended until the variable is instantiated. If it is an EX cell, a *%read* message is passed to the cluster that it references. When the *%answer_value* message returns, the EX cell identified by *ReturnAddress* is overwritten by the value, and the import table entry corresponding to the EX cell can be freed. This is why the cell and the entry are separate.

When an active unification tries to unify an external reference cell X with a term Y,

%unify(X, Y)

is sent to the referenced cluster. It is a request to unify the data referenced by X with a term Y. The cluster that receives the above message performs the active unification after translating the two terms into internal representations. Care must be taken with the unifications between two unbound variables in different clusters, because they may make reference loops between clusters. This problem can be solved: first, compare the two cluster identifiers, then make sure that the reference pointers point in the same direction, in descending (or ascending) order of cluster identifiers [15].

6.6 Memory management in PIM

6.6.1 Incremental garbage collection by MRB

While KL1 can describe synchronization and communication between parallel processes without side-effects, naive implementations of KL1 as well as other concurrent logic

[4]The *%read* and *%answer_value* messages correspond to the *%read_value* and *%return_value* messages in [14].

programming languages [7,24,23] consume memory area very rapidly. For example, whole array elements must simply be copied when only one element is updated because destructive assignment is not allowed. As a result, garbage collection (GC) occurs very frequently. In addition, the locality of memory references is not good during GC by widely used methods, so that cache misses and memory faults occur often. In sequential Prolog [29], this problem is not very serious because of the backtracking feature. However, since concurrent logic programming languages have no backtracking, an efficient incremental GC method is important in their implementation.

The multiple reference bit (MRB) method [5] was proposed as an incremental GC method for concurrent logic programming languages[5]. The MRB method maintains one-bit information in pointers indicating whether the pointed data object has multiple references to it or not. This multiple reference information makes it possible to reclaim storage areas that are no longer used. By keeping information in the pointers rather than in the objects that are pointed to, no extra memory access is required for reference information maintenance.

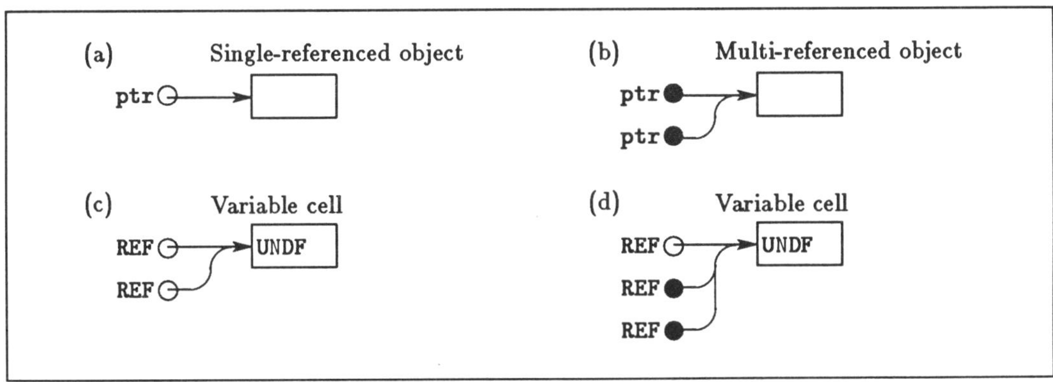

Figure 6.6: References in the MRB scheme

Figure 6.6 shows the data representation in the MRB scheme. A single-referenced object (a) and a multi-referenced object (b) can be distinguished by the MRB flag on pointers, *MRB off* by ○and *MRB on* by ● Because of the single assignment nature of KL1, an unbound variable cell usually has one reference path for instantiating and one or more reference paths for referencing its value. Therefore, an unbound variable cell with only two reference paths is pointed by MRB off, as in Figure 6.6(c). On the other hand, an unbound variable with more than two reference paths has only one or no pointer with MRB off, as in Figure 6.6(d).

The MRB information on variables or structure pointers is maintained through their unification. When a unification consumes a reference path to a single-referenced data

[5]Another incremental GC method, called lazy reference counting (LRC) [9], was designed. LRC uses two-word indirect pointers with a reference counter.

object, the storage area can be reclaimed after the unification. For example, the goal reduction by a clause:

$$p(\,[X|Y]\,)\;:-\;\textit{true}\mid q(X,Y).$$

is committed when the argument of the goal p is the pointer to a cons cell. Its elements are retrieved as the arguments X and Y of the body goal q, consuming one reference path to the cons cell. If the pointer to the cons cell shows *MRB off*, the storage area for the cons cell can be reclaimed during goal reduction.

Although the MRB scheme gives up the storage reclamation for the data objects that were once multi-referenced, the MRB scheme can greatly reduce the memory consumption rate with small run-time overhead. The MRB scheme also makes available several optimization techniques, such as destructive array element update without using the method in Barklund and Millroth (1987). In addition, the MRB scheme can be used for the export and import procedures in section 6.5.2. Because single-referenced data objects may not be exported more than once, we introduce two kinds of export and import tables, one each for single-referenced objects and multi-referenced objects. While the export and import tables with the hashing function are used for multi-referenced data objects that can be found by the MRB scheme in each cluster, a simpler external reference mechanism is used for single-referenced objects.

6.6.2 Garbage collection within a cluster

Data structures or variables in KL1 are stored as shared data in each cluster memory. The MRB scheme enables storage reclamation for these data structures. Thus, free lists for data structures and variable cells are maintained. Storage allocation and reclamation are very frequent operations, So each processing element has a set of free lists for frequently used cells, enabling each free list access to be done independently in each processing element.

We use another type of garbage collection that is performed locally within a cluster accompanied with the incremental garbage collection by MRB. This is because the MRB scheme leaves some garbage. We first implemented a simple garbage collection, the *copying* scheme, on our experimental KL1 system.

We designed a parallel mechanism that enables all processing elements to collect garbage in a cluster. When a certain processing element has a shortage of memory space during its goal reduction, it reports this event to other processing elements after it finishes the current goal reduction. This is because garbage collection is difficult to start during goal reduction. Shortage of memory space should therefore be detected before all the memory area is used up. After all processing elements stop their goal reductions, they start the copying operations, tracing all active cells in the shared memory of a cluster.

Here, the copying roots are the ready goals in ready-goal-stacks[6].

6.6.3 Distributed garbage collection by WEC

Since export table entries for multi-referenced data objects cannot be freed by local garbage collection within a cluster of the type described in section 6.6.2, there must be an inter-cluster garbage collection mechanism to free those entries that have become garbage.

The weighted export count (WEC) scheme was designed as incremental inter-cluster garbage collection. The WEC scheme can also be seen an application of weighted reference counting [2,30]. Note that a naive implementation of the standard reference counting scheme does not work correctly in a distributed environment.

The WEC scheme assigns weighted export counts (*wec*) to references (pointers) as well as to referenced data [15]. More precisely, positive values are assigned to external references (import table entries and references encoded in messages), and negative values are assigned to export table entries, so that the following condition is kept for every export table entry E (see figure 6.7.):

$$(weight\ of\ E) + \sum_{x:reference\ to\ E} (weight\ of\ x) = 0$$

The weight of E will become zero only when there is no reference to E. As a result, export table entries can be incrementally reclaimed through the message operation with *wec*.

6.7 Abstract instruction set: KL1-B

To build an efficient parallel inference machine, execution on each processing element must be as efficient as possible. Therefore, KL1-B was designed first based on sequential execution[7]. It was extended for parallel execution.

Most instructions in KL1-B include run-time data type checks. The actions that follow the run-time type check are very different. Therefore, all the memory words and all the argument/temporary registers hold tagged words of the form:

$$\langle tag(MRB, Type), value \rangle .$$

The *MRB* in each tag is maintained to show the multiple reference information. *Type* shows the data type information.

[6] The export tables in section 6.5 are also the roots of copying operations.

[7] An explanation of each KL1-B instruction can be found in [5] and [16].

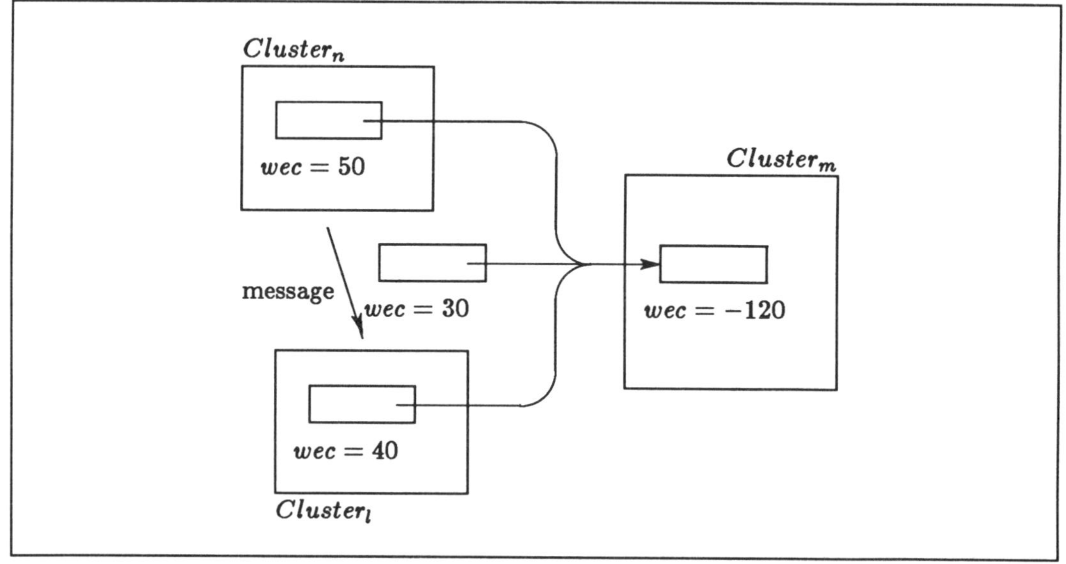

Figure 6.7: WEC scheme

6.7.1 Compiled code in KL1-B

A data structure called a *goal-record* is used for representing a goal. A goal-record consists of its argument list, a pointer to the compiled code corresponding to its predicate name, and control information. The argument list includes atomic values or pointers to variables or structure bodies in the heap.

A goal reduction is initiated by a KL1-B instruction[8], $proceed_B$, popping a goal as a current goal from the ready-goal-stack. Here, we assume that the arguments of a current goal are located in argument registers (Ais).

A set of candidate clauses for a predicate is compiled into a sequence of KL1-B instructions[9] as shown in figure 6.8.

For the current goal, candidate clauses are tested sequentially by head unification and guard execution to choose one clause whose body goals will be executed.

A KL1-B code for a set of candidate clauses includes passive unification instructions for head and guard parts, active unification instructions, argument preparation instructions and goal fork instruction for body part, and garbage collection instructions. The guard part is compiled so that argument registers are never destroyed before commitment. In-

[8]In this article, each KL1-B instruction is written with postfix B, for example: $proceed_B$.

[9]The actual compiled code has a different form when indexing instructions are used.

$Label_1$:	Code for the first clause
	passive unification instructions for the head and guard parts
	(commit)
	garbage collection instructions
	active unification instructions for the body part
	argument preparation instructions
	goal fork instructions
$Label_2$:	Code for the second clause
	...
	...
$Label_n$:	Code for the last clause
	...
$Label_{n+1}$:	*$suspend_B$ pred*

Figure 6.8: Form of compiled codes in KL1-B

structions are arranged so that reference paths to data objects can be maintained correctly in terms of the MRB scheme. Table 6.1 shows the principal KL1-B instructions.

6.7.2 Passive unification

Passive unification instructions include the instructions for goal arguments (*$wait\_XXX_B$*), and for structure elements (*$read\_XXX_B$*). The indexing instructions are also used to avoid duplicated operations between the head and guard part execution of candidate clauses.

Dereferencing is required at the beginning of passive and active unification instructions. The data type of an argument register is first tested to see whether its content is an indirect pointer or not. If it is an indirect pointer, the pointed cell is dereferenced until an instantiated value, an unbound variable cell, or an external reference is reached.

If the instantiation of a variable (including an external reference) is required during the execution of the passive part, the test for this clause is abandoned. The variable that caused the suspension is saved in a suspension stack, then execution proceeds to the next candidate clause.

The *%read* message is not sent, in principle, in passive unification instructions even when the value of a certain external reference cell is required; instead, such a message will be sent in the *$suspend_B$* instruction, because other candidate clauses may be committed.

Table 6.1: Principal KL1-B instructions

KL1-B Instruction	Comment
Passive unification and suspension	
$wait\_value_B$ Ai, Aj	Wait for two instantiated terms, Ai and Aj, then unify them.
$wait\_const_B$ Ai, C	Wait for a constant value C.
$wait\_list_B$ Ai	Wait for a pointer to the list.
$read\_car/cdr\_var_B$ Ai, Aj	Read the car (or cdr) of a list cell pointed by Ai into Aj.
$try\_me\_else_B$ *Label*	Set a branch label *Label*.
$suspend_B$ *Goal*	Suspend *Goal*.
MRB maintenance and garbage collection	
$mark_B$ Ai	Set the MRB of Ai to on.
$collect\_value_B$ Ai	Reclaim along with the reference path from Ai.
$collect\_list_B$ Ai	Reclaim a list cell Ai.
Active unification	
get_value_B Ai, Aj	Actively unify Ai with Aj.
get_const_B Ai, C	Unify Ai with a constant C.
$get\_list\_value_B$ Ai, Aj	Unify Ai with a list pointed to by Aj.
Argument preparation	
put_var_B Ai, Aj ; set_value_B Gi, Aj	Make a new variable pointing from Ai/Gi and Aj.
put_value_B Ai, Aj ; set_value_B Gi, Aj	Move the variable from Aj to Ai/Gi.
put_const_B Ai, C ; set_const_B Gi, C	Put a constant C in Ai/Gi.
put_list_B Ai ; set_list_B Gi	Allocate a list cell in Ai/Gi.
$write\_car/cdr\_var_B$ Ai, Aj	Make a new variable pointed to by Aj and the car (or cdr) of a list Ai.
$write\_car/cdr\_value_B$ Ai, Aj	Move Aj to car (or cdr) of a list Ai.
$write\_car/cdr\_const_B$ Ai, C	Write a constant C in car (cdr) of a list Ai.
Goal fork	
$proceed_B$	Pop a goal from the ready-goal-stack.
$execute_B$ *Goal*	Jump to the code for *Goal*.
$enqueue\_goal_B$ *Goal*	Push a forked goal *Goal* to the ready-goal-stack.
$enqueue\_with\_priority_B$ *Goal*, *Pri*	Push *Goal* to the ready-goal-stack of the priority *Pri*.
$enqueue\_to\_processor_B$ *Goal*, *Node*	Throw *Goal* to *Node*.

Note: Ai, Aj: Argument registers Gi: Gi-th argument of a forked goal
C: Atoms, integers and nil are handled by individual instructions.

6.7.3 Suspension

If no clause is selected for the current goal, the ***suspend***$_B$ instruction tests the suspension stack. If there is no variable, a failure exception occurs at the shoen. Otherwise, the current goal becomes a suspended goal. First, variables that cause the suspension are popped up from the suspension stack. Then, the current goal is linked to these variables, setting the tag of the variable by HOOK, to realize a non-busy waiting synchronization mechanism between KL1 goals.

When an external reference is found in the suspension stack, the ***%read*** message is sent to the node where the exported data resides (see figure 6.5). The goal waits for the ***%answer_value*** message as a suspended goal.

The processing element that received ***%read*** message returns the value of the exported data with the ***%answer_value*** message. However, the exported data may be an unbound variable cell. In this case, the action of replying to the ***%read*** message is suspended by linking a ***reply_record*** to the unbound variable cell. The reply-record can be seen as a special goal record to reply with the ***%answer_value*** message.

6.7.4 MRB maintenance and garbage collection

Active unification may produce a chain of variable cells pointed to by indirect pointers. These variable cells pointed to by an indirect pointer with *MRB off* can be reclaimed during deferencing. Therefore, each dereferencing operation includes the MRB test and, possibly, a reclamation operation.

The MRB is maintained in each KL1-B instruction. In addition, several garbage collection instructions are introduced in KL1-B. The compiler detects candidate places where reference paths are added. ***mark***$_B$ is used to set MRB to ***on***. When the compiler finds a unification in which a reference path to a data object is consumed, it inserts a *collect_XXX*$_B$ instruction at an appropriate place. *Collect_list*$_B$ is a typical KL1-B instruction which corresponds to the goal reduction by the clause in section 6.6.1. Note that the cons cell can be reclaimed after the clause is committed. Therefore, *collect_list*$_B$, which reclaims the cons cell if it is a single-referenced cell (*MRB off*), is put after the passive unification instructions as shown in figure 6.8.

6.7.5 Active unification and resumption

If a clause is selected, the body part of that clause is executed. Execution of the body part includes two kinds of operations, ***active unification*** and ***body goal fork***. Figure 6.9

put_list$_B$	*Aj*	% allocate a cons cell
write_car_const$_B$	*Aj, foo*	% write the car part
write_cdr_variable$_B$	*Aj, Ak*	% allocate a new variable
get_list_value$_B$	*Ai, Aj*	% active unification

Figure 6.9: An active unification example

shows the typical compiled code for the active unification in such a clause as:

$$\ldots \mid X = [\,foo \mid Y\,],\ \ldots$$

The structures for active unifications or the arguments for body goals are prepared by argument preparation instructions, *put_XXX*$_B$, *write_XXX*$_B$, and *set_XXX*$_B$. New variable cells or structures, such as the right-hand side of the above unification, may be allocated from free lists or in free memory area by these instructions. Unlike the original WAM, structure elements should not be used directly as undefined variable cells, to avoid fragmentation. This is because the incremental garbage collection by MRB may reclaim a structure body and its elements at a different timing. Thus, when a structure element should be initiated as a new variable, the new variable cell is allocated separately from the structure body, and a pointer to the cell is stored inside the body.

The last instruction in figure 6.9, *get_list_value*$_B$, is a typical KL1-B instruction for active unification. This instruction has one of four kinds of actions, selected by checking the data type. When *Ai* is an uninstantiated variable without suspended goals, *Aj* (a pointer to a cons cell made by the first instruction in Figure 6.9) is assigned to the variable cell. Note that unbound variables are located in shared memory. Thus, the instantiation of unbound variables is done by locking and unlocking the variable cells [22]. Here, it is important to shorten the period of locking the unbound variable. Therefore, the compiler generates the compiled code as shown in Figure 6.9, where the right-hand side structure is created first. As a result, the unbound variable is locked only within the *get_list_value*$_B$ instruction.

If *Ai* is an uninstantiated variable with suspended goals, these suspended goals are resumed by moving the goal-records linked from the variable to the ready-goal-stack again before instantiating to *Aj*. (See figure 6.3.) When reply_records are linked to that variable, the *%answer_value* messages for each reply_record are sent to the cluster which is waiting for the instantiated value.

Ai may be an external reference. In this case, the *%unify* message is sent to the node which exported the variable. The node which received the *unify* message performs active unification on the behalf of the sender processor.

When *Ai* is a pointer to a list cell, general unification is performed. Otherwise, unification fails and an exception occurs.

6.7.6 Goal fork and slit-checking

Several goal fork instructions are provided to push and pop a goal-record to and from a ready-goal-stack, or to execute goal reductions repeatedly. As shown in Figure 6.3, a KL1-B instruction $proceed_B$ pops up a goal record (a current goal) from the ready-goal-stack when the previous goal reduction did not fork any body goals. The KL1-B code corresponding to the goal predicate is executed. Assume that there are two body goals in a KL1 clause as:

$$p :- \langle guard \rangle \mid q, r.$$

The reduction of the left-most body goal, q, will follow just after the current goal reduction, while the other goal(s), r, is pushed to the ready-goal-stack.

Other body goals are pushed by the $enqueue\_goal_B$ instructions. When scheduling priority is specified by the pragmas, the KL1 compiler generates a KL1-B instruction, $enqueue\_with\_priority_B$. When the pragmas for load distribution are specified in a KL1 program, KL1-B instructions $enqueue\_to\_processor_B$ are used. This instruction sends a message, *%throw*, to the specified cluster instead of enqueuing its own ready-goal-stack.

The following events are incidental in KL1 execution: a garbage collection requirement (section 6.6.2), an inter-processor communication request, and a goal fork with the highest priority (section 6.3.3). These events are only detected by *slit-checking* in the $execute_B$, $proceed_B$ and $suspend_B$ instructions, i.e. the actions corresponding to these events are delayed until a certain goal reduction finishes, even if the event occurred during a goal reduction. This is because garbage collection is difficult to start during a goal reduction. In inter-processor communication or for a goal fork with highest priority, the corresponding actions do not have to be performed immediately, so they may be delayed until after the goal reduction finishes.

As described in section 6.4.2, a foster-parent in a cluster holds the shōen status as well as information about the computing resources assigned for the foster-parent. Before $execute_B$, $proceed_B$ or $suspend_B$ starts a goal reduction, it checks the shōen status of the current goal, and the computing resources left in that foster-parent.

6.8 PIM hardware architecture

6.8.1 Targets of the PIM hardware architecture

Our performance target in the R&D of PIM hardware architecture was to execute KL1 programs with more than 100 times the performance of conventional machines. To achieve this goal, we studied new processing element architectures as well as new parallel architectures to connect more than 100 processing elements. The target processing element performance is 200K to 500K RPS[10], so that 10 to 20M RPS is expected to be the total performance for practical applications.

Several pilot machines are now being developed for the PIM research for the final stage of the FGCS project. The PIM/p is one of the PIM pilot machines, which is planned to have 128 processing elements. The rest of this section focuses on the hardware architecture of the PIM/p.

6.8.2 The pilot machine: PIM/p

In the parallel architecture design for the PIM/p, we aim to build a parallel processing architecture where the locality in communication cost can easily be used from software. We introduced a hierarchical structure, as shown in Figure 6.10. Eight processing elements (PEs) form a cluster with shared memory. The PIM/p consists of 16 clusters connected by inter-cluster network.

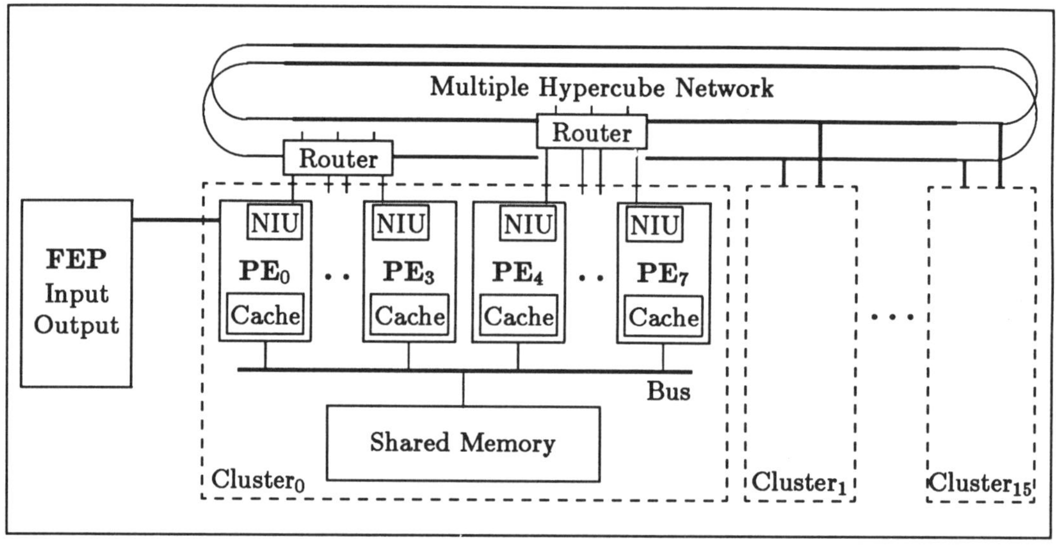

Figure 6.10: The pilot machine: PIM/p

[10]RPS: KL1 goal reductions per second

6.8.3 PIM/p processing element

A PIM/p processing element is implemented on a single board with about 20 static RAMs and several custom CMOS LSIs, a CPU, a network interface unit (NIU), cache controller units (CCUs), and a floating point processor unit (FPU), as shown in Figure 6.11. The basic machine cycle target is 50 nanoseconds.

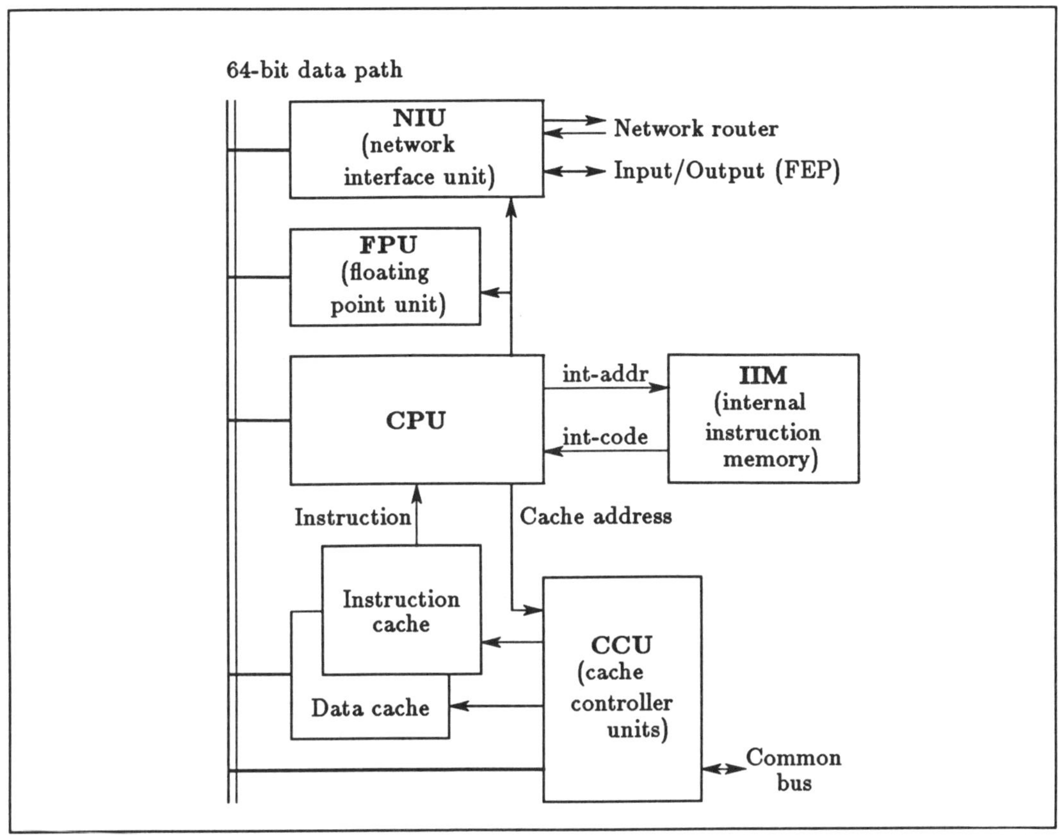

Figure 6.11: PIM/p processing element configuration

The processing element includes two caches: an instruction cache and a data cache. The contents of both cache memories are identical. They are provided to enable the CPU to fetch both data and instructions every machine cycle. The cache controller units (CCUs) manage both the instruction cache and the data cache. The cache address array is updated by both commands from the CPU and a common bus.

The CPU has two instruction streams: one from the instruction cache, called external instructions, and the other from the internal instruction memory (IIM), called internal instructions. *External instructions* are used to represent compiled codes of user programs.

Internal instructions are stored in the internal instruction memory (IIM) of each processor, in the same way as in the microprogrammable processor. Small programs in IIM can specify the complex actions of KL1-B instructions. Both instructions include KL1 support instructions as well as simple RISC-like instructions. They are invoked by external macro-call instructions. Hopefully, the CPU will execute an instruction every 50 nanoseconds using a four-stage pipeline in most cases.

Slit-check and interrupt

A hardware mechanism for *slit-checking* (see section 6.7.6) is incorporated into the processing element of PIM/p. A normal hardware interrupt causes automatic save of program status: however, slit-checking does not. Each processing element has a dedicated register, each bit of which can keep an individual event. The slit-checking mechanism has an additional one-bit flag to show whether any events happened or not, which can be tested by one conditional branch instruction. On general-purpose computers, slit-checking might be implemented using normal interrupt mask/unmask operations and a cumbersome interrupt handler, which would incur too great a cost for the KL1 system. By incorporating the hardware slit-checking mechanism, the processing element can avoid frequent mask/unmask operations and interrupt handling overhead.

Registers

The processing element includes 32 general-purpose registers with some dedicated registers. Each general-purpose register has an 8-bit tag and 32-bit data. The dedicated registers include a condition code register for the result of ALU execution and a slit-check register. Most flags, such as the condition code, are placed in the tag part of the dedicated registers. Therefore, these flags can be tested by the tag-branch instructions.

A CPU has virtual registers, called indirect registers, in addition to the above registers. Through the indirect registers, internal instructions can easily handle the operands of a macro-call instruction that has just invoked the internal program code. In other words, each indirect register corresponds to the operand position of the macro-call instruction. It can represent either the immediate value or the contents of a register specified in the operand of the macro-call instruction.

6.8.4 Cache system

Processing elements within each cluster share one address space. Therefore the design of a local coherent cache is a key issue in increasing the efficiency of local execution on each

Table 6.2: Basic CPU commands to the cache

CPU command	*Comment*
Read	Ordinary memory read.
Write	Ordinary memory write.
Read_Invalidate	When cache-to-cache transfer occurs, the source cache block is invalidated. Otherwise, same as Read.
Read_Purge	After CPU reads, the cache block is purged. The shared blocks in other caches are also purged.
Direct_Write	If the cache misses at the block boundary, write data to the cache without fetching from memory. Otherwise, ordinary memory write.
Lock_Read	Lock address, then memory read.
Write_Unlock	Memory write, followed by unlock.
Unlock	Unlock address.

processing element, and it enables high-speed communication within a cluster. Although several coherent cache protocols have been proposed so far [1,8,3,19], we designed a cache protocol for KL1 parallel execution based on the simulation results [10]. The simulation results have shown that KL1 programs require more write accesses than conventional languages. Therefore, we chose a write-back protocol which can reduce common bus traffic more than a write-through protocol. When a cache block is updated, the consistency with other caches is kept by invalidating the shared cache blocks in other caches. In addition, we extended some cache functions from ordinary cache protocols using the characteristics of the KL1 parallel execution. Table 6.2 shows the basic CPU commands to the cache.

Cache commands for KL1 support

In parallel implementation of KL1, some data structures can be found out when they are not accessible. A typical example is an explicit communication between processing elements. First, a sender processor creates a message in its own cache. The message is sent to a receiver processor as a *cache-to-cache* data transfer. Although the message in the sender processor is useless after message transfer, it remains as shared cache blocks between both processors' caches. Therefore, when the receiver processor makes a message in the same area, another cache will be invalidated. The CPU command, *Read_Invalidate*, is provided to avoid invalidation caused by invalidating at cache-to-cache data transfer.

In normal write operations, *fetch-on-write* is used. However, when data structures are created in an unused memory area, it may not be necessary to fetch-on-write. This is because the memory contents have no meaning, and because the new data structure is not shared by other processors. The *Direct_Write* command is introduced to avoid useless cache block fetch from shared memory. The *Read_Purge* command invalidates its own cache block just after the CPU reads the last cache block word, so that the *Direct_Write* command can be used for already-used memory area that is already in use.

Hardware lock

Lock operations are essential for implementing KL1 in the shared memory multiprocessor. This is because exclusive memory access is required to instantiate variables in active unifications (see section 6.7.5) or to link suspended goals to them (see section 6.7.2). Although lock conflicts seldom occur, lock latency is high in KL1 execution. The simulation results in Matsumoto et al. (1987) show that the *Read_Lock* frequency is about 7 % for data access, so a *lightweight* lock operation is required.

The PIM/p cache enables a *lightweight* lock and unlock operation by using the cache block status, lock address registers, and busy-wait locking scheme. When the CCU receives a *Lock_Read* command from the CPU, the CCU checks the corresponding address tag and status tag. If the address hits and its status is *exclusive*, the address can be locked without using the common bus. The locked address is held in a lock address register.

6.8.5 Hyper-cube network and network interface unit

As discussed in sections 6.5 and 6.7, inter-cluster communication may be required during a KL1-B unification instruction on each processing element. That communication may include various kinds of messages. We designed the inter-cluster network aiming at enough performance for both short and long message packets, and inter-cluster processing where it is required. The hyper-cube structure [4] has been introduced to connect clusters in PIM/p, placing each cluster on the hyper-cube node. This is because the hyper-cube structure enables us to shorten the inter-cluster distance with reasonable hardware costs. In addition, the network router can be implemented distributedly on each cluster.

The network was designed aiming at an inter-cluster communication throughput of 40 M byte/s. We chose the following configuration considering the limitations in hardware implementations. A network router was designed for a six-dimensional hyper-cube connection. While four dimensions are enough to connect 128 processing elements (16 clusters), the router switch will be available for future extensions. Each communication path has a throughput of 20 M byte/s one byte every 50 nanoseconds, in both directions. To obtain 40 M byte/s throughput, the inter-cluster network has been doubled. Therefore, two network routers are provided for each cluster, one for four processing elements.

Each processing element has a network interface unit (NIU) as a co-processor of the CPU. The NIU has two packet buffers, one for each direction, whose contents can be transferred to and from CPU registers. A packet is sent to the other processing element from the NIU by the CPU requests. The buffer status in a NIU, full or empty, can be reported to the CPU by the slit-checking mechanism. Therefore, these message handling operations can be done on each processing element.

6.8.6 PIM/p instructions

The instruction set for the PIM/p processing element has been designed for the efficient implementation of KL1. The design started by analyzing the behavior of the KL1-B instructions [26].

Tagged architecture

As discussed in section 6.7, run-time data type checks are essential for KL1-B instructions, so we introduced the tagged-architecture in the CPU design. The tag part in a KL1 variable cell can be implicitly loaded and stored with the data part by using basic memory access instructions. In addition, a new tag can be given in memory access instructions and ALU computation. The memory access giving a new tag is a primitive operation in the KL1-B argument preparation instructions of KL1-B.

The run-time test of the type tag is a primitive operation to implement KL1. Most unification includes a multi-way branch for the goal argument type. Some Prolog machines, such as the PSI [18], have a hardware-supported multi-way branch function. However, the processing element of PIM/p does not have such hardware. This is because (1) it is difficult to adopt a hardware-supported multi-way branch to a pipeline processor, and (2) branches taken in run-time are biased. Even a normal two-way branch can be useful enough by selecting an appropriate branch condition. Therefore, the PIM/p instruction set has only two-way branch instructions, but various tag conditions can be specified in them. A branch condition can be specified as a logical operation between two register tags, or between a register tag and an immediate tag. In addition, some branch instructions have an immediate tag mask in their operands.

Conditional macro-call instruction

The next issue is how to implement polymorphic functions in KL1-B, because most KL1-B instructions include very different actions that follow the run-time data type check. The RISC-like instruction set can be executed using short pipeline cycles, and in hardware design cost is relatively low. However, considering the naive expansion of KL1-B using RISC-like instructions, the static code size of compiled programs will be very large. This problem can be solved by incorporating the features of microprogrammable processors such as PSI [18]. Therefore, we designed RISC-like instructions with conditional macro-call instructions for the PIM/p processing elements, so that the advantages of both in the RISC-like instructions and microprogrammable processors are available in the KL1-B implementation on the PIM/p.

Macro-call instructions were introduced to implement high-level KL1-B instructions. A macro-call instruction can be regarded as a *lightweight* subroutine call or as a high-level instruction realized by the microprogram. A macro-call instruction invoke a small program in the internal instruction memory (IIM) depending on given conditions, which has the form:

$$\texttt{MCALL}\ \textbf{if}\ \textit{cond},\ \textit{address}\ \textbf{with}\ \texttt{reg}_0,\ \texttt{reg}_1/\texttt{immed}_1,\ \ldots,\ \texttt{reg}_n/\texttt{immed}_n$$

where:

address :	Entry address of the internal instruction memory
$\texttt{reg}_i/\texttt{immed}_i$:	register number or constant for the macro-call argument
cond :	condition for the macro-body invocation.

A tag condition, *cond*, can be specified as a logical operation between a register tag, $\texttt{reg}_0$ and a register tag, $\texttt{reg}_1$, or an immediate tag, immed.

MRB GC support

The principal operations such as incremental garbage collection by MRB and dereferencing are supported by dedicated RISC-like instructions. In MRB incremental garbage collection, each variable cell or structure is allocated from a free list. When reclaimed, its memory area is linked to a free list. To support these free list operations, the PUSH and POP instructions are used. PUSH can link a variable cell or a structure to the free list, and POP can allocate it from the free list, in one machine cycle.

The MRB of each pointer and data object must be maintained correctly in all unification instructions. Here, the most primitive operation is MRB maintenance during dereferencing. In dereferencing, the MRB of the dereferenced result should be *off* if and only if MRBs of both the pointer and the cell are *off*. In this case, the indirect word cell can be reclaimed immediately because there are no other reference paths to it. Two dedicated instructions, MRBorRead and DEREF, support this operation. MRBorRead accumulates both the address register's MRB and the destination register's MRB, then sets the result in the destination register. DEREF performs MRB accumulation along with the POP operation.

Special cache access

As stated in section 6.8.4, the coherent cache of the processing element has extended functions for KL1 parallel execution. The instruction set includes memory access instructions corresponding to each cache function: `DirectWrite`, `ReadPurge`, `ReadInvalidate`, and `ExclusiveRead`. Exclusive memory access instructions, `LockRead` and `WriteUnlock`, are also provided. Incorrect use of these instructions may cause fatal errors. Therefore, the use of these instructions will be limited to internal instructions.

The processing element performance estimated from the compiled code is over 600 K RPS for the append program. Note that the estimated performance includes the incremental garbage collection cost using MRB.

6.9 Summary

This paper outlined the parallel inference machine architecture. KL1 parallel implementation issues, such as distributed resource management, goal scheduling and distribution, memory management, and distributed unification, were discussed, based on the logic programming framework. These have been implemented on the parallel software workbench, the Multi-PSI systems. This paper described the design of the PIM pilot machine hardware, including its processing element instruction set. The LSIs are now being implemented.

Acknowledgement

All the parallel inference machine systems research has been performed with the collaboration of all PIM and Multi-PSI researchers in the FGCS project. Most ideas for the KL1 parallel implementations came from the accumulation of their discussions.

I wish to thank all researchers of the companies participating in the PIM R&D project: Fujitsu Limited, Mitsubishi Electric Corporation, Hitachi Ltd., and Oki Electric Industry Co. Ltd. One of the PIM pilot machines, PIM/p, shown in this report was designed and implemented by cooperative work with Mr. A. Hattori, Mr. T. Shinogi, Mr. K. Kumon and all of their colleagues at Fujitsu Limited.

Finally, I would like to thank the ICOT Director, Dr. K. Fuchi, and the chief of the fourth laboratory, Dr. S. Uchida, for their valuable suggestions and guidance.

6.10 References

[1] J. Archibald and J. Baer. Cache coherence protocols: Evaluation using a multiprocessor simulation model. *ACM Transaction of Computer Systems*, 4(4):273–298, 1986.

[2] D.I. Bevan. Distributed Garbage Collection using Reference Counting. In *Proceedings of Parallel Architectures and Languages Europe*, pages 176–187, June 1987.

[3] P. Bitar and A. M. Despain. Multiprocessor cache synchronization. In *Proc. of the 13th Annual International Symposium on Computer Architecture*, pages 424–433, June 1986.

[4] G. Broomell and J.R. Heath. Classification categories and historical development of circuit switching topologies. *ACM Computing Surveys*, 15(2):95–133, 1983.

[5] T. Chikayama and Y. Kimura. Multiple Reference Management in Flat GHC. In *Proceedings of the Fourth International Conference on Logic Programming*, pages 276–293, 1987.

[6] T. Chikayama, H. Sato, and T. Miyazaki. Overview of the Parallel Inference Machine Operating System (PIMOS). In *Proc. of the International Conference On Fifth Generation Computing Systems 1988*, Tokyo, November 1988.

[7] K. Clark and S. Gregory. Notes on Systems Programming in PARLOG. In *Proc. of the International Conference on Fifth Generation Computer Systems*, pages 299–306, Tokyo, 1984.

[8] J. R. Goodman. Using cache memory to reduce processor-memory traffic. In *Proc. of the 10th Annual International Symposium on Computer Architecture*, pages 124–131, 1983.

[9] A. Goto et al. Lazy Reference Counting: An Incremental Garbage Collection Method for Parallel Inference Machines. In *Proc. of the Joint Fifth International Logic Programming Conference and Fifth Logic Programming Symposium*, pages 1241–1256, Seattle, WA, August 1988.

[10] A. Goto, A. Matsumoto, and E. Tick. Design and Performance of a Coherent Cache for Parallel Logic Programming Architectures. In *16th Annual International Symposium on Computer Architecture*, Jerusalem, May 1989.

[11] A. Goto et al. Overview of the Parallel Inference Machine Architecture (PIM). In *Proc. of the International Conference On Fifth Generation Computing Systems 1988*, Tokyo, Japan, November 1988.

[12] A. Goto and S. Uchida. Current Research Status of PIM: Parallel Inference Machine. TM 140, ICOT, 1985. (Third Japan-Sweden workshop on Logic Programming, Tokyo).

[13] A. Goto and S. Uchida. Toward a High Performance Parallel Inference Machine – the Intermediate Stage Plan of PIM–. In *Future Parallel Computers*, pages 299–320. LNCS 272, Springer-Verlag, 1986.

[14] N. Ichiyoshi, T. Miyazaki, and K. Taki. A distributed implementation of flat GHC on the Multi-PSI. In *Proceedings of the Fourth International Conference on Logic Programming*, 1987.

[15] N. Ichiyoshi et al. A New External Reference Management and Distributed Unification for KL1. In *Proc. of the International Conference On Fifth Generation Computing Systems 1988*, Tokyo, November 1988.

[16] Y. Kimura and T. Chikayama. An Abstract KL1 Machine and its Instruction Set. In *Proceedings of the 1987 Symposium on Logic Programming*, pages 468–477, 1987.

[17] K. Nakajima et al. Distributed Implementation of KL1 on the Multi-PSI/V2. In *Proceedings of the Sixth International Conference on Logic Programming*, Lisboa, June 1989.

[18] H. Nakashima and K. Nakajima. Hardware architecture of the sequential inference machine: PSI-II. In *Proceedings of 1987 Symposium on Logic Programming*, pages 104–113, San Francisco, 1987.

[19] M.S. Papamarcos and J.H. Patel. A low-overhead coherence solution for multiprocessors with private cache memories. In *Proceedings of the 11th Annual International Symposium on Computer Architecture*, pages 348–354, 1984.

[20] K. Rokusawa et al. An Efficient Termination Detection and Abortion Algorithm for Distributed Processing Systems. In *Proceedings of the 1988 International Conference on Parallel Processing*, volume 1 Architecture, pages 18–22, August 1988.

[21] M. Sato and A. Goto. Evaluation of the KL1 Parallel System on a Shared Memory Multiprocessor. In *Proceedings of IFIP Working Conference on Parallel Processing*, Pisa, Italy, April 1988.

[22] M. Sato, A. Goto, et al. KL1 Execution Model for PIM Cluster with Shared Memory. In *Proceedings of the Fourth International Conference on Logic Programming*, pages 338–355, 1987.

[23] E.Y. Shapiro, editor. *Guarded Horn Clauses*, pages 140–156. MIT Press, 1987.

[24] E.Y. Shapiro. A subset of Concurrent Prolog and Its Interpreter. TR 003, ICOT, 1983.

[25] E.Y. Shapiro. Systolic programming: A paradigm of parallel processing. In *Proceedings of the International Conference on Fifth Generation Computer Systems*, pages 458–470, 1984.

[26] T. Shinogi et al. Macro-call Instruction for the Efficient KL1 Implementation on PIM. In *Proc. of the International Conference On Fifth Generation Computing Systems 1988*, Tokyo, Japan, November 1988.

[27] Y. Takeda et al. A Load Balancing Mechanism for Large Scale Multiprocessor Systems and its Implementation. In *Proc. of the International Conference On Fifth Generation Computing Systems 1988*, Tokyo, November 1988.

[28] K. Taki. The parallel software research and development tool : Multi-PSI system. In *France-Japan Artificial Intelligence and Computer Science Symposium 86*, pages 365–381, October 1986.

[29] D.H.D. Warren. An Abstract Prolog Instruction Set. Technical Note 309, Artificial Intelligence Center, SRI, 1983.

[30] P. Watson and I. Watson. An Efficient Garbage Collection Scheme for Parallel Computer Architecture. In *Proceedings of Parallel Architectures and Languages Europe*, pages 432–443, June 1987.

Chapter 7

Concurrent logic languages for the design and implementation of parallel AI systems

Rajiv Trehan [1]
Department of Artificial Intelligence,
University of Edinburgh
80 South Bridge
Edinburgh EH1 1HN
United Kingdom

Abstract The development of new architectures with several processing and memory units and new models of computation promise to alleviate some of the limitations of conventional Von Neumann architecture. There are two clear implications for artificial intelligence: increased execution speed and more natural decomposition of applications. An improvement in execution speed results in models and applications being tested that would not have been feasible on previous generations of computers. Enhanced modelling capabilities have been addressed indirectly in the development of AI. Successful problem modelling has several requirements such as the ability to define the application more naturally and to be able define the flow of execution control in the application. Most importantly, many problems are parallel rather than sequential and so are better thought of in terms of a parallel rather than a sequential framework.

A key area of research in understanding how this new technology can be applied to AI problem solving is through using logic languages. The Japanese Fifth Generation

[1]Supported by the Science and Engineering Research Council under a Research Studentship.

Computer Project uses logic programming as the link between information processing and parallel architectures.

In this article we give an overview of work carried out in investigating a class of parallel logic language known as the Committed Choice Non-Deterministic (CCND) languages.

7.1 Introduction

Artificial Intelligence (AI) by its nature is a multi-disciplined field bringing together subjects areas such as Philosophy; Natural Language; Vision; Logic; Robotics; Computer Science; Engineering and Physics. The main tool of the Artificial Intelligence researcher has been the digital computer, enabling theory to be put into practice.

Currently most digital computers are based on the Von Neumann architecture; a single central processing unit with a small amount of memory and a large amount of separate memory (which holds the data and the program). The limits of such computers are widely recognised: the speed of a signal in a wire; the physical limits of integration; heat dissipation and memory accessing.

The development of new architectures with several processing and memory units and new models of computation promise to alleviate some of these limitations. There are two clear implications for Artificial Intelligence: increased execution speed and more natural decomposition of applications. An improvement in execution speed results in models and applications being tested that would not have been feasible on previous generations of computers such as:

the use of AI in embedded real-time systems, which are time critical;

the development of systems which are based on higher levels of abstraction, hence they tend to be more removed from the machine they are to execute on;

the use of development tools illustrates both these points, tools will only be used in real-time and the code they generate will tend to be more abstract (as the tool adds another level of complexity).

Enhanced modelling capabilities have been addressed indirectly in the development of AI. Successful problem modelling has several requirements such as the ability to define the application more naturally and to be able to define the flow of execution control in the application. Most importantly, many problems are parallel rather than sequential and so are better thought of in terms of a parallel rather than a sequential framework. For example, being able to parse a string and build a semantic structure as well as refer to a world model in an incremental fashion requires control over how these parts execute and interlink. Implementing such a model in a sequential framework requires the programmer to consider how to mimic the parallel execution and control required. This adds an additional level of conceptual complexity to the problem when realising the solution as a program.

A key area of research in understanding how this new technology can be applied to AI problem solving is through using logic languages. The Japanese Fifth Generation Computer Project uses logic programming as the link between information processing and parallel architectures [Uchida 82]. Logic programming languages provide a procedural interpretation for sentences of first order logic, mainly using a class of sentence called Horn clauses. The first and most widely used of the family of Horn claused based languages is Prolog [Clocksin & Mellish 81], [Sterling & Shapiro 86]. Prolog currently provides a sequential means of evaluating Horn clause based programs. This sequential search being efficiently realised in a stack based implementation [Warren 83] giving in excess of 100,000 Logical inferences per second (Lips). However, Horn clauses are open to a wide variety of parallel evaluation models, there are two main types of parallelism that can be exploited. The parallel reduction of a conjunction of goals is known as AND-parallelism. All the goals in a conjunction of goals must successfully reduce (i.e. the 1st goal & 2nd goal & .....& Nth goal must all be fully reduced). The second type of parallelism is where a goal tries to reduce by matching with all the various OR-clauses in the system in parallel; this is known as OR-parallelism (i.e. reducing via the various OR-branches of the search tree in parallel). Trying to exploit these forms of parallelism has led to two forms of parallel evaluation model. The first form evaluates a query using a parallel reduction of Horn clauses which is opaque to the programmer; the parallelism is implicit in the underlying execution model. The second form offers explicit control of the parallelism to the programmer, who then has to indicate, by annotation, the parallelism required in the evaluation.

The first form of parallelism addresses the execution performance to be gained by using multi-processor architectures but as the user language and semantics remain unchanged offer no improved modelling capabilities. The second approach requires the programmer to control and model parallel execution and achieve improved execution performance.

In this article we give an overview of work carried out in investigating a class of parallel logic language known as the Committed Choice Non-Deterministic (CCND) languages which offer explicit control over parallel execution.

This review has been split into 3 main sections. The first presents the CCND languages and considers how they support communication and non-determinism. The second considers how these languages have been used to design and test concurrent AI systems. Finally, we consider issues related to implementation of algorithms developed in a CCND framework and evaluation of parallelism.

7.2 Concurrent logic languages

In this section we give a brief introduction to the CCND languages. Several flavours of language have been proposed [Shapiro 83] [Gregory 87] [Ueda 86a], these essentially differ in the means of synchronisation of communication. A tutorial introduction to some of the concepts and programming methods for these languages can be found in [Conlon 89].

A CCND program is a finite set of guarded horn clauses of the form:

```
R(a1,...,ak) :- G1, ..., Gn : B1, ..., Bm      (n,m >=0)
```

The different CCND languages give different names for the various components of the guarded horn clause. We use the following terminology for all the languages:

R(a1,...,ak) is a head goal;

R is its functor name;

k is the number of arguments (referred to as arity);

G1,..., Gn form the guarded goals;

":" is known as the commit operator;

B1,..., Bn are known as the body goals.

The "commit operator" generalises and cleans the "cut" of sequential Prolog; the "cut" is used to control and reduce the search of OR-branches in Prolog. The "commit operator" forms the means of pruning OR-branches in a parallel search.

A general query in the CCND languages has the following form:

```
B :- C1, C2, ... Cn
```

In the CCND model the general feature of the evaluation of a conjunction of goals is as follows. A given goal in the conjunction **Ci** is evaluated by unifying the goal with the clauses in the system. Those clauses whose head successfully unify are now possible solution paths for this goal. The guarded goals for the possible solution paths are then (investigated) evaluated in parallel. The first such guarded system to successfully terminate results in commitment to the body goals of the given clause. These body goals are essentially added to the original conjunction for evaluation. This is known as a ***reduction***. The evaluations of the other OR-clauses are discarded. In the CCND languages concurrency is achieved by reducing several goals in parallel. At the clause level, this form of parallelism is **AND-parallelism** or more precisely **Streamed AND-parallelism**.

7.2.1 Communication and synchronisation

Communication is achieved by the assignment of values to variables shared by several goals (processes). Assignment of shared variables in the guard evaluation of a clause may result in several copies of the variable having differing bindings. Only one binding will be carried forward on commitment to a given clause. Hence the evaluation of the guard proves to be a key point in how the CCND languages offer communication. The CCND languages differ in the semantics of the guarded goals and the synchronisation mechanisms employed for the instantiation of shared variables.

This form of parallelism can be realised in many programs where there is an incremental producer of items and a consumer process which consumes these items incrementally. The parallelism is realised by the incremental evaluation of some structure. This is evident in an example where a list is being produced using a recursive procedure and consumed incrementally, using a recursive procedure. Figure 7.1 is an example of a produce-consumer type algorithm which exploits "Streamed AND-parallelism".

```
producer(Current, List) :-
    List = [Current|Rest],
    Next is Current + 1,
    producer(Next, Rest).

consumer([Head|Rest]) :- process(Head), consumer(Rest).

process(Item) :- write(Item).

    :- producer(Start, List),consumer(List).
```

Figure 7.1: An example of "streamed AND-parallelism"

Note that `consumer/1` must suspend until the shared variable is instantiated to a list, the `process/1` goal must suspend until the head of the list is instantiated. So in offering this form of parallelism, issues of communication, synchronisation and suspension must be considered. The major difference between the CCND languages lies in their synchronisation.

Concurrent Prolog (CP)

In Concurrent Prolog [Shapiro 83] synchronisation is achieved by declaring certain shared variables as **read only**. These **read only** variables can only be instantiated by the producer process, consumer processes will suspend until they can be evaluated without instantiating a **read only** variable.

Concurrent Prolog permits parent variables to be bound in evaluation of the guard the bindings being made to a local environment. On commitment the system tries to unify the local bindings with the binding environment of the parent process. This requires the commitment stage to be atomic [Saraswat 87b], that is all bindings that would result by unifying local and parent environments should be made in one step or not at all. Such languages are known as **unsafe**, as the local bindings that are made are speculative until commitment has taken place.

Parlog

In Parlog [Gregory 87] synchronisation is achieved by declaring (modes) the inputs and outputs to every clause in the system. A goal can only attempt to be reduced by a clause if the input arguments for that predicate can be unified with the head of the clause without causing any instantiations in the goal being evaluated and if the output arguments are not instantiated. If head unification or guard evaluation require any instantiations of input arguments that OR-clause evaluation is suspended. Parlog is **safe**, as it does not permit the binding of goal parent variables in the guard.

Guarded Horn clauses (GHC)

In GHC synchronisation is achieved by giving special significance to the semantics of the commit operator. The basic idea is to ensure **safety**, so no output instantiations should occur until the evaluation has committed to a given OR-clause. If the evaluation tries to instantiate a variable in the goal being evaluated before commitment, the evaluation suspends. By adopting this form of synchronisation, the part of the clause before the "commit operator" forms a test for input instantiation.

7.2.2 Support for non-determinism

Logic programming languages offer many modelling capabilities. In particular logic programming languages attempt to model the non-determinism found in logical conjectures, i.e. making the correct logical deduction when faced with several choices. The search capability of logic programming languages has proven to be powerful for defining and implementing algorithms, concisely and elegantly.

The CCND languages appear to trade the non-determinism involved in supporting the OR-choice selection (backtracking) in Prolog languages for synchronisation of communication. In [Trehan & Wilk 87] we carry out an evaluation of how search can be achieved in Prolog and the CCND languages. In the following sub-sections we provide a summary of that work which considers how the CCND languages support three recognised forms of non-determinism, namely: ***don't care*** non-determinism; ***don't know*** non-determinism and ***generate and test*** non-determinism.

Don't care non-determinism

Don't care non-determinism is where choice of any evaluation path will lead to a solution. Take for example the merge predicate (the unordered combination of two lists) figure 7.2.

```
merge([],L,L).
merge(L,[],L).
merge([H|T],L,[H|Y]) :- merge(T,L,Y).
merge(L,[H|T],[H|Y]) :- merge(T,L,Y).
```

Figure 7.2: Unordered combination of two lists in Horn clauses

CCND realisation

In the CCND execution model the first clause that can commit does commit, so the evaluation of the above predicate will produce an unordered list. The other feature is that the lists can be thought of as streams, so this process serves to merge the two streams into one (hence the name merge). The evaluation of the merge goal suspends waiting for either one of its input arguments to be instantiated to a list (an input on a stream), when either argument becomes instantiated (a message) it is added as the head of the output list (the output stream) and the tail forms the new list (rest of the input stream) to be merged. Hence the CCND languages provide a good approximation to this form of non-determinism.

Don't know non-determinism

Don't know non-determinism is where there is a choice of possible solution paths. However, at a choice point it is not known which path will lead to a solution. (Here we restrict ourselves to choice points in which no instantiations need to be made, we treat these cases in the next sub-section on "*Generate and test* non-determinism").

A typical example of such a search is testing if two trees are isomorphic. Basically two trees are isomorphic if:

> either both trees are empty;
>
> or, if they have the same root node and both left and right subtrees are isomorphic;
>
> or if they have the same root node and the left subtree of one is isomorphic with the right subtree of the other and vice-versa.

These three statements can be represented by Horn clauses as in figure 7.3.

```
isomorphic(terminal, terminal).
isomorphic(tree(Node, Ltree1, Rtree1), tree(Node, Ltree2, Rtree2)) :-
    isomorphic(Ltree1, Ltree2), isomorphic(Rtree1, Rtree2).
isomorphic(tree(Node, Ltree1, Rtree1), tree(Node, Ltree2, Rtree2)) :-
    isomorphic(Ltree1, Rtree2), isomorphic(Rtree1, Ltree2).
```

Figure 7.3: Isomorphic tree program expressed in pure Horn clauses

Each node in the tree is either labelled a terminal, for a node whose parent is a leaf node, or has two subtrees. If we use this Horn clause definition to test if two trees are isomorphic, then we cannot pre-determine which of the latter two clauses, will be used to prove the isomorphism.

CCND realisation

The algorithm for testing if two trees are isomorphic requires an OR-choice to be made. To insure that the correct solution path is committed to, the OR-search has to be resolved within the guard. So the Horn clause algorithm in figure 7.3, would be transformed into a CCND language by making use of **deep guards**, as shown in figure 7.4.

```
mode isomorphic(?, ?).

isomorphic(terminal, terminal).
isomorphic(tree(Node, Ltree1, Rtree1), tree(Node, Ltree2, Rtree2)) :-
    isomorphic(Ltree1, Ltree2), isomorphic(Rtree1, Rtree2) : true.
isomorphic(tree(Node, Ltree1, Rtree1), tree(Node, Ltree2, Rtree2)) :-
    isomorphic(Ltree1, Rtree2), isomorphic(Rtree1, Ltree2) : true.
```

Figure 7.4: Isomorphism algorithm expressed in a CCND language (Parlog)

This use of OR-parallel search in the guard is a good approximation to this type of non-determinism, as the guard evaluations are carried out in parallel so solutions that lie textually after an infinite search path will be considered.

Generate and test non-determinism

Another type of non-deterministic algorithm exploited in logic programming algorithms is known as *generate and test.* Here one process generates a possible solution to a problem and another process places certain test conditions upon the solution. The non-determinism lies at the point where the possible solution is generated, as it cannot be predetermined whether the possible solution will pass the test stage.

```
male_and_(Person) :-
    male_height(Person, Height), tall(Height).

tall(Height) :-
    Height >=180.
male_height(john, 150).
male_height(jack, 175).
male_height(jim , 190).
```

Figure 7.5: *generate and test* algorithm expressed in Horn clauses

Figure 7.5 is a simple *generate and test* algorithm. Here, the male_height/2 is a search over a database which returns *Person, Height* pairs. The tall/1 predicate verifies that this person is tall. However, at the point when the *Person* and *Height* pairs are generated it cannot be determined if the tall test will succeed.

CCND realisation

In CCND languages, this sort of non-determinism is not so easily modelled. The basic problem is that the generate goal has to commit to a given clause in order to generate a possible solution (make an instantiation) for testing. However, the generate goal may commit to the wrong solution and with CCND languages, once the evaluation has committed to a given solution path, all other paths are ignored. This problem has resulted in several techniques aimed at implementing search algorithms in CCND languages [Ueda 86b] [Ueda 87] [Tamaki 87] [Okumura & Matsumoto 87].

7.3 Design

One of the reasons for adopting parallel models of computation is the possible improvement in the realisation of certain algorithms or problems. Apart form considering the issues of parallel search, highlighted in *section 7.2.2*, we were interested in how these languages may be used to support cooperating problem solvers or expert systems.

The first stage of this work was to investigate how these languages support objects, processes, and communication [Trehan *et al* 88] and how shared data structures could be supported in various styles of CCND language [Trehan & Mellish 89]. This study was parallelled by a review of features of Distributed Artificial Intelligence (DAI) systems and their possible software requirements [Hern 89]. More recently we have applied the programming techniques developed and the study of DAI systems to implement a Distributed Decision Support System and a Contingent Plan Tracking System. The rest of this section gives an overview of the use of objects and shared data structures in the CCND languages.

7.3.1 Taxi scheduling – an investigation of object models

Object Oriented Programming (OOP) is a programming and design methodology in which the system is constructed as a collection of objects, each object performs actions based on interactions with the rest of the system. These objects interact by sending messages to one another. By placing structure (e.g. hierarchy) on the objects, features like inheritance can be offered (i.e. if an object cannot process a message it can ask some generic object how to process the message).

Our basic view of objects and their mapping to a CCND languages is that proposed in [Shapiro & Takeuchi 87], namely:

an object exists as a CCND goal through the goal recursively calling itself;

the state of an object is defined by its input arguments' instantiations;

an object sends a message by partially instantiating a shared variable (stream) between itself and the object it wishes to communicate with;

an object receives a message by consuming a partial instantiation of a shared variable (stream) — this may cause the object to perform some action;

an object changes state by changing its arguments in recursive calls — note that if another object has access to the arguments of a goal it may be able to change the state of that object by suitably instantiating these arguments;

an object may have its state changed by sending a message to it — note that this is not the only way to change the state of an object (as another process can have access to an object's state variable);

objects can create other objects by reducing to a conjunction of goals — each new goal is a new object;

objects can create instances of themselves by spawning sub-classes or sub-goals when recursing;

an object can either be active or suspended, where suspended objects are waiting for incoming messages.

Shapiro and Takeuchi suggest a mechanism for default programming and inheritance of object properties via message delegation. When an instance of an object is created, it is connected to its super-class by a default stream. If the object receives a message to which it cannot respond it sends the message to its super-class.

The work of Shapiro and Takeuchi was analysed by Kahn [Kahn *et al* 86] and a preprocessor to support many of the features of OOP suggested. The object-level language POOL [Davison 87] is a realisation in Parlog of the ideas of Shapiro and Takeuchi (inheritance) and Kahn et. al. (declarations).

A contrasting view of objects was taken by [Furukawa *et al* 83]. In this model an object is taken to be a knowledge base manager; a process which manages a set of program clauses. Relationships can be defined between knowledge base managers, producing an object hierarchy. The object language Mandala is a realisation of this model in CP. In Mandala, objects attempt to solve queries using the information (CP clauses) held in their knowledge bases.

Possible object models

Within this general framework of objects several styles of object could be employed. Objects could be restricted to using message passing to obtain information about other objects in the system. Objects could have access to information in other objects by sharing variables that represent object state. We have listed the possible features that CCND objects may have. A given object model may only adopt a sub-set of these features. In the following sub-sections we give names to three possible object models. Note that the behavior and performance of objects in a system depends upon the class of objects that they are interacting with.

Closed objects

In this type of object all the information and knowledge that an object has access to, is local. If an object wishes to get information about another object a request for information must be sent to that object. Moreover, if an object wishes to change information in another object it must request the change by sending a message to that object.

This is suitable for systems in which objects do not frequently need to know the state of another object; the messages that are sent to an object are usually processing requests based on an object's internal information.

Open objects

Objects can share information through having common access to data structures. This is possible by use of the logical variable. Two processes with a common variable in their arguments both have access to instantiations made to that variable. However, if this type of object model is used, care must be taken to ensure that both objects do not try to update the shared data.

This model is suitable for systems in which the state of one object is dependent on the state of another object.

Informed objects

If we choose a "Closed Object" model, then to overcome the problem of frequently requesting information about the internal state of another object, objects can store relevant information about other objects. This style of object is particularly useful if the information being requested is relatively static (i.e. it does not change over several requests).

There is redundancy in that several objects now hold duplicate information. Also, care must be taken to ensure consistency of duplicate information. This consistency could be achieved by regular update polling, where objects holding information about other objects could, at regular intervals, poll and update duplicate information. However, this "regular interval" becomes a critical parameter in the system and it is difficult to make a good choice. An alternative is for the object whose data is duplicated, to be made responsible for sending update messages whenever the shared information is to be updated.

Possible communication mechanisms

One way communication (complete messages)

Objects that can communicate are represented as conjunctive goals (processes) which share a variable; this variable acting as the communication channel. The synchronisation mechanism required for the CCND languages means that a given stream can only have one producer, although it may have several consumers. Streams offer one way communication. So if two objects need to communicate with each other two streams are required.

Two way communication (incomplete messages)

Two way communication can be achieved on a single stream by using the technique of incomplete messages. If a message from one object to another contains a variable, which the sender object keeps a copy of, then the recipient of the message is able to reply by fully instantiating the incomplete message. This mechanism requires an implicit protocol to be maintained, between both objects, on the use of incomplete messages. This approach is useful when one object requires information from another object; the result being returned by fully instantiating the incomplete message. However, using this mechanism to provide two way communication results in two streams, one contained within the other.

Examples

To examine the use of these different object models and communication mechanisms we implemented three taxi schedulers in Parlog. The basic systems contained taxis, customers, taxi and customer generators, a controller and a user interface. Taxis and customers are created by the generator objects at the request of the user interface object. The customers are then allocated a free taxi by the controller object. An allocated taxi object iterates on its state until it arrives at the position. The customers position state is then controlled by the taxi which iterates to the customers destination where the customer disembarks and dies (that is the customer processes no longer exists). The taxi can then be reallocated by the controller.

Implementation one

In this system all the taxis and customers are **closed objects**. The controller is an **informed object**, holding information about taxis and unallocated customers. The initial information to the controller is provided by the generator objects. As, each object changes state the controller is informed of this change hence insuring consistent data. Alternatively the controller could have polled all the taxis and customers to insure data was consistent (but this defeats the purpose of using an **informed controller**). Taxis inform customers of position updates by message passing.

Implementation two

In this system all the objects are **closed objects**. Customers continually send requests for taxis to the controller. The controller in turn must poll all the taxis in the system for state information. The polling is achieved by generating a communications manager for each taxi, this results in a pipeline of managers each supporting a given taxi. Poll requests to the taxis use **back communication** for replies. The function of the communications managers is to split a request for information to its taxi and to the remaining managers and create the resulting reply route. This technique was chosen as it allowed multiple requests to be handled without sequentialisation (to ensure replies are answering associated requests). Taxis inform customers of position updates by message passing.

Implementation three

In this system the taxis and customers are **open objects** and the controller is an **informed object**. The initial information to the controller is provided by the generator's object. A taxi is capable of seeing inside and updating the customer's position implicitly; hence providing a means of explicit control of state. This required a mechanism by which control of slots and value could be systematically maintained (while under the control of the taxi the customer should only be able to read its position slots).

Comments

The investigation of object models and communication resulted in the development of several techniques that would be generally useful when constructing communicating systems in the CCND languages, these include:

Mechanisms for addressing classes of objects using sequential or concurrent communication techniques.

A mechanism for representing the behavior of objects under changed circumstances.

A method for one process to access and control the state of another without the controlled process having to perform unnecessary computation.

7.3.2 Binary trees – use of shared data structures

In this section we present some of the points raised in using shared data structures in the CCND languages. A more complete analysis of shared data structures is given in [Trehan & Mellish 89] which considers how chart parsing can be achieved in the CCND languages. The investigation highlights two styles of language, ***unsafe*** and ***safe***, and proposes a third ***safe+system streams***. The example we use to consider these language is that of a shared ordered binary tree to store integers. For a given node in the tree, nodes in the left subtree contain integers which are smaller than the integer labelling this node, and the nodes in the right subtree contain integers which are greater than the integer labelling this node. Terminal nodes are variables. The example programs in this paper have not been annotated with specific synchronisation primitives or mode declarations, we assume the generic features of the particular languages systems when executing a given program. For example, ***unsafe*** languages allow global variables to be bound in the guard while in ***safe*** languages attempting to bind in the guard results in suspension.

Unsafe

The ***unsafe*** predicate in figure 7.6 allows several processes to add integers to a shared binary tree. The predicate takes an integer and an ordered binary tree. The integer either already exists in the tree or should be added to the tree. The first two clauses traverse the binary tree, comparing the integer to be added to the current node value and hence traversing either the left or right subtrees. The last clause has a dual purpose. If the second argument (the binary tree) is instantiated, the clause serves as a test if the integer to be added already exists in the tree. If the second argument is uninstantiated the clause serves to make an ***unsafe*** binding of the terminal node, currently a variable, in the binary tree. The unification of this local binding with the global variable will be made on commitment. The commitment has to be an atomic action.

```
add_binary_tree(Element,tree(Value,Left,Right)) :-
    Element < Value
    :
    add_binary_tree(Element,Left).
add_binary_tree(Element,tree(Value,Left,Right)) :-
    Element > Value
    :
    add_binary_tree(Element,Right).
add_binary_tree(Element,tree(Element,_,_)).
```

Figure 7.6: Predicate to add an element to an ordered binary tree

Consider behavior of two processes which make additions, *4* and *3*, to a shared binary tree, namely *tree(7,L,R)*:

```
add_binary_tree(4,tree(7,L,R)),add_binary_tree(3,tree(7,L,R)).
```

Both processes will traverse the binary tree to the left subtree `L`, resulting in two goals `add_binary_tree(4,L)` and `add_binary_tree(3,L)`. Now consider the evaluation of these goals. The evaluation of both goals via the first two clauses will suspend, because the variable `Value` is currently unbound. So, both will make speculative bindings of the parent variable `L` via the last clause; the first binding `L` to `tree(4,_,_)` and the second binding `L` to `tree(3,_,_)`. The system will then, on commitment, try to make both local bindings global. However, using atomic commitment one of the processes will succeed and the other will fail. If the second process succeeds, `L` will be bound to `tree(3,_,_)`. So, the two suspended clauses for the first processes can be rescheduled for evaluation as `Value` is now bound to 3. This will result in this evaluation committing to the second clause, as `4 > 3`. Finally, this process will bind the right subtree of the newly created node to `tree(4,_,_)`. So, the final state of the binary tree is:

```
tree(7,tree(3,_,tree(4,_,_)),_)
```

Safe

In a *safe* language the binary tree addition predicate in figure 7.6 would fail or suspend. *Safe* languages do not permit the binding of global variables in the guard. In the case where the last clause is used to add an element to a binary tree, rather than testing if an element already exists, either the evaluation of the third clause suspends awaiting the second argument to be bound or the binding of the global variable has to be transferred to the body. However, if the binding is transferred to the body, two processes could try to bind the same variable to different terms. In this case one of the processes will fail.

The manipulation of a global data structure, like a global binary tree, by several writer processes has to be supported by a manager process, (perpetual process), see [Shapiro & Takeuchi 83]. This manager is the only process which could write to the shared data structure, hence resolving the problem of binding conflicts that will occur with several processes writing to a shared resource. The processes that wish to update the shared data structure send requests to the manager process. The requests from each of the writer processes are merged together to form a single request stream to the manager process.

```
manager_binary_tree([add(X)|Rest],continue,BinaryTree) :-
    add_binary_tree(Element,Flag,BinaryTree),
    manager_binary_tree(Rest,Flag,BinaryTree).

add_binary_tree(Element,Flag,tree(Value,Left,Right)) :-
    Element < Value
    :
    add_binary_tree(Element,Flag,Left).
add_binary_tree(Element,Flag,tree(Value,Left,Right)) :-
    Element > Value
    :
    add_binary_tree(Element,Flag,Right).
add_binary_tree(Element,Flag,BinaryTree) :-
    var(BinaryTree)
    :
    bind(BinaryTree,tree(Element,_,_),continue,Flag).

bind(X,X,Y,Y).
```

Figure 7.7: Manager process for a binary tree

Figure 7.7 contains a perpetual process that manages a binary tree. The process consumes a stream of requests, in this case requests for additions. For each request the manager invokes a process to add the element to a binary tree. Once the addition, or confirmation, has taken place the process can then process the next request. The addition and the recursive call to the manager have been sequentialised using a short circuit technique [Hirsch *et al* 87]. The writer processes that wish to make additions to this data structure send requests to the manager, which in turn make the updates. So, requests from write processes have to be collected together into a single request stream. The commonest way of collecting the requests together is via merge processes, as in figure 7.2. Consider two processes that generate streams of integers which are to be added to a shared binary tree, as in figure 7.8. The request streams from the two processes are merged together and the *resultant stream* is consumed by a manager process for the binary tree, as in the query shown in figure 7.8.

For large numbers of writer processes the problems associated with how to interconnect the writer processes allowing each fair access to the shared resource, has been the attention of considerable research [Kusalik 84] [Ueda & Chikayama 84] [Gregory 87] [Shapiro & Mierowsky 87] [Shapiro & Safra 87] [Saraswat 87c].

Two main issues arise when faced with an interconnection of merge processes. Ensuring that a given request stream is not starved indefinitely and that the delay in propagating a request to the final stream is small.

```
random(Seed,Requests) :-
    generate(Seed,Number,NewSeed),
    Request = [Number|NewRequests],
    random(NewSeed,NewRequests).

:-  random(1,Ra),random(2,Rb),merge(Ra,Rb,Requests),
    manager\_binary\_tree(Requests,continue,BinaryTree).
```

*(*merge/3 *and* manager_binary_tree/3 *are defined in figures 7.2 and 7.7)*

Figure 7.8: A perpetual process which generates a stream of random integers

Safe+system streams

The use of streams of requests, merge processes and manager processes, appears to be the only way of supporting multiple writers in *safe* languages. Moreover the use of streams and merge processes are required to support *many-to-one* communication. The general feature of both these uses of streams is to combine requests from many sources on to one final stream, the *resultant stream.*

```
random(Seed,Resultant_handle) :-
    generate(Seed,Number,NewSeed),
    add_to_stream(Resultant_handle,Number),
    random(NewSeed,Resultant_handle).

:-  make_stream(resultant,Requests),
    random(1,resultant),random(2,resultant),
    manager_binary_tree(Requests,continue,BinaryTree).
```

the above query assumes add_to_stream/2 *will suspend if*
the stream handle has not been identified,
i.e. make_stream(resultant,Requests) *has not been evaluated.*

Figure 7.9: A perpetual process which uses proposed stream primitives

Consider another view of this *resultant stream*, that is a list with a tail variable to be instantiated. This view of the *resultant stream* was employed in [Saraswat 87c] to mimic the merging of several streams together in constant time. Basically, processes that wish to write to the *resultant stream* use the multiple writers capabilities of *unsafe* languages. Each writer has a copy of the stream, additions to the stream take place by a writer recursing down the stream until it finds the tail variable which is then instantiated to a list containing the required message and a new tail variable. For efficiency the writer can keep a copy of the new tail variable for future additions. This technique requires *n* process reductions, where *n* is the number of new elements that have been added to the stream since the last addition. However, this approach is not applicable to *safe* languages, as they do not support multiple writers.

Streams could be supported by the system, resulting in a language we identify as *safe+system streams.* This system could provide special primitives for multiple writers to a *resultant stream.* This requires the system to know that a given stream, or variable, is a *resultant stream.* The system could then keep track of the end of the stream via a pointer to the tail variable. Any additions to the stream would automatically update the pointer. So system primitives could be provided which add an element to a given *resultant stream* directly. The consumption of a *resultant stream* by any process proceeds as normal, as it is still a stream.

We propose two basic primitives required to support *resultant streams* by the system. The first `make_stream(STREAM_ID,STREAM)` identifies a stream as a *resultant stream.* The second `add_to_stream(STREAM_ID,Element)` directly adds an element to this *resultant stream.* Using these primitives the predicate example in figure 7.8, is transformed into figure 7.9.

7.4 Implementation

We now turn our attention to the implementation of CCND languages and their use as a vehicle for developing concurrent algorithms. The CCND languages provide a powerful vehicle for the design, testing and debugging of a wide variety of computation and communication models. They possess many features that are particularly useful when developing concurrent AI systems:

- declarative reading;
- elegant model of communication;
- elegant means of synchronisation;
- partial search capabilities;
- easy support for several models of objects;
- dynamic process creation;
- dynamic communication creation;
- symbolic capabilities;
- pattern matching.

However, the implementation of these languages is difficult and still an open and active research problem. The implementation of these languages has undergone a series of evolutionary steps. The first implementations were meta-interpreters on top of Prolog [Shapiro

83] [Tanaka *et al* 86] [Pinto 86]. Subsequently, compilers to Prolog were produced [Clark & Gregory 85] [Ueda & Chikayama 85] [Saraswat 87a]. More recently these languages have been implemented via abstract machine emulators written in 'C' [Foster *et al* 86] [Levy 86] [Chikayama & Kimura 87], giving a speed-up over the original meta-interpreters and compilers. Most recently, distributed implementations of the CCND languages have been investigated [Foster 88] [Crammond 88] [Taylor *et al* 87]. However, although these systems appear to give relative performance gains over single processor architectures they are still slow compared with the best sequential implementations of Prolog.

We have approached the issue of implementation of algorithms and languages from two perspectives. First the specification of algorithms in CCND languages which are later translated into OCCAM programs. Secondly the analysis of the dynamic execution of our range of applications and programming technique in order to provide for language implementors. In the following subsection we give an overview of these two directions.

7.4.1 OCCAM – low level realisation of AI process models

The CCND languages provide a powerful vehicle for the design, testing and debugging of a wide variety of computation and communication models. As such they could be thought of as a design tool for parallel AI systems. This view is particularly true when faced with target systems like OCCAM [INMOS 84] [Bowler *et al* 87] [Kerridge 87] and the Transputer. OCCAM is a difficult language for developing AI systems, because it:

is imperative in nature;

has poor symbolic processing capabilities;

requires statically (compile time) defined data and processes;

does not support interactive and incremental program development;

it only supports synchronous point-to-point communication.

It should be noted that OCCAM has advantages which make it desirable as a target language:

Transputer realisation (speed);

a mathematical foundation;

a calculus for program analysis.

In the paper [Scott & Trehan 89] we consider the translation of Parlog programs to OCCAM. In this work we draw on a common view of Parlog and OCCAM processes as a route to a translation of certain forms of Parlog to OCCAM.

Basic schema

Processes level description

The translation first involves describing the Parlog program as a network of processes. Each Parlog process is defined in terms of its use of streams, its initial state and its action.

Parlog network diagram

The next stage is a network diagram; a diagram of the processes and their interconnect. The evolution of the processes network is considered over several process cycles. This results in an understanding of process creation and interconnect.

OCCAM network diagram

The Parlog network diagram is then translated into an OCCAM network digram. Here issues like the dynamic creation of processes must be translated into a static network of process **shells**, or **virgin processes**. These **shells** will be initialised with state information and hence mimic Parlog process creation. Parlog also allows for asynchronous one-to-many communication. This requires Parlog streams to be translated into communication buffers and the use of de-multiplexers, (**splitters**) to support multiple readers.

Applicability

The applicability of this translation schema relies on the Parlog program having several attributes, namely:

- the Parlog program should be developed in an object oriented style;
- the use of guards should be strictly for *if-then-else* type processing on input messages (in line with the functioning of an object);
- process creation should not be non-deterministic in nature, that is different clauses (*don't care* non-deterministic) for a predicate should not result in different process networks;
- the use of two way communication, see *section 7.3.1* (**back communication**) is forbidden.

Example

In [Scott & Trehan 89] we consider the translation of a parallel chart parser developed for Parlog [Trehan & Wilk 88]. Using algorithmic decomposition three different uses of Parlog were identified: **shared streams** (many-to-one communication); **pipeline creation** (linear processes spawning); **worker generation** (process and communication creation).

These three uses of Parlog have been translated into OCCAM using the schema mentioned. As a result we were able to translate the Parlog chart parser to OCCAM. Here we give the simplest example of the three **shared streams**.

Shared streams example

The Parlog program fragment is as follows:

```
program(B,C) :-
    producer(A),
    consumer1(A,B),
    consumer2(A,C).
```

Process description and PARLOG network diagrams

Since the program fragment is short we will deal with stages 1 and 2 of the schema simultaneously. `program/2` simply creates three processes; `producer/1`, `consumer1/2` and `consumer2/2`. We will assume that all three are perpetual processes. `producer/1` produces items on stream A. `consumer1/2` receives items from stream A, processes them, and outputs items on stream B. Similarly, `consumer2/2` receives items from stream A, processes them, and outputs items on stream C. `consumer1/2` and `consumer2/2` share stream A. A process network diagram of the program fragment is given in figure 7.10.

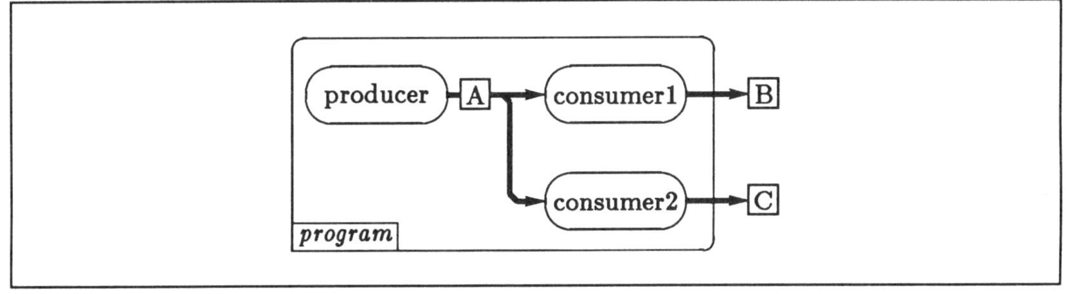

Figure 7.10: PARLOG multiple consumers process network

OCCAM process diagrams and program

In order to share a channel between two (or more) processes in OCCAM we invent a process. The process has one input channel and two output channels. The input channel is the channel that we wish to share. The process receives a value on the input channel and sends identical copies on both of its output channels. We call this process a **splitter** since, in a sense, the shared channel has been split into two identical copies of itself.

The OCCAM process diagram is shown in figure 7.11. In general, each process that shares a channel with another will have an associated **splitter**.

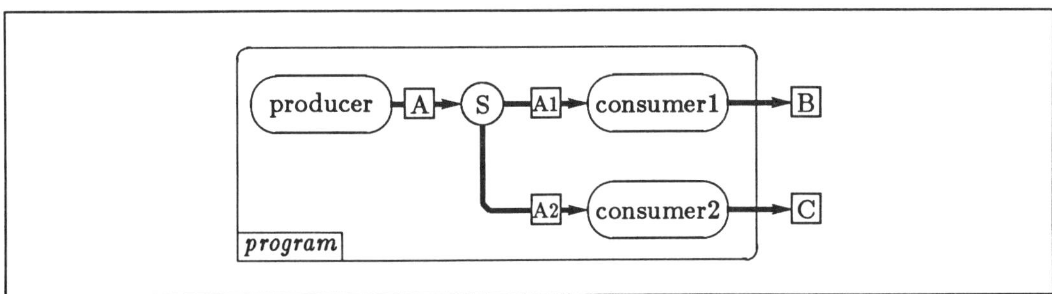

Figure 7.11: OCCAM multiple consumers process network

The OCCAM equivalent program fragment is as follows:

```
PROC program(CHAN OF INT B,C)
  CHAN OF INT A, A1, A2 :
  PAR
    producer(A)
    splitter(A,A1,A2)
    consumer1(A1,B)
    consumer2(A2,C)
:
```

```
PROC splitter(CHAN OF INT A, A1, A2)
  WHILE TRUE
    SEQ
      A ? x
      PAR
        A1 ! x
        A2 ! x
:
```

7.4.2 Evaluation – information for implementors

The CCND languages provide a model of computation which supports both limited OR-parallelism and concurrent AND-goal evaluation. In this section we consider the inherent parallelism that is available in the evaluation of programs implemented in the CCND languages. This inherent parallelism has several uses: a theoretic measure of the parallelism against which particular implementations can be gauged; it provides information for programmers on the relative merits of various programming techniques; it provides information on the suitability of various execution alternatives, like suspension, pruning and scheduling. To obtain a measure of the inherent parallelism available in program execution we adopt a breath-first execution model on an unlimited number of processors. We also consider some of the execution alternatives like, scheduling, open to implementors this provides us with a set parameters which indicate the relative merits of these alternatives. We first consider the current parameters collected during program execution and discuss their limitations. This forms the basis of some new parameters and improved meta-interpreters for their collection.

Limitations of current measurements

Three parameters, cycles, suspensions and reductions, were suggested by Shapiro [Shapiro 83] when he first proposed Concurrent Prolog. The limitations of these parameters and their collection are now discussed to justify some of our new statistics.

Cycles

Current meta-interpreters evaluate the guarded goals as if they were single calls which incur no cycle count. So, the cycle count can only claim to measure the depth of the search space when evaluating *flat code* [Mierowsky *et al* 85], [Foster & Taylor] which have no data dependencies in the guard. Any goals suspended awaiting the evaluation of a *deep guard* will only suspend for one cycle and not the number of cycles it takes for the deep guard to be evaluated. So, this cycle count measures the depth of top-level commitments and not the depth of the evaluation tree.

Another limitation is that the process queue in the meta-interpreters is evaluated left to right, any bindings made by the evaluation of goals in the queue taking place immediately. So, these bindings will be available to any remaining goals in the process queue. This will allow goals that require these bindings to reduce in the current cycle, whereas they would have suspended for one cycle if all the AND-goals were evaluated concurrently, i.e. breadth-first.

Reductions

Current meta-interpreters do not count a call to the underlying Prolog system as a reduction. However, these do contribute to the overall work done in evaluating programs. By ignoring their contributions the comparison of programming techniques which make use of system primitives in the guard is meaningless or at best misleading.

Another limitation is that current meta-interpreters evaluate the OR-alternatives for a given predicate top-down, committing to the first clause whose guarded goals succeed. So, reductions can only be counted for the OR-clauses that have been attempted. Hence, the reduction count depends on the order of the clauses. In a breadth-first evaluation of the CCND languages each set of guarded goals for a given predicate should be evaluated in parallel, with the evaluation committing to the first clause whose guarded goals and head unification have succeeded.

Suspensions

In the Shapiro meta-interpreter the process queue is evaluated from left to right in each cycle, breadth-first. Any bindings made by the evaluation of goals in the queue take place immediately. So, these bindings are available to the goals which remain to be processed in this cycle. The bindings may allow a goal to reduce in the current cycle which would have otherwise suspended assuming a parallel evaluation of the AND-goals.

Suspended goals can be reactivated on several criteria which result in differing amounts of overhead depending on the nature of the execution: current meta-interpreters perform **busy waiting**, where the suspended goals are requeued. So, the same process may suspend several times awaiting the same input in each case. Using this suspension mechanism all the suspended evaluations in each cycle are counted, rather than the new suspensions that occur in each cycle. However, a **non-busy waiting** strategy could have been used. Here, suspended goals are hooked (or tagged) to the variables that they were suspended on so that they can be reactivated when sufficient variables become instantiated. Using this suspension mechanism the new suspensions that occur in each cycle will be counted.

Basis for new parameters

Many of the limitations and inaccuracies of the statistics generated by current meta-interpreter implementations are due to the execution mechanisms employed to model these languages. The collection of more meaningful statistics has required the development of an improved meta-interpreter. The features of this interpreter are as follows:

both AND and OR-parallelism is modelled;

each of the guarded goals for a given predicate is tried and relevant statistics collected;

the statistics from the evaluation of the guarded goal are used to pick the solution path (currently this is the shallowest successful guard, i.e. first guard that would have succeeded in a breadth-first execution);

the AND-goals that form the process queue each undergo one reduction in a cycle; any bindings made as the process queue is evaluated occur only when all the AND-goals have been attempted;

evaluation of a system goal which makes a call to the underlying Prolog system is counted as one reduction;

bindings made using calls to the underlying Prolog system are made only when all the AND-goals in this cycle have been attempted;

the meta-interpreter makes a distinction between suspension and failure;

the commitment of a goal to a given clause is prevented for the number of cycles the guard took to evaluate.

We still make idealisations about CCND execution, namely:

head unification takes no time;

reducing a goal which is a guard to *true* allows us to reduce the goal's parent, in the same cycle.

The first idealisation is not too much of a simplification when handling **flat code**, as the head unification can be included as part of a reduction. However, for **deep guards** this execution model may result in several head unifications being invoked in one cycle. Note that earlier meta-interpreters also assumed this idealisation. The second idealisation could be thought of as assuming a compiler optimisation similar to tail recursive optimisation in Prolog. Note, that the issue of how long a commitment should take was not addressed in earlier meta-interpreters because user defined guards were treated as system calls taking *zero* cycles to evaluate.

Apart from the inaccuracies introduced through limitations in the execution model, the parameters proposed by Shapiro (*cycles*, *suspensions* and *reductions*) do not give any indication of the effect that alternative implementation strategies may have had. In the following subsections we consider some of these alternatives. The new parameters that we propose aim to provide information about the relative merits of these choices.

Pruning OR-branches

The evaluation of a goal invokes several guarded systems, one for each clause that the goal successfully head unifies with. The evaluation commits to the first clause whose guarded system successfully terminates. On commitment, the other guarded systems invoked by the goal evaluation can be terminated or ignored. Terminating the alternative OR-clauses (**pruning**) requires the system to stop the computation being carried out in the alternative branches. This may prevent these branches spending time in needless computation. However, if the guarded goals for the clauses are balanced, that is evaluate in the same time, or all the clauses but one fail before the remaining clause commits, then **pruning** the OR-search will not save any computation in the alternative guards. Ignoring the other alternative OR-clauses (**no-pruning**) when a goal commits, requires the system to disregard any commitment requests from the other alternatives should their guarded systems also terminate successfully. This may save some computation (in sending a terminate message to the other guard evaluations) if the guards are balanced or in cases where only one clause can be committed to.

Even if **pruning** the OR-clauses reduces some computation it may be worth attempting only if the amount of work saved is comparable to the overhead of terminating the other OR-clause evaluations. This comparison will be architecture and implementation dependent.

Pruning OR-clauses is likely to be most beneficial for programming techniques and applications that employ an uneven guarded computation. Such programs usually employ **deep guards** [Gregory 87]. However, it should be noted that even **flat guards** may benefit from **pruning**. This occurs when some of the (**flat**) guards have data dependencies which result in them taking longer to evaluate than other guards, or if some guards make use of costly system predicates while others do not. However, programs with **flat guards** are likely to have an even guard evaluation.

Suspension mechanisms

A goal evaluation suspends if the evaluation of the guarded goals, or head unifications, for the clauses that this goal could reduce by suspend. Suspending the evaluation can be achieved in several ways, the two extremes being **goal suspension** and **clause suspension**. **Goal suspension** involves suspending the parent goal of a computation when all of the clauses it could reduce by suspend. Note that this parent goal may actually be the guarded goal of some other evaluation.

Alternatively each of the clauses (guarded computations and head unifications) could be suspended, known as **clause suspension**. The trade-off between these two extremes is basically a space-time consideration. Suspending a goal requires less space than suspending the evaluation of each of the clauses, which may involve suspending a tree of computation in the case of **deep guards**. However, if some computation is performed in the evaluation of the guarded goals before they eventually suspend this computation will be lost if the goal is suspended. The computation carried out in the guard evaluation will be repeated when the goal is rescheduled for evaluation.

Another choice is how and when suspended goal evaluations are scheduled. When the evaluation of a goal suspends it could be tagged to the variables which when instantiated would allow this goal to be evaluated, known as **non-busy waiting**. It is complex to implement full **non-busy waiting**; that is to suspend a goal until just enough variables are bound to allow the goal to reduce. This is because some clauses, like merge/3, only suspend on one variable, whereas others like `equals/2` require both arguments to be bound. The other extreme would be to immediately reschedule the suspended evaluation, i.e. **busy waiting**.

Employing a **non-busy waiting** suspension mechanism is appropriate if suspended goals remain so for several cycles. For example, in prime number generation by sifting, [Gregory 87] most of the filter processes will be suspended most of the time. Employing a **busy waiting** suspension mechanism is appropriate if the suspended goal is only likely to be suspended for a short period, for example in a producer-consumer type algorithm in which the producer and consumer take approximately the same time.

New profiling parameters

The profiling parameters we are putting forward aim to reflect the effect of the various options available in **pruning OR-branches** and different **suspension mechanisms**. The basic parameters are still suspensions and reductions. However, these are given for the different combinations of suspension mechanism and pruning strategy.

So the basic top-level parameters put forward are suspensions and reductions using the following execution models:

> **busy waiting, no-pruning** and **goal suspension**;
> **busy waiting, no-pruning** and **clause suspension**;
> **busy waiting, pruning** and **goal suspension**;
> **busy waiting, pruning** and **clause suspension**;
> **non-busy waiting, no-pruning** and **goal suspension**;
> **non-busy waiting, no-pruning** and **clause suspension**;
> **non-busy waiting, pruning** and **goal suspension**;
> **non-busy waiting, pruning** and **clause suspension**.

7.5 Conclusions

In this paper we have given a summary of the activities of several directions of work which we have undertaken with respect to a class of languages known as Committed Choice Non-Deterministic. The investigation has highlighted several different aspects of the CCND languages and their usage.

> The issues of search are bound up with those of non-determinism. The sequential logic programming language Prolog is able to find the correct solution path when faced with any form of non-deterministic choice. However, the search is incomplete, solution paths that exist after some infinite branch in the search space will not be considered.
>
> The Committed Choice Non-Deterministic logic languages, provide an AND-parallel and limited OR-parallel evaluation model. These languages are based on *don't care* non-determinism. *Don't know* non-determinism can be mapped directly by using **deep guards**; i.e. placing the relevant OR-search within the guarded goals. However, *generate and test* non-determinism cannot be directly mapped to the CCND model. The problem is that to generate a solution the evaluation has to commit to a given solution path. Once the evaluation has committed, alternative bindings cannot be generated.
>
> The general investigation into object oriented styles of programming which views perpetual processes as objects gave rise to three models of objects. The use of the three object models in supporting a taxi scheduler system provided a vehicle to develop several programming techniques related to the differing object models.
>
>> Mechanisms for addressing classes of objects using sequential or concurrent communication techniques.

A mechanism for representing the behavior of objects under changed circumstances.

A method for one process to access and control the state of another without the controlled process having to perform unnecessary computation.

All the CCND languages easily and directly support ***one-to-many*** communication by single writers to a shared variable. However, only Concurrent Prolog (an ***unsafe*** language) is able to directly support ***many-to-one*** communication, using its facilities for multiple writers to a shared variable. Shared data structures can be supported by the other CCND languages (*safe* languages) by merging requests for updates to a manager process. The manager process then updates the shared resource.

We considered how shared data structures and streams can be supported in the different CCND languages. As a result of this analysis we proposed that streams and in particular multiple writers to streams could be supported by the system efficiently. The resulting language we name as *safe+system streams*. The analysis of applications implemented in the three different styles of language highlight benefits of supporting multiple writers to a stream by the system, in terms of: suspension overheads; available parallelism and total number of cycles required.

The CCND languages provide a powerful vehicle for the design, testing and debugging of a wide variety of computation and communication model. We have considered the development of AI algorithms in the CCND languages with are later translated into OCCAM programs for efficient execution. The translation draws on a common view of Parlog and OCCAM processes as a route by which certain forms of Parlog program can be translated.

We have considered the measurements that should be collected to capture the nature of a CCND computation. As a result we have developed a two stage analysis system: an AND/OR-interpreter, which evaluates the program breath-first producing a dump file and an analyser program which reconstructs a parallel view of the program execution. The statistics obtained are more accurate in two respects. The first is in the modelling of a parallel AND/OR execution on an unlimited number of processors; this allows us to consider the inherent features of our algorithm. The second is in identifying the nature of the execution: **pruned** or **non-pruned**; **busy** or **non-busy** and **goal** or **clause** suspension.

Acknowledgements

The author would first like to thank Dr. Paul Willk and Dr. Chris Mellish for general interest and supervison of much of the work covered in this paper. The AI Application Institute, University of Edinburgh, for use of computing facilities. Tom Conlon; Jim Crammond; Ian Foster; Steve Gregory; Jacob Levy; Ross Overbeek; Peter Ross; Ehud Shapiro and David Warren for discussion and comments about various aspects of this work.

Emilio Agustin; Luis Hern; Richard Baker; Michael Buckley; Andrew Hamilton; Henry Pinto; Robert Scott and Denis Suen for providing valuable input in terms of comments and implementations. Andy Bowles; Eleanor Bradley; Tim Duncan and Robert Scott for reading earlier versions of this paper.

7.6 References

[Bowler *et al* 87] Bowler, Kenway, Pawley and Roweth. *An Introduction to OCCAM2 and the MEIKO Computing Surface.* Teaching paper, University of Edinburgh, Department of Physics, 1987.

[Chikayama & Kimura 87] , T. Chikayama and Y. Kimura. Multiple Reference Management in Flat GHC. In J. Lassez, editor, *Fourth international conference of Logic Programming*, pages 276–293, MIT Press, Melbourne, 1987.

[Clark & Gregory 85] , K. Clark and S. Gregory. Notes on The Implementation of Parlog. *The Journal of Logic Programming*, 1:17–42, 1985.

[Clocksin & Mellish 81] K. Clocksin and C. Mellish. *Programming in Prolog.* Springer-Verlag, 1981.

[Conlon 89] T. Conlon. *Programming in PARLOG.* Addison and Wesley, 1989.

[Crammond 88] J. Crammond. Implementing Parallel Logic Languages on Multi-Processor Architectures. Forth comming PhD. Thesis, Department of Computer Science, Heriot-Watt, Edinburgh, 1988.

[Davison 87] A. Davison. *POOL: A Parlog Object Oriented Language.* Technical Report PAR 87/5, Department of Computing, Imperial College, London, 1987.

[Foster & Taylor] I. T. Foster and S. Taylor. *Flat Parlog: a basis for comparison.* Technical Report DOC 87/5, Department of Computing, Imperial College of Science and Technology, London, 1987.

[Foster 88] I. Foster. *Parlog as a Systems Programming Language.* Unpublished PhD thesis, Department of Computing, Imperial College of Science and Technology, London, 1988

[Foster *et al* 86] I. Foster, S. Gregory, G. Ringwood and K. Satoh. A Sequential Implementation of Parlog. In E. Shapiro, editor, *Third International Conference on Logic Programming*, pages 149–156, Springer-Verlag, London, 1986.

[Furukawa *et al* 83] K. Furukawa, A. Takeuchi, S. Kunifuji, H. Yasukawa and M. Okhi. *Mandala: A Logic Based Programming System.* Technical Report TR 076, Institute For New Generation Computer Technology, Tokyo, 1983.

[Gregory 87] S. Gregory. *Parallel Logic Programming in Parlog.* Addison-Wesley, 1987.

[Hern 89] L. E. C. Hern. On distributed artifical intelligence. *The Knowledge Engineering Review*, 21–57, October 1989.

[Hirsch *et al* 87] M. Hirsch, W. Silverman and E. Shapiro. Computation Control and Protection in the Logix System. In E. Shapiro, editor, *Concurrent Prolog: Collected Papers*, chapter 20, pages 28–45, MIT Press, 1987. Volume 2.

[INMOS 84] INMOS. *OCCAM Programming Manual.* Prentice Hall, 1984.

[Kahn *et al* 86] K. Kahn, M. Miller and D. Bobrow. *Objects in Concurrent Logic Programming Languages.* Technical Report, Knowledge Systems Area, Intelligent System Laboratory, Xerox PARC, 1986.

[Kerridge 87] J. Kerridge. *OCCAM Programming: A Practical Approach.* Blackwell Scientific Publications, 1987.

[Kusalik 84] A.J. Kusalik. Bounded-wait merge in Shapiro's Concurrent Prolog. *New Generation Computing*, 1(2):157–169, 1984.

[Levy 86] J. Levy. A GHC Abstract Machine and Instruction Set. In E. Shapiro, editor, *Third International Conference on Logic Programming*, pages 157–171, Springer-Verlag, London, 1986.

[Mierowsky *et al* 85] C. Mierowsky, S. Taylor, E. Shapiro, J. Levy and M. Safra. *The Design and Implementation of Flat Concurrent Prolog.* Technical Report CS85-09, Weizmann Institute of Science, Rehovot, Israel, 1985.

[Okumura & Matsumoto 87] A. Okumura and Y. Matsumoto. Parallel Programming with Layered Streams. In *Fourth Symposium on Logic Programming*, San Francisco, 1987.

[Pinto 86] H. Pinto. *Implementing Meta-Interpreters and Compilers for Parallel Logic Languages in Prolog.* Project Report PR-14, Artificial Intelligence Applications Institute, University of Edinburgh, Edinburgh, 1986.

[Saraswat 87a] V. A. Saraswat. *Compiling CP(↓,|,&) on top of Prolog.* Technical Report CMU-CS-87-174, Carnegie Mellon, October 1987.

[Saraswat 87b] V. A. Saraswat. The concurrent logic programming language cp: definition and operational semantics. In *SIGACT-SIGPLAN Symposium on Principles of Programming Languages*, ACM, January 1987.

[Saraswat 87c] V.A. Saraswat. Merging Many Streams Efficiently: The Importance of Atomic Commitment. In E. Shapiro, editor, *Concurrent Prolog: Collected Papers*, chapter 16, pages420–445, MIT Press, 1987. Volume 1.

[Scott & Trehan 89] R. Scott and R. Trehan. Translating from Parlog to OCCAM2 : a Schema. *Concurrency: Practice and Experience*, 1(1), 1989.

[Shapiro & Mierowsky 87] E. Shapiro and C. Mierowsky. Fair, Biased, and Self-Balancing Merge Operators: Their Specification and Implementation in Concurrent Prolog. In E. Shapiro, editor, *Concurrent Prolog: Collected Papers*, chapter 14, pages 392–413, MIT Press, 1987. Volume 1.

[Shapiro & Safra 87] E. Shapiro and S. Safra. Multiway Merge with Constant Delay in Concurrent Prolog. In E. Shapiro, editor, *Concurrent Prolog: Collected Papers*, chapter 15, pages 414–420, MIT Press, 1987. Volume 1.

[Shapiro & Takeuchi 83] E. Shapiro and A. Takeuchi. Object Oriented Programming in Concurrent Prolog. *New Generation Computing*, Vol.1(No.1):25–48, 1983.

[Shapiro & Takeuchi 87] E. Shapiro and A. Takeuchi. Object Oriented Programming in Concurrent Prolog. In E. Shapiro, editor, *Concurrent Prolog: Collected Papers*, chapter 29, pages 251–273, MIT Press, 1987. Volume 2.

[Shapiro 83] E. Shapiro. *A Subset of Concurrent Prolog and Its Interpreter.* Research Paper TR-003, Institute For New Generation Computer Technology, Tokyo, 1983.

[Sterling & Shapiro 86] L. Sterling and E. Shapiro. *The Art of Prolog.* MIT Press, 1986.

[Tamaki 87] H. Tamaki. Stream-based Compilation of Ground I/O Prolog into Committed Choice Languages. In J. Lassez, editor, *Fourth international conference of Logic Programming*, pages 376–393, MIT Press, Melbourne, 1987.

[Tanaka *et al* 86] J. Tanaka, K. Ueda, T. Miyazaki, A. Takeuchi, Y. Matsumoto, and K. Furukawa. *Guarded Horn Clauses and Experiences with Parallel Logic Programming.* Technical Report TR-168, Institute For New Generation Computer Technology, Tokyo, 1986.

[Taylor *et al* 87] S. Taylor, S. Safra and E. Shapiro. A Parallel Implementation of Flat Concurrent Prolog. In E. Shapiro, editor, *Concurrent Prolog: Collected Papers*, chapter 39, pages 575–604, MIT Press, 1987. Volume 2.

[Trehan & Mellish 89] R. Trehan and C. Mellish. *Shared Data Structures in the Committed Choice Non-Deterministic Languages.* Technical Report, Department of Artificial Intelligence, University of Edinburgh, 1989. Submitted to: North American Conference on Logic Programming.

[Trehan & Wilk 87] R. Trehan and P. Wilk. *Issues of Non-Determinism in Prolog and the Committed Choice Non-Deterministic Languages.* Research Paper RP-378, Department of Artificial Intelligence, University of Edinburgh, 1987. Also: Artificial Intelligence Applications Institute, University of Edinburgh, Technical Report-TR-43.

[Trehan & Wilk 88] R. Trehan and P. F. Wilk. *A Parallel Chart Parser for the Committed Choice Non-Deterministic (CCND) Logic Languages.* Research Paper RP-366, Department of Artificial Intelligence, University of Edinburgh, 1988. Also: Artificial Intelligence Applications Institute, University of Edinburgh, Technical Report TR-36, Presented at: 5th International Logic Programming Conference Seattle.

[Trehan *et al* 88] R. Trehan, P. Wilk and M. Buckley. *Object Models in the Committed Choice Non-Deterministic Logic Languages.* Research Paper RP-368, Department of Artificial Intelligence, University of Edinburgh, 1988. Also: Artificial Intelligence Applications Institute, University of Edinburgh, TR-37. Presented to the British Computer Society Parallel Processing Specialist Group, February 1988

[Uchida 82] S. Uchida. *Toward a New Generation Computer Architecture*, Technical Report TR-001, Institute For New Generation Computer Technology, Tokyo, 1982. Also: VLSI Architecture, Prentice-Hall, 1984.

[Ueda & Chikayama 84] K. Ueda and T. Chikayama. Efficient stream/array processing in logic programming languages. In *International Conference on Fifth Generation Computer Systems*, pages 317–326, Tokyo, 1984.

[Ueda & Chikayama 85] K. Ueda. and T. Chikayama. Concurrent Prolog Compiler on Top of Prolog. In *Symposium on Logic Programming*, pages 119–126, IEEE Computer Society, 1985. Also: New Generation Computing, Vol. 2, No. 4, pp 361–369.

[Ueda 86a] K. Ueda. *Guarded Horn Clauses*. Unpublished PhD thesis, Department of Information Engineering, University of Tokyo, Tokyo, 1986.

[Ueda 86b] K. Ueda. Making Exhaustive Search Deterministic. In E. Shapiro, editor, *Third international conference of Logic Programming*, pages 270–282, Springer-Verlag, London, 1986.

[Ueda 87] K. Ueda. Making Exhaustive Search Programs Deterministic, Part II. In J. Lassez, editor, *Fourth international conference of Logic Programming*, pages 356–375, MIT Press, Melbourne, 1987.

[Warren 83] D. H. Warren. *An Abstract Prolog Instruction Set*. Technical Note 309, SRI International, 1983

Chapter 8

Multi-transputer implementation of CS-Prolog

P. Kacsuk and I. Futo
Multilogic Computing Ltd.
H-1015 Budapest
Csalogany u. 30–32.
Hungary

Abstract The aim of the paper is to describe the design considerations and techniques that were used for implementing CS-Prolog in a multi-transputer environment connected to a PC as a host computer. First the main language features of CS-Prolog are briefly summarized. The solution of the 8-queens problem illustrates how a CS-Prolog program looks like and how to achieve coarse-grain OR-parallelism in the system.

The distributed control mechanism of CS-Prolog is explained. This mechanism can be viewed as a distributed generalization of the sequential LRDF strategy and assures systematic travel through the whole Search Tree of Prolog programs.

It is thoroughly discussed in the paper how the functions and data structures of the CS-Prolog system are distributed between the host and the transputers. The activity of the host computer is briefly explained. Message types and their roles are summarized.

A Prolog interpreter with a scheduler and a communication subsystem is placed on each transputer. At last a detailed description is given about the implementation layers of the Prolog system and the communication subsystem.

8.1 Introduction

CS-Prolog is a parallel extension of Prolog where the concept of processes are involved in the language. CS-Prolog shows many similar features with occam 2 [1] and Parallel C [2]. All these three languages are based on the communication concept of Hoare's CSP [3] and are intended to be implemented on parallel, communicating process architectures like multi-transputer systems.

In CS-Prolog it is possible to assign a process to a goal and to execute the goal as a Prolog program in parallel with other goals (processes). The communication and synchronization of these parallel processes is done by messages. There is no way for the processes to communicate by means of a common shared database or logical variables. The processes can be suspended waiting for messages and they can send messages to activate other waiting processes. Unlike in occam 2 the communication is asynchronous, the sender process can go on without waiting for the reception of the message. Processes can be created and deleted during program execution. In case of failure CS-Prolog ensures the selection of new alternatives by backtracking.

The aim of this paper is to describe the design considerations and techniques we used for implementing CS-Prolog in a multi-transputer environment connected to a PC as a host computer.

Section 8.2 briefly summarizes the main language features of CS-Prolog. Section 8.3 explains the distributed control mechanism of CS-Prolog programs. Section 8.4 describes how the functions and data strucures of the CS-Prolog system are distributed between the host and the transputers. Section 8.5 enumerates the message formats used for interprocessor communication. In Section 8.6 a detailed description of the transputer implementation layers can be found.

8.2 The language concept of CS-Prolog

The basic notions of CS-Prolog are the same as in occam:

a) process

b) communication

c) time

In CS-Prolog each process represents a Prolog goal to be resolved. To each process an independent Prolog interpreter/compiler is assigned to execute the goal of the process in parallel with other processes. Conceptually CS-Prolog is a two-level language. On the higher level the notion of process is available to describe parallel activities. On the lower level the behavior of each process is given by a Prolog program. The declarative semantics of Prolog is preserved within each process meanwhile the process is able to receive and send information from/to its environment (processes). Processes can be created and deleted during program execution. In case of failure backtracking ensures the selection of new alternatives.

The communication and synchronization of the parallel Prolog processes is done by messages. Unlike in other parallel logic programming languages [4], [5], [6] there is no way for the processes to communicate by means of a common shared database or logical variables. The processes can be suspended waiting for messages and they can send messages to activate other waiting processes. Unlike in occam 2 the communication is asynchronous, the sender process can go on without waiting for the reception of the message.

The time concept of CS-Prolog is significantly different from the occam concept. Instead of using the global real-time concept, CS-Prolog applies the local virtual-time concept. This means that all processes can have their own local times (simulated time) which might be different during the parallel progress of processes. The local time is typically used for distributed discrete event simulation.

8.2.1 CS-Prolog built-in predicates

The process, communication and time concepts of CS-Prolog are defined by means of a collection of built-in predicates which are described in detail in [7]. Here only a short overview of the most important built-in predicates is given:

`new(G,N,T,S,E)`
: A new process is created with goal G and name N on transputer T. The starting local time is S end the resolution of G should be finished by the local time E. The N,T,S,E arguments are optional. If T is missing, then the process is allocated to the transputer of the caller.

`delete_process(P)`
: Each processes whose name can be unified with P is deleted.

`active_process(AP,T)`
: Identifies the caller process AP and the transputer T where it is running.

`send(M,PL)`
: The caller process sends message M to the process being in the process list PL. M should be a fully instantiated term by the moment of the call. It prevents the sender from receiving a binding value produced by the receiver process. This is the main difference between the communication concept of CS-Prolog and Delta Prolog.

`wait_for(M)`

The caller waits for a message which is unifiable with M. After backtrack a new message can not be accepted (deterministic execution).

`wait_for_dnd(M)`

Delayed, nondeterministic version of `wait_for`. After backtrack a new message can be accepted. The implementation of `wait_for_dnd` assures that all possible solutions of a CS-Prolog program can be resolved by backtracking.

`hold(T)`

The local time of the caller process is increased by T.

`run(G)`

Starts the multiprocess scheduler making it possible to run Prolog processes in parallel.

CS-Prolog is a superset of ordinary Prolog. Without using the built-in predicates enumerated above CS-Prolog programs work just like any other Prolog programs on uniprocessors.

8.2.2 Parallelism in CS-Prolog

The process level parallelism offered by CS-Prolog insures a new type of parallelism, called communicating parallelism (similar to Hoare's concept of communicating sequential processes [3]) which is not available in other Prolog languages. By means of communicating parallelism OR- and AND-parallelism can be achieved. The granularism of parallelism can be controled by the user encapsulating Prolog programs of different size into one process.

8.2.3 Example: The 8-queens problem

To illustrate how a CS-Prolog program looks like and how to realize parallel activities, the solution of the 8-queens problem is shown below. The problem is a well-known, typical AI problem: place eight queens on a chessboard that no queen attacks any other queens. Suppose we search one possible solution of the problem for each queen's position in the first column. The next program illustrates how to use CS-Prolog to achieve coarse-grain OR-parallelism.

```
"Main process"

queens_problem:-
        solve([1,2,3,4,5,6,7,8]),
        new(display_result(8),display).

solve([]).
solve(Ylist):-
        del(Y1,Ylist,Ylist2),
        new(one_solution([1/Y1,2/Y2,3/Y3,4/Y4,5/Y5,6/Y6,
            7/Y7,8/Y8],queens(Y1),Y1),
        solve(Ylist2).

"queens_process"

one_solution(Ylist):-                % there is a solution
        solution(Ylist), /,
        send(Ylist,[display]).
one_solution(Ylist):-              % there is no solution
        send([1/Y|[]],[display]).

solution([]).
solution([X/Y|Ylist]):-
        solution(Ylist),
        member(Y,[1,2,3,4,5,6,7,8]),
        noattack(X/Y,Ylist).

"display process"

display_result(0).
display_result(N):-
        N2 is N - 1, wait_for([1/Y1|Ylist]),
        write("solution for Y1="), write(Y1), nl,
        write_list(Ylist),nl, display_result(N2).

? run(queens_problem).
```

The explanation of the "solution" predicate and the definition of the "del", "member", "noattack" predicates can be found in [8] on pages 108-111.

The CS-Prolog prgram shown above generates 8 processes corresponding to the 8 possible positions of the first queen. Each process searches for the positions of the other 7 queens in parallel. Notice that each process is allocated to different PEs identified by Y1 in the "new" built-in procedure calls. Since the eight processes are independent to each other this technique corresponds to the processor farm technique used in numerical problems.

8.3 Distributed control mechanism

The control mechanism of sequential Prolog systems are based on the LRDF (Left-to-Right Depth-First) control strategy that assures systematic travel through the whole Search Tree of Prolog programs. Similarly we would like to define a distributed LRDF strategy assuring the systematic search for CS-Prolog programs.

8.3.1 Distributed foreward execution

The basic control mechanism of CS-Prolog is identical with the LRDF strategy of sequential Prolog systems. The difference appears when the interpreter reaches a so-called communication point, which is a CS-Prolog built-in predicate effecting the execution of other Prolog processes. Two types of communication points are available in CS-Prolog:

- new : creating a new process
- send: sending a message to other processes

In both cases the execution of the caller process continues without delay and as a result of these procedures parallel processes can start or resume on other transputers.

8.3.2 Distributed backtracking

A major problem with the implementation of CS-Prolog (and of any distributed Prolog languages) is how to ensure the backtracking facility in a distributed environment. The main difference between the distributed foreward execution and the distributed backtracking is in their parallelism. While the former is parallel in nature, the latter is sequential. Distributed backtracking is done sequentially, controled by one of the transputers until a new alternative ensuring the parallel reactivation of the other processes can be found by the process executing the distributed backtrack.

In CS-Prolog two kinds of backtracks are distinguished:

1. local backtrack

2. global backtrack

Backtrack between two communication points is called local and has no direct effect on the behavior of other processes. Backtrack passing a communication point is called global and immediately alters the behavior of other processes. According to the origin of the backtrack on a given transputer again two kinds of backtracks can be distinguished:

1. failure backtrack

2. deadlock backtrack

Failure backtrack occurs when a process failed. Deadlock backtrack is needed when the system reaches a point where each Prolog process is either in state finished or waiting for a message and there is no transient message in the multi-transputer network. This situation is called global deadlock. In global deadlock one process is choosen (called forced process) for executing deadlock backtracking while the others are waiting for reactivization by the forced process.

The main difference between the failure backtrack execution and the deadlock backtracking is in their parallelism. While the former is parallel in nature, the latter is sequential. Many processes can execute failure backtrack in parallel while others are going foreward. Deadlock backtracking is done sequentially, controled by one of the processes until it finds a new alternative ensuring the parallel reactivation of the other processes.

Similarly we can distinguish two kinds of choice points:

1. normal choice point

2. communication choice point

The normal choice point represents untried alternative clauses in a predicate. Communication choice points are created when "`wait_for_dnd`" procedures are executed.

Based on the introduced notions the algorithm of the distributed backtracking is as follows:

1. If during failure backtrack a process passes a communication point, an anti-message is sent to the receiver processes or to the created process causing forced failure backtrack for these processes. The backtrack of the original process continues to its last choice point.

2. If during failure backtrack a process arrives to a communication choice point, then

```
if
there are further matching messages for the process
then
   the next message is selected and the process goes
   into state running foreward
else
   the process becomes waiting on the communication choice point.
```

3. If during deadlock backtrack the forced process passes a communication point, forces the receiver or created process to become the new forced process and to execute the deadlock backtrack.

4. If during deadlock backtrack the forced process arrives to a communication choice point, then

```
if
   there are further matching messages for the process
then
   the next message is selected and the process goes into
   state running foreward and reactivates the other processes
else
   the process passes the communication choice point
   and continues the deadlock backtrack.
```

8.4 Distribution of work

The first and most important design decisions in a distributed implementation of a process oriented language are

a) how to map the processes into the processor space

b) how to distribute work between the host computer and the processor space

c) how to allocate data structures into the memory space.

8.4.1 Mapping of CS-Prolog processes

There are two basic solutions for mapping processes in a multiple processor space:

a) Static mapping, where the execution of each process is restricted to a given transputer.

b) Dynamic mapping, where processes can be moved between transputers during the execution.

Though the b) alternative insures more flexibility and better load balancing occam 2 and Parallel C realizes the static mapping. In case of CS-Prolog moving a process from one transputer to another would require the movement of a large amount of data usually stored in three Prolog stacks (Environment, Copy and Trail) representing the history of the process execution. This would speed down the computation therefore we also have chosen the static mapping technique for CS-Prolog.

In case of static mapping the next question to be solved is how to choose transputers for processes. Again two possible alternatives can be considered:

a) User controled mapping, where the user should decide how to map the processes into the processor space. To control the mapping language tools are available for the user.

b) Run-time system controled mapping, where the run- time system decides on the process allocation based on run-time informations such as the current load balancing of the system.

The advantage of version a) is that the run-time system can be kept simple and fast. In many cases the user who designed the parallel algorithm is able to control the process allocation in a much more effective way than even an intelligent run-time system. Obviously a drawback of version a) that the user is burdened by the task of process allocation.

Both occam 2 and Parallel C use version a). In occam 2 the PLACED PAR serves for controlling the process mapping, while in Parallel C a special configuration file is used for this purpose.

In CS-Prolog processes are dynamically created by the "new" built-in predicate. The optional third argument of this predicate is used for specifying the transputer where the new process should be executed. This argument can be a variable getting value during the execution. This way the CS-Prolog solution is somewhere between version a) and b). When the third argument is missing, the new process is mapped on the parent's transputer. Detailed description of process creation in CS-Prolog can be found in [7]. Like in occam and in Parallel C the mapping of processes does not effect the logical behavior of CS-Prolog programs but has a great influence on the overall system performance.

On each transputer any number of concurrent Prolog processes can be executed together, sharing the processor time. To dispatch the processor among the processes a CS-Prolog scheduler is used [7]. Unlike in occam and Parallel C each Prolog process has the same priority in CS-Prolog. Processes are not distinguished since the initial goal of CS-Prolog is successfully resolved when all the created Prolog processes are successfully terminated.

8.4.2 Function distribution between host and transputers

Since all the IO devices are connected to the host computer any operations concerned with IO activities should be executed by the host. According to this rule in the distributed CS-Prolog system the host realizes the user environment and the IO built-in predicates. The CS-Prolog system always works in one of the following modes:

- environment mode
- execution mode

The purpose of the environment mode is to prepare the system for executing a CS-Prolog program. The following main activities can be done in the environment mode:

- program loading with syntactic checking
- program editing
- defining the initial goal statement
- starting the execution of the initial goal

In environment mode the host is the active part of the host – multitransputer system. The only task of the transputer network in this mode to transmit the prolog clauses (program) packed into DATABASE messages in a broadcast way to each transputer of the system. The environment mode finishes when the initial goal statement is sent to the ROOT transputer. The ROOT is the only transputer connected to the host and this way it plays a distinguished role in both execution modes. In case of the environment mode the ROOT initiates the broadcast messages for the other transputers.

The execution mode starts when the Prolog interpreter on the ROOT receives the "start initial goal" message and begins the execution of the initial goal. The other transputers are activated by the "new" built-in predicates of CS-Prolog creating Prolog processes on different transputers. Whenever a Prolog process on a transputer reaches an IO built-in predicate it generates an "io service message" and sends to the host. It is the responsibility of the host to execute the IO predicates and this is the only role of the host in the execution mode.

8.4.3 Data distribution

In case of CS-Prolog the following main data structures are used:

a) Source Table representing the CS-Prolog source code

b) Prog Table describing the clauses of the CS-Prolog program in term format.

c) Constant Table containing Prolog names

d) Operator Table defining Prolog operators

e) Environment stack representing the history of a CS-Prolog process

f) Copy stack storing the dynamically created compound terms

g) Trail containing information to undo variable bindings in case of backtrack

h) Scheduling lists for managing the concurrent CS-Prolog processes

Since the Source Table represents the source text of the program it only plays role in the environment mode and therefore is only located in the host memory.

The b) and c) tables together represent the inner format of the prolog database. Static and dynamic clauses of the database are distinguished in the system. Static clauses are defined by the original program text and they are visible for each Prolog process, therefore a copy of them is stored in each transputer's memory. Since static clauses are commonly used by all of the transputers they are not allowed to be removed by any Prolog processes. One copy of these tables is stored in the host memory too in order to assist program editing in environment mode and IO operations in the execution mode. Static clauses are broadcasted by the host during the program loading and editing phases of the environment mode.

Dynamic clauses are created by different processes during the execution of the goal sequence. Dynamic clauses are local to the creator process so they are only stored in the local memory of the creator and they can only be removed by their creator process. As a result dynamic clause operations (assert, retract, etc.) do not require any intertransputer communication.

New operators can be added to the Operator Table either in environment or execution mode. In the latter case the "add_operator" built_in predicate is responsible for creating new operators by sending to the host an ADD_OP message containing the operator definition. The host syntactically checkes if the operator is acceptable and in this case the operator is added to the Operator Table of the host and a broadcast message is generated by the host for the transputers. Based on this broadcast message the operator is added to the Operator Tables of the transputers. Deletion of operators are executed in the same way.

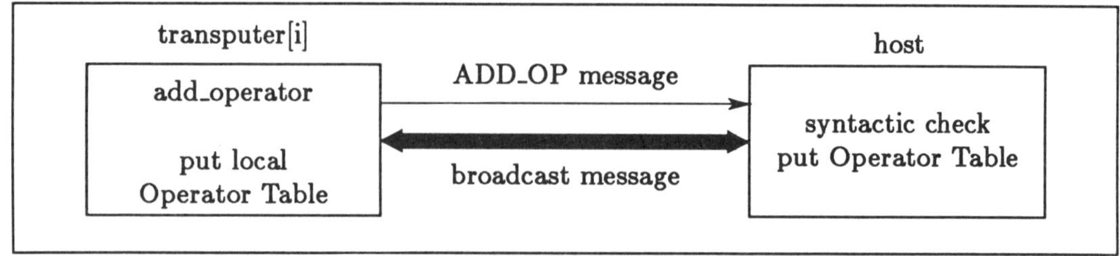

Figure 8.1: Distributed execution of add_operator built-in predicate

e)–h) data structures represent the dynamic behavior of the Prolog processes in the execution mode. These data structures are stored on the transputers but not on the host since it is the task of the transputers to run CS-Prolog processes.

8.5 Communication subsystem

There are 4 basic types of messages in the multi-transputer system:

- user
- broadcast
- acknowledge
- deadlock token

The so-called user messages serve for passing information between two transputers or between a transputer and the host. Two subclasses of the user messages can be distinguished according the progress direction of the sender interpreter. Positive messages are sent in the case of forward progress and negative messages during backtrack. Functionally the user messages support the distributed implementation of the send, new, io, database and control built-in predicates.

Broadcast messages are used for transmitting information to all transputers of the multi-transputer system. Typically broadcast messages appear in the program loading, process allocation and Operator Table management. From the point of view of broadcast transmission transputers are connected in a logical tree where the root of the tree is always the ROOT transputer.

Acknowledge messages and deadlock token messages support the detection of the global deadlock situation, which plays a central role in distributed backtrack (see Section 8.3.2). The system is in global deadlock when both the Prolog interpreters and the communication subsystem are without any work, i.e. there is no Prolog process to resume by any interpreter, no message on its way to reach the destination transputer and there is at least one process waiting for a message.

The global deadlock detection algorithm is a distributed one where the transputers are organized in a logical ring. A so-called deadlock token is circulated in the ring. The deadlock token is passed by a transputer if its interpreter is in local deadlock and all the messages sent by this interpreter have arrived in their destination transputers. If the deadlock token can reach the emission transputer having passed through the ring finding all transputers in local deadlock means that the system is in global deadlock.

The possible message types are summarized in Figure 8.2.

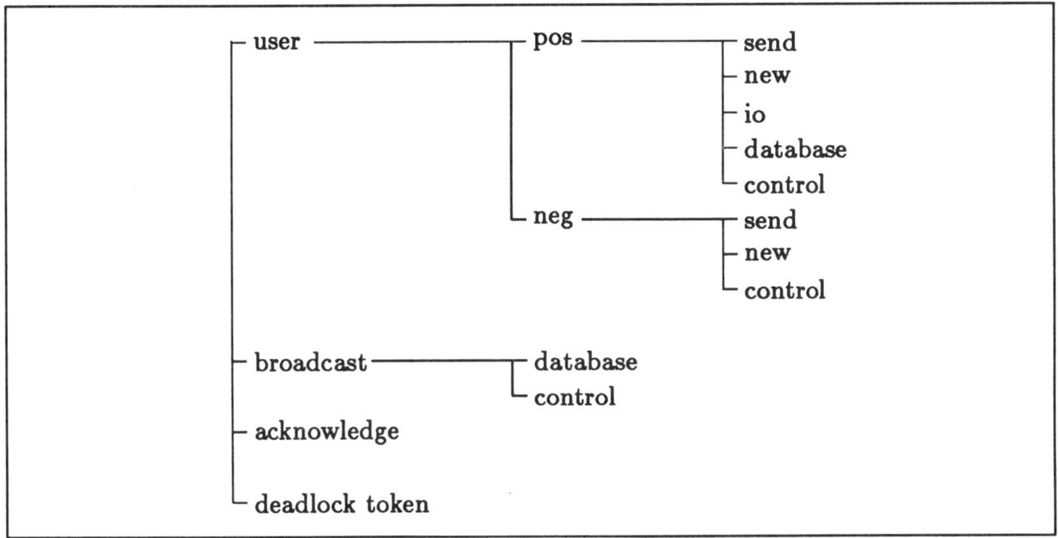

Figure 8.2:

8.6 Implementation layers on transputers

The implementation of the CS-Prolog system is folded into 4 layers on each transputer:

- Communication Subsystem Layer (CSL)
- Communication Control Layer (CCL)
- Prolog Control Layer (PCL)
- Prolog Interpreter Layer (PIL)

8.6.1 Communication subsystem layer (CSL)

CSL is the nearest layer to the phisical hardware and responsible for hiding the phisical topology of the transputer network. It realizes a logical network topology defined by the user and stored in the Topology Description Table.

CSL assures the following features of the intertransputer communication:

a) Messages can be of unlimited size but should be composed from packages with maximum size of 256 bytes.

b) The order of packages belonging to the same message does not change during the communication.

c) Packages are guaranted to arrive to the target transputer except for the case of hardware error.

d) No communication deadlock can arise in the network.

8.6.2 Communication control layer (CCL)

The tasks of CCL are as follows:

a) To receive USER and BROADCAST messages from the Prolog Control Layer, to disintegrate them into packages shorter than 256 bytes and to send them to the CSL.

b) To receive messages from the CSL and to process them based on their types.

c) To generate and send ACK (acknowledgement) messages for the USER and BROADCAST messages.

d) To receive and handle DEADLOCK TOKEN messages.

e) To detect local and global Prolog deadlock.

The ACK and DEADLOCK TOKEN messages are generated and processed in the CCL. The main reason for introducing the CCL was to detect the global Prolog deadlock as it is described in Section 8.2 and 8.3. The basic system processes of CCL are shown in Figure 8.3.

Outgoing messages are taken from the Message Out Table (MOT) of PCL. Incoming messages are put into the Message In Table (MIT) of PCL. In order to assist CCL in determining the local deadlock state of the node the interpreter sets a Deadlock State Flag whenewer it can not find any Prolog process to run.

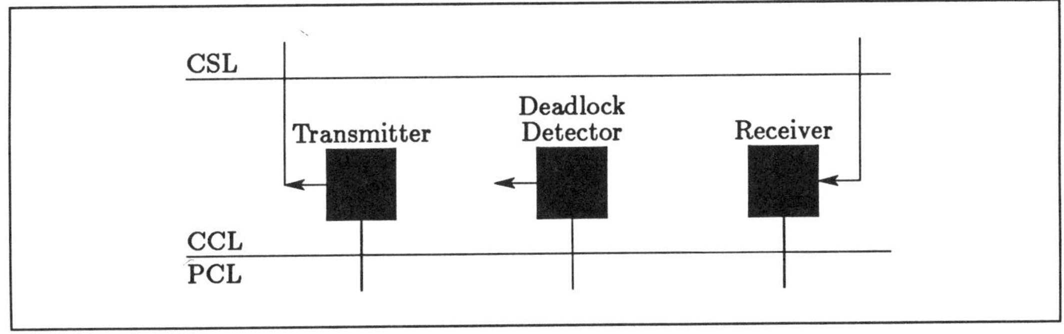

Figure 8.3:

8.6.3 Prolog control layer (PCL)

The task of PCL is to organize the work of the Prolog interpreters running on different processors into an integrated system resolving the initial goal statement of CS-Prolog. The simplified structure of PCL is shown in Figure 8.4 where black boxes represent system processes and white boxes are the data structures.

The main tasks of PCL are as follows:

- PCL has to administrate the process allocation on transputers. For this purpose the so-called Process Allocation Table (PAT) contains pairs of process names and their associated transputers where they were created. Whenever a message is sent to a Prolog process running on a different transputer it is the task of the PAT Handler to determine based on PAT where to actually send the message.
- Based on the type of the incoming messages Message Sorter places them in one of the Message Input Tables (MIT) or sets one of the State Vector Flags.

The MIT holds the incoming user messages and according to these messages it is divided into six parts:

1. Table of incoming NEW type messages (NEW_MIT)
2. Table of incoming SEND type messages (SEND_MIT)
3. Table of incoming I/O type messages (I/O_MIT)
4. Table of incoming DATABASE type messages (DBASE_MIT)
5. Table of incoming CONSUMED type messages (CONS_MIT)
6. Table of incoming RESUME type messages (RESUME_MIT)

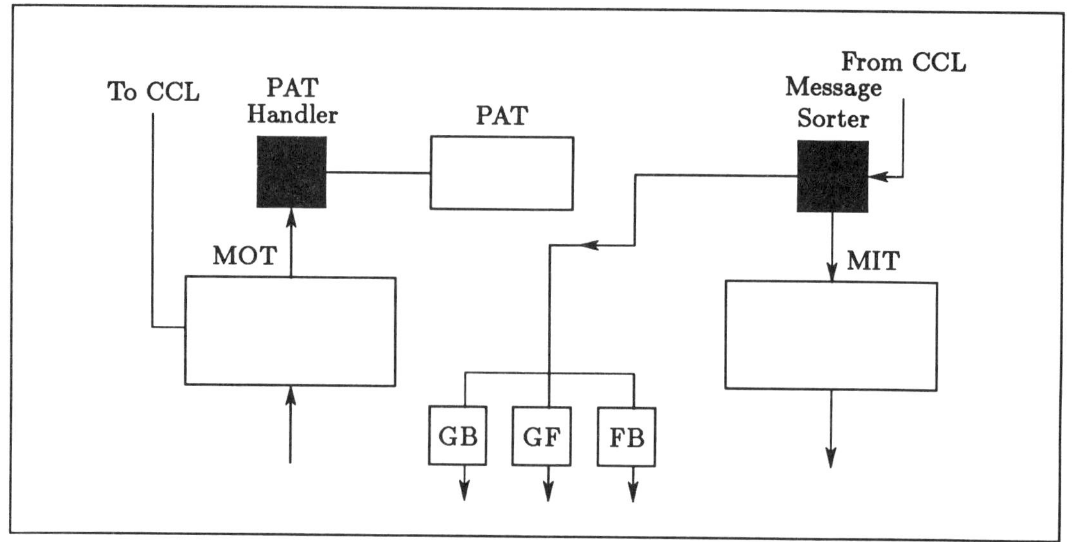

Figure 8.4:

The structure of MIT is shown in Figure 8.5. CONS_MIT and RESUME_MIT play role in the realization of the TRANSIENT BACK state. The State Vector Flags serve for realizing the state transition diagram of the multiputer schedulers. They are the Global Backward Flag (GB), the Global Forward Flag (GF) and the Forced Backtrack Flag (FB).

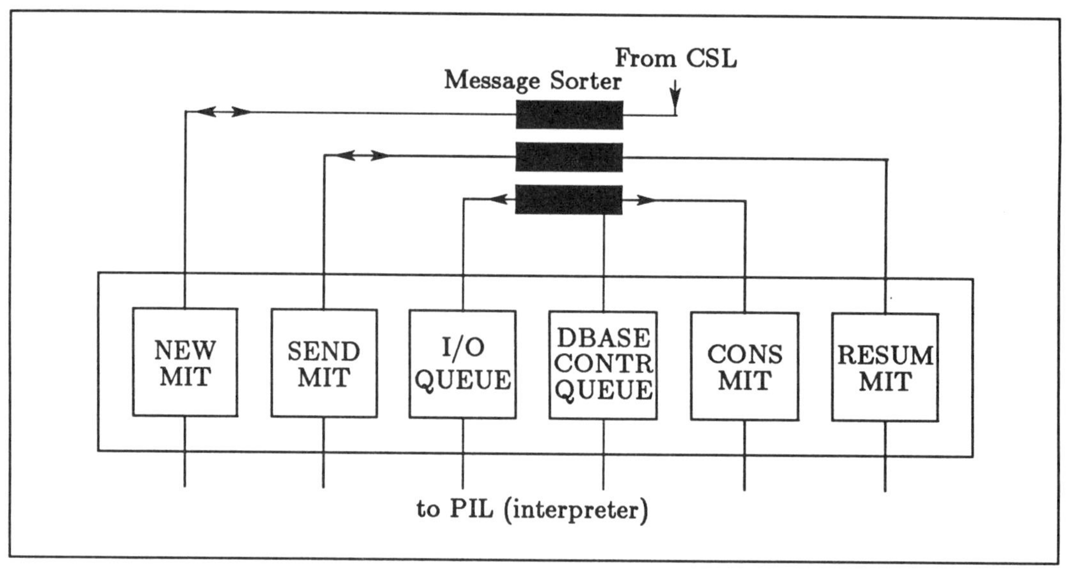

Figure 8.5:

8.6.4 Prolog interpreter layer (PIL)

PIL contains the Prolog interpreter and the Prolog data structures described in Section 8.4.3. PIL also realizes the Process Level and Monoputer Level Scheduling [7]. The interpreter and scheduler basically work within the PIL, they call the underlying layers only in the following cases:

- creating a process by the "new" built-in predicate
- sending a message to a process running on another transputer
- executing IO built-in predicate
- detecting local deadlock

PIL always generates USER type messages and places them into the Message Out Table (MOT) of PCL.

8.7 Conclusion

CS-Prolog is a parallel extension of Prolog defined for implementing Prolog on communicating process architectures. CS-Prolog makes it possible to exploit coarse grain parallelism in Prolog environment by defining processes for resolving different goals in a cooperative way.

The distributed implementation of CS-Prolog is radically different from other proposed parallel implementations of logic programming languages. A demonstration version of the distributed CS-Prolog interpreter has been available since September 1988. The alpha version of the multi-transputer interpreter is expected by the end of January 1989.

8.8 References

[1] INMOS Limited 'occam 2 Reference Manual', Prentice Hall, 1988

[2] 3L 'Parallel C User's Manual', 1988

[3] Hoare, C A R 'Communicating Sequential Processes', Prentice Hall, 1985

[4] Clark, K L and Gregory, S 'PARLOG: Parallel Programming in Logic', Research Report DOC84/4 Dep. Of Computing, Imperial College, University of London

[5] Shapiro, E Y 'A Subset of Concurrent Prolog and its Interpreter', Technical Report TR-003, Inst. for New Generation Computer Technology, Tokyo, 1983

[6] Ueda, K 'Guarded Horn Clauses' Lecture Notes in Computer Science, Springer-Verlag, Berlin Heidelberg, 1986

[7] Futo, I and Kacsuk, P 'CS-Prolog on multitransputer systems', Int. Journal Microprocessors and Microsystems, Vol 13 No 2 March 1989

[8] Bratko, I 'Prolog Programming for Artificial Intelligence', Addison-Wesley, 1986

Chapter 9

Transputer Common-Lisp: a parallel symbolic language on transputer[1]

Bruno Pagès
Laboratoires de Marcoussis
CGE Research Center
Route de Nozay
91460 Marcoussis France
Tel: 33 1 64 49 15 77
Fax 33 (1) 64 49 06 95
e-mail : pages@crcge1.cge.fr

Abstract In this paper we give the definition and description of the implementation of Transputer Common-Lisp, a subset of Common-Lisp [Steele 84] on Transputer. Transputer Common-Lisp is composed of a Common-Lisp compiler and interpreter, a Stop-and-Copy garbage collector, and distributed multi-tasking supports with load balancing and message routing.

The aim of Transputer Common-Lisp is to define a flexible language allowing the studies and experimentations of different technical points within parallelism, such as topology [Baude 89], message routing, dynamic load balancing, and also language definition (actor language for instance).

[1]This study is supported by Esprit Project 440 and Alcatel fundings.

For that, we did define and realize Transputer Common-Lisp deliberately using all the characteristics of the Transputer. For instance, Common-Lisp tasks are Transputer tasks, and the channels can be used in Lisp with several manners (for example with streams). For parallelism we have selected explicit parallel or concurrent execution mechanisms of Common-Lisp forms. The execution management is based on the use of a fixed number of tasks on each processor, this can be transparent to the user.

9.1 Introduction

Lisp has been a popular programming language for 30 years and is the most popular language for Artificial Intelligence Applications. Lisp is a very good programming tool within the context of sequential execution, but we want to use it in the parallelism domain, particularly with distributed architectures.

Then, the aim of Transputer Common-Lisp realization is not to obtain only a nth implementation of a mono-task mono-processor Common-Lisp on a nth processor. We want to study the implementation of Common-Lisp, and the corresponding extensions, within the context of a distributed architecture without shared memory, composed of a big number of processors. Transputer Common-Lisp is not the final aim of our researches, it is also a tool for studies made at the *Laboratoires de Marcoussis* on the distributed architectures: Actor language, inter-processors communications and processor load balancing.

Among Lisp dialect we have selected Common-Lisp for its qualities as language, because it is normalized, and available on many computers, then very widespread. Furthermore, we already have a good knowledge in Common-Lisp implementation.

Common-Lisp definition is almost fully written in Common-Lisp itself and partly independent of the target machine. This Common-Lisp software part is named a *root*. Transputer Common-Lisp implementation uses this root, which has been used previously to implement Common-Lisp on the MAIA machine (Machine for the Artificial Intelligence Applications), jointly developed by the *Laboratoires de Marcoussis* and the *Centre National des Télécommunications* at Lannion [MAIA 85].

The first part of this paper describes the basic choices in relation with the Transputer architecture. Then we describe the implementation of a concurrent Common-Lisp in relation with the Transputer characteristics. The paper finishes with the description of the parallel execution mechanisms of Common-Lisp forms, and extension functions about channels.

9.2 Basic choices in the transputer use

The first problems of the Transputer Common-Lisp implementation are the same as those found in the implementation of any recursive language which support parallel and concurrent executions. To obtain an efficient implementation, the processor characteristics must be cleverly taken into count, which is particularly true in the Transputer case because it is not a classical processor.

9.2.1 Transputer characterization

Within the context of this implementation, we think that the most important Transputer characteristics are the following :

The instruction set is reduced, for instance there is no ***push*** instruction, very much used in the implementations of recursive language such as Lisp.

The Transputer has a hardware multi-tasking, with a ***time-sharing*** of the low priority tasks, linked with the use of the ***j*** and ***lend*** instructions. A memory area, called ***workspace***, is associated with each task.

It is possible to use external or internal channels, whose management is strongly linked with the multi-tasking, to stop or restart the tasks using them. The external channel use is obviously obligatory to send informations to an other Transputer.

Contrary to most processors, there is no working register, the calculi are made with a three word evaluation stack, which is not saved during the process switch. We will see that we use pseudo-registers located in Transputer internal memory.

The Transputer has some single-float and double-float instructions.

Each Transputer has an internal very fast memory of 4 Kbytes, the memory cycle is 50 nano seconds. Obviously, this memory area must be reserved for the most frequent uses.

Moreover on our board ([Inmos 87 a]) each Transputer has an external slow memory with a memory cycle of 300 nano seconds to obtain a total real memory size of 8 Mbytes.

There is no virtual memory, then the total memory size is 8 Mbytes, which is a small memory to use Common-Lisp. This problem is one of the most important in the Transputer Common-Lisp implementation.

There is no instruction or data cache, these devices minimize the memory accesses and then increase the program performances. In return, it is possible to know exactly what happens during execution.

There is no *trap* or similar mechanisms, when using invalid memory addresses (for instance when the two less significant bits of an address used to read a word are not both zero).

No optimization linked with the execution instruction order (for instance delayed jumps)

Then, we must now define Common-Lisp task, and the implementation of the classical storage structures (stacks and registers) on Transputer.

9.2.2 Tasks

We want to realize a Lisp supporting parallel executions on several processors, but also concurrent executions on each Transputer (in order to increase the total number of tasks, but also to facilitate processor programming, separating for instance the *router*, and user programs). Here, the problems introduced by the concurrence are much important than these introduced by the parallelism.

For obvious memory size reasons, each Transputer has only one Transputer Common-Lisp definition, and all the tasks share a same environment. The Lisp task implementation must be as efficient as possible, and compatible with the channel use. The channel integration is a very important point of the Transputer, because they are used by the tasks not only to communicate. Because the channel management and the multi-tasking are linked, it is possible to stop and to restart tasks, without active wait.

Then we have decided to stick against the Transputer. The Lisp tasks are Transputer tasks and have their own *workspace*, the dispatching is made by the Transputer, without any additional management. Of course, this choice creates some problems, which are now examined.

We remind that for the Transputer a task is constituted of a private memory area (indicated when the task is active by the Wprt register) and an instruction address. To dispatch the tasks, and to manage the channels and timers, the Transputer uses the memory words from Wptr-4 to Wptr. For instance when an active task is dispatched, its program counter is saved at the address Wptr-1. Then, this memory area is not the user property, and it is impossible to use it.

A task is dispatched because it makes an explicit wait on a channel or a timer, or because it has passed its quantum of time (about 1 ms) and it executes a *j* or *lend* instruction. Then it is possible to avoid task commutation to realize exclusive sections. But it is not possible, or conceivable, to know exactly when a *j* or a *lend* produces a dispatching. Then it is not possible, for instance, to execute a particular program just before and after each commutation, we will look at this point when we talk about special binding.

On a same Transputer, the Lisp tasks share a global environment, containing the symbols for instance, and possess their own special binding stacks and pseudo registers. We now describe these two last points.

9.2.3 Stacks

It is impossible to implement a recursive language as Common-Lisp without stack. We saw that the Transputer has no stack instruction (for instance ***push*** or ***pop***), and no register to memorize stack pointers. We also know that a Lisp task is a Transputer task, and that the task scheduling is made by the Transputer, with the previously cited results.

Then on the Transputer there is not really a stack, except perhaps the memory area designated by the Wptr register, because we have the *ldl* and *stl* which can be viewed as stack element access and write instructions, and *ajw* can be seen to change the stack pointer. But we don't use the ***workspace*** as a stack, we use it as a scratchpad which is peculiar to each task, we will look at this point in the following section. Simply remark that if Occam can use Wptr as a stack base, this is impossible with Lisp where the necessary area size cannot be established at compile time, because the functional calls are unconstrained.

As for many RISC processors, the stack management is handmade, each stack has its own memory stack area, and a stack pointer refers to the last pushed word.

9.2.4 Registers

The Transputer itself has no register, but it is imperative to have pseudo registers (for instance the stack pointers) peculiar for each task, obviously their uses must be very efficient. For that they are stored in the *workspace* of each task, which are in the fast internal memory. Then each task scheduling is a register automatic commutation, with a nil cost. A register access is made by the *ldl* instruction, obviously the most used registers (for instance the *nil* address and stack pointers) are placed in the first 15 locations to avoid *pfix* instructions.

Some constant addresses (for instance *nil*) are also stored in pseudo registers to increase the program performances.Then getting the symbol *nil* address with its *tag* reclaims only 1 byte and 3,5 cycles (we count 1,5 cycles to load 1 instruction of 1 byte), because it needed only the *ldl* instruction execution. Without a REG-NIL pseudo register the generated code is seven *pfix* and one *ldc*, and reclaims 8 bytes and 20 cycles.

Because stack pointers are speudo-registers, the stack management are the following :

Without overflow test, the Areg (top of the evaluation stack) push in a Lisp stack is made with the following sequence (we suppose that the stack grow to the decreasing addresses) :

```
ldl   stack-pointer
adc   -4
stl   stack-pointer
ldl   stack-pointer
stnl  0
```

then 6 bytes are needed. To limit the binary size, and increase the program performances, the compiler groups together the pushings, when it can do so, in order not to change the stack pointer for each pushed word.

A stack grows to the decreasing addresses to easily access an under top. For instance the access of the first stack under top is made by the two following instructions :

```
ldl   stack-pointer
ldnl  1
```

The general use of Transputer is defined, we can tackle the Transputer Common-Lisp implementation specific problems. We begin by the Common-Lisp implementation problems, then we describe the multi-tasking.

9.3 Common-Lisp

For the sake of briefness, the whole Transputer Common-Lisp implementation is not describe, and we stress on the problems linked with the Transputer use.

Because a full and efficient Common-Lisp implementation requires much memory, and we only have 8 Mbytes on our boards, we have made some removals from the Common-Lisp standard to obtain Transputer Common-Lisp. The most important removals are the ***ratio bignum*** and ***complex*** types, and the fact that all arrays are ***simple-arrays*** (they cannot contain ***fill-pointer*** or be ***displaced***).

As any Lisp, Common-Lisp is not only a language, it contains a memory management with its ***garbage collector***, which is described first. Each Lisp object has a testable type, this is very important, and must be considered from the beginning of the implementation design, we will describe how we proceed. At last we will give some informations about the variable bindings and functional calls.

9.3.1 Garbage collector

Because we have no real time claim, the Transputer Common-Lisp *garbage collector* is not an incremental *garbage* and we chose a simple, efficient and classical Stop and Copy. It is very well-known, then we don't describe it, and only give its implementation particularities for Transputer Common-Lisp.

The allocation memory is shared in two areas : a dynamic area (itself shared in two areas because we use a Stop and Copy) and a static area. Objects allocated in the static area are not reprocessed, then they are not moved at each *garbage* and their addresses are fixed.

All the objects which must be retained by the *garbage collector* are reached from a root, constituted by the static area, all the used stack parts and some particular registers of all tasks. It is imperative that all the pointers reached by the *garbage collector* allow to establish without ambiguity the type of the corresponding object. In order that the task registers might be shared into two groups, the registers of the first one are *garbaged* and must only contain tagged pointers, in the second one the registers must not contain any pointers to objects allocated in the dynamic area. Obviously this distinction is impossible with the Transputer evaluation stack, then it is not garbaged and when the *garbage collector* can intervene, this stack must not contain any pointers to objects allocated in the dynamic area. All the pointers do not correspond to objects allocated in the dynamic area, the *garbage* can also finds pointers to objects allocated in the static area, code or stack addresses. The distinction between all the pointers is made by zoning, the memory map for a 8 Mbytes board is the following :

80000000 (internal memory)	Reserved memory for Transputer internal running. Procedures called by compiled codes. Tags table. Several important addresses tables. Ten task workspaces.
80001000	Transputer Common-Lisp stacks.
80029004	Static area.
801EC000	Two half dynamic areas.
80680000	Binary area.

The *garbage collector* is a subroutine called by the first task which cannot allocate an object in the dynamic area. Obviously it is impossible to make other allocations, or to use an object, during the *garbage* collection. Then, the *garbage* must work without a break, and it does not use the instructions which can cause a dispatch. It is also possible to change the task priority, but we prefer the previous manner, where the Transputer is not absolutely stuck.

To decrease the *garbage* intervention time, its binary code is copied each time in a internal memory area which is restored at the end of the *garbage* collection (the saving of time is about 2). There is no other case where the internal memory is used as a cache.

The static area is used by the compiled codes, because all the data directly referenced in a compiled program are allocated in this area. For instance in the program *(defun foo()'(1))* the list *(1)* is allocated in the static area, and the generated code is a sequence of seven *pfix* instruction codes and a *ldc* instruction code to obtain its address, with the *cons tag*. Obviously, these object addresses are placed by the Common-Lisp binary loader, and the compiler unknowns them.

9.3.2 Object type determining

In classical languages, for instance C, the type of all the data must be known at compile time and these types are not testable during the execution. On the other hand, in a Lisp compilation, the data types can be unknown, and they are testable (for instance with the *type-of* function). The type is used very often, to make type check (for instance the *rplaca* function checks that the first argument is a *cons*), or to establish an object type (for instance for a generic function which has a specific treatment for each type as *write*). Then the type treatment must be very efficient.

There is three main ways to differentiate the data type :

zoning : in this case each data type is linked with an specific allocation area, then a type checking is a limit checking. But Common-Lisp has many types and would necessitate many areas, then a memory loss, and a slow type determining. Moreover, this method requires *fixnums* and characters encoded on particular memory area (for instance the binary area) not already used to allocate, but their values would be limited. It is also possible to allocate *fixnums* and characters, but the cost for the *fixnums* which are very much used, is too important (however some implementations use this method, for instance *Kyoto Common-Lisp*).

The **typing** : In this case a mark particular with each type is placed in the objects themselves. The main disadvantage of this method, beside the memory place used by each object, is its slowness, because each type checking requires a memory access.

At last the third method uses **tag** bits. In this case the object type is stored in all the pointers referencing the object, not in the object itself. The disadvantages of this method are the required space in the pointer, and at a lower level of importance the necessity to remove the *tag* before each use as an address. We have chosen this method because there is no problem to use it on the Transputer.

All the Transputer Common-Lisp objects are based on 32 bit words. To understand the object representations and the choice of the *tags*, it is necessary to note the following points:

> Because of the word addressing mode used, the two less significant bits of any pointer are equal to 0. Therefore it is possible to use these bits to contain *tag* bits.
>
> The memory size of our board is 8 Mbytes, and this memory is consecutively addressed after the internal memory, furthermore the 8 most significant bits of any pointer are equal to 128 (a fixed value). Therefore it is possible to use these bits to contain *tag* bits.
>
> *Fixnums* and *conses* are probably the most used types, their representation must be as simple as possible to find quickly their types and to use them,
>
> therefore, the more the *fixnum* representation is close to Transputer number representation, the more arithmetic operations are efficient.

According to the data types, we use the 2 less significant bits and sometimes the 5 most significant bits in the following way : *Fixnums* have the two less significant bits equal to 0, *Conses* have the two less significant bits equal to 2. For the other data types, the two less significant bits are equal to 3, but the five most significant bits are used (then with this representation, the greater usable memory size is 64 Mbyte). The two less significant bits can be equal to 1 only during the *garbage* collection (used as an object mark). To promptly obtain the value of these *tags*, which occupy 32 bits, they are placed in a table memorized in the Transputer internal memory, its address is stored in a pseudo register of each task *workspace*. This pseudo register is one of the first 15 locations to avoid *pfix* instructions. We will see that there is an other table accessed in the same manner.

In the Transputer documentation [Inmos 87 b] the result of a memory access with a non word address is given undefined. In fact, with our boards, it is not necessary to remove the *tag* bits from an address before its use. The saving of time is very small (about 3 %), but the binaries are smaller, then we leave the *tag* bits.

We give some objects representation :

A **Fixnum** is a 30 bits quantity (two's complement notation). The coding and decoding use shift operations. With this representation, it is not necessary to decode fixnums before addition and comparison operations.

31	2 0
number in two's complement notation	00

A **cons** has two words to memorize its car and cdr. To have the two less significant bits equal to 2, the address coding is the *cons* address minus 2. Then it is enough to execute the simple instruction adc 2 to decode a *cons*.

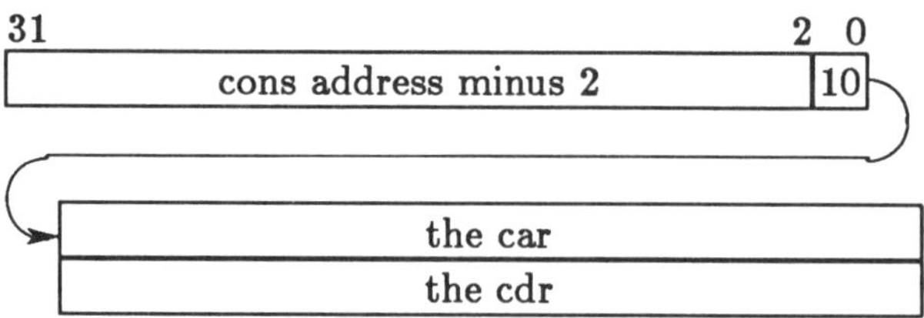

For the **simple-vector** whose element type is *t*, the first word contains the number of elements encoding in a *fixnum*, the other words contain the elements.

31 2 0

11001 | simple vector address | 11

vector length = n | 00

element 1

element 2

- - - - -

element n

When the representation type is omitted in the *defstruct* definition (the representation type is linked with the *keyword :type*), **structures** are the following representation. The first word contains the number of the following words. The second word contains the structure name, which is a symbol. The other words contain the *slots* values.

31 2 0

10100 | structure address | 11

vector length = n + 1 | 00

structure name

slot 1

- - - - -

slot n

9.3.3 Compiled code execution model

The compiled code execution model uses six stacks :

The control stack REC, which contains the function and subroutine calls return addresses.

The escape task ECH, which contains escape name, and other informations as the stack pointers backup (it is possible to memorize them in an other stack as REC).

The binding stack LOC, which contains lexical bindings, and which can be used for the dynamic bindings.

The backup dynamic bindings stack SPE, which is needed because we use a ***superficial binding with cval***, we will look at this point later.

The arguments stack ARG.

At last the multiple values stack VAL, used when the number of value is greater than 1.

On Transputer, these six stacks are grouped together in three stacks, in order to save memory space : REC-ECH-LOC, SPE et ARG-VAL. Only the first group is Transputer dependent. SPE cannot be grouped with an other stack, because the ***progv special*** form allows to do a number of dynamic bindings unknown at the compilation.

9.3.4 Lexical bindings

The most used stack is the lexical binding stack LOC, supported by REC-ECH-LOC. New bindings are made by pushing of the values, the stack pointer is restored to unbind them (the values are lost). Then all the necessary memory is not reserved in advance, which could use too memory space, not to mention the necessary cleanings in relation with the ***garbage collector*** (this problem appears with the register stacks). Then a lexical variable access is a REC-ECH-LOC stack under top access, its deep is statically established at compile time. To have a positive gap and avoid *nfix* instruction which is expensive in time and space, this stack grows to the decrease addresses.

To not reserve three memory area for each task, what obligatory implies memory loss, the ARG-VAL stack grows to the increase addresses, and shares the same memory area as REC-ECH-LOC, their stack pointer goes from one to the other in the pushing direction.

9.3.5 Special bindings

The special bindings implementation is one of the main problems linked with concurrent executions. In mono or multi-tasking, there are two manners to implement them :

The *deep binding* : in this method, the link between the variable and its value is not direct, the value is not in a constant place. One can use *hash-tables*, *A-lists* (association list) or *P-lists* (property list) where the variable is the key, or a stack containing successively a variable name and its value. It is also possible to make a dictionary with two lists or two stacks (this method is used in *Smalltalk* for instance). The *deep binding* can be used in mono or multi-tasking, but it is very slow, because it is necessary to search the bindings during the execution.

The *superficial binding* : in this method the value is stored in a constant place directly linked with the variable. The access time is constant and short, then we use the *superficial binding*.

In the case of a mono tasking Common-Lisp, the value is generally stored in one of the symbol fields, called *cval*. To use a *cval* with concurrent executions, each commutation task must be preceded by the backup of all the bindings of the interrupted task, and restored the bindings of the task which restart. We cannot use this method (section 9.2.2). Then, to use the *dynamic bindings* method, and for other reasons which we will discuss in the multi-tasking section, the number of task is fixed to 10. Then there are 10 *cvals*, grouped in a vector. To save memory space, these vectors are only allocated for the symbols linked with special variables. To have fixed addresses, these vectors are allocated in the static area. Obviously the code generated by the compiler for a special variable access must be usable by any task, then it is of the following type :

```
ldc   vector-address   ; with the necessary pfix
ldl   task-number      ; a pseudo register
add
ldnl  0
```

Obviously the vector address in unknown at compile time, this one is placed by the Common-Lisp binary loader.

9.3.6 Functional calls

In a functional language such as Common-Lisp, the functional calls must be particularly well treated by the compiler. To be efficient, the generated code for functional call must be as small as possible. An other important Common-Lisp concept, but in contradiction with the previous one, is the *debugging*, which requires to memorize some informations at the functional calls. But the debugging and effective use phases are different, then the compilers have several compilation modes, linked for instance with the *optimize* or *inline* proclamations and declarations. The cost of a functional call is due at the check that the called function is defined and compiled, at the branch address determining, at last at the bindings with all the necessary checks. To decrease this cost, many implementations (Lucid Common-Lisp for instance) have an option to eliminate the number of argument check, when it is fixed. We don't follow this method, because we consider that these checks must be realized during the compilation, moreover this method applies to the less expensive case only, neglecting the terrific *keyword* cases. On the other hand the *inline* proclamations and declarations are generally neglected by the implementations, except some *open-coding* or *tail merging* cases. In fact one of our previous work concerns the *inline* calls of any function (for instance written by a user, not only the standard functions), obviously we use this technique on the Transputer.

Our point of view is the following : the *not-inline* calls are reserved for the *debugging*, then they are slow, and put informations for the *debugging*. For these calls, all the checks are made during the executions, these calls can be traced, and when a function is redefined the new definition is used. The *inline* calls are used to have efficient codes, but sure however. But these calls cannot be *traced* and when a function is redefined, the new definition is not used, as it is authorized by the Common-Lisp standard.

Not-inline calls

In the following explanations, we don't consider the local functions (*labels* or *flet*) and the use of the *multiple-value-call special form.*

When a function is *not-inline* called, there is no assumption about it, perhaps the function is not defined. The code generated by the compiler calculates and places the value of the arguments in the ARG-VAL stack, and stores their number in a pseudo register. Next the branch address is obtained from the *symbol-function*, this is made by a subroutine to decrease the generated code size. These subroutines are placed in the internal and fast Transputer memory. As for the *tags*, their addresses are placed in a table stored in the internal memory, and its table address is stored in a pseudo register. The subroutine receives in argument the address of the symbol designating the called function, takes the function definition in the *fval* field (see the symbol representation), checks that it is a compiled function, takes the branch address and jumps to it. Moreover some informations for the *debug* are memorized. When the *symbol-function* is not a compiled function, the interpreter is called, to manage the other cases (the function is not defined, or not compiled).

The code generated at the beginning of the function body saves the return address (the *jump* uses the *gcall* instruction), takes the arguments in the ARG-VAL stack, realizes the bindings according to the *lambda-list* and the necessary checks.

Inline calls

Only the bare essentials is made at the execution of an *inline* call, the rest is made during the compilation. Then :

There is no generated code checking that the function called is defined and compiled. The branch address is obtained with seven *pfix* and a *ldc*, obviously these instructions are placed by the Common-Lisp binary loader, or by the function linked with the *(setf (symbol-function -) -)* form.

All the checks about the validity of a call (for instance number of argument) are made during its compilation, not during execution.

The bindings are directly made according to the *lambda-list* and the type of the variables (lexical, dynamic or enclosed). Then the ARG-VAL stack is not used.

The more the bindings are complicated, the more the saving of time is important with an *inline* call. The following function runs five times faster when the *ktak* internal calls are *inline* :

```
(defun ktak(&key x y z)
   (if (not (< y x))
       z
       (ktak :z (ktak :y x :z y :x (1- z))
             :y (ktak :z x :x (1- y) :y z)
             :x (ktak :x (1- x) :z z :y y))))
```

A functional call can be compiled *inline* when the function called and the call itself are defined in the same file, or when the function is already compiled and loaded, to have all the necessary informations. Obviously when the *lambda-list* uses *&key*, in the functional call the *keywords* don't need to be calculated.

When the binary loader loads an *inline* call, this one checks if the called function is defined and compiled. When the function is not defined or compiled, the loader cannot place the right address and it uses the address of an error subroutine, which indicates the name of the corresponding function. Otherwise, the loader checks that the expected and effective binding modes correspond. If it is not the case, the loader uses the address of the previous subroutine, otherwise it places the *inline* entry address, obviously this last is not equal with the *not-inline* entry address.

When the user defines a compiled function, the function called linked with *defun* or the *(setf (symbol-function –) –)* form modifies the *inline* calls to the corresponding function which uses the subroutine.

The compiler takes into account the *inline* and *not-inline* proclamations and declarations, except for the local functions whose calls are always *inline*. By default all the pre-defined functions are proclaimed *inline*. The default case of the user functions is linked with the *optimize* proclamation. When this last is *(optimize '(speed 3))* , by default the user function calls are *inline*.

Moreover the compiler treats the *tail merging* (for instance the *self tail merging*), and takes into account functional and type proclamations or declarations.

Open-coding

In the case of small and very often used functions, for instance *car*, it is not desirable to generate a functional call, because it represents an important part of the function execution total time. To avoid these calls, many Common-Lisp implementations, including Transputer Common-Lisp, use the *open-coding* method, where the function calls are replaced by the function bodies themselves. Obviously this method can only be used with very small functions, because their sizes are very linked with the processor used we say a few words about it.

The Transputer has no *trap* or other mechanisms which can be used to avoid to generate check code. For instance, to read a memory word with an odd address does not cause an exception, as the 68000 family (Motorola) or the Sparc (Fujitsu) do it. In this case the generated code for a *car* function call would have been :

```
              ; Areg contains the supposed cons
adc    2      ; decode the cons
ldnl   0      ; exception if Areg was not a cons
```

Then the number of needed instructions for a small function as car is relatively important. To decrease the size of the binaries, the code generated for some *open-coding* is a subroutine call. These calls are much less expensive than functional calls, because their arguments are placed in the Transputer evaluation stack or pseudo registers and not in a Lisp stack, their bodies are in the faster Transputer internal memory, and their addresses are obtained with a table in the internal memory, as for the *tags*.

For instance the *cons* procedure address is obtained in the following manner :

ldl infos-base ; 0 < infos-base < 16
ldnl addr-cons ; 0 < addr-cons < 16

which uses 2 bytes and 13 cycles (we count 1,5 cycles to load 1 instruction of 1 byte) and not the 8 bytes and 20 cycles reclaimed with a *pfix* and *ldc* sequence.

We stop here the description of the Common-Lisp implementation. Then we have a Common-Lisp supporting concurrent executions. When Transputer Common-Lisp is *booted*, only the *top-level* task is created, and only the first Transputer is used. Next it is possible to boot the other Transputers (for this the useful memory part is sent with an external link), and to create the 9 other tasks on each Transputer with a specific first code address, for instance to use our multi-tasking management now described.

9.4 Multi-tasking

When the parallelism is introduced in a language, two of the first questions that arise are :

Is the parallelism implicit or explicit ?

What is the grain of parallelism ?

In our case the parallelism must be introduced in an already defined language, Common-Lisp, and we want to minimize the modifications which must be made. The Transputer Common-Lisp aim is not to be a very high level parallel language, taking all into account behind user's back. Transputer Common-Lisp must be a flexible language allowing the studies and experimentations of different technical points within parallelism. If necessary, the user must be able to control precisely the execution. Therefore the parallelism is explicit, and stands at the Lisp forms level.

For that, there are two ways to design a multi-tasking : in the first way, the user can allocate (next kill) tasks running in parallel, and in the second one the user has some functions to realize parallel evaluations on pre-existent tasks.

We think that the first way is not adjusted to obtain good performances and a reasonable use of memory space for a small computer like the Transputer. As a matter effect the reserved memory size for each task is large (stacks, *workspace* linked with the Wptr Transputer register), then it is impossible to have many tasks, and a right use of internal memory which is very fast but very small. We think that having a large number of tasks running concurrently is too expensive in memory size, and not really useful, we therefore prefer to have tasks on a lot of processors, rather than to have a lot of tasks on a few processors. Moreover, we have already seen the advantages of a fixed number of task in connection with the dynamic bindings.

Therefore we prefer to fix the number of tasks, and have parallel and concurrent runnings, whose number is apparently independent of the real number of tasks, with several Transputers. The fixed number of task is 10 to have a reasonable use of memory space, and a right use of Transputer internal memory.

Then we give two functions which requires a parallel running (*send* and *execute*) and a function used for asking the results (*receive*), the multi tasking management undertake to find a task for the running.

For all that, it is necessary to have a *message routing* to enable the tasks to receive the requests for running and to return the values. Because of the Transputer channel implementation, the natural *routing* mechanism is *store and forward*. The transmited messages are constituted by one byte (written by *write-char*) or several bytes (written by *write* or similar functions). In this last case the messages are cut in packets smaller than 1024 characters, for bufferisation problems and to avoid that one message monopolize a network part. The cut is made by the sender task because of the *routing streams* definition, the bufferisation uses string as *with-output-to-string*. Because messages are Lisp forms, then are structured, it is useless that the *router* knows all the message size. On our boards, all the Transputers are linked with a *pipe* by the external links 1 and 2, then the *message routing* use these links. The others links are used to connect Transputers in any topology by way of a *crossbar*. When describing the network topology, the user can decided on each Transputer to keep or not the external links 0 and 3 for its own use. With the given topology the system establish the shortest paths. Because it is closely linked with Lisp and it manages packets, the *router* is efficient.

In a first time we will describe the parallel executions functions, next the use of channels in Transputer Common-Lisp. At last we will describe the shared environment problems and exclusive sections.

9.4.1 Parallel executions

To make parallel or concurrent evaluations of Common-Lisp forms, we give three main functions :

(send form &optional tr)

This function requests to evaluate *form* in parallel by any task on any Transputer if *tr* is omitted, or by a task on the Transputer *tr* otherwise. This function returns a *stream* to communicate with the selected task, and used by the function *receive.*

(execute form &key tr other)

This function is similar to the previous one except that the produced values are lost. *tr* is used to specify the Transputer number where the *form* will be evaluated. If there is no free task to execute form at this time, the value of *other* is considered :

> If *other* is *nil*, *form* is immediately evaluated,
>
> otherwise *form* will be evaluate only when a task become free.

This function returns no values.

(receive stream &key error here)

stream must have been created by *send.* This function returns the values made by the evaluation of *form* of the corresponding *send.* When *receive* is executed, there are three possibilities :

> The evaluation of *form* is completed and the values have reached the local Transputer, the task doesn't wait.
>
> The evaluation of *form* is not completed, or all the values have not reached the local Transputer, the task waits for them.
>
> Otherwise no task is free to evaluate *form.* Then if *here* is *:abort* the evaluation is not made and the *receive* function returns *:abort* and *form.* Otherwise if *tr* was omitted at the *send*, or if *here* is not *nil*, the task evaluates *form.* Otherwise the task waits until an other task becomes free to evaluate the form.

In the normal use, *tr* is omitted in the *send* form or *here* is not *nil*, (and not *:abort* of course), then the evaluation of *form* is guaranteed, whatever the number of free tasks. Then if there is no free task to execute the form before the *receive* function call, the form is executed by the current task itself instead of waiting that an other task become free and finishes the execution.

The keyword *error* is considered when an error occurred during the reading or evaluation of *form.* If no error occurred, *receive* function returns the results of the evaluation. Otherwise :

> if *error* is omitted, the *error* function is called by the current task, with all the arguments of *error*, or with the first argument of *cerror*, depending of the circumstances.
>
> if *error* is *nil*, *receive* returns the call of *error* or *cerror*, in an *interpreted* form of course.
>
> otherwise the value of *error* is returned.

For instance who can define the *fibonacci* function (obviously it is not the better definition) :

```
(defun mfib(n)
   (if (< n 3)
       1
       (let((x (send '(mfib ,(1- n)))))
           (+ (mfib (- n 2))
              (receive x)))))
```

We also have :

(who stream)

Who takes a *stream* produced by *send*, and returns *nil* if no task is selected to evaluate the corresponding form, the task number and Transputer task number otherwise.

It is important to remark that it is not because there is no free task during the *send* that the evaluation will not be executed in parallel, the key time is when the *receive* is executed. An execution can automatically start between the *send* and *receive* calls. When a task is required and more than one task is free, the least used Transputer is chosen (except when the Transputer is set of course). For all these reasons, the choice is made by a global *allocater*, which is a Common-Lisp task placed on one Transputer. This *allocater* knows how many tasks are active on each Transputer and manages the parallel execution requests. To enable a task to find a task after an unsuccessful attempt during a *send* or an *execute*, an other system Lisp task is present on each Transputer.

We have seen in the description of the *stream* returned by the *send* function, that the *streams* are naturally used for the information sending between the tasks, because these informations can be any Lisp form. These particular *streams* use the *message routing*, we will see an other type of *stream* which permits to use directly external and internal channels.

But before, we must remark that it is not possible to use the *read* and *write* functions, as they are normally defined in Common-Lisp, to transmit any object. The produce of the *write* function is not always readable. Then we defined the extension variable **non-printable**, its default value is *nil*. When the printer cannot write an object without traditional #< and the **non-printable** value is not *nil*, the printer writes a list which contains the **non-printable** value, followed by the string printed without the **non-printable** variable, at last the object type. For instance :

```
(let((*non-printable* :mark))
    (prin1 (find-package 'user)))
```

writes *(:mark "#<The USER Package>" package)*

The read-write functions have an other disadvantage, they are slow because they are complex. In this way, the time required to *send* and *receive* any information is too long, just think about the writing and reading of a float for instance. To have efficient input/output functions, the following extension functions are defined :

*(fast-write obj &optional (stream *standard-output*) (*non-printable* :non-printable))*

Writes *obj* with a representation in accordance with the representation of compiled objects in binary files. This representation is very efficient, for example a float is directly represented with the value of its 32 bits.

*(fast-read obj &optional (stream *standard-input*))*

To read a produce of *fast-write* only.

9.4.2 The streams

Then, in addition to the usual Common-Lisp *streams*, we define two other types of *stream* : one for using the *message routing*, and a second one for the channels.

Routing streams

These *streams* are returned by the *send* function, but it is also possible to explicitly create them, to allow two tasks to communicate using the *message routing* :

(open-routing n-task n-transputer)

returns a bi-directional *streams* which links the local task and the task corresponding to *n-task n-transputer* (perhaps the current task itself !). When both *n-task* and *n-transputer* equal 0, the *stream* is only usable for input, and enable to receive characters from any task. But to be careful, the characters are read in arrival order to the task.

(with-open-routing(var n-task n-trans) [declarations] &rest body)

is to *open-routing* that *with-open-file* is to *open*.

They support the standard input/output functions, which are modified, for example the semantics of *listen* is widen to these *streams*, this function returns *t* if a character is buffered by the *router* from the corresponding selected task, *nil* otherwise. A character is absolutely available when the *stream* is produced by *send*, and the corresponding form execution is done.

The channel streams

The channel streams are equivalent with the Occam channels. Contrary with the *routing streams* the communications are synchronous. Therefore the following functions are defined :

(alloc-channel)

which returns a *fixnum* referring a new internal channel, which is in fact the address of a *cons* allocated in the static area.

(open-channel chan &key direction)

This function returns a *stream* as *open* do it. The default *direction* is *:input*. *chan* is a channel returned by *alloc-channel*, or the address of an external channel (the direction and the address must be corresponding) or *nil* (in this case *alloc-channel* is called).

(with-open-channel (var &optional chan) [declarations] &rest body)

with-open-channel is a macro similar to *with-open-file*, chan follows the previous agreements.

All the input/output functions can be used with these *streams*.

The channels can also be directly used, without the *stream* interface, with the following functions :

(sys::channel-write obj chan)

sends the pointer to *obj*, or *obj* if it is a *fixnum* or a character, not an external representation as write dot it.

(sys::channel-read chan)

chan is the address of a channel, this function returns the read object.

These functions should be carefully used, it is very dangerous to send the address of a dynamic object on a channel because the *garbage collector* cannot see it. We also have :

(sys::channel-listen chan)

returns *t* if another task writes a word in chan, *nil* otherwise.

(sys::channels-listen lchan)

lchan is a list of channel addresses, the function returns *t* if at least one of these channels is used for a write, otherwise *nil*.

(sys::channel-wait lchan)

lchan is a list of channel addresses, the current task is locked until one of these channels is used for a write. This function returns no value.

9.4.3 Mutual exclusions

Because there is more than one task on each Transputer, the executions of Lisp form are not purely parallel and can be concurrent, then they use a shared environment. In these conditions, it is imperative to have mutual exclusions, and we give two ways : the *test and set* and the *regions*. The main functions are :

(test-and-set cons)

If the *car* of the *cons* is *nil*, it is modified to *t* and *t* is returned, otherwise *cons* is not modified and *nil* is returned.

(enter-region region)

There are 3 cases :

If the *region* is free, the current task takes the *region*, with an overlapping number equal 1.

If the *region* is already taken by the current task, the overlapping number is increased.

Otherwise the task is pushed to the *region* waiting list and the task is suspended, the waiting is made with an internal channel.

In all cases, two values are returned, the first one is the overlapping number, and the second one is *nil* if the task did wait, t otherwise.

(exit-region region)

It is an error when the task doesn't take the *region*. There are 2 cases :

If the *region's* overlapping number is greater than 1, it is decreased and the new overlapping number is returned. The task still takes the *region*.

Otherwise the task looses the *region*, if the waiting list is not *nil*, the task which has made the oldest request receives a word on its channel to wake it, and it takes the *region*. The function returns 0.

(make-region)

This function returns a new free *region*.

Because the *region* implementation is a typical example of the internal channels used in the task management, we describe it.

A *region* is a Common-Lisp structure containing the task which takes the *region* or *nil*, the overlapping number and the waiting list. The main problem in their implementation is to stop and restart a task which uses a *region*, for this we use internal channels.

Reading from an internal channel (which obviously is not used for an output) is enough to stop a task, without active wait, also each task has private internal channel (having only one channel is enough because a task can only wait from one *region* at the same time). Then, when a task uses *enter-region* with a *region* already used by an other task, this task reads from its channel, moreover the task number is pushed in the *region* waiting list.

The *exit-region* function manages the task restart. When a task releases a *region*, and its waiting list is not empty, this one writes in the channel corresponding with the oldest waiting task.

Then the *region* implementation is very simple, and its cost is very small.

The shared system data structures, for instance the *packages*, are protected toward the concurrent executions. But the user data structures, for instance the *P-lists* and the *hash-tables*, are not protected.

We know that symbols are shared, the *special variables* initialization and their use when they are not bound must be described. It brings us to describe the *defvar*, *defparameter* and *defconstant* macros, and the *defglobal* non standard macro. In the following when we speak of tasks, we have in mind *tasks of the same Transputer.*

When you use the *defparameter* form, you make a multiple *setq* , all the *cvals* are modified in the given value, without any copy. Then at the beginning all the tasks get to the same value.

The *defvar* case is immediately inferred from the *defparameter* case. By extrapolation of the Common-Lisp definition, only the not already initialized *cvals* are modified.

When the value of a *special variable* is modified, this modification is local. Then Transputer Common-Lisp has *global variables*, these variables are global for all the tasks on the same Transputer. A variable cannot be special and global at the same time, the *global variables* cannot be bound, use *set* or *setq* to change (for all the tasks) their value. The *(defglobal var &optional value)* form proclaims var global, and initializes it to value when it is *unbound*. For these variables, all the tasks use the same particular entry in the *cvals* vector.

The value of the constants (*defconstant*) are also shared by all the tasks on the same Transputer.

The presented multi-tasking and its implementation are relatively simple, it uses a *message routing* written in Common-Lisp, then easily modifiable. Because the channels have a very important role, it is possible to use them at different levels.

Then this management is not frozen, and the previous description is adapted to an average number of processors. To manage many processors only one global *allocater* is not enough, to only quote the main point.

9.5 Conclusion

The most part of Transputer Common-Lisp (about 90 %) is written in Common-Lisp, the rest is written in assembler. The assembler is used when it is impossible to use Lisp, or for performance reasons.

The compiler directly generates instruction codes, therefore we do not use an intermediate language (for instance Occam), mainly for generated code performances and because we can do anything we want only in assembler.

Is the Transputer a good processor to implement a concurrent Common-Lisp ? The first impression, when one see the Transputer instruction set with the eyes of an implementer using specialized machine (such as MAIA) or usual machine (CISC processor), is near the panic. Because the instruction set is not only reduced but the usable hard or soft resources, for instance stack and register, seem non-existent. Obviously the instruction set and the Occam language are totally linked, but the Transputer is enough adaptable (particularly because each task has its own *workspace*) to implement a concurrent Common-Lisp, which its foundations are, that is the least one can say, opposite with the Occam philosophy.

The most important weak points toward Transputer Common-Lisp implementation are first linked with the instruction format, so acquiring a code or data address (which is very often made) requires 8 bytes (7 *pfix* and 1 *ldc*). In view of the normal Transputer, there is no virtual memory, then the memory size is small *vis-à-vis* Common-Lisp, and it is a well-known fact that running fast and using a small memory, are two opposing things. At last, principally for cost reasons, a Transputer board is simple, the (external) memory is very slow : on our memory boards the memory cycle is 300 ns, reading a word requires only 150 ns for a *Sun 4 110* and 200 ns for a *Sun 3 75*, moreover these computers have instruction caches. So a program which only uses the Transputer internal memory has very good performances, but it is not the same when the external memory must be used, which is our case.

The Transputer Common-Lisp performances, as we can see with the unavoidable Gabriel *benchmarks* [Gabriel 85] are comparable or better than *Lucid Common-Lisp* on *Sun 3 75*. We give the execution real time for the compiled version of the *benchmarks*. Obviously the real time and *cpu* time are equal for the Transputer, and we don't use the multi-tasking of Transputer Common-Lisp. For the Lucid Common-Lisp executions, we use a *Sun 3 75* with 8 mega bytes of real memory, it runs on *Unix 4.2*, the Lucid Common-Lisp version used is 2.1.1 and the compiler flags are set to *speed* 3 and *safety* 0, we use the *change-memory-management* function to avoid *garbage*. Of course we know that we compare two incomparable versions of Common-Lisp, Transputer Common-Lisp is made for parallel execution and we pay that somewhere. Moreover in the Lucid Common-Lisp execution sometimes we have no type check (for instance when you use the *car* function), contrary to Transputer where it is necessary to use declarations to avoid checks. But the aim of this table is just to have an idea of Transputer Common-Lisp performances. Then we have :

Benchmark	Transputer C-L	Lucid C-L
Boyer	16 sec	19 sec
Div-by-2	2.1 sec and 2.7 sec	2.4 sec and 3.0 sec
dd-Derivative	6.4 sec	6.0 sec
Traverse (total)	145 sec	75 sec
Triangle	356 sec	426 sec
Puzzle	21 sec	62 sec
Tak	1.0 sec	0.64 sec
Stak	2.7 sec	2.7 sec
Ctak	1.9 sec	2.3 sec
Dhrystone	0.9 sec	1.3 sec

The *Traverse benchmark* seems bad for Transputer Common-Lisp, it is because we use the *benchmarks* without modification. Transputer Common-Lisp have an option to avoid check for *structure* accesses, with it the time becomes 80 sec.

The *Tak benchmark* is bad for the Transputer Common-Lisp toward Lucid Common-Lisp because the used code is very small then it stays in the *Sun* instruction caches.

The *Puzzle benchmark* is faster in Transputer Common-Lisp than in Lucid Common-Lisp because the two-dimensional arrays have a particular representation in our implementation.

The *Dhrystone benchmark* is not a Gabriel's *benchmark*, but a Common-Lisp translation of the C version of *Dhrystone 2.0*, published in the News.

9.6 References

[Baude 89] BAUDE F. *Topologies for Large Transputer Networks : Theorical Aspect and Experimental Approach*, Occam User Group 10 Conference, 1989.

[Gabriel 85] GABRIEL, R.P. Computer Systems Series. Volume : *Performance and evaluation of* LISP *Systems.* The MIT Press, 1985.

[Inmos 87 a] IMS B405 *Data Sheet*, INMOS.

[Inmos 87 b] *The Transputer instructions set - a compiler writers' guide*, INMOS.

[Maia 85] SANSONNET J.P. - CLERE P. - PAPON E. - BOURGAULT S. - GRANDJEAN B. *A Real Time Oriented Machine for* A.I. *Applications.* IEEE Computer Society Press. 1985

[Steele 84] GUY L. STEELE JR. *Common-Lisp the Language*, Digital Press. 1984

Chapter 10

The Application of Artificial Intelligence to Robotics

C.B.Besant
Department of Mechanical Engeering
Imperial College
London SW7 2AX.

Abstract The first and some of the second generation of robots have been notoriously difficult to use because of the low level techniques available for programming them. These techniques have involved teach-by-show methods or the use of textual languages. Both of these methods are tedious to use since so much detail in terms of robot instructions have to be provided to the robot controller. Higher level programming systems such as Object Level and Task Level methods are now rapidly appearing which allow a user to program a robot in a more simplistic manner by, for example, a description of actual tasks. These new methods rely on artifical intelligence techniques for planning through reasoning and the use of a knowledge base. An outline of these methods and their application is presented.

10.1 Introduction

It was in the mid-1950s that Devol developed a manipulator whose operation could be programmed and changed. The manipulator could therefore follow a sequence of motion steps determined by instructions in the program. The first industrial robot was introduced by Unimation in 1959, based on Devol's concept. The key to this robot was the use of a computer in conjunction with a manipulator to produce a machine that could be "taught" to automatically carry out a variety of tasks and that could be reprogrammed and retooled to perform other tasks at a relatively low cost.

Robots have seen wide use in the automobile and other industries where there existed a requirement for repetitive work of a precision nature, ranging from welding to pick-and-place to even assembly applications.

However, robots have not lived up to their promise as a highly flexible tool and this is mainly due to the difficulties encountered in programming them. Even though much research has gone into the development of textual languages for robots, it still remains a time-consuming task to program a robot for a particular job. Furthermore, complex tasks such as continuous path work or difficult assembly jobs are almost impossible to perform since so much information needs to be generated and carefully checked for satisfactory performance. Thus the first and most of the second generation of robots are far from being the flexible tools that industry requires for small to medium batch manufacture.

There are new techniques for solving the problems of programming robots to allow flexibility in their use by minimising set-up times. These techniques include the use of artificial intelligence in some form. The various aspects relating to the programming of robots will be discussed and the importance of using AI techniques illustrated.

10.2 Functions of a robot controller

It is worth outlining the various functions that have to be performed by a robot controller in order to understand some of the problems associated with the programming of the manipulator. The manipulator joints are powered by an actuator that is normally a dc or ac motor, with velocity feedback being provided by a tachogenerator and position via an encoder or resolver.

The computer within the controller has to perform the following functions:

a) Closed loop control of the joints to ensure that the motion of the joints meet the prescribed plan in terms of acceleration, velocity and speed.

b) Solution of the kinematic equations so as to either relate joint positions with end effector positions and angles — forward kinematics; or to relate end effector angles and positions with joint positions or angles — inverse kinematics.

c) To provide dynamic compensation for inertia, coriolis and gravity effects.

d) To read and analyse data for sensors.

e) To perform planning tasks.

f) To effect a programming language for easy use of the manipulator.

g) To provide communication with other systems.

All of these topics are receiving considerable attention in terms of research. However, the programming of robots and the planning functions will mainly be considered in this paper.

10.2.1 Robot languages

There are four principal types of programming languages and these are:

1) Joint level

2) Robot level

3) Object level

4) Task level

Joint level programming is related to "teach by showing". This is the lowest form of robot programming and consists of teaching the robot through the desired motions and recording the positions along the trajectory. These positions or set points are smoothed by a numerical method and the robot motion can be "played back" to repeat the motion.

The robot level language is based on the use of a textual language that allows the user to describe robot motions and positions in cartesian space independent of the manipulator configuration. A task is thus described explicitly as a sequence of robot motions. A typical textual language is VAL by Unimation. A textual language can cope with sensor feedback such as vision or force.

The user of such languages needs to acquire considerable skill if difficult tasks are to be attempted. It requires the input of much information for only relatively simple tasks and is therefore time-consuming to use.

Object level robot languages are high level languages and are arrived at by simplifying the programming process. The goal of object level programming is to specify the desired task in terms of operations on the objects rather than specifying the motion of the robot. An object level programming system has some knowledge of the objects and the robot, known as the world model, so that the user can define the sequence of tasks in less detailed instructions than the robot level language, and it can compute collision free trajectories. Extensive research is now taking place at this level and the principal problems are in world modelling, automatic grasping, collision free path planning and sensory programming.

The highest level of robot programming is at task level. Task level systems rely heavily on design data defining the objects, and from this data together with knowledge of the robot, the system automatically constructs a plan to perform an entire task and generate the appropriate information for the robot to enable it to perform that task. Again, this is a typical area for research, and both task and object level languages involve a degree of AI.

10.3 Knowledge-based programming systems

The application of knowledge-based techniques will now be considered in relation to object and task level programming. At this level the system will have a reasoning capability that is related to the knowledge base. In object level programming the user will perform the task planning but will describe the task at a function level. In practice, each level of programming is built on the lower levels in a hierarchical fashion.

10.3.1 Architecture of a knowledge-based system

The architecture of a knowledge-based system is shown in figure 10.1 and it contains the following three sub-systems:

a) Task planner:

   The task planner transfers a task-oriented problem description, such as an assembly task, into a sequence of object level commands that can be solved by a robot program synthesiser.

b) World model data base:

   A world model data base describes the geometric and physical properties of the objects and robot together with a representation of the state of the operating workspace.

c) Program synthesiser:

   The program synthesiser receives the object-oriented commands generated by the tasks planner and translates them into a robot control program.

High level programming is now usually performed on an off-line Graphic Robot Simulator rather than on-line in order to prevent shutting down the robot whilst a new program is being developed. Typical of the graphical simulators is that described by Katajima [1].

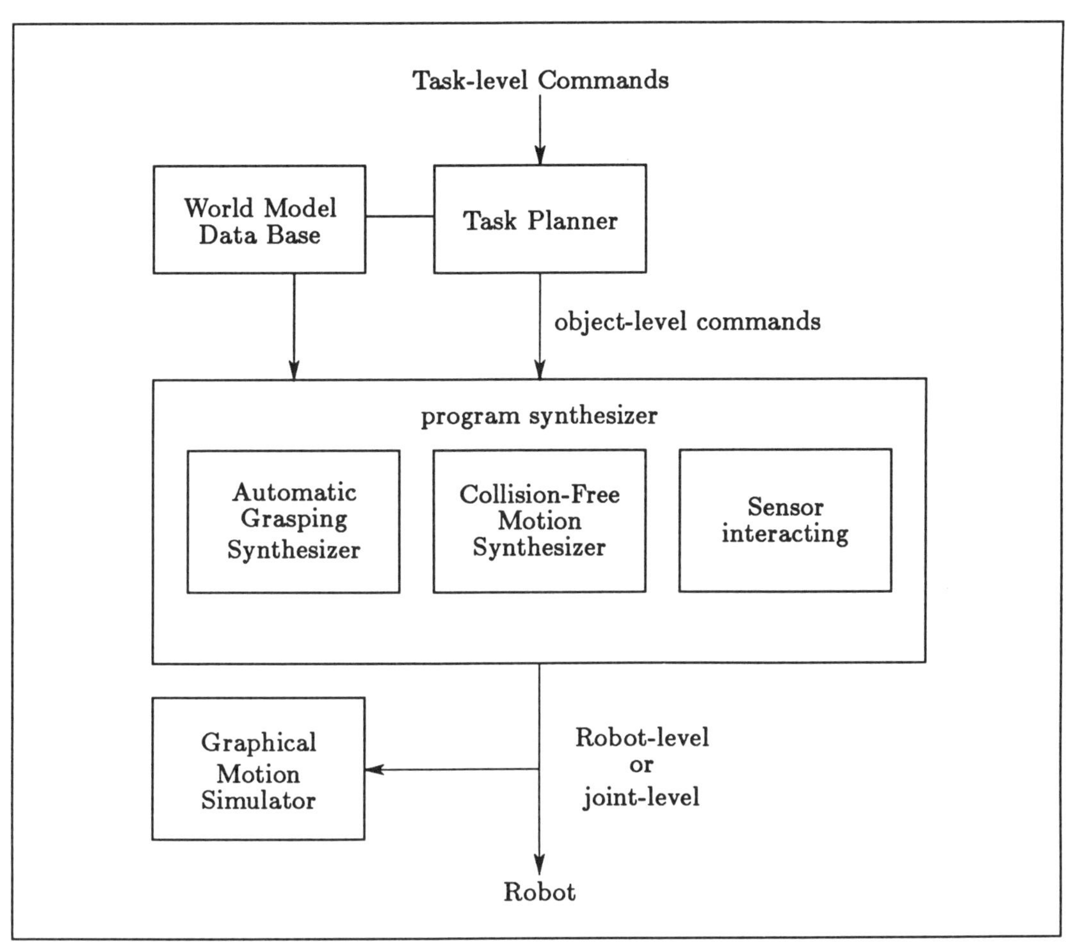

Figure 10.1: Architecture of knowledge-based robot language system

10.3.2 AUTO-GRASP: An off-line programming system

AUTO-GRASP is a high level off-line robot programming system that is under development at Imperial College [2]. It is essentially an object level system although it is planned to increase its capability to task level. It is implemented in a LISP environment and it enables users to prepare robot programs using object level functions down to joint level.

The operation of this system is based on a common data base strategy that can be interfaced to different software modules where each module has some function that accepts or modifies data within the data base. A block diagram of the system is shown in figure 10.2 and it contains the following features:

a) It is independent of robot type and can therefore be used with a wide range of robots.

b) A graphical display with a comprehensive range of facilities to allow visualisation of a robot task implementation.

c) A polyhedral geometric modeller that includes environmental and task modelling tools together with a representation of physical attributes.

d) Joint, robot and object level programming modes.

e) An automatic grasping system that determines the procedure for grasping an object with a parallel jaw gripper.

f) An interactive or debug facility that allows testing of a developed program.

10.3.3 World modelling

There are a variety of methods that can be used to model the objects, robot and its environment. The important fact to note is that the modelling must be such that the required information exists in a knowledge base so that geometric reasoning operations, such as motion planning, automatic grasp configuration determination and motion checking can be performed.

World Modelling can be built up from a Vision System or via CAD. In AUTO-GRASP, CAD Solid Modelling techniques are extensively used for defining objects and the environment.

There are many different ways of Solid Modelling [3], ranging from Cell Decomposition and Sweep Representation to Constructive Solid Geometry and Boundary representation. In AUTO-GRASP the solid modeller is implemented in a LISP environment and has the following features:

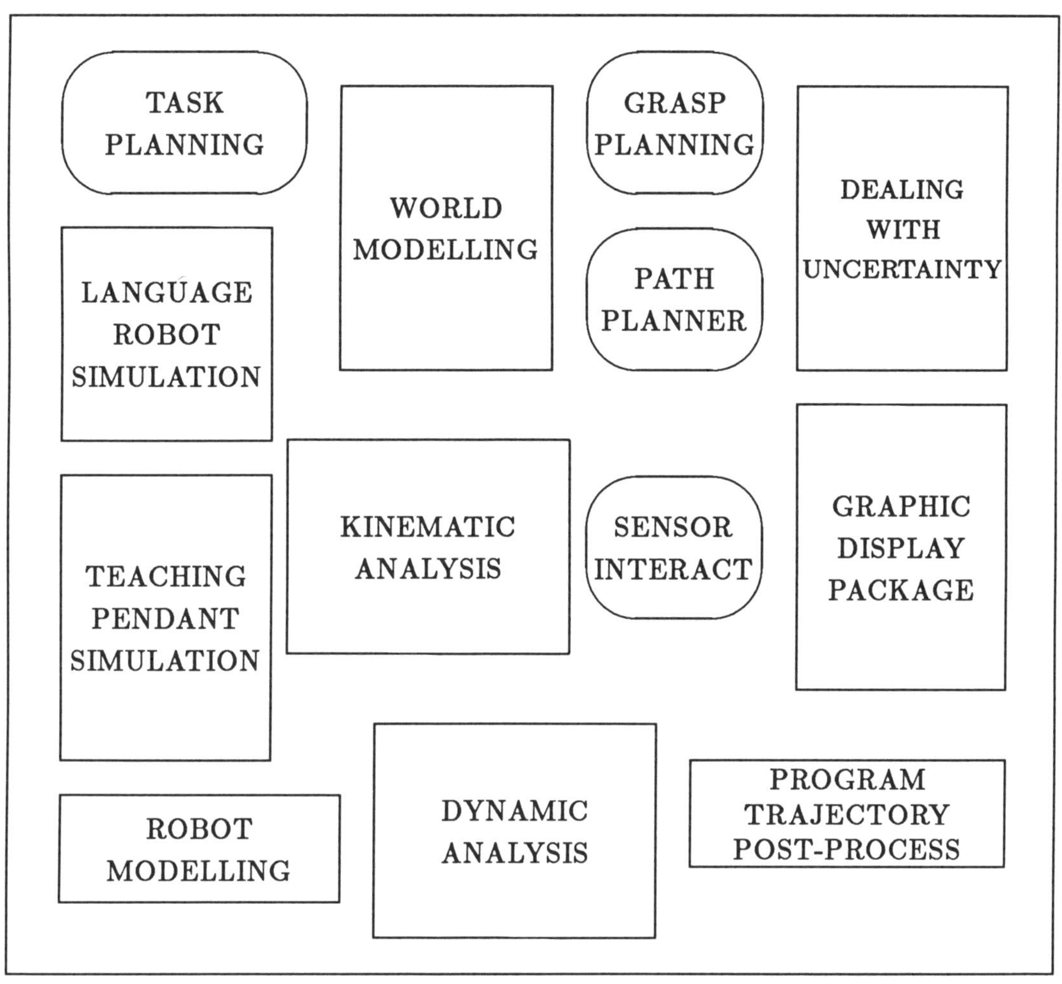

Figure 10.2: Block diagram of AUTO-GRASP

1) Solid modelling of objects is in the form of polyhedral bodies. The face list of the polyhedral may include cylindrical and spherical faces in addition to planer faces.

2) Interactive shape creation facilities are available and CAD or Vision data may also be read from another source.

3) Tools are available for representing the environment and the task. The relationship between objects in the environment can be specified together with their final positions, and a task can be described as a sequence of environmental situations.

4) Physical and technological attributes such as centre of gravity and coeffiecients of friction on surfaces, are also included.

5) A wide range of reasoning algorithms are available to determine the desired attributes of surfaces or edges. The topological validity of objects can also be checked.

10.3.4 Database

A common data base maintenance strategy is a feature of AUTO-GRASP. The data base is implemented in LISP, and all kinds of common LISP features such as arrays, structures, symbols and associated lists are used as the principal means of data storage.

A solid object and each of its elements are referred to by a symbol and stored under property lists. Typical lists for various elements are shown in table 10.1.

	vertex	line	curve	plane	cylindrical	spherical	object
name	Vertex-n	edge-n	edge-n	face-n	face-n	face-n	object-n
value	"Vertex"	"line"	"curve"	"plane"	"cyl"	"sph"	"object"
DEFINI-TION ATTR	Coordin-ates	Vertex-list	vertex-list curvity	edge-list	edge-list curvity axis	edge-list curvity1 axis-1 curvity2 axis-2	face-list hole-list
TOPOLO-GICAL	edge-list face-list	face-list	face-list	vertex list	vertex list	vertex list	edge-list vertex-list
GEOM-ETRICAL	position vect.	length centre direction	length centre direction1 direction2	gross centre normal	gross centre normal-1 normal-2	gross centre normal-list	centre volume
PHYSCL				friction coeft.	friction coeft.	friction coeft.	mass

Table 10.1: Represented attributes of elements

The world model can be created from a file of data from CAD system. The file is stored in a particular format that is specified in table 10.2. Alternatively, the model can be created using interactive facilities that are embodied in AUTO-GRASP, and some of these facilities are given in table 10.3.

10.3.5 Robot program synthesis

The synthesis of a robot program from implicit object level task specification into explicit robot level commands is one of the most important and difficult of knowledge-based language systems. The grasping motion synthesis is a significant problem in robot motion synthesis because the way in which objects are grasped affects all subsequent

Element	INPUT FORMAT	Parameters
vertex	(x y z)	c : curvature
line	(1 ((x1 y1 z1)(x2 y2 z3)))	cc : curve centre
curve	(c (v1 v2)(c cc ca))	ca : curve angle
plane	(pln (e1 e2 ... en) rest)	one of these three
cyl-face	(cyl (e1 e2 ... en)(axis c cc ca) rest)	curve parameters is
sph-face	(sph(e1e2...en)(axis c cc ca)1(axis c cc ca)2rest)	sufficient.
object	(obj (f1 f2 ... fn)(h1 h2 ... hn))	rest : restricted area

Table 10.2: Element input format

Function	Parameters
make-vertex	(x y z & opt name)
make-line	(v1 v2 & opt name)
make-curve	(v1 v2 & opt name & rest c cc ca)
make-plane	((e1 e2 ... en) & opt name)
make-cyl	((e1 e2 ... en) axis & opt name & rest c cc ca)
make-sph	((e1 e2 ... en) axis-1 axis-2 & opt name & rest c1 c2)
make-polyhedra	((f1 f2 f3 ... fn) & opt(h1 h2 ... hn) & opt name)
make-element	(element x y z & opt name)
rotate-element	(element roll pitch yaw & opt name)

Table 10.3: Element creation and manipulation function

operations. It will be used to illustrate the problem of program synthesis. The end result from the synthesis phase is an executable robot-level program consisting of a set of grasp commands together with motion commands. However, before the motion planner can perform the synthesising task, it must convert the symbolic tasks specification into a usable form [4], [5].

Most grasping algorithms relating to a parallel jaw gripper are based on the same general method and are variations of the following procedure:

1) A set of candidate grasping configurations are chosen based on:

   Object geometry, e.g. a good place to grasp is on either side of parallel surfaces.

   Stability, e.g. one heuristic criterion is to ensure that the object's centre of gravity lies within the gripper fingers.

Uncertainty reduction.

2) The sets are then pruned according to reachability by the robot and collision with other objects.

3) The final configuration is selected based on:

Stability of grasp

Best collision-free choice in the presence of positional errors.

Various laboratories have provided solutions to the grasping problem. Among them are Nguyen [6] at MIT who proposed a force-closure and stable grasp system in 3D, and the IMAG laboratory in France [7], where a heuristic guided search method was proposed for the determination of the optimum grasp faces of an object.

In AUTO-GRASP, an automatic grasping algorithm has been developed that has the following features:

1) It contains a full 3D solid model representation of the objects including objects with cylindrical and spherical surfaces.
2) A heuristically guided search algorithm that is successively applied at these different stages which establish:
    a) The candidate sets of parallel surfaces
    b) The sets which are not achievable
    c) The achievable sets which satisfy a specified grasp quality.
3) Consideration of physical aspects such as stability and slippage.
4) Consideration of constraints that are imposed by the environment and the task on the object.
5) A 3D collision checking algorithm to ensure that desired grasp configurations are reachable and that a collision free path exists.
6) Facilities to input object data definitions from CAD systems as well as interactively creating it.
7) The ability to reason not only the two face gripping pairs but also other types of pairs such as face-edge.

The importance of establishing the heuristic rules or criteria for a parallel jaw gripper is important if computation is to be minimised. Some of these heuristic criteria are convexity, topological connections, task constraints and environmental constraints.

A flow chart describing the grip search in AUTO-GRASP is shown in figure 10.3.

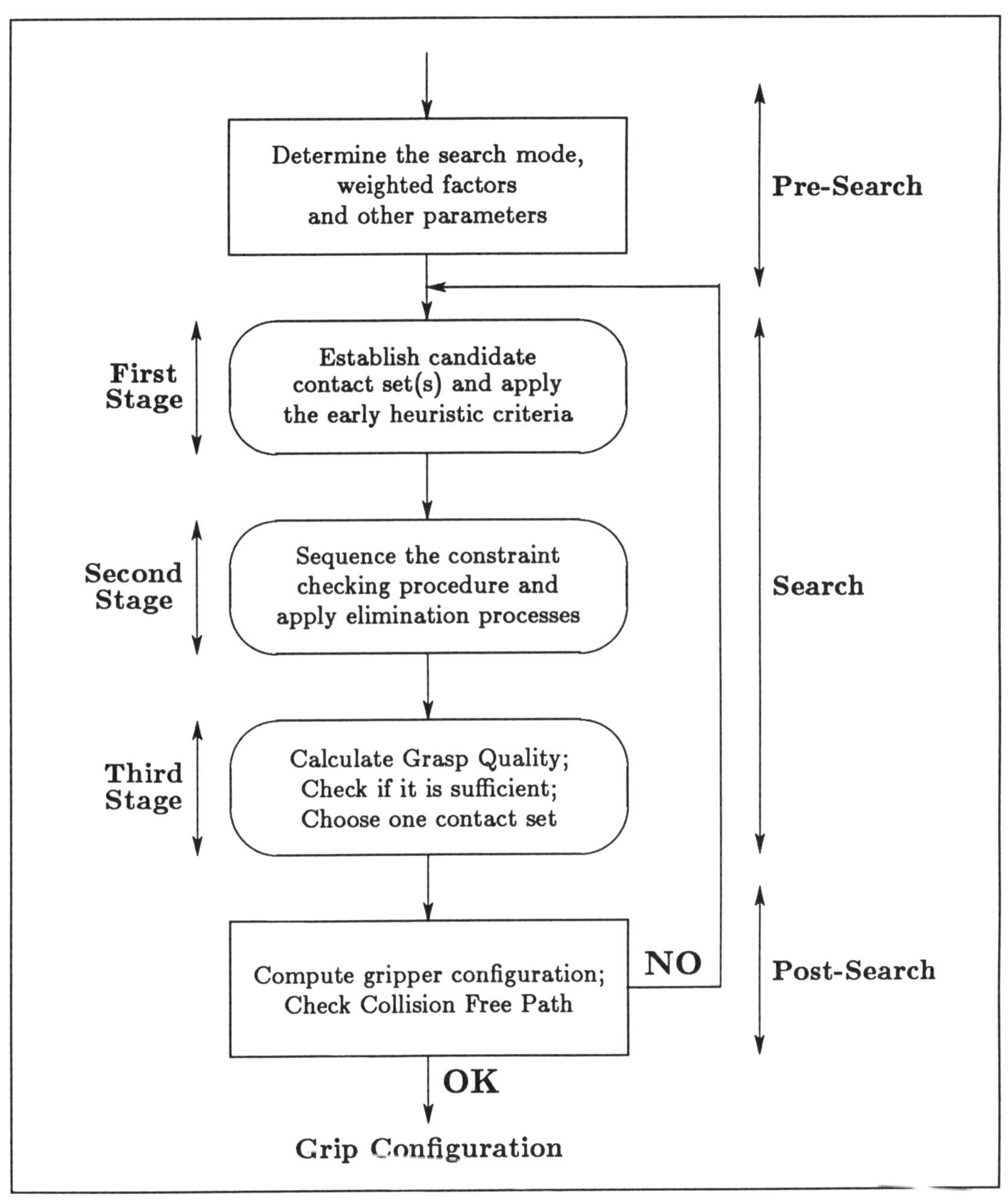

Figure 10.3: Flow chart of the AUTO-GRASP grip search

10.4 Collision-free motion planning

Path planning is another area that is fundamental to the programming of robots. When an object is grasped, the robot must move it to its destination and this motion can be divided in four parts:

1) A guarded departure from the current state.
2) A free transfer motion to the desired place without collision.
3) A guarded approach to the destination.
4) A compliant motion to achieve the goal configuration.

Automated path planning of a collision-free path is not easy, particularly if full three dimensional determination is required as with anthropomorphic robots. There are a variety of methods for determining collision-free paths.

One of the most common methods is the Configuration Space Method which has been substantially developed by Luzano Perez [8], [9]. In this method of manipulator motion planning, the problem is represented in such a way that the object to be moved is a point which moves through configuration space or Cspace as it is often called. In order to achieve this, a common approach is to "grow" physical objects into corresponding obstacles in the Cspace of the object. If, therefore, an object represented by a point A is moved and B is a physical obstacle, then the obstacle for the point A in the Cspace of A is the set of all tuples of parameters that correspond to a collision between A and B in physical cartesian space. This set of parameter tuples is called the Cspace obstacle for A due to B.

Once the configuration obstacles have been outlined, strategies can be adopted for finding a path for the moving point A, ie. the object. One method is to construct a Visibility Graph whose vertices are the Cspace representations for the initial and final configuration of A together with points on the Cspace obstacle boundaries where its edges represent the existence of straight lines of legal positions in Cspace connecting these positions. Path planning is thereby converted into searching for a path between two vertices of a graph. An example is given in figure 10.4.

Another method proposed by Brooks [10] called generalised cones, makes use of pairs of edges of obstacles to compute the spines of generalised cones, called freeways, as shown in figure 10.5. Possible motions of the moving object are constrained along the freeway and at each point a subset of orientations is permitted. Brooks [11] has extended the method to 3D by solving the problem in a series of planes.

At Imperial College, Muck [12] proposed a method called Constraint Space Path Planning. In this method, both the robot and obstacle are represented by convex polygons. The free space in the environment is segmented into a set of triangular and convex quadri-

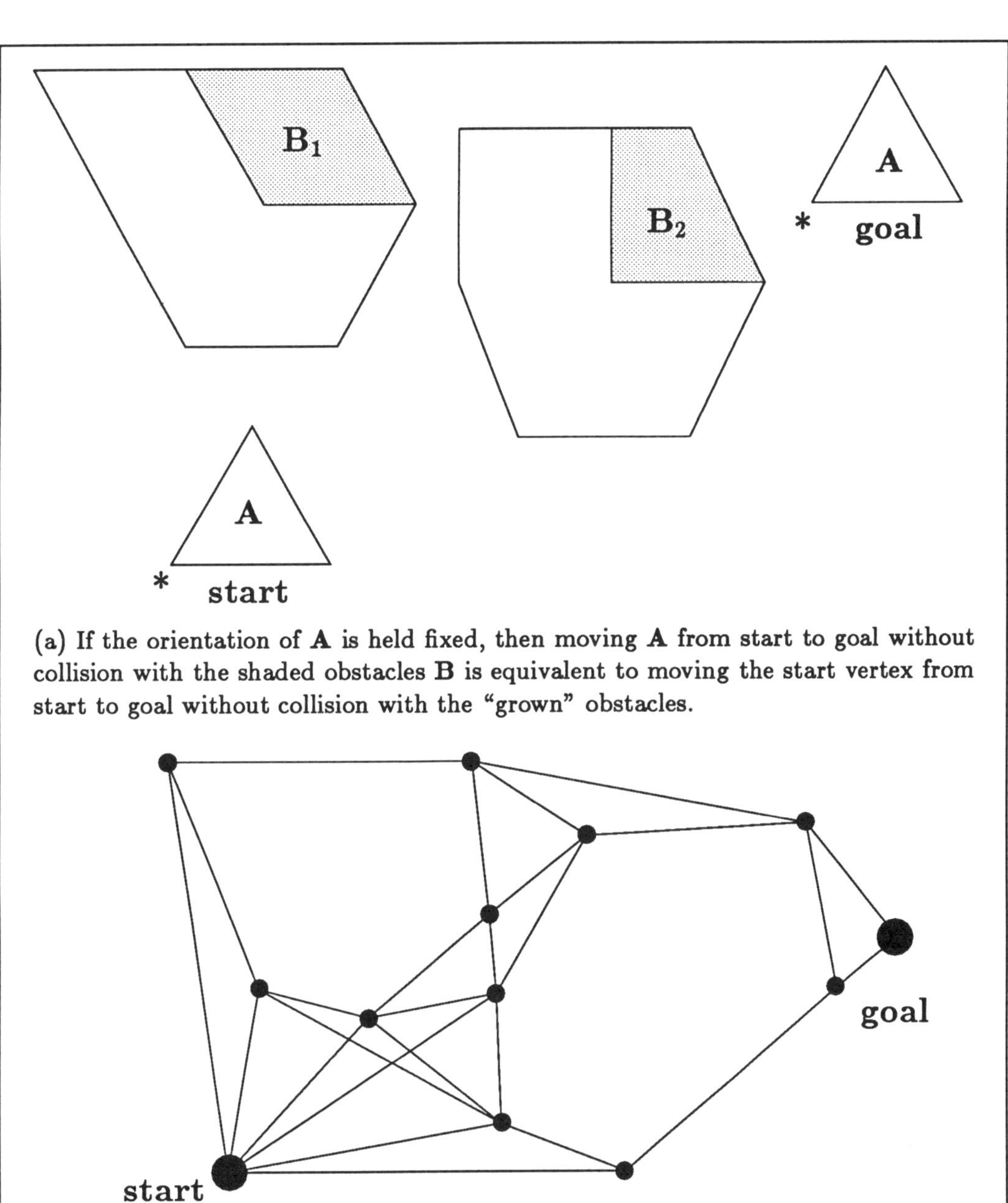

Figure 10.4:

lateral polygons that are called Free Space Polygons. A Constraint Space Point (CSP) is defined as a point in space and a unique legal range of motion is associated with that point. Hence, a configuration point, which represents the sets of robot collision-free ro-

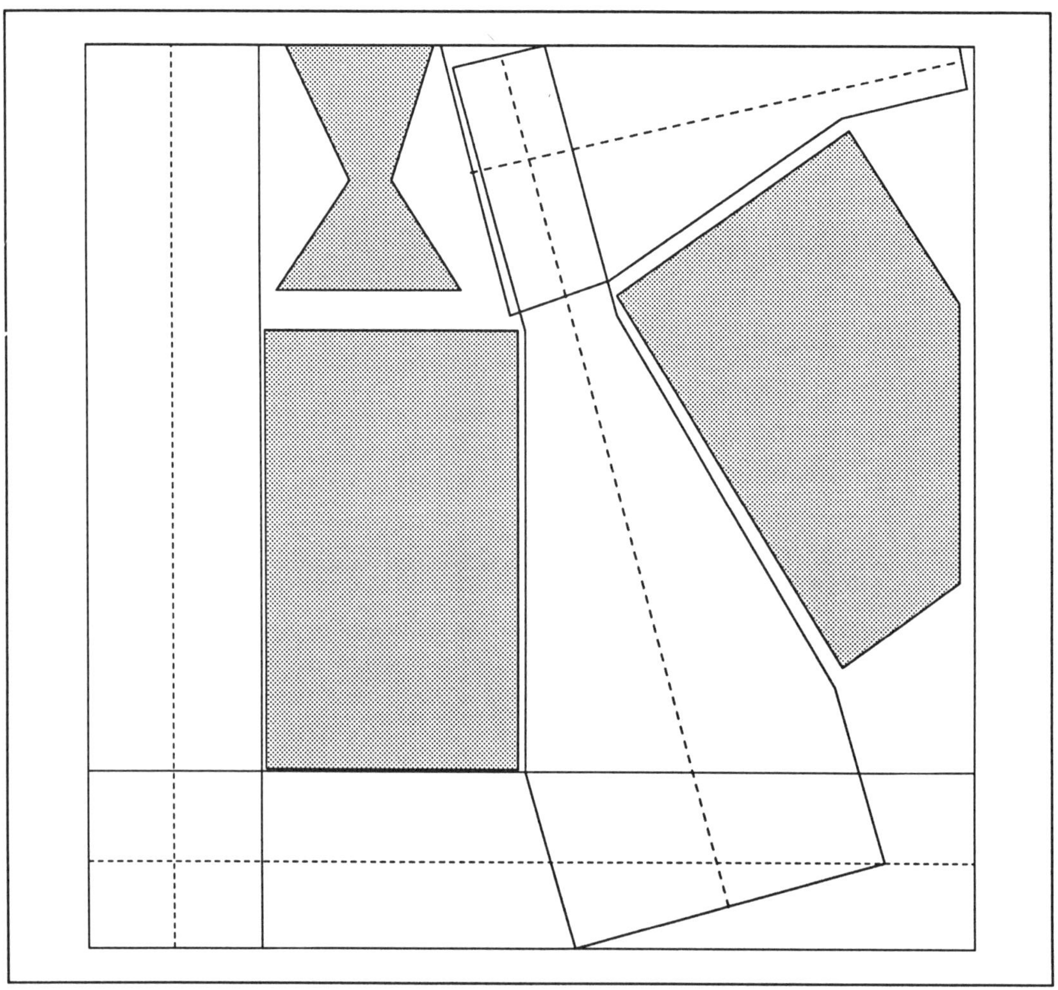

Figure 10.5: Generalized cones generated by two obstacles and workspace boundary

tation ranges about a reference point in space of n number of legal ranges is a union of n constraint points. This means that in the regions between obstacles, constraint points may be established such that the robot can move within its legal range.

The actual path planning can be viewed as a two step process. First a Connectivity Graph is constructed, where a node is created in each free space polygon containing geometric and other information about the local area it represents and the lines joining the nodes represent the connectivity graph (Figure 10.6). The second stage is to search the connectivity graph using an A* search process to optimise the actual route from the robot starting point to the goal. An A* search is a heuristically guided search process that determines the optimum route in terms of shortest distance and other criteria.

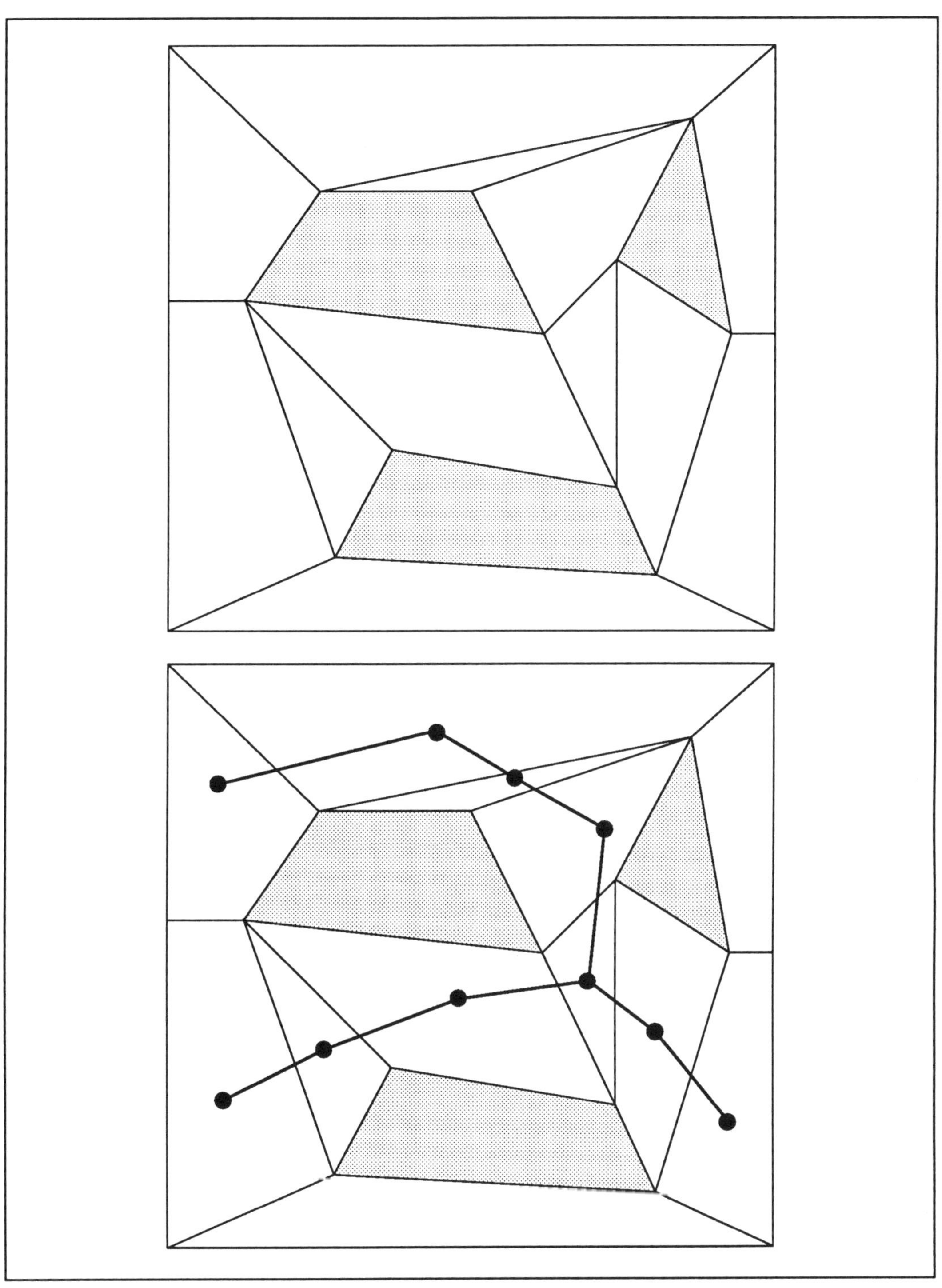

Figure 10.6: Free space polygon and connectivity graph

10.5 Automatic task planning

Task planning transforms a problem description, such as an assembly task, into a sequence of object-level commands. Here, planning means deciding a course of action and is an area where AI plays an important role.

One of the early AI systems for task planning is STRIPS [13] which was developed at the Stanford Research Institute. There are other systems such as BUILD [14], AUTOPASS [15] and RAPT [5]. The RAPT system was developed at Edinburgh University and is a system for transforming symbol specifications of geometric goals. It is focussed on the problem of assembly where parts are recognised using vision technology.

The objective of most task planners is that the system should be able to plan the task with the minimum of user input. In the AUTOPASS system only the relationships between components such as PART OF, ATTACHMENT, CONSTRAINT and ASSEMBLY are specified. Thus, based on the description, a data base is generated in which components and assemblies are represented by nodes in a graph structure. The branches of the graph are the relationships amongst the components. There are various methods for solving the planning route, ranging from state-space representation with search tree techniques [4] to forward and backward graph searching methods [16].

10.6 Conclusions

If robots are to fulfil their true potential in industrial applications then flexibility in their use will be a major factor. Object and Task level planning techniques will be the key to achieving flexibility since set-up or programming time will be minimised so that very small batches down to the batch-of-one will be a reality.

10.7 References

[1] Katajima, K. 'Interactive Robot Simulator for High-Level Tasks; Computer-Aided Design', Vol. 20, No.2, March 1988

[2] Guler, G.S. 'The Application of Artificial Intelligence to the Programming of Robots'; Ph.D Thesis, University of London, 1988

[3] Mortenson, M.E. 'Geometric Modelling'; John Wiley & Son Inc., 1985

[4] Ambler, A.P. and Popplestone, R.J. 'Inferring the Positions of Bodies from Specified Spatial Relationships', Artificial Intelligence, Vol. 6, 1975

[5] Popplestone, R.J. 'An Interpreter for a Language for Describing Assemblies'; Artificial Intelligence, Vol. 14, 1980

[6] Nguyen, V. 'Constructing Force-Clsure Grasps in 3D'; IEEE Conference on Robotics, 1987

[7] Dufay, B. and Langier, C. 'Geometric Reasoning in Automatic Grasping and Contact Analysis'; Proceedings of 5th International IFIP/IFAC, May 1982

[8] Lozano-Perez, T., and Westey, M.A. 'An Algorithm for Planning Collision-Free Paths among Polyhedral Obstacles'; Communication of the ACM, Vol. 22, No. 10, Oct. 1979

[9] Lozano-Perez, T. 'Spatial Planning – A Configuration Space Approach'; IEEE Transactions, Vol. C-32, No. 2, February 1983

[10] Brooks, R.A. 'Solving the Find-Path Problem by Good Representing of Free Space'; IEEE Transactions, Vol. SMC-13, March 1983

[11] Brooks, R.A. 'Planning Collision Free Motions for Pick and Place Operations'; MIT AI Memo No.725, May 1983

[12] Muck, K.L. and Besant, C.B. 'Motion Planning in Constraint Spaces'; IEEE Conference on Robotics, April 1988

[13] Fikes, R.E. and Nilsson, N.J. 'STRIPS : A New Approach to the Appliction of Theorem Proving to Problem Solving', Artificial Intelligence, Vol.2, 1971.

[14] Fahlman,S.E., 'A Planning System for Robot Construct Tasks', Artificial Intelligence, Vol.5,No.1, 1974.

[15] Lieberman,L.I. and Wesley,M.A., 'AUTOPASS: An Automatic Programming System for Computer Controlled Mechanical Assembly', IBM Journal of Research and Development, July 1977.

[16] Nielsson,N.J., 'Principles of Artificial Intelligence', Spring-Verlag,1980.

Chapter 11

Fast robot kinematic modelling via transputer networks

A. Y. Zomaya
A. S. Morris
Robotics Research Group
Department of Control Engineering
University of Sheffield
Mappin Street
Sheffield S1 3JD
U.K.

Abstract The rapid development in VLSI technology makes it possible to implement time consuming algorithms in real-time situations.

Parallel processing approaches can now be used to reduce the processing-time for models of very high mathematical structure such as the kinematic modelling of robot manipulators. The development system used to implement the algorithms consists of an INMOS TRANSPUTER (a VLSI single chip computer) running the OCCAM concurrent programming language. This system is used to construct and evaluate the performance and cost effectivness of several proposed methods to solve for the JACOBIAN algorithm. Parallelism is introduced to the algorithms by using different task-allocations and dividing the whole job into subtasks. Detailed analysis is performed and successful results are obtained for the case of 6 dof (degree of freedom) robot arm (Stanford Arm). Execution time comparisons between Von Neumann (uniprocessor) and parallel processor architectures are also included to show the superiority of the latter approaches.

11.1 Introduction

The last few years have seen remarkable achievements in the field of robotics and related technology. The control of most existing robot arms is relatively simple and well defined, based on a servo mechanism at each joint. However, sophisticated control algorithms are needed to improve the speed and precision of robot manipulators. Hence, several schemes had been proposed by researchers but without actual implementation because of the excessive comutations involved (Fu, Gonzales, and Lee 1987).

The position of the robot arm is most naturally expressed in joint coordinates whereas the usual point of interest is the position of the end-effector expressed in cartesian coordinates.

Therefore, the transformation from joint to cartesian coordinates and visa versa is very important. This transformation is accomplished by using the *Jacobian* and *Inverse Jacobian* formulations which play a major role in many control techniques (Whitney 1969, 1972, 1987; Luh, Walker, and Paul 1980; Wu and Paul 1982), solving inverse kinematics (Tsai and Orin 1987; Angeles 1985; Ang and Torrassis 1987), and assisting in the general description of the kinematic behavior and static forces equilibration of robot manipulators (Paul 1981; Craig 1986; Wolovich 1987). Different techniques have been proposed to solve for the Jacobian and its inverse (Renaud 1981; Paul 1981; Warldon 1982; Featherstone 1983; Elgazzar 1985; Lenarcic 1984; Mitra and Mohalanabis 1984; Orin and Schrader 1984; Paul and Zhang 1986; Leahy, Nugent, Saridis, and Valavanis 1987). However, only a few attempts have been made to incorporate parallelism to speed up the computations and achieve satisfactory real-time standards and efficient performance (Orin, Chao, Olson, and Schrader 1985), unlike the area for robot dynamics which gained a lot of attention and good algorithms were developed (Luh and Lin 1982; Lathrop 1985; Lee and Chang 1986; Vukobratovic, Kircanski, and Li 1988; Zomaya and Morris 1989). The purpose of this work is to introduce new computational techniques for real-time control implementations embodying Jacobian calculations within acceptable sampling rates of no less than 60 Hz.

The problem is solved for a 6 dof Stanford Arm. The results and discussions are presented in the following order; Section 11.2 presents the computer architecture used in implementing this work. Section 11.4 highlights the problem of the Jacobian computation from published literature. Parallelism is introduced to solve the problem in sections 11.5 and 11.6. Conclusion and further comments are given in section 11.7.

11.2 The transputer and parallel processing

Recent years have witnessed rapid development in VLSI technology which is weighting all the arguments in favour of parallel processing techniques (Kuck 1977; Kung 1982;

Zakharov 1984; Hwang and Briggs 1985). This is achieved by distributing the task over a number of processors, ideally in such a way that all the processors used are fully utilised. To accomplish that, general and special purpose systems which employ parallel architectures have evolved to meet the increasing demand for more computing power and higher processing speed.

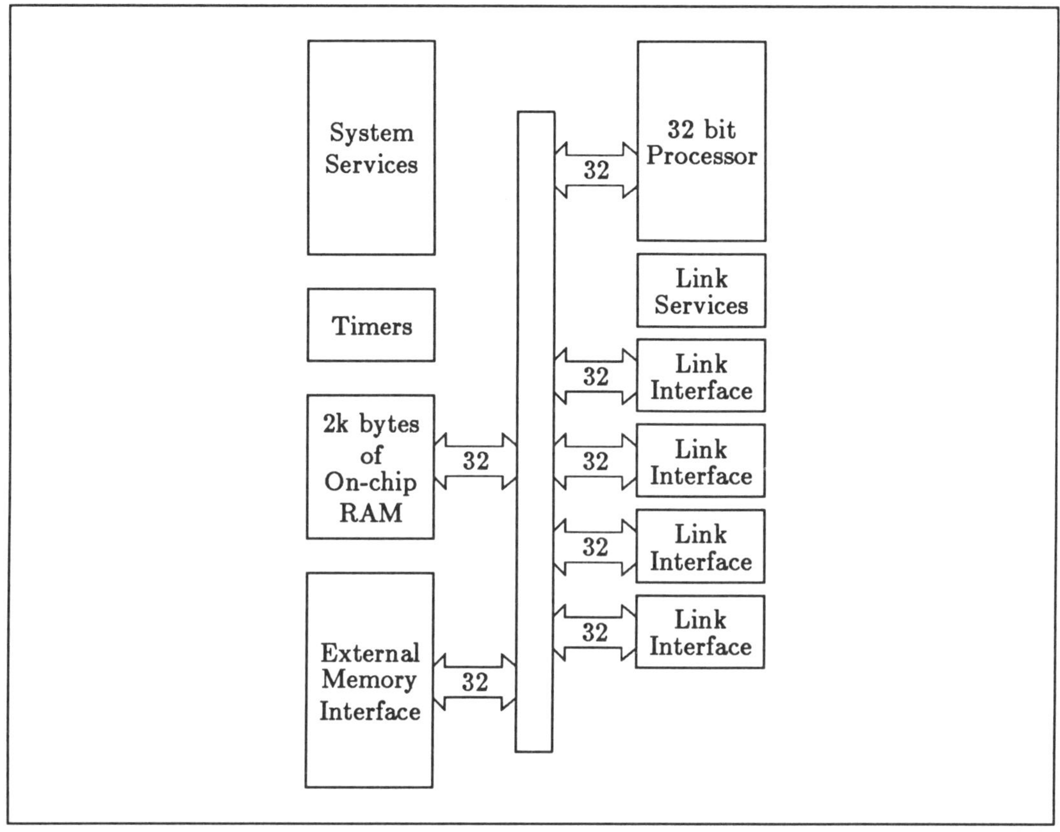

Figure 11.1: The INMOS T414 transputer

The INMOS TRANSPUTER is a pioneering device that fills this gap, and it can be considered to be the ideal component for fifth generation computers. The T414 Transputer in (Figure 11.1) is a 32 bit microcomputer with 2 Kbytes on chip RAM (50 ns static RAM) for high speed processing, a configurable memory interface, 4 bidirectional communication links, and a timer. It provides high performance arithmetic and micro code support for floating point operations and achieves an instruction rate of 10 MIPS (millions of instructions per second) by running at a speed of 20 MHz. The T800 (Figure 11.2) with an extra 2 Kbytes and a 64-bit floating point unit. This makes the Transputer one of the first designs that incorporate several hardware features to support parallel-processing. This allows for any number of Transputers to be arranged together to construct a parallel-processing system, and permits for massive concurrency to be used without further complexity. To provide maximum speed with minimal wiring, the Transputer uses point to point serial communication links for direct connection to other Transputers.

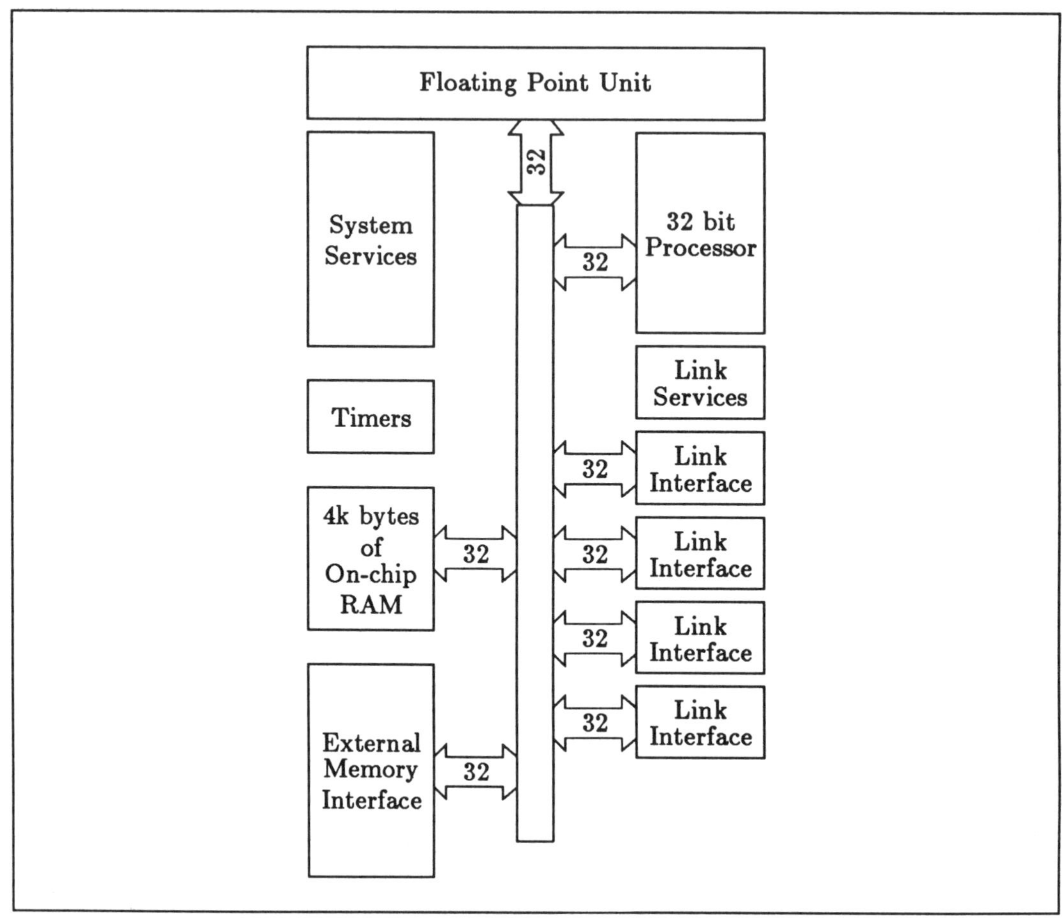

Figure 11.2: The INMOS T800 transputer

OCCAM is a high level language developed by INMOS to run on the Transputer (INMOS 1984, 1985, 1986; IEE Workshop 1988; Kerridge 1987), and it is as important as assembly language is for the ordinary microprocessor, because Transputer features are best exploited by using OCCAM. It is simple, block structured, and supports both sequential (SEQ) and parallel (PAR) features on one or more Transputers which can be used to facilitate the simulation, modelling and control of complicated physical systems (Jones 1985; Hamblen 1987).

11.3 General background

A robot consists of a chain of (N) rigid links.The links (Figure 11.3) are arranged such that link (i) is connected to a preceding link (i-1) and a following link (i+1). In robot manipulators, two types of joints exist, translational and revolute joints. The translational joints are such that the adjacent links translate linearly to each other along the joint axis, while the revolute joints allow adjacent links to rotate with respect to each other about the joint axis. Therefore, the link (i) motion with reference to the link (i-1) depends only on one variable, rotation Θ_i or translation d_i.

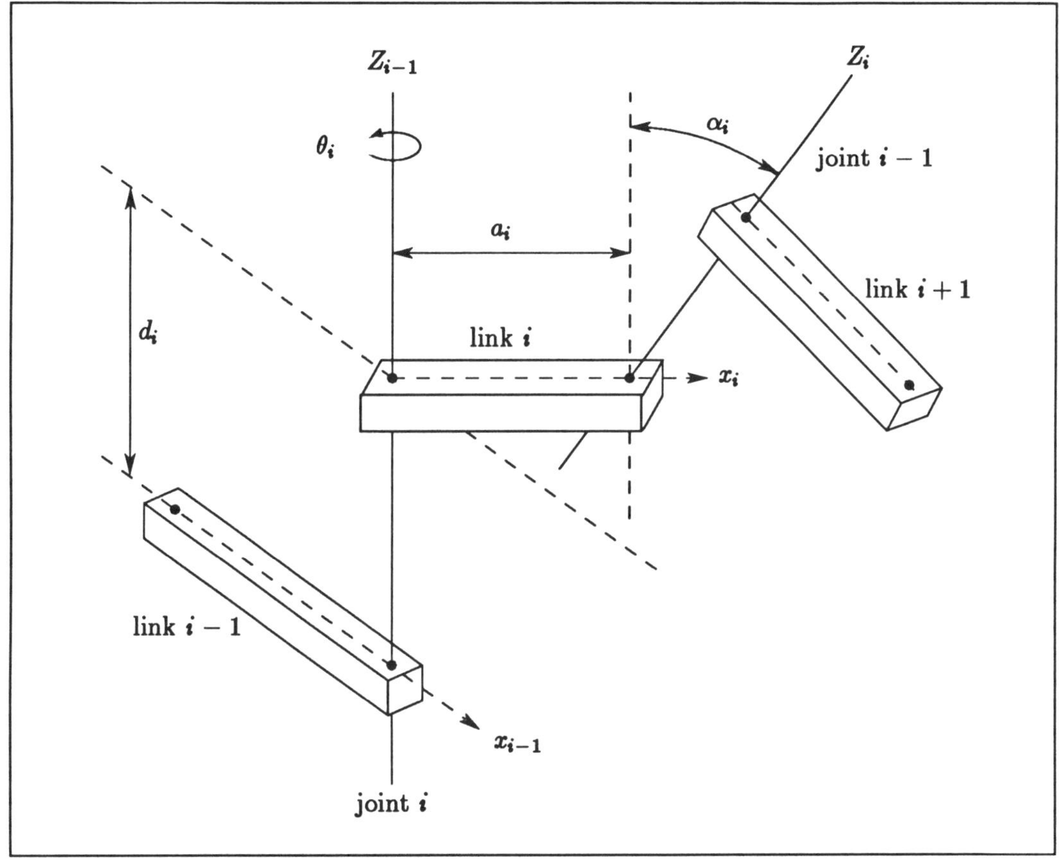

Figure 11.3: The relation between different links

Generally, the robot base is considered to be link (0). The last link (N) carries a gripper (hand) or a tool (drill, pincer) and is called the end effector of the robot. The location of an object in space is determined by six degrees of freedom (dof), three of which represent position and the other three orientation. If a task is performed in space without constraints, 6 dof are necessary. But if the task is performed in a plane, only 3 dof are necessary. The joint variables of the robot arm are limited between both initial and final values which depend on the robot structure. As a result, the number of points which can be reached by the end effector is also limited. The set of points that can be reached is called the work space of the robot. In general, it is a volume with complex form calculated from the limit values of the joint variables. For a task to be workable, all the paths constituting that task must be contained within the working space.

Robots play a major role in today's modern Computer Integrated Manufacturing Systems (CIMS). The British Robot Association defines a robot as "a programmable device designed to both manipulate and transport parts, tools or specialized manufacturing tasks". The choice of the computer architecture used to control the robot is of great importance. Most of the algorithms used for controlling the various aspects of the motion of a robot are complicated and involve trigonometric functions, multiplications and/or inversion of matrices. In addition, many of these calculations have real-time constraints in that they must be computed within some small time period (e.g. 10 msec) or the robot control loop may become unstable.

The use of *Distributed Computing* techniques by employing several computing units, interacting in real-time to provide the required computational speed and power, finds an immediate application in robotics. There is a vast plethora of literature on distributed computing, and many, if not all of the concepts described are directly applicable to robotics. In this paper a trial is made to introduce these concepts to robot Jacobian control (Figure 11.4) to emphasize the role which can be played by distributed architectures in enhancing the real-time speeds by distributing the whole of a task over several cooperating processors.

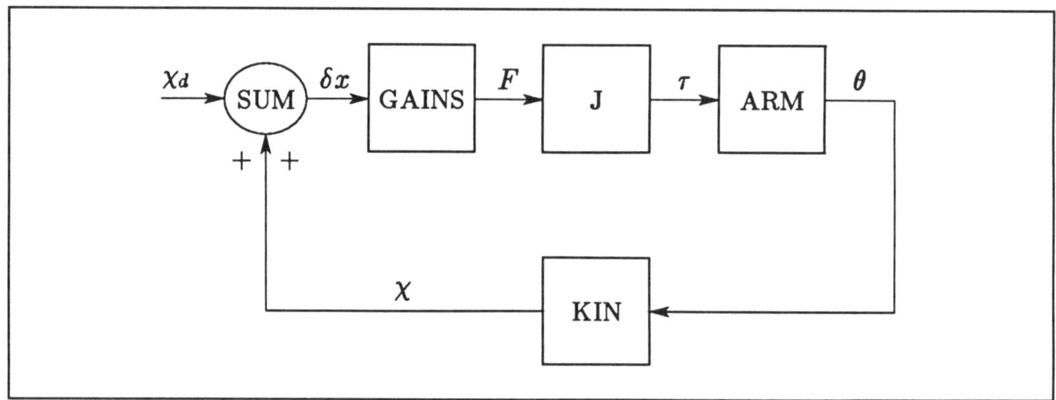

Figure 11.4: Jacobian control scheme

11.4 Problem formulation

11.4.1 The Jacobian

Several remarks are in order with regard to the Jacobian (J). First, it relates changes in joint space to changes in cartesian space. Hence, (J) is necessary in any cartesian-based control scheme. Second, it is not a constant matrix, but depends on the arm configuration. This fact makes real-time computation a major challenge.

$$\Delta x = J(\theta) \, \Delta\Theta \tag{1}$$

where x is the cartesian coordinates vector, and

Θ is the position vector of joint angles.

Orin and Schrader (1984) reviewed some of the methods used to compute (J) and some other techniques were proposed by (Lenaric 1984; Mitra and Mahalanabis 1984; Leahy, Nugent, Saridis, and Valavanis 1987). In this paper the adapted method is the one first outlined by Whitney (1972) and later refined by Paul (1981) because of its simple and algorithmic nature.

11.4.2 Nomenclature

The well known conventions first proposed by Denavit and Hartenberg (DH) (1955) are used throughout this paper. The main idea is to assign a coordinate frame to each link with the z-axis along the joint axis. This gives rise to four transformations; the rotation angle (Θ_i) which rotates about the z_{i-1}, translation of distance d_i along the z_{i-1} (offset distance), a_i the shortest distance between z_{i-1} and z_i (link length), and rotation angle (α_i) about the x_i (twist angle) (table 11.1).

From these parameters a 4 $\times$ 4 homogeneous transformation matrix is produced.

$$A_i = \begin{bmatrix} \cos\Theta_i & -\sin\Theta_i \cos\alpha_i & \sin\Theta_i \sin\alpha_i & a_i \cos\Theta_i \\ \sin\Theta_i & \cos\Theta_i \cos\alpha_i & -\cos\Theta_i \sin\alpha_i & a_i \sin\Theta_i \\ 0 & \sin\alpha_i & \cos\alpha_i & d_i \\ 0 & 0 & 0 & 1 \end{bmatrix} \tag{2}$$

For a revolute joint, Θ_i changes while d_i, a_i, and α_i remain constant. For a translational joint d_i is changing and $a_i = 0$. To achieve transformation between different coordinate

LINK PARAMETERS				
Link	Θ	a	d	α
1	Θ_1	0	0	−90
2	Θ_2	0	d_2	90
3	d_3	0	d_3	0
4	Θ_4	0	0	−90
5	Θ_5	0	0	90
6	Θ_6	0	0	0

Table 11.1: Link parameters between different frames for a Stanford-like manipulator

frames a matrix $boldT_n$ is defined such that

$$\begin{aligned} T_n &= A_1 A_2 A_3 A_4 A_5 A_6 \\ &= \begin{bmatrix} R_i^{i-1}(\Theta, axis) & P_i^{i-1} \\ 0^T & 1 \end{bmatrix} \end{aligned} \quad (3)$$

where R_i^{i-1} is a 3×3 matrix that describes the orientation and rotation between successive coordinate frames.

P_i^{i-1} is a 3 *times* 1 vector which denotes pure translation.

By using these matrices the derivation of (J) for a 6 dof robot arm, as given by Paul (1981), is as follows:

$$T_6^0 = \prod_{i=1}^{6} A_i \quad (4)$$

$$T_6^1 = \prod_{i=2}^{6} A_i \quad (5)$$

$$T_6^2 = \prod_{i=3}^{6} A_i \quad (6)$$

$$T_6^3 = \prod_{i=4}^{6} A_i \quad (7)$$

$$T_6^4 = \prod_{i=5}^{6} A_i \quad (8)$$

$$T_6^5 = A_6 = \begin{bmatrix} n_x & o_x & a_x & p_x \\ n_y & o_y & a_y & p_y \\ n_z & o_z & a_z & p_z \\ 0 & 0 & 0 & 1 \end{bmatrix} \tag{9}$$

Accordingly, for a revolute joint (i), each column of (J) is of the form

$$J_i = \begin{bmatrix} n_y^i p_x^i - n_x^i p_y^i \\ o_y^i p_x^i - o_x^i p_y^i \\ a_y^i p_x^i - a_x^i p_y^i \\ n_z^i \\ o_z^i \\ a_z^i \end{bmatrix} \tag{10}$$

For a translational joint (i);

$$J_i = \begin{bmatrix} n_z^i \\ o_z^i \\ a_z^i \\ 0 \\ 0 \\ 0 \end{bmatrix} \tag{11}$$

Hence, the (i^{th}) column of the Jacobian can be described as follows :

$$J_i = \left[\delta_i \begin{pmatrix} n_y^i p_x^i - n_x^i p_y^i \\ o_y^i p_x^i - o_x^i p_y^i \\ a_y^i p_x^i - a_x^i p_y^i \\ n_z^i \\ o_z^i \\ a_z^i \end{pmatrix} + (1 - \delta_i) \begin{pmatrix} n_z^i \\ o_z^i \\ a_z^i \\ 0 \\ 0 \\ 0 \end{pmatrix} \right] \tag{12}$$

where

$$\delta_i = \begin{cases} 1 & \textit{if i is revolute joint} \\ 0 & \textit{if i is translational joint} \end{cases} \tag{13}$$

11.5 Parallel Jacobian computation

Parallel processing can be divided into four levels (Hwang and Briggs 1985)

Job or program level.

Task or procedure level.

Interinstruction level.

Intrainstruction level.

In this section the first and the second levels are used and addressed. The first level depends upon developing parallel processable algorithms where multiple programs are used to solve a large problem. The second level is achieved among procedures or tasks within the same program which involves the decomposition of a program (algorithm) into multiple tasks.

To show how parallel processing can be used to compute (J), three methods for dividing the task are described to achieve an optimal configuration. The main difference between the three methods is how the algorithm is divided, that is, the amount of work carried out by each processor and the overhead caused by the communication between the processors in the network. Real-time results are included to compare uniprocessing and multiprocessing architectures.

11.5.1 Method 1

For this method a tree structured network is used (Figure 11.5) were (P_0) is the master processor (controller) and the other three processors P_1, P_2, and P_3 are slave processors (the names processor and transputer are used interchangably).

The master processor is connected to a personal computer (PC) which works as a link between the user and the network. P_0 sends the position variables (Θ_i) and receives the columns of (J) from the slave processors in the network. The main role of P_0 is to supervise the network and to check for any faulty event. The job of calculating the different columns of (J) is divided as shown:

- P_1 : compute the fourth, fifth, and sixth columns of (J) using eq.(7-9) respectively.
- P_2 : compute the second and third columns of (J) using eq.(5,6) respectively.
- P_3 : compute the first column of (J) using eq.(4).

The whole procedure will work as follows:

P_0 sends Θ_1,Θ_2 to P_3, Θ_3, Θ_4 to P_2, and Θ_5,Θ_6 to P_1, and this is performed in parallel. Then, P_0 will start receiving (J) columns from the different processors, i.e.

```
SEQ
  PAR
     ... Send Θ1 and Θ2 to P3
     ... Send Θ3 and Θ4 to P2
     ... Send Θ5 and Θ6 to P1
```

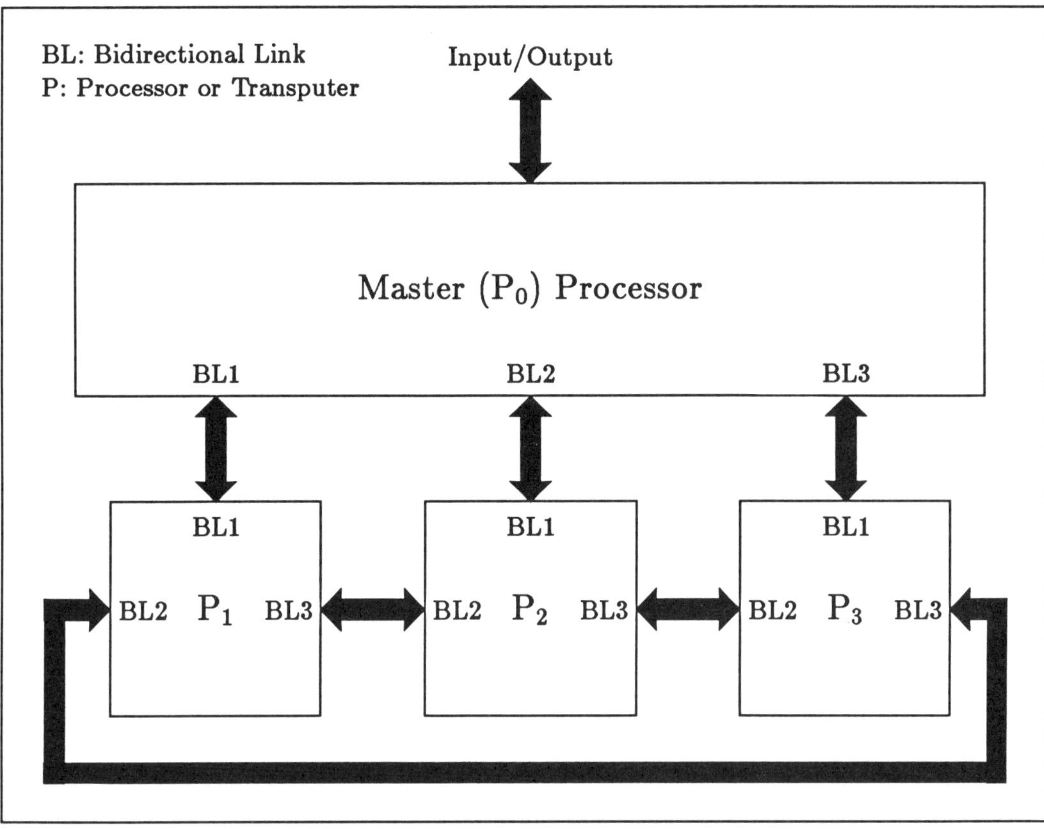

Figure 11.5: Three processor network

```
PAR
    ... Receive J1 from P3
    ... Receive J2 and J3 from P2
    ... Receive J4, J5, and J6 from P1
```

This stage is divided into 3 substages working in parallel together, but each substage is running sequentially

(a) Processor P_1

```
SEQ
    ... Form A5 and A6
    ... Multiply A5 by A6 to form T6^4
    ... Send T6^4 to P2 and P3 and receive A4 from P2
    ... Multiply A4 by T6^4
    ... Form J4 from (A4 * T6^4)
    ... Form J5 from T6^4
    ... Form J6 from A6
    ... Send J4, J5, and J6 to P0
```

(b) Processor P_2

```
SEQ
  ... Form A3 and A4
  ... Multiply A3 by A4 and store in T1
  ... Send T1 and A4 to P3 and P1 rspectively,
      and receive (A5 * A6) from P1 and A2 form P1
  ... Multiply the matrices to form T6^2 and T6^1
  ... Form J2 from T6^1
  ... Form J3 from T6^2
  ... Send J2 and J3 to P0
```

(c) Processor P_3

```
SEQ
  ... Form A1 and A2
  ... Multiply A1 by A2 and store in T1
  ... Send A2 to P2 and receive (A3 * A4)
      and (A5 * A6) from P2 and P1 respectively
  ... Multiply the matrices to form T6^0
  ... Form J1 from T6^0
  ... Send J1 to P0
```

In the previous method four processors were used to solve the problem, one as controller and the other three carrying out operations. Each processor is considered as a separate unit executing its operation sequentially but at the same time the other processors are doing the same thing. Hence, the whole network is running in parallel. Any number of methods could be used to divide the problem but the best allocation would be, of course, to solve the problem as fast as possible. To do so, each processor should be kept busy performing useful computations. If a large amount of data must be transferred between the processors, a potential communication bottleneck may occur which would slow down the network. To avoid that, only the first 3 rows of the (4 *times* 4) transformation matrices are transferred between different processors. Another restriction is the matrix by matrix multiplication. In this case the operation is performed in a way which avoids useless multiplications and additions, i.e.

$$
\begin{aligned}
T_i^{i-1}\,T_{i+1}^{i} &= \begin{bmatrix} R_i^{i-1} & P_i^{i-1} \\ 0^T & 1 \end{bmatrix}\begin{bmatrix} R_{i+1}^{i} & P_{i+1}^{i} \\ 0^T & 1 \end{bmatrix} \\
&= \begin{bmatrix} R_i^{i-1}\,R_{i+1}^{i} & R_i^{i-1}\,P_{i+1}^{i} + P_i^{i-1} \\ 0^T & 1 \end{bmatrix}
\end{aligned} \tag{14}
$$

11.5.2 Method 2

This method is used with the same network configuration (Figure 11.5) as that of method 1. The main difference is a reduction in the communication between slave processors by redistributing the job and using different task-allocations. This will allow each processor to work independently most of the time and so achieve better processor-utilisation. Therefore, each processor is spending its time doing useful computations instead of waiting to receive data from other processors. The following job schedule is used

- P_1 : compute the fifth and sixth columns of (J) using eq.(8,9) respectively.

- P_2 : compute the third and fourth columns of (J) using eq.(6,7) respectively.

- P_3 : compute the first and second columns of (J) using eq.(4,5) respectively.

The algorithm will proceed as follows

P_0 sends Θ_1,Θ_2 to P_3, Θ_3, Θ_4 to P_2, and Θ_5,Θ_6 to P_1. Then, P_0 will start receiving (J) columns from the different processors, i.e.

```
SEQ
  PAR
    ... Send Θ1 and Θ2 to P3
    ... Send Θ3 and Θ4 to P2
    ... Send Θ5 and Θ6 to P1
  PAR
    ... Receive J1 and J2 from P3
    ... Receive J3 and J4 from P2
    ... Receive J5 and J6 from P1
```

This stage is divided into 3 substages working in parallel together, but each substage is running sequentially

(a) Processor P_1

```
SEQ
  ... Form A5 and A6
  ... Multiply A5 by A6 to form T6^4
  ... Send T6^4 to P2 and P3
  ... Form J5 from T6^4
  ... Form J6 from A6
  ... Send J5 and J6 to P0
```

(b) Processor P_2

```
SEQ
  ... Form A3 and A4
  ... Multiply A3 by A4 and store in T1
  ... Send T1 to P3 and receive T6^4 from P1
  ... Multiply A4 by T6^4
  ... Multiply T1 by T6^4
  ... Form J3 from (T1 * T6^4)
  ... Form J4 from (A4 * T6^4)
  ... Send J3 and J4 to P0
```

(c) Processor P_3

```
SEQ
  ... Form A1 and A2
  ... Multiply A1 by A2 and store in T1
  ... Receive (A3 * A4) and (A5 * A6) form P2 and P1 respectively
  ... Multiply (A3 * A4) by (A5 * A6) and store in T2
  ... Multiply T2 by A2
  ... Multiply T2 by T1 to form T6^0
  ... Form J1 from T6^0
  ... Form J2 from (A2 * T2)
  ... Send J1 to P0
```

It is important to note that, the sending and receiving of matrices and data is performed in parallel. For example, if matrices T_a and T_b are sent from P_1 to P_2 and P_3 respectively and T_c is received by P_1 form P_3, this operation is coded as follows:

```
  SEQ i = 1 FOR 3
SEQ j = 1 FOR 3
  PAR
    C1.2 ! Ta [i][j]
    C1.3 ! Tb [i][j]
    C3.1 ? Tc [i][j]
```

where C1.2, C1.3, and C3.1 are communication channels implemented by OCCAM and correspond to actual hardware communication links connecting the different transputers.

11.5.3 Method 3

A different network and a different task-allocation (Figure 11.6) is used for this method to give more independence to each processor and eliminate any communication between the slave processors, so that the communication bottleneck is minimised.

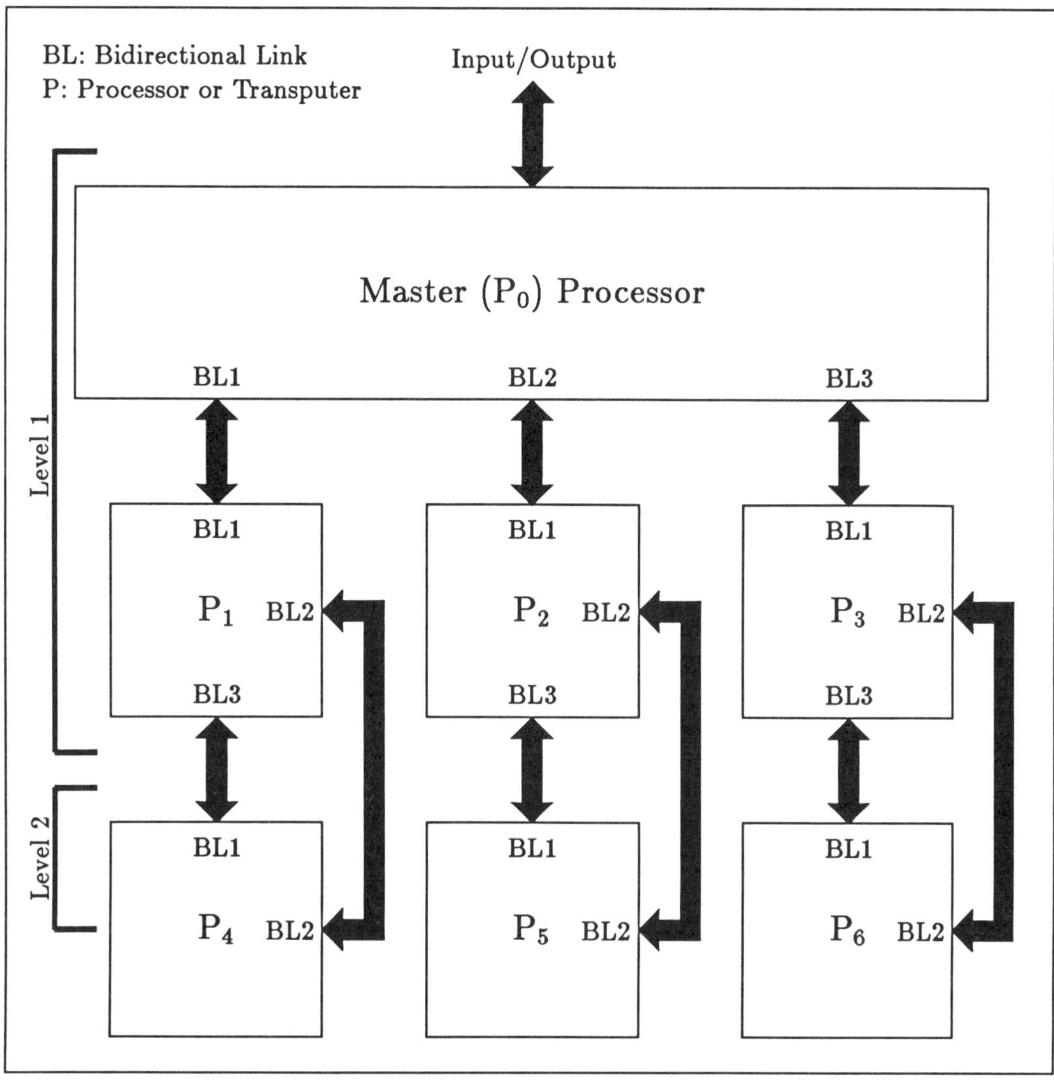

Figure 11.6: Six processor network

In this configuration the first level of the network is a simple tree-structure, but each slave processor in Level 1 is a master for another slave processor in Level 2. Equations (4) to (9) are distributed on the six processors such that each processor works on computing one column of (J), i.e. one processor is assigned to each link. In this case the structure of the OCCAM program is the same for the six processors except for a slight difference in the data flow path, that is, level 1 slave processors communicate directly with the controller P_0 but slave processors in level 2 "talk" to P_0 through their master processor (i.e. P_6 talks to P_0 through P_3). This difference appears where position variables (Θ_i) are sent from P_0 to the network and Jacobian columns (J_i) are received from the different processors.

Now three types of procedures are given to illustrate the OCCAM portions which run on each processor:

1. Processor P_0

```
SEQ
  PAR
    ... Send Θ1,..., Θ6 to P3
    ... Send Θ3,..., Θ6 to P2
    ... Send Θ5,..., Θ6 to P1
  PAR
    ... Receive J1 and J2 from P3
    ... Receive J3 and J4 from P2
    ... Receive J5 and J6 from P1
```

2. Processor P_2 (example of a processor in level 1)

```
SEQ
  ... Receive Θ3,..., Θ6 form P0
  ... Send Θ4,..., Θ6 to P5
  ... Form A3,..., A6
  ... Multiply the chain of matrices (A3 * A4 * ...A6)
  ... Form J3
  ... Receive J4 form P5
  ... Send J3 and J4 to P0
```

3. Processor P_5 (example of a processor in level 2)

```
SEQ
  ... Receive Θ4,..., Θ6 form P2
  ... Form A4,..., A6
  ... Multiply the chain of matrices (A4 * A5 * ...A6)
  ... Form J4
  ... Receive J4 form P2
```

The whole procedure is shown in a block diagram (Figure 11.7)

Its important to note that in writing OCCAM code, efficiency is the main aim if real-time implementations are required. Hence, no redundant calculations are performed and the (DH) parameters reside on each Transputer in the network to minimise the communication overhead (Kung 1985).

11.6 Results

The previous three algorithms are implemented using OCCAM to show their suitability for real-time applications. The results are compared with a sequential version in FORTRAN and executed on a SUN 350 workstation (SUN Inc. 1984) with additional floating point hardware. The results are given in (table 11.2).

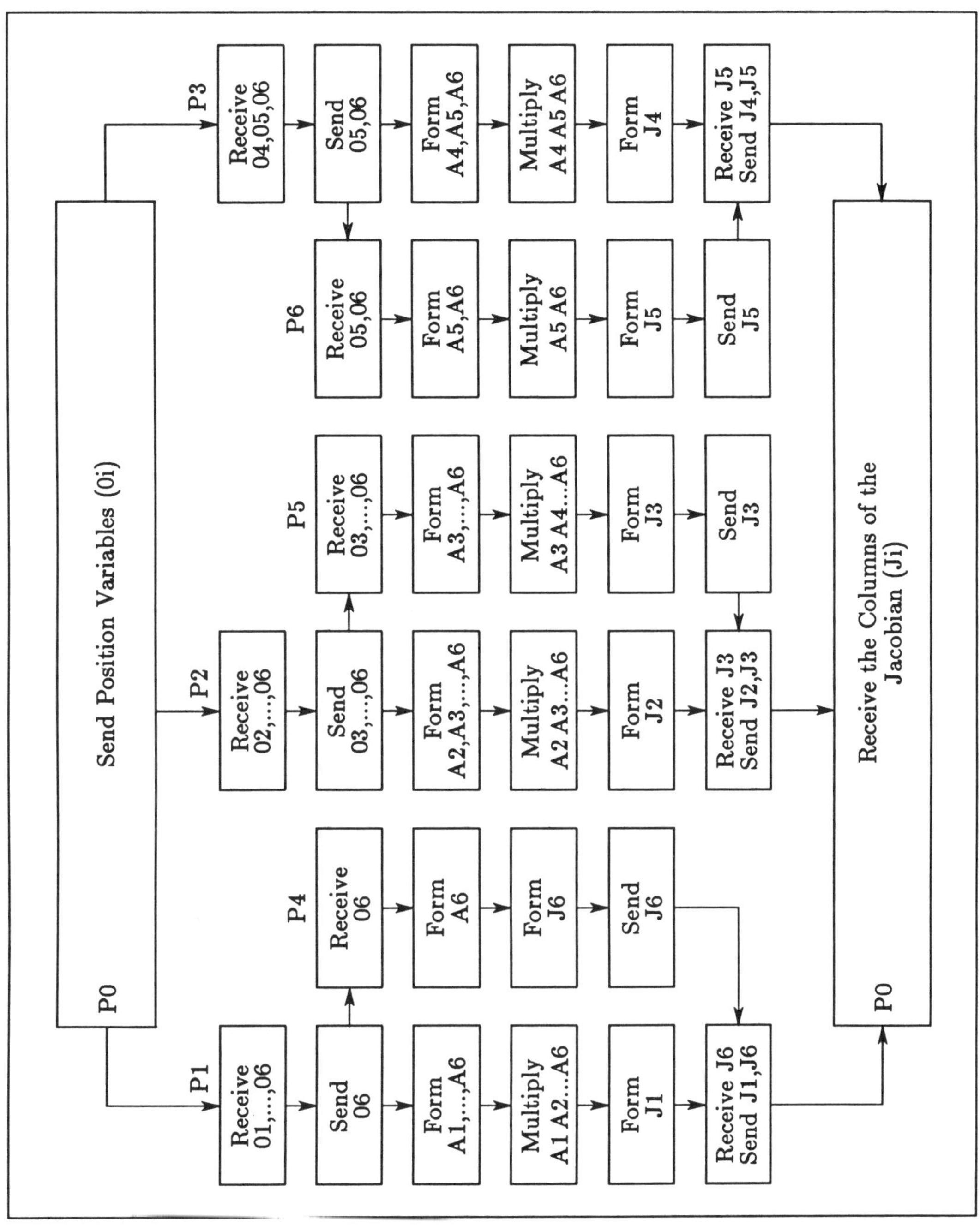

Figure 11.7: Block diagram description of method 3

It can be noticed from (table 11.2) that the methods 1, 2, and 3 are adequate for real-time applications, and this shows the superiority of parallel processing techniques.

Algorithm	Processing time (msec)
Sequential	15.0
Method 1	3.84
Method 2	4.67
Method 3	0.256

Table 11.2: Execution time (T414)

Method 3 is 58 times faster than it's sequential counterpart. The choice between the three methods will be made according to the speed requirements needed (Figure 11.8).

11.6.1 Extra computing power

If the (T800) is used instead of the (T414) this will lead to a better performance and speed up (table 11.3). Theoretically, the processing time ratio between the (T414) and the (T800) is about (1:10). This is true if only (multiplications/additions) are involved. However, this is not always the case in practical situations because of the communication overheads and the efficiency in writing OCCAM code. This will reduce the ratio to about (1:5)(Figure 11.9).

Algorithm	Processing time (msec)
Sequential	15.0
Method 1	0.768
Method 2	0.973
Method 3	0.0533

Table 11.3: Execution time (T800)

Some points about the values of Exectution-time (T_P) quoted above should be noted. Firstly, the goal of enhancing the performance of the network is attained by making sure that information can flow to and from the processsing elements with sufficient speed, rather than by maximizing the computational bandwidth of the processing elements (the number of operations per second that the processor can deliver). This is accomplished by organizing the processors which need to communicate with one another in such a way as to make the transfer of data smooth and cost effective. Hence, the situation of two

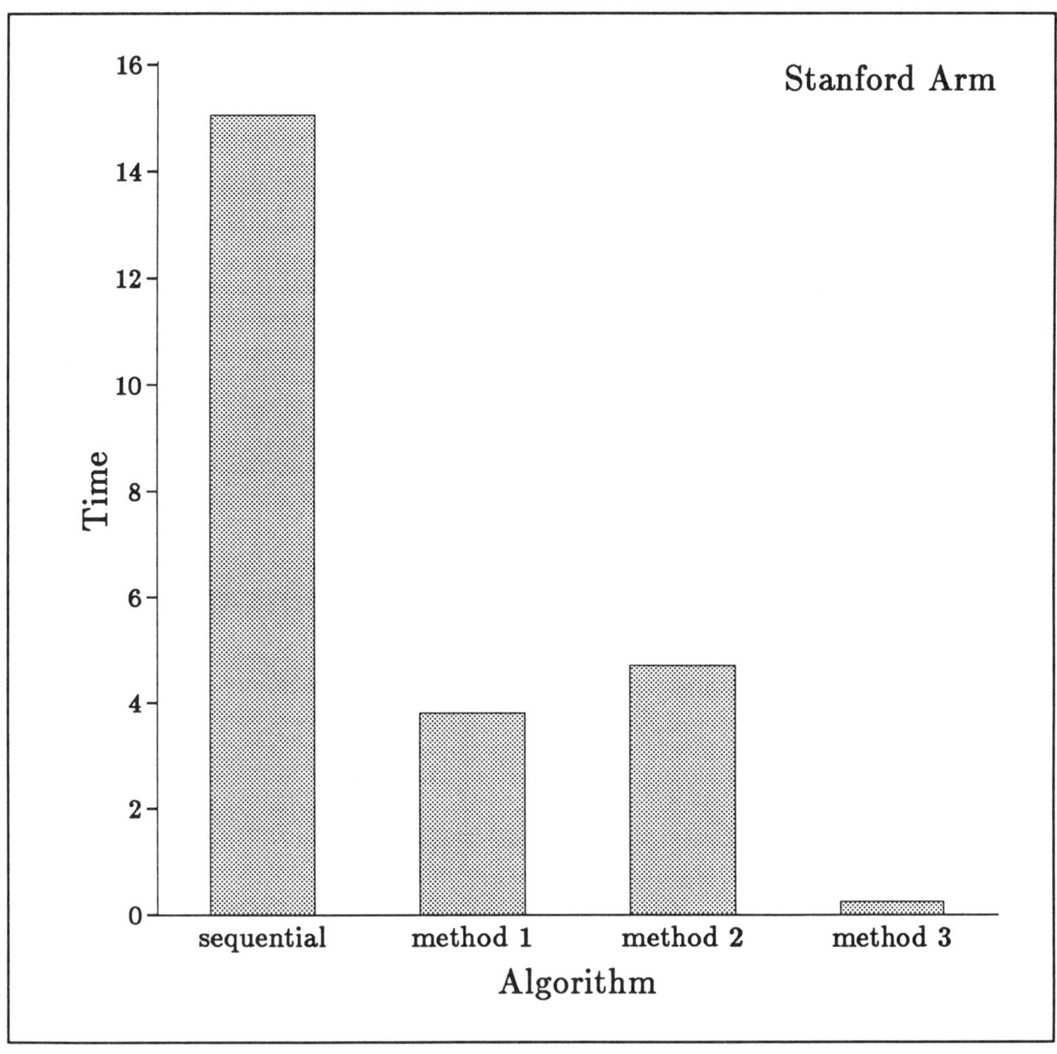

Figure 11.8: Processing time for the T400 case

processors communicating with each other through a third processor is avoided.

Secondly, the different subtasks must be divided so that the processors spend most of the time on useful computations whilst at the same time minimizing the communication between the different processors as much as possible.

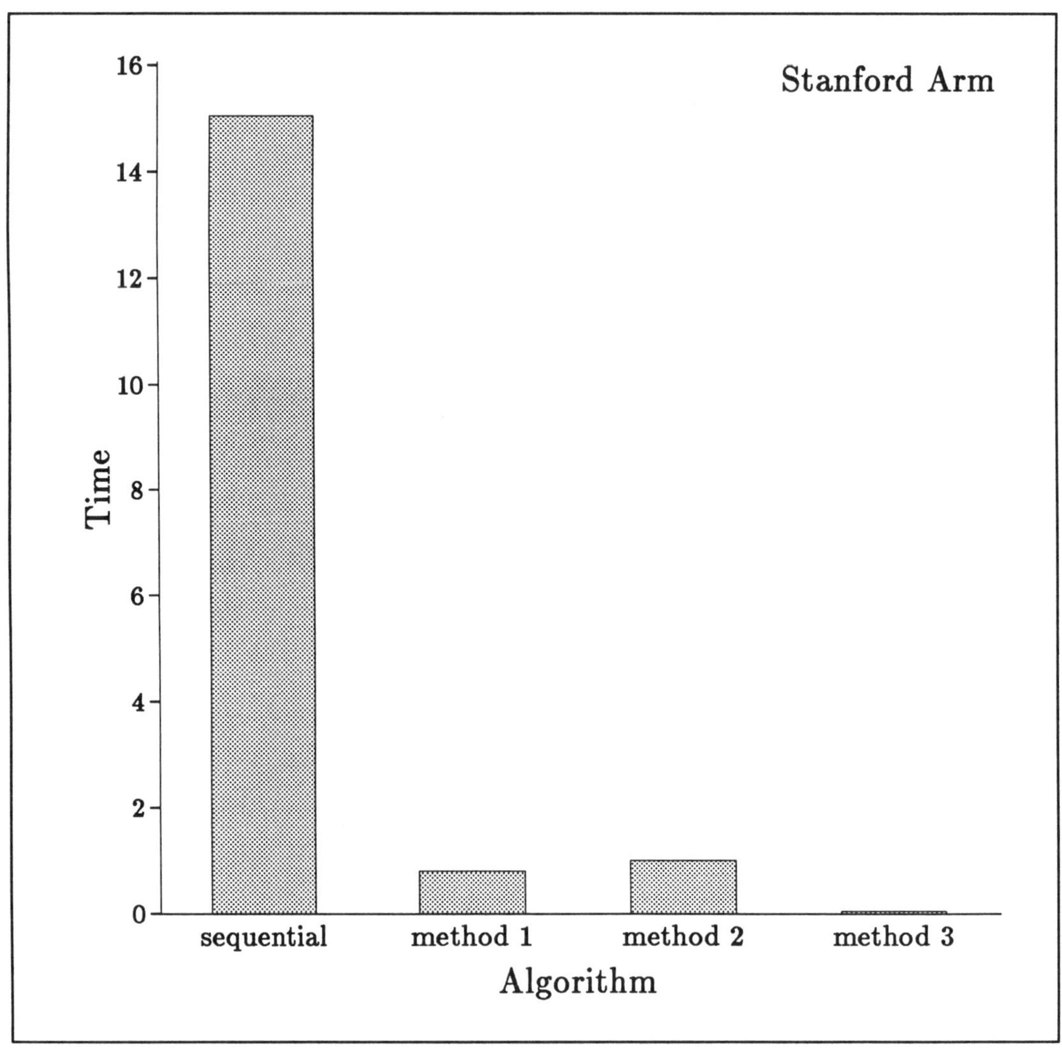

Figure 11.9: Processing time for the T800 case

11.7 Summary and conclusion

The Kinematic modelling of typical robot manipulators such as the Stanford arm is systematic and simple in concept but complicated in respect of the computational burden inherent in real-time control applications. The work addressed in this paper deals with one of important aspects of this problem, that is the computation of the Jacobian matrix within acceptable control sampling rates.

A suitable algorithm for computing the Jacobian has previously been presented by

Paul (1981). Three alternative ways of distributing the computation of this algorithm on a general purpose distributed computing system have been suggested in this paper. The computational efficiency of these methods has been compared with that for an equivalent sequential implementation. This comparison has demonstrated the efficiency of all three methods and shown the feasibility of using them in real-time situations.

A few notes have to be kept in mind while distributing a whole of a task (algorithm) to work on several processors:

The data flow paths and the communication between the different processors constitute a major bottleneck in many situations.

The division of the workload between the different co-processors.

The idle-time that each processor spends waiting for input from other processors.

The required computing power which decides the size and complexity of the network.

The amount of parallelism and sequentialism inherent in the algorithm.

The efficiency in coding the algorithm (software development).

The work described has demonstrated how the recent advances in computer technology, particularly in new VLSI architectures, can be utilised in the implementation of Jacobian based control schemes. Suitable foundations have been set for the development of a wide range of control algorithms, unhindered by the computational restrictions.

11.8 References

ANG, M. H. and TOURASSIS, V.D., (1987).
"General Purpose Inverse Kinematics Transformations for Robotic Manipulators," *J. Robotic Systems*, vol. 4, no. 4, pp. 527–549.

ANGELES, J., (1985).
"On the Numerical Solution of the Inverse Kinematic Problem," *Int. J. Robotics Research*, vol.4, no. 2, pp. 21–37.

CRAIG, J. J., (1986).
Introduction to Robotics: Mechanics and Control, Addison-Wesley, Reading, Mass.

DENAVIT, H. and HARTENBERG, R., (1955).
"A Kinematic Notation for Lower Pair Mechanisms Based on Matrices," *J. Applied Mechanics*, no. 22, pp. 215-221.

ELGAZZAR, S., (1985).
"Efficient Kinematic Transformation for the PUMA 560," *IEEE J. Robotics and Automation*, vol. 1, no. 3, pp. 142–151.

FEATHERSTONE, R., (1983).
"Position and Velocity Transformation between Robot End-Effector Coordinates and Joint Angles," *Int. J. Robotics Research*, vol. 2, no. 2, pp. 35–45.

FU, K. S., GONZALES, R.C., and LEE, C. S. G., (1987).
Robotics: Control, Sensing, Vision, and Intelligence, McGraw-Hill, New York.

HAMBLEN, J. O., (1987).
"Parallel Continous System Simulation Using the Transputer," *Simulation*, vol. 49, no. 6, pp.249–253.

HWANG, K. and BRIGGS, F. A., (1985).
Computer Architecture and Parallel Processing, McGraw-Hill, New York.

IEE, (1988).
Parallel Processing in Control – The Transputer and other Architectures, IEE Workshop, UCNW, Bangor, Wales, U.K.

INMOS, (1984).
OCCAM Programming Manual, Prentice-Hall, Englewood Cliffs, N.J.

INMOS, (1985).
IMS T414 Transputer, Reference Manual.

INMOS, (1986).
IMS T414 Transputer, Preliminary data.

JONES, D. I., (1985).
"OCCAM Structures in Control Applications," *Trans. Inst. of Measurements and Control*, vol. 7, no. 5, pp. 222–227.

KERRIDGE, J., (1987).
OCCAM Programming: A Pratical Approach, Blackwell.

KUCK, D.J., (1977).
"A Survey of Parallel Machine Organization and Programming," *Ass. of Computiong Machinery (ACM)*, vol. 9, no. 1, pp. 29–59.

KUNG, H. T., (1982).
"Why Systolic Architectures," *IEEE Computer*, pp. 37–46.

KUNG, H.T., (1985).
"Memory Requirements for Balanced Computer Architectures," *J. of Complexity*, vol. 1, no. 1, pp. 147–157.

LATHROP, R. H., (1985).
"Parallelism in Manipulator Dynamics," *Int. J. Robotics Res.*, vol. 4, no. 2, pp. 80–102.

LEAHY, M. B., NUGENT, L. M., SARDIS, G. N., and VALAVANIS, K. P., (1987).
"Efficient PUMA Manipulator Jacobian Calculation and Inversion," *J. Robotic Systems*, vol. 4, no. 2, pp. 185–197.

LEE, C. S., and CHANG, P. R., (1986).
"Efficient Parallel Algorithm for Robot Inverse Dynamics Computation," *IEEE Trans. on Systems, Man, and Cybernetics*, vol. 16, no. 4, pp. 532–542.

LENARCIC, J., (1984).
"A New Method for Calculating the Jacobian for a Robot Manipulator," *Robotica*, vol. 1, no. 4, pp. 205–209.

LUH, J. Y. S., WALKER, M. W., and PAUL, R. P., (1980).
"Resolved Acceleration Control of Mechanical Manipulators," *IEEE Trans. Automatic Control*, vol. 25, no. 3, pp. 468–447.

LUH, J. Y. S. and LIN, C. S., (1982).
"Scheduling of PArallel Computation for a Computer Controlled Mechanical Manipulator," *IEEE Trans. on Systems, Man, and Cybernetics*, vol. 12, no. 2, pp. 214–234.

MITRA, S. K. and MAHALANABIS, A., (1984).
"Fast Computation of Jacobian and Inverse Jacobian of Robot Manipulators," in *Proc. of SPIE Int. Soc. of Optical Eng., Intelligent Robots and Computer Vision*, vol. 521, pp. 235–242.

ORIN, D. E. and SCHRADER, W. W., (1984).
"Efficient Computation of the Jacobian for Robot Manipulators," *Int. J. Robotics Research*, vol. 3, no. 4, pp. 66–75.

ORIN, D. E., CHAO, H. H., OLSON, K. W., and SCHRADER, W. W., (1985).
"Pipeline/Parallel Algorithms for the Jacobian and Inverse Dynamics Computations," in *Proc. IEEE Int. Conf. on Robotics and Automation*, pp. 785–789.

PAUL, R. P., (1981).
Robot Manipulators: Mathematics, Programming, and Control, MIT Press, Cambridge, Mass.

PAUL, R. P., and ZHANG, H., (1986).
"Computationally Efficient Kinematics for Manipulators with Spherical Wrists Based on the Homogeneous Transformation Representation," *Int. J. Robotics Research*, vol. 5, no. 2, pp.32–44.

RENAUD, M., (1981).
"Goemetric and Kinematic Models of a Robot Manipulator: Calculation of the Jacobian and its Inverse," in *Proc. 11th Symp. Industrial Robots.*

SUN, MICROSYSTEMS INC (1984).
FORTRAN Programmer's Guide for the Sun Workstations, Mountain View, CA 94043.

TSAI, Y. T. and ORIN, D. E., (1987).
"A Strictly Convergent Real-time solution for Inverse Kinematics of Robot Manipulators," *J. Robotic Systems*, vol. 4, no. 4, pp. 477–501.

VUKOBRATOVIC, M., KIRCANSKI, N., and LI, S. G., (1988).
"An Approach to Parallel processing of Dynamic Robot Models," *Int. J. Robotics Res.*, vol. 7, no. 2, pp. 64–71.

WARLDON, K. J., (1982).
"Geometrically Based Manipulator Rate Control Algorithms," *Mechanism and Machine Theory*, vol. 17, no. 6, pp.379–385.

WHITNEY, D. E., (1969).
"Resolved Motion Rate Control of Manipulators and Human Protheses," *IEEE Trans. Man Machine Systems*, vol. 10, no. 2, pp. 47–53.

WHITNEY, D. E., (1972).
"The Mathematics of Coordinated Control of Prosthetic Arms and Manipulators," *Trans. ASME J. Dynamic Systems, Measurement, and Control*, vol. 94, no. 4, pp. 303–309.

WHITNEY, D. E., (1987).
"Historical Perspective and State of the Art in Robot Force Control," *Int. J. Robotics Research*, vol. 6, no. 1, pp. 3–14.

WOLOVICH, W. A., (1987).
Robotics: Basic Analysis and Design, Holt, Rinehart and Winston, The Dryden Press, Saunders College.

WU, C. H. and PAUL, R. P., (1982).
"Resolved Motion Force Control of Robot Manipulators," *IEEE Trans Systems, Man, and Cybernetics*, vol. 12, no. 3, pp. 266–275.

ZAKHAROV, V., (1984).
"Parallelism and Array Processing," *IEEE Trans. Computers*, vol. 33, no. 1, pp. 45–78.

ZOMAYA, A. Y. and MORRIS, A. S., (1989).
"Robot Inverse Dynamics Computation Via VLSI Distributed Architectures," *Research Report No. 350, Dept. of Control Enginerring, University of Sheffield*, Sheffield S1 3JD, U.K.

Chapter 12

Transputer-based behavioral module for multi-sensory robot control

Zhang Ying
Department of Computer Science
University of British Columbia
Vancouver, B.C.
Canada, V6T 1W5
e-mail zhang@cs.ubc.ca

Abstract Current robots have very limited abilities to adapt to the environment, to survive in unstructured situations, to deal with incomplete and inconsistent information, and to make real-time decisions. One reason for this is the limited power of computation; the other reason is the unsuitable representation with rigid programming style.

In this paper, we propose a novel representation for multi-sensory robot control built on transputers using parallel and distributed processing. The scheme for this representation is based on the *Behavioral Module* which consists of perception, cognition and action. The robot control system can be decomposed into multiple behavioral modules which are distributed over transputers.

We show that object-oriented concurrent languages in general, FCP++ and parallel C++ in particular are good candidates for programming behavioral modules. Each perception, cognition or action is corresponding to a process which is independent of other processes, but communicates with each other by message passing. Each behavioral module is defined as a concurrent object which is an integration of data and processes. The system is under asynchronized control. Motors and sensors coordinate each other by internal data dependency and the ***suppression*** [2] mechanism.

This work contributes to current Robotics research in the following two aspects:

As a new methodology for robot programming and system development.

As a new technique for designing and generating synthetic or computational behaviors for robots.

The goal of this research is building *Open Robot Systems* which can work in uncertain, inconsistent real-time situations.

12.1 Introduction

Parallel distributed systems in AI and robotics

The power of parallel and distributed processing comes from both *effectiveness* and *expressiveness*. Basically, there are two kinds of parallel and distributed processing:

1) Based on fine-grained massively parallel hardware. This kind of architecture is suitable for lower level vision, numerical array computation, neural networks etc.

2) Based on coarse-grained loosely distributed hardware. This kind of architecture is suitable for higher level cognition model, distributed Artificial Intelligence [13], Open Systems [11] [12] and robot control [3] [2] [6] [10] [17] [5].

Robot systems are inherently distributed since multiple sensors and manipulators are physically on different processors. In previous approaches, the computer was taken as a central computation machine, while sensors and manipulators were considered as input-output peripherals. In a distributed model for robot systems, the processes of sensors and manipulators are designed to be independent of, but communicates with each other. In the sequential programming paradigm,

$$control = data\_structure + algorithm$$

while in the parallel and distributed programming paradigm,

$$control = process\_structure + communication\_protocol$$

In conventional control theory, **feedback** is the central theme; while in distributed systems, the **coordination** among multiple processes and the environment should be the general mechanism.

Open robot systems and the programming methodology

We call a robot system an *Open Robot System* if the robot can:

1) work in unstructured and unpredictable environments;

2) deal with incomplete and inconsistent information;

3) take complicated jobs and respond to real-time change.

We call this kind of robots *open systems* because they work in a *non-closed* world. As an open robot, it should be able to coordinate with other robots working in the same environment or communicate with human beings; it has incomplete knowledge about its environment but can get various information by its multiple effective sensors; it has no accurate dynamic model nor fine trajectory planner, but can chase moving objects, avoid unpredictable obstacles, and achieve its goal; it should also have the capability of protecting itself from being damaged. This kind of robots is extremely useful for space exploration, under sea application, and forest harvesting.

The problem of developing an open robot system is increasingly recognized as a critical area in Robotics. The solution will be challenging to the fundamental theory of Artificial Intelligence. While little work on representing such a robot system has been done, some interesting contributions have recently been made along this line:

On the theoretical side, Agre and Chapman [1] claimed that pure planning and reasoning are not suitable for dealing with inconsistent, uncertain and immediate situation, rather, *reaction* and moment-to-moment *improvisation* play a central role during most activity. Rosenschein [19] formalized this kind of idea by situated-automata, which analyses knowledge in terms of the relation between the states of a machine and states of its environment over time.

In task planning, Georgeff and Lansky [8] designed a system for reactive reasoning and planning, which considered the run-time change of the environment. Schopper [20] proposed a universal planning framework, which only encoded the goal state rather than both the initial and goal state in classical planning. Kealbling [15] developed a language, based on goal reduction rules, which did not generate plans but achieved the specified goals during execution.

Brooks [2] and his colleagues have done very interesting work on building sensor-based robots by a multi-layered control architecture — the *subsumption architecture*. Connell [4] described a behavior based arm controller which is run on a set of loosely coupled microprocessors. The overall behavior of the arm is totally reactive to its changing environment. Brooks et al. [3] explored the functions and structure of their second-generation robot which is capable of real-time three-dimensional vision, while simultaneously carrying out manipulator and navigation tasks. Similarly, Smithers and Malcolm [22] chose a behavioral approach to robot task planning and off-line programming and declared the importance of sensor-based robot system.

However, up to now, there is no general and suitable representation for Open Robot Systems. Few robot languages exist now can handle parallel and distributed problem solving, react to changing environment in real-time, and provide inherent motor sensor coordination. A new kind of robot programming style is needed for building this kind of robots.

Outline of this paper

In this paper, we present a novel representation scheme for multi-sensory robot control. **Section 12.2** discusses some issues on the approach of behavioral modeling; **Section 12.3** and **Section 12.4** deal with the robot programming on transputers using concurrent object oriented languages in general, FCP++ and C++ in particular, by illustrating the approach of building behavioral modules for high and lower levels of robot control respectively. And last, the mapping of processes or behavioral modules to physical transputer configurations is discussed in **Section 12.5**.

12.2 The approach of behavioral modeling

Unlike the previous approach, which decomposes the system into task-based subsystems — i.e. sensor, effector, knowledge base, reasoning and planning mechanism etc., we are focused on behavior-based decomposition — i.e. systems are composed of behaviors which are the integration of perception, cognition and action. Under this kind of decomposition, we can build incrementally complex behaviors and connect them in an appropriate way. This architecture is much clearer and easier than the approach that adds unrelated facts and rules to a single database and makes more and more complicated sensors and effectors.

General methodology for behavioral modeling

The overall system consists of two orthogonal hierarchies [9]. One hierarchy is behavioral specification. In robot systems, this could be multi-layered decomposition, based on *task achieving behaviors* [2]. The other hierarchy is implementational decomposition. For robot systems, this is a refining procedure by which the specified behaviors can be decomposed into processes in lower level behavioral modules, and last to the motor control.

1) System's decomposition of Behavioral Modules:

Behavioral Modules are logical or physical concurrent objects. From higher to lower levels, for instance, we can have **robot**, **base**, **arm**, **hand**, **joint**, etc. as the type of behavioral modules. The overall functions of these modules are exhibited by input-output patterns; the internal structures are transparent between different modules. The behavior of the **robot** could be implemented by lower level behaviors of **base**, **arm** and **hand**, the behavior of the **arm** could be further implemented by the behaviors of **joints**. The communication between different layers are all through message passing (Figure 12.1).

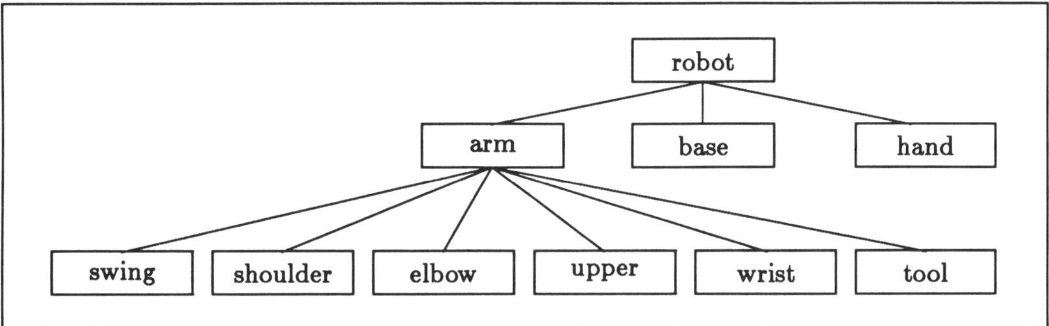

Figure 12.1: The implementational decomposition of the robot

2) Behavioral specification in Behavioral Modules:

Each behavioral module consists of a set of concurrent processes, including action, perception, and cognition. Basically, there are two kinds of processes. One is permanent process, which is created whenever the module is instantiated. The other one is dynamically generated temporal process, which is created for certain tasks and dies when the task finishes. On the other hand, there are two kinds of action and perception. One is active action or perception, which is task dependent. The other is reactive action or perception, which is task independent, but for primitive surviving or adapting mechanism. In general, dynamical process is corresponding to active action or perception; while permanent process is for reactive action or perception.

Behavioral specification describes the internal process structure, i.e., how various processes are communicated through the permanent or dynamical channels in order to achieve certain kind of input output behaviors.

General behavioral modeling under concurrent object oriented framework

Concurrent object-oriented programming provides both ***concurrency*** and ***modularity***. The pre-eminent concept in programming under this framework is:

Programming is a way of designing each individual process and module, and constructing processes into modules, and modules into systems. As a result, the robot programming language provides **process** *and* **module** *libraries instead of the internal* **function** *library.*

So far, concurrent object-oriented approach is the trend for programming of distributed and asynchronized systems [7]. It would be the general programming methodology for Behavioral Modeling.

12.3 Logical concurrent objects for high level behavioral module design

High level cognition models for multi-sensory robots

For a multi-sensory open robot system, the following characteristic should be embedded in the high level cognition model:

1) Concurrent multi-intelligent-agent architecture.

Concurrent multi-agent architecture provides a kind of organization with a large collection of computational services and interactions. On the other hand, each service is independent, without central coordination, trust, or complete knowledge of each other [14].

The result system based on this model is robust, easy to deal with uncertainty and local failures and be possible to accomplish tasks under inconsistent and incomplete situations.

2) Universal planning and decision making by parallel reduction rules.

Planning and plan executing is the wrong decomposition for real-time, reactive system. Reasoning and decision making using a complete theorem prover is also not suitable for inconsistent and incomplete situations.

Universal planning and decision making is a way of achieving goals with step-by-step improvement [20], i.e. if under condition C to achieve goal G, the appropriate response is action A, or the best decision is D. In general, this can be represented by guarded Horn clause:

```
G :- C|G1, G2,...Gn.
```

where Gi is a sub-goal, an action or a decision. "," represents "and" parallelism.

3) Communication by message passing paradigm with decentralized control.

An open robot is composed of multiple physically distributed services. A centralized control would become a serious bottleneck [11]. And it is difficult to maintain a global memory for overall communications.

The advantage of using message passing and decentralized control is to keep the locality. This ensures that each component can be kept relatively independent. The control law and communication interface would be simple and clear.

FCP++ for high level behavioral module design

FCP— Flat Concurrent Prolog is a logic programming language which replaces the backtracking search mechanism of Prolog with communicating concurrent processes [14]. It can represent incomplete messages, unification, direct broadcasting and concurrency synchronization, with the declarative semantics by a sound theorem prover [21]. It is a good candidate as the language for Open Systems [14].

FCP++, a concurrent logic object oriented language based on FCP was designed and implemented [24]. FCP++ inherits all the capabilities of concurrent logic programming techniques supported by FCP. Besides, it provides a new and powerful tool for building object-oriented systems:

1) class definition

2) function for making instance

3) function for halting instance

4) method definition

5) message passing by commands

6) message passing by data through channels

The syntax for these functions is in Appendix 1.

Suppose we design a robot working in a forest environment. The robot's job is to move logs from one place to another. We consider the different level of behaviors, corresponding process structures and communication protocols.

Suppose the robot is composed of an arm and a hand.

```
class(robot,[state, sensor, arm, hand]).
```

Where *arm* and *hand* are objects of **class arm** and **hand** respectively, *state* is the robot internal state, *sensor* is a computional service which is able to get the internal or external conditions of the robot.

In task level behavior, we ignore the path planning, or obstacle avoiding, rather, leave these to lower levels. We are interested in general task specification restricted to this level. We use a behavior chart instead of sequential task planning (Figure 12.2).

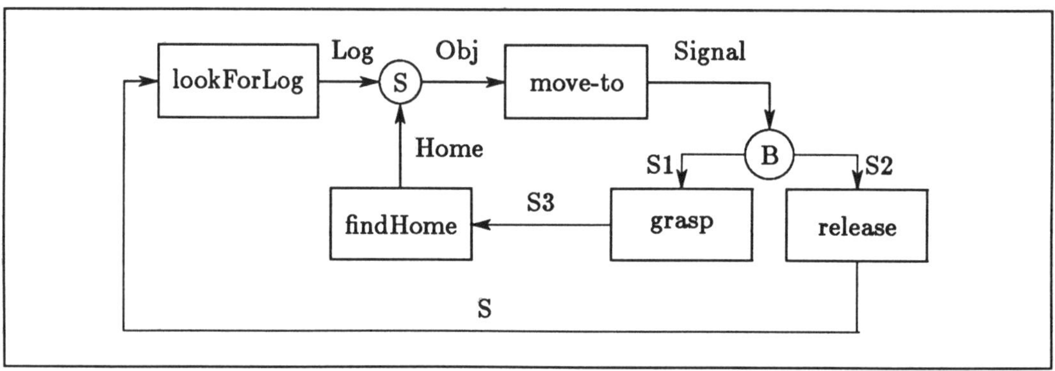

Figure 12.2: The behavior chart for moving logs

The corresponding program would be:

```
robot::init ->
            sensor:lookforLog(Log, [s|S?]),
            sensor:findHome(S3?, Home),
            suppress(Log?, Home?, Obj),
            arm:move_to(Obj?, Signal),
            branch(Signal?, S1, S2),
            hand:grasp(Log?,S1?, S3),
            hand:release(Log?,S2?, S).
```

Even in task level, using sensor to obtain the accurate positions is not appropriate. Sensors are used to give the continuous information, which guides the manipulators step by step to achieve the goals.

For example,

```
arm::move_to([Object|Obj], Signal) ->
            sensor:trace(Object, POS),
            arm:move_by(POS?, Signal).
```

Where **sensor:trace** is a process which iteratively sets the position points to drive the servo to the **Object**. **arm:move_by** acts on the servo until the relative position is zero.

The design on FCP++ for robot control is still on early stage. However, the power of this representation is very impressive. In the long run, we will use FCP++ or other similar language, for example, STRAND [23] as the major programming language for the transputer-based robot control.

12.4 Parallel C++ on transputers for low level behavioral module design

Parallel C on transputers provides the function of defining and executing processes, channels for message passing and PV operations for shared memory approach. C++ provides the facility of defining classes, its corresponding methods and initiating or destroying objects. We combine Parallel C and C++ by first preprocessing Parallel C++ code and translating it into Parallel C, then using C Compiler [16] and loading the code on the transputers.

We implement every behavior module as an object of C++, which consists of the internal states and a set of public operations. The communication between the different modules is by explicit channels or a limited amount of shared memory. In the later case, we should make sure that these modules must be mapped to the same transputers. Each perception or action is a process, which is pre-defined, but dynamically created in any functions. In particular, we can create all sets of processes in the initialization function of the module, so that whenever a module is initialized, it's processes and communication channels are established.

In the environment of forest, the task doesn't need high speed, high accuracy in trajectory and position. However, the robot should be able to deal with unpredictable changes in unstructured environment, for example to avoid moving objects, especially human beings, to grasp and move unknown weight loads. The suitable control for this kind of application requires:

1) Reactive

2) Adaptive

3) Fault tolerant.

In the current stage, we leave the robot controller as it is, by only considering the control on the kinematics level — pseudo-control.

We use Functional Joint Control [18] on joint level for the arm's kinematics. This method is iterative in nature and highly parallel. It is successful for functionally decomposable arms [18].

The program is written for a six-link PUMA-like robot. We define each joint as a class, from the base to the hand, SWING, SHOULDER, ELBOW, UPPER, WRISTFLEX, and TOOLS.

Each joint has two permanent processes. One process is always updating the current state of the joint. The other one always checks the difference between the current joint angle and the goal joint angle, and sends out the relative movement of the joint. The current and goal Cartesian positions are shared by six joints, which is updated by lower level position sensors and higher level arm's command respectively.

The module structure and process structure are shown in Figure 12.3.

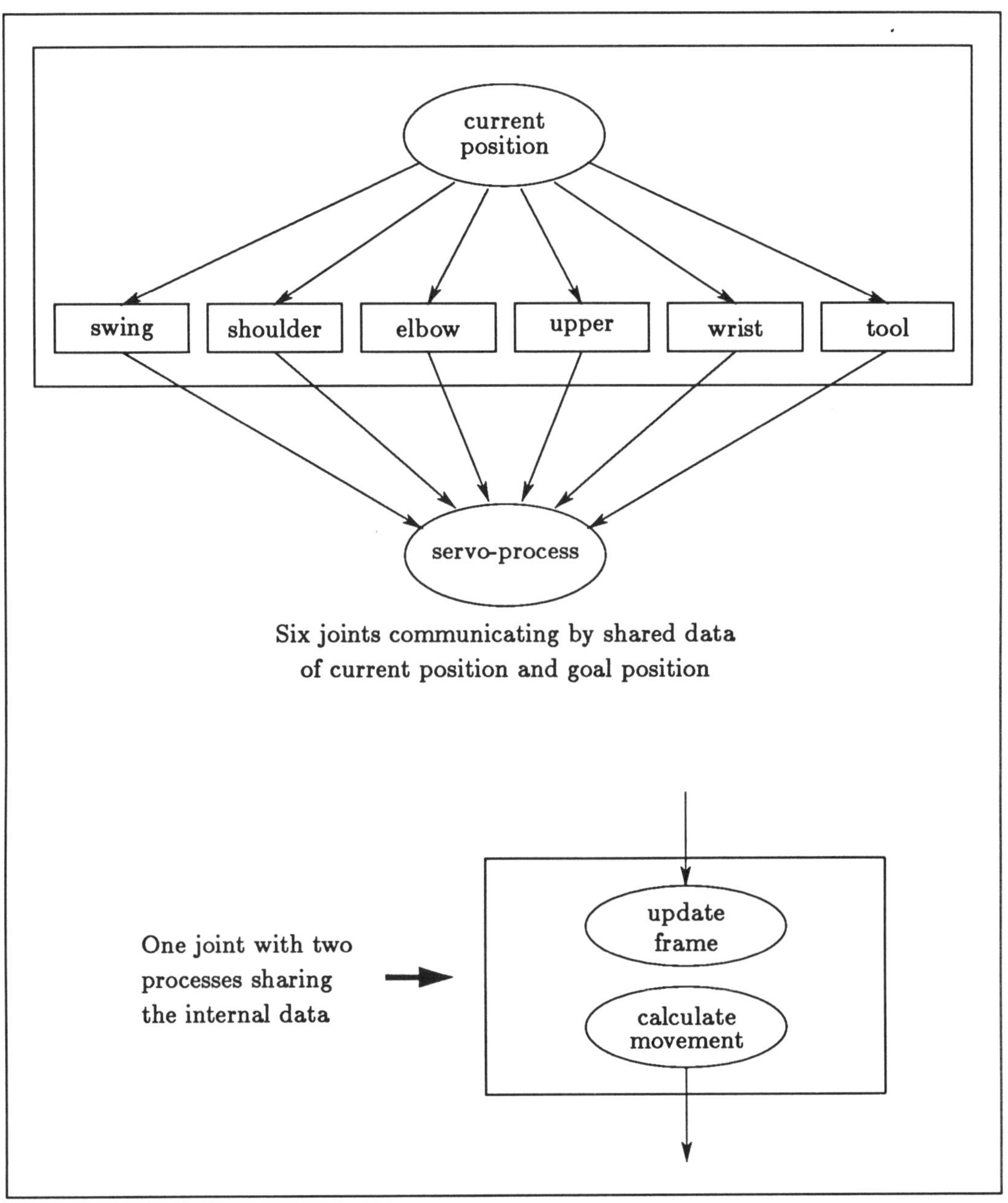

Figure 12.3: The module and process structure of six joints

In the main program of the transputer, we initialize these six joints and their corresponding channels.

```
main()
{     Process *p1,*p2,*p3;
      Channel *in[6], *out[6];
      Channel *armIn, *armOut, *servoIn, *servoOut;
      ...

/*    initialize soft channels                          */
      for(i=0;i<6;i++) {
         in[i] = ChanAlloc();
         out[i] = ChanAlloc();
      }

/*    initialize hard channels                          */
      armIn = LINK0IN;
      armOut = LINK0OUT;
      servoIn = LINK1IN;
      servoOut = LINK1OUT;

/*    generate the processes to send out the joint */
/*    movement, set goal positions, and update the */
/*    current positions                                 */
      p1 = ProcAlloc(servo_process, 1000, 2, out, servoOut);
      p2 = ProcAlloc(set_goal_process, 1000, 1, armIn);
      p3 = ProcAlloc(current_position, 1000, 3, servoIn, in armOut);
      ProcRun(p1); ProcRun(p2); ProcRun(p3);

/*    initialize the six joint modules                  */
      SWING           swing(in[0], out[0]);
      SHOULDER        shoulder(in[1], out[1]);
      ELBOW           elbow(in[2], out[2]);
      UPPER           upper(in[3], out[3]);
      WRISTFLEX       wrist(in[4], out[4]);
      TOOLS           tool(in[5], out[5]);
      ...
}
```

12.5 Mapping of processes to processors

We take mapping as the last stage of behavioral module design. There is no general approach of mapping modules and processes into transputers. It is an *ad hoc* problem, since we should consider not only the software configuration, but also the hardware configuration.

However, there are some restrictions on this particular domain:

1) Modules which have the shared memory communication have to be mapped into one transputer.

2) One module and its corresponding processes should be mapped into one transputer.

3) Modules which share the communication channels would be better to be mapped into transputers which have direct hardware links.

The hardware connection of our robot to the transputers is through one transputer link, i.e. one link of the transputer is directly connected to RS232 board. Based on the efficiency of communication, we map all the modules to transputers as Figure 12.4.

There are two pre-eminent problems in multi-transputer control scheme:

1) Communication between processes in different transputers. We solve this problem by serializing the data and using the appropriate protocols. We also implemented the "fair" merge functions for this problem.

2) Coordination between different operations and processes. Because of the delay of message passing and certain amount of time for one robot command, we should figure out the waiting time between different operations, so that no operation would be "over" executed. This problem could be solved only by doing experiments on real robots. Good design is also important though.

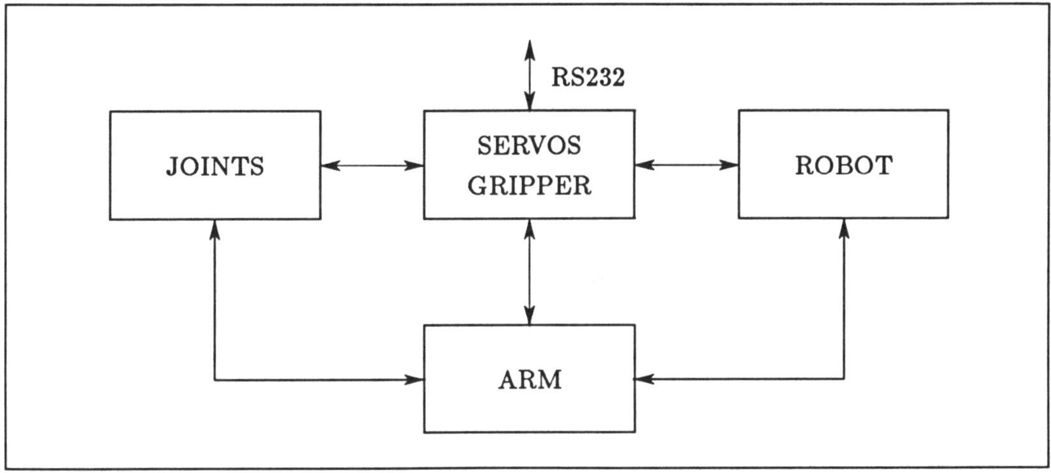

Figure 12.4: Mapping processes to processors

12.6 Conclusion

We have proposed here an approach of designing behavioral modules for robot control with concurrent objects, and implemented part of this system on transputers. This approach has the advantage of modularity and flexibility with the powerful representation over the previous approaches. The current state of our research is focused on both high and low levels. We will combine them later, when we get a suitable environment of Concurrent Prolog or Parallel Prolog on transputers.

Acknowledgment

Many people have made contributions to this paper. First, I would like to thank Prof. Alan Mackworth for his kind guidance and support, Prof. Peter Lawrence for various discussions and comments on this paper. I also got lots of help from the transputer groups in Computer Science and Electrical Engineering Department at UBC. Jim Little, Runping Qi and Felix Jaggi carefully read the paper, and made valuable suggestions from the content to the organization of the paper. Last but not least, I would like to give my thanks to all the referees for their constructive criticism and comments on the early version of the paper.

12.7 References

[1] Philip E. Agre and David Chapman, Pengi: An Implementation of a Theory of Activity, In *IJCAI-87*, pages 268–272, 1987.

[2] Rodney A. Brooks. A Robust Layered Control System For a Mobile Robot. *IEEE Journal of Robotics and Automation*, (1), March 1986.

[3] Rodney A. Brooks and Jonathan H. Connell and Peter Ning. *HERBERT: A SECOND GENERATION MOBILE ROBOT*. Technical Report 1016, AI Lab, MIT, January 1988.

[4] Jonathan H. Connell. A Behavior-Based Arm Controller. draft.

[5] James L. Crowley, Coordination of Action and Perception in a Surveillance Robot, *IEEE Expert*, Winter 1987.

[6] Alberto Elfes and Sarosh N. Talukdar, A Distributed Control System for the CMU Rover, In *IJCAI 83*, 1983.

[7] Geoffrey Fox, Theory and Practice of Concurrent Systems, In *Proceedings of the International Conference on Fifth Generation Computer Systems*, 1988.

[8] Michael P. Georgeff and Amy L. Lansky. Reactive reasoning and planning. In *AAAI-87*, pages 677–682, 1987.

[9] D. Harel and A. Pnueli, On the Development of Reactive System, In K.R. Apt, editor, *Logics and Models of Concurrent Systems*, Springer-Verlag Belin Heidelberg, 1985.

[10] Tom Henderson and Chuck Hansen and Bir Bhanu, A Framework for Distributed Sensing and Control, In *IJCAI 85*, 1985.

[11] Carl Hewitt. Offices Are Open Systems. In B. A. Huberman, editor, *The Ecology of Computation*, pages 5–23, Elsevier Science Publishers B.V.(North-Holland), 1988.

[12] B. A. Huberman, The Ecology of Computation. In B. A. Huberman, editor, *The Ecology of Computation*, pages 1–4, Elsevier Science Publishers B.V.(North-Holland), 1988.

[13] Michael N. Huhns, editor. *Distributed Artificial Intelligence. Research Notes in Artificial Intelligence*, 1987.

[14] Kenneth M. Kahn and Mark S. Miller. Language Design and Open Systems. In B. A. Huberman, editor, *The Ecology of Computation*, Elsevier Science Publishers B.V.(North-Holland), 1988.

[15] Leslie Pack Kealbling. Goal as Parallel Program Specifications. In *AAAI-88*, 1988

[16] Jeffrey Mock. Process, Channels and Semaphores (Version 2). 1988. Manual for Parallel C from Logical System.

[17] Richard P. Paul and Hugh F. Durrant-Whyte and Max Mintz, A Robust, Distributed Sensor and Actuation Robot Control System, In *Robotics Research 3*.

[18] Joseph Kin-Shing Poon, *Kinematic Control of Robots with Multiprocessors*, Technical Report, 1988. Ph.D. thesis.

[19] Stanley J. Rosenschein. Formal Theories of Knowledge in AI and Robotics. *New Generation Computing 3*, 345–357, 1985.

[20] M. J. Schoppers. Universal Plans for Reactive Robots in Unpredictable Environments. In *IJCAI-87*, pages 1039–1046, 1987.

[21] Ehud Shapiro, editor. *Concurrent Prolog*. MIT press, 1987.

[22] T. Smithers and C. Malcolm. *A BEHAVIOURAL APPROACH TO ROBOT TASK PLANNING AND OFF-LINE PROGRAMMING*. technical Report 306, DAI, University of Edinburgh, June 1987.

[23] Susan Watts. Parallel thinking takes on the human genome. *New Scientist*, November, 1988

[24] Y. Zhang, FCP++ — A Concurrent Logic Object Oriented Language based on FCP. 1988. Project Report.

12.8 Syntax for FCP++

Following is the syntax for FCP++, which would be translated into FCP by a preprocessor written in Quintus Prolog.

Italics is used to indicate a part of a template which users are to fill in. Completely upper case italic items are to be filled in with variables, lower case with constants, and identifiers starting with a capital letter followed by some lower case letters with any kind of term.

class definition

class(name,[*var1,var2,...,varn*])

function for making instance

className:make([*Value1, Value2,..., Valuen*], *INSTANCE*<:>**state**(*Id*))

function for halting instance

className:halt([*Value1, Value2,..., Valuen*])

className:halt([*Value1, Value2,..., Valuen*])− > *Body*

method definition

className::*MessagePattern*

className::*MessagePattern*− >*Body*

message passing through instance

INSTANCE:*MessagePattern*

message passing through communication channel

var:>*Message*

var<:*Message*

getting object identifier

INSTANCE<:>*ID*

Chapter 13

PUSSYCAT : a parallel simulation system for cellular automata on transputers

Eddy Pauwels
University of Brussels
Pleinlaan 2
B-1050 Brussels
tel : +32-2-6412968
e-mail : epauwels@info.vub.ac.be

Abstract Initially, cellular automata were introduced to model complex dynamical aspects of physical systems. This approach was much simpler than modelling these systems by means of differential equations, as these equations are in general hard to solve. This paper introduces an environment for the simulation of cellular automata on a transputer network.

The environment consists of three parts:

- *user interface* : The user interface presents routines for the creation of the rules and initial states of the automata.
- *graphical interface* : This interface collects all the information from the workers and displays them on a graphical monitor.
- *workers farm* : This part simulates the automata and reports the output to the graphical interface. In the current implementation 40 workers are interconnected in a torus.

The original cellular automaton model has been extended in a number of ways, so that a wider range of applications can be investigated. A first extension is the introduction of multiple levels, which means that the user is able to create a stream of interdependent cellular automata. In multi-level mode, the output of one automaton determines the rules that will be used in the automaton below it. Using the graphical interface, it is possible to inspect both the data-level automaton and one of the rule-level automata. A second extension makes it possible for cells to communicate with neighbours, other than the adjacent cells. This facility is useful when examining reaction-diffusion and collision system models. A third extension enables the user to use and display earlier states of a cell, which is very important for the creation of reversible rules. A fourth a nd final extension multiplies the number of states one particular cell can take. Instead of two, it is possible to give a cell 256 different states. This extension together with the first one implies that a cell can have up to 256 different rules associated with it.

13.1 Introduction

Ever since computers became available, computer scientists have tried to improve these machines, so they would be faster and more user-friendly, and so they could be used in a larger variety of applications. There is one kind of application where the need for a faster computer has been especially great, namely parallel processes. Until recently, the only way parallel applications could be investigated was by working in time sharing on a sequential computer. One of the most recent successes in the research for new hardware are the parallel computers.

Research domains where a lot of inherently parallel processes are encountered are physics and biology. In these fields, cells interact with each other. Scientists have tried to come up with models to analyse these interactions. One of these models has been given the name of *cellular automaton.*

This paper introduces an environment on a transputer network for the development of cellular automata. But before looking at the implementation, it is necessary to give a brief description of these automata.

13.1.1 What are cellular automata?

Cellular automata are dynamical systems[1] with a simple microscopic construction, but very complex macroscopic behavior.

[1] A dynamical system is a system that evolves in time. Because a lot of computation has to be done at every step, a discrete timescale is introduced.

They are mathematical models which can be used to model natural systems. For example, figure 13.1 shows a cellular automaton which is used to simulate the behavior of fluid dynamics.

A cellular automaton consists of a large number of simple, identical cells with local interaction. Local interaction means that every cell can communicate with neighbouring cells by exchanging information like, for instance, their current state. Each cell has a finite set of possible values (these values are usually represented as 'dead' or 'alive', but sometimes more than two values are used). The value of one particular cell can be determined by the previous values of its neighbours and its own previous value. The rule which calculates the next value or state of a cell is the same for every cell in the grid.

13.1.2 Why are these automata so important?

In the very beginning, cellular automata were used to model dynamical aspects of physical systems, by implementing rules which simulate the microscopic behavior of the cells involved. This approach was much simpler than modelling these aspects by means of macroscopic differential equations, as these equations are hard to solve. When we look at present-day applications of cellular automata, we see that they are all used to model a physical dynamical system, like the one in figure 13.1.

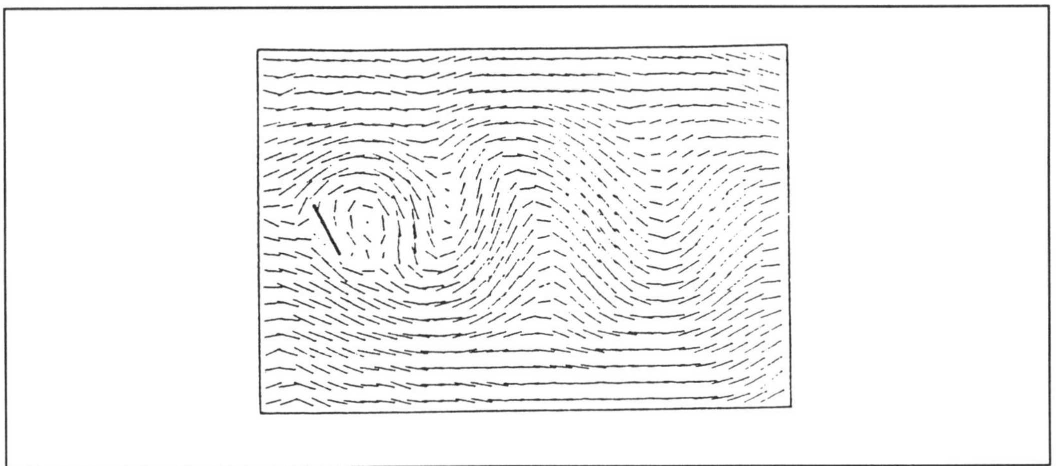

Figure 13.1: Picture of fluid dynamic simulation

Because of the wide range of possibilities of modelling complex behavior with simple rules, AI researchers have become more and more interested in these automata.

13.1.3 Why an environment?

During the development process of a cellular automaton, every time a possible rule is deduced, a program has to be made[2], and inserted into a larger (master) program.

After that, the program has to be re-compiled. Only when all these actions have been performed, the program can be run to observe its behavior. This whole process is very time-consuming. If we could design an environment that could take over a lot of this work, much time would be saved for research on rules and models. This is the task that we have tried to fulfill in this project. When the researcher has constructed his rule, he can pass it to the environment, and the environment does the rest automatically. A special language for the construction of rules has been developed. As a result of this, the developer can now work independently from the programming language the environment is written in[3].

13.1.4 Choice of the hardware environment

To choose an optimal hardware environment (in the range of all environments that are available in our laboratory) we have to look at the problem more closely.

There is one thing that has to be done for every cell, but there can be a vast amount of cells working together. When a sequential computer is used to perform this task, you have to wait a long time for an output, since such a computer has to perform the rule for each cell in the grid, one after the other. When a grid is taken with, say, 500 as the length of the grid, and 200 as the width, this means that the same rule must be evaluated 100000 times. So, sequential computers do not offer an optimal environment for the task.

A second argument against a sequential computer can be derived from the environment we want to create. Since the environment we are developing can be seen as an interpreter of rules, we have to consider the loss of performance of this strategy compared to the compilation of a program which simulates the same rule. Because the rules have to be interpreted for each cell, the decrease of speed on a sequential computer will be unacceptable.

The only alternative left is a parallel computer[4]. The advantage of working on such an architecture, is that you can perform a number of operations simultaniously. The most suitable computer one can think of for this task is certainly the connection machine. Unfortunately, these machines are not widely available yet, because they are too expensive

[2]this is not necessarily so if the program is written in a non-imperative language, like LISP for instance.

[3]this is not entirely true in the current implementation, but this is caused by the fact that arrays cannot be dynamically allocated in the OCCAM language.

[4]or the design of a special hardware like in CAM for instance, but this alternative is too expensive.

in maintenance, so we have to look for a better compromise between price and performance.

At the AI laboratory of the University of Brussels, one of the parallel architectures available at present, is a transputer network from INMOS. The network contains forty transputers, a graphical board, and a root transputer called "front-end transputer". Each transputer can have up to four links by which it can communicate with other transputers. The front - end transputer is connected to an IBM-AT personal host computer. You can choose the connections between the transputers by shifting the leads[5].

13.1.5 Extensions to the original concept

Before presenting the reader with the environment and its implementation, we will first describe the extensions we made to the original cellular automata model.

Additional levels

Usually each cell in a cellular automaton evolves according to one rule, as shown in figure 13.2. The extension we made in the environment is that instead of taking one rule for each cell, each cell gets its rule from a cellular automaton one level higher (see figure 13.3). In Complex Systems[6] a similar extension up to two levels is presented. The advantage of our extension is that more research can be done, because a wider scope of possible experiments become available.

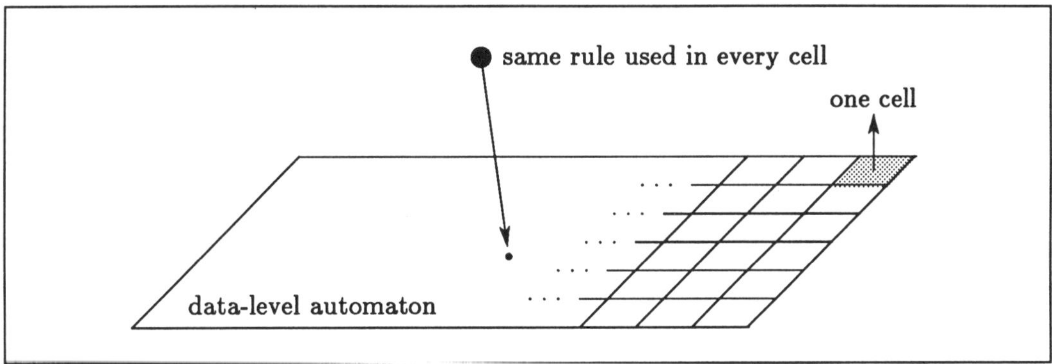

Figure 13.2: Updating cells in accordance to one rule

[5]though the choice is restricted.

[6]Complex Systems. Volumel Number 2, April 1987 p. 245-256

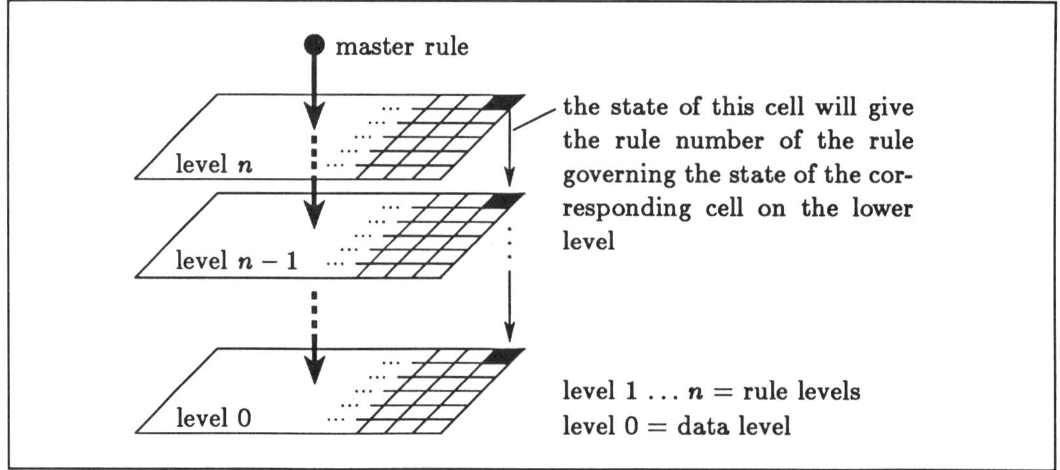

Figure 13.3: "More than one level" cellular automaton

Introducing a history

In the typical cellular automaton model, the parameters of the updating rule are the current lives of the neighbours of a cell. What we have introduced is that each cell holds a history of itself, so an additional dimension for parameters is created (see figure 13.4). Another advantage of this is that the evolution of the lives of one cell can be observed longitudinally. CAM, a cellular automata machine described in Physica D[7], includes a similar, but more restricted mechanism. For instance, cells can only be 'on' or 'off' and the history is limited to eight lives. None of these restrictions are present in the environment we devised. Restrictions only make it more difficult for the developer to do what he wants to do, so an attempt has been made to avoid as much restrictions as possible. This will have its consequences for the performance of the system as a whole, but flexibility is also important for a good environment. The current implementation is a good trade-off between all relevant parameters, namely performance, system restrictions, and flexibility.

Number of states

In our system, each cell can have up to 256 different states. The advantage of this extension is that once more we have added an extra dimension.

To illustrate this we will give an example. Suppose we want to represent the path-

[7]You can also get information about CAM in Cellular Automata Machines written by Tommaso Toffoli and Norman Margolus. [Toffoli 1987]

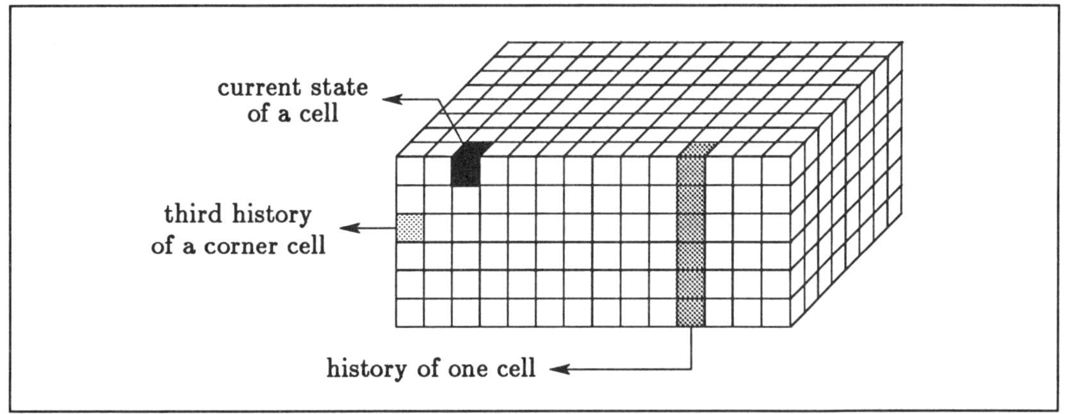

Figure 13.4: A grid in which every cell holds a history of itself

finding problem[8]. The obstacles are represented as black squares, they can't move. An open space cell is represented as white squares. The movable block is represented as a gray one. This examples illustrates that a lot of information can be asserted by giving the entities of the system different values (or colors in case of the example)

Extension of the rules

Possible extensions of the original rules in cellular automata have already been suggested. We described the extension of letting rules take states of a cell, other than the current state, as a parameter.

Another extension we made to the environment is the possibility to communicate information further than to the nearest neighbours (see also figure 13.5. The parameter which determines how wide two cells may be separated, can be set by the user.

In the extension proposed here we are not really true to our principle that restrictions should be avoided, because we introduce one ourselves. It is not possible to reach every cell from one particular one. The marked cells in figure 13.5 will make this clear. One of the modifications we will make to the current environment will probably be to eliminate this limitation, if users find it necessary to do so.

In the next section we will introduce the environment and its global implementation. We show how the program is mapped on the transputer network, and what the responsibilities are of each of the subprograms. We finally give some small experiments we

[8]A block has to be moved from one place to another through a space containing obstacles. The problem is to find the shortest way to do this.

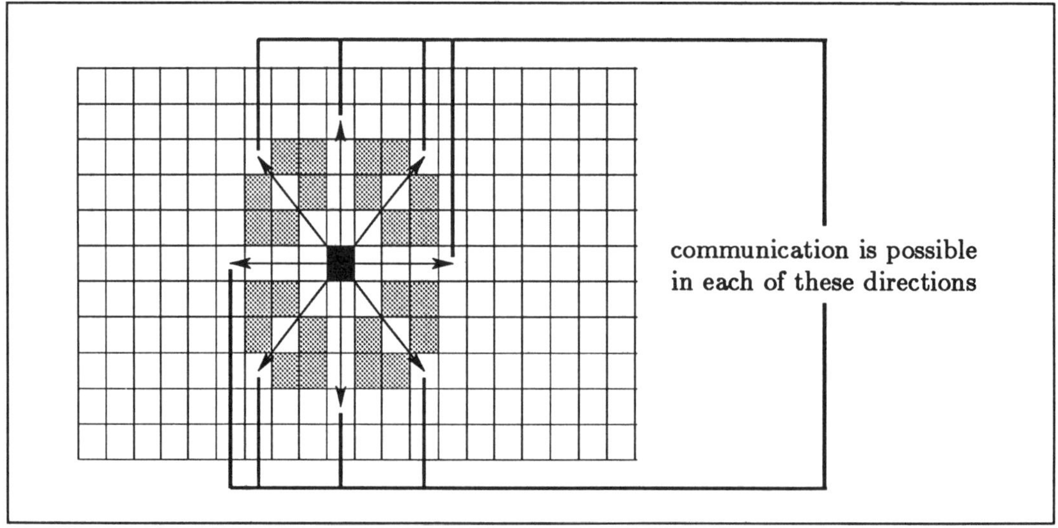

Figure 13.5: Extension of the locality of rule parameters

implemented using the environment.

13.2 Global implementation

13.2.1 Mapping on the network

The global mapping of all processes is illustrated in figure 13.6. The ***user interface*** is placed on the front-end transputer, because of its connection to the IBM host computer. The user interface program serves as a communication intermediary between user, screen, keyboard, and the graphic transputer.

The graphic transputer is the one connected to the front-end transputer. This is a transputer containing a graphic card and additional memory. This unit is connected to the monitor where output will be shown. The program that runs on this processor is called the *graphical interface*. This program contains all the procedures for screen composition as well as procedures for collecting information[9] from the rest of the network. The names of the channels that connect the transputers are indicated beside the lines.

All the other transputers (40 units in the configuration used at our AI laboratory) are connected in the form of a torus. The left and right top-row transputers however,

[9]Each piece of information is a screen block from a particular transputer in the network containing the output of its part of the grid.

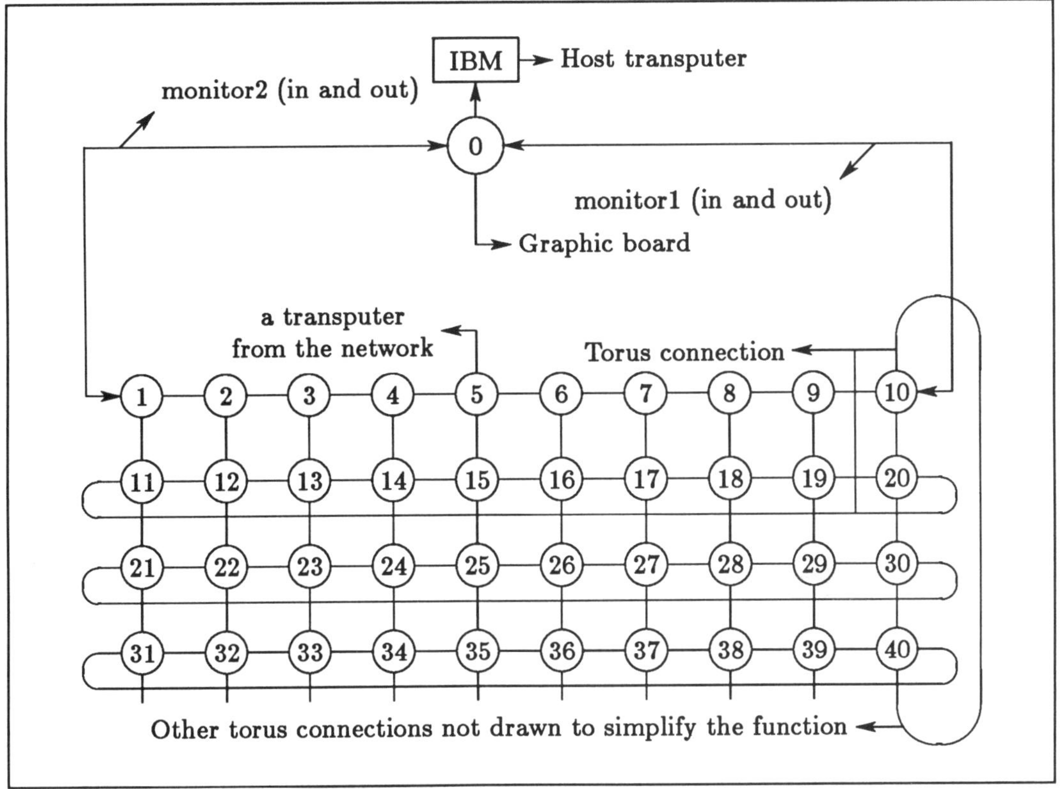

Figure 13.6: Mapping of the interface on the network

are connected to the graphical unit, to allow output. This discontinuity in the torus necessitates an extension to the actions performed by the graphic transputer. When you want to leave the option of taking the automaton grid as a torus (which is one of the options), the graphical interface must be capable of exchanging information between the left edge of the left top-row-transputer and the rightedge of the right top-row transputer.

The channels between the transputers in the network are called :

left.to.right	top.to.bottom
right.to.left	bottom.to.top

The process running on each of the forty transputers is called process and simulates a part of the grid of the cellular automaton.

In the presentation hereafter we expand upon all of the processes involved in the system and their global structure.

13.2.2 The user interface

This program serves as an intermediary between the user and the main program, placed on the graphic transputer. This means that the program gets its instructions from the main program, performs the necessary communication actions and, after that, returns the collected information to the main program. The structure of the user interface program is one large IF- statement similar to a large CASE- statement in PASCAL.

The possible commands that it must be able to execute are :

- asking the user whether the initial configuration of a certain level should be random or not.
- if the answer to the previous question is negative, the main program composes a user-directed initial configuration. It sends a command to the user interface to run a section in which the user can choose from a number of actions, in order to create an initial state.
- asking the user what other level, beside the data-level, should be sent to the screen.
- assisting the user in creating the rules for each level and sending a coded version of them to the main unit.

At present, a special purpose text editor is being designed for helping the user creating rules. In addition, a filing mechanism is under development, to make it possible to store patterns and rules on disk for later use.

13.2.3 The graphical interface

This part of the program contains three parallel programs. One program is concerned with the regulation of information flow between the left and right top-transputers[10], and also with collecting screen information from all transputers.

When all this information has been received, the process relays its information to another program called *show.vision.buffer*, which transforms the input it receives and hands the result on to the third program, which is an interface between transputer and monitor. This third program contains all the graphical routines.

What kind of transformation does the show.vision.buffer perform? To answer this question, we first have to give some more details about the program.

[10]This is needed when the torus option is on, as mentioned earlier.

Details about the program concerning screen composition

The total number of pixels on the monitor restricts the size of the automatongrid to 500×200[11]. This implies that a lot of space would be lost if the automaton grid were only a 100×100 one, because a two-dimensional array is needed to represent the monitor. What the program automatically tries is to enlarge the pixels of the grid so that the grid fits as neatly as possible into the display area. In the example of the 100×100 grid, a pixel would be transformed into a 5×2 pixel. In this way, the pixels are easier to see and therefore the automaton can easilier be analysed. Every time an automaton sends its state-of-life to the screen, the grids that are sent from each transputer, have to be enlarged[12].

Enlargement in length The enlargement in length is done by a process in each transputer because this is very time-consuming (see figure 13.7). This is because you have to copy each pixel a number of times, and an ordinary loop in OCCAM is rather slow[13] By dividing the process in a way that lets each transputer do a part of the transformation work, performance can be improved. In this way, the grids that are transported from one transputer to another over physical links, are larger than before. Normally one would expect that, as physical links are involved here, the process would be slowed down considerably. Fortunately however, this is not the case. The communication over links is so fast[14], that the few more bytes that have to be transported, hardly have any effect on the global speed of the system.

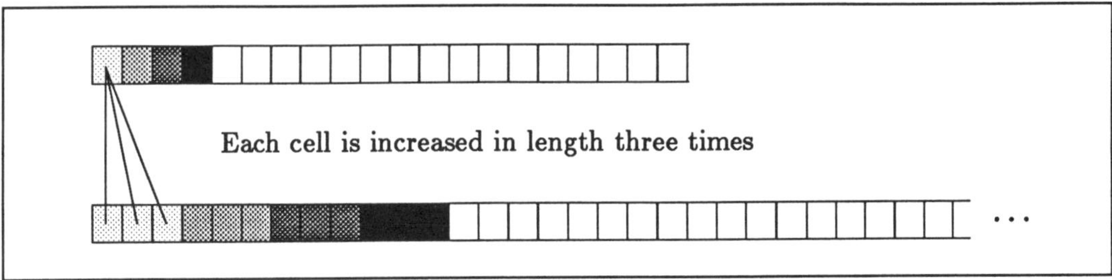

Figure 13.7: Enlargement of an array in length

[11]In fact, our monitor has a 512×512 grid. So, there is room for two such grids, but both are in use. The first one serves for the data-level automaton output, the other for the rule-level one.

[12]5 times in length and twice in width in the example of the 100×100 grid.

[13]By eliminating a loop, I once managed to speed up my program 5 times!

[14]this can reach up to 20 Megabit/sec

Enlargement in width What show.vision.buffer does is quite simple. It takes each row from every grid, copies it a number of times[15], and puts it into the final, totally composed grid, as illustrated in figure 13.8. It is important to note that this process copies rows[16]. This is implemented in OCCAM as a block move and therefore much faster than pixel copying. Since we have increased the information in length in each transputer, the length of one row is the original length multiplied by the horizontal enlargement. This is another reason why we decided to increase the length somewhere else. Now, we can copy larger rows in one block move (see also figure 13.8).

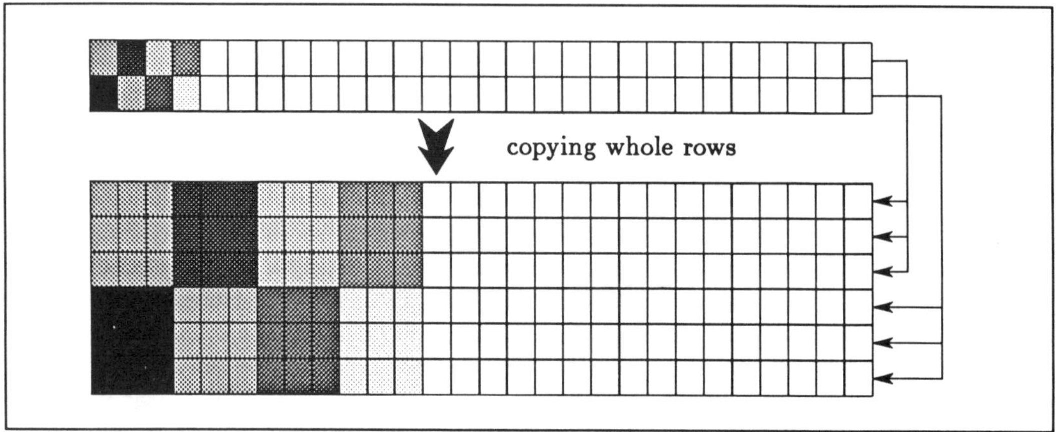

Figure 13.8: Expansion in width of the grid

Since this proces is responsible for most of the speed problem, it was important to think carefully about how to implement this in an efficient way.

13.2.4 The automaton generator

This is the most interesting part of the interface. Each transputer in the network contains such a program. It simulates a part of the automaton. Figure 13.9 represents the global structure of the program.

Tasks

Three different tasks must be accomplished. The automaton on each level has to be simulated. This is done for each level in a procedure called automat.generator. To be able

[15]twice in the example given earlier.

[16]instead of pixels, as done in each transputer

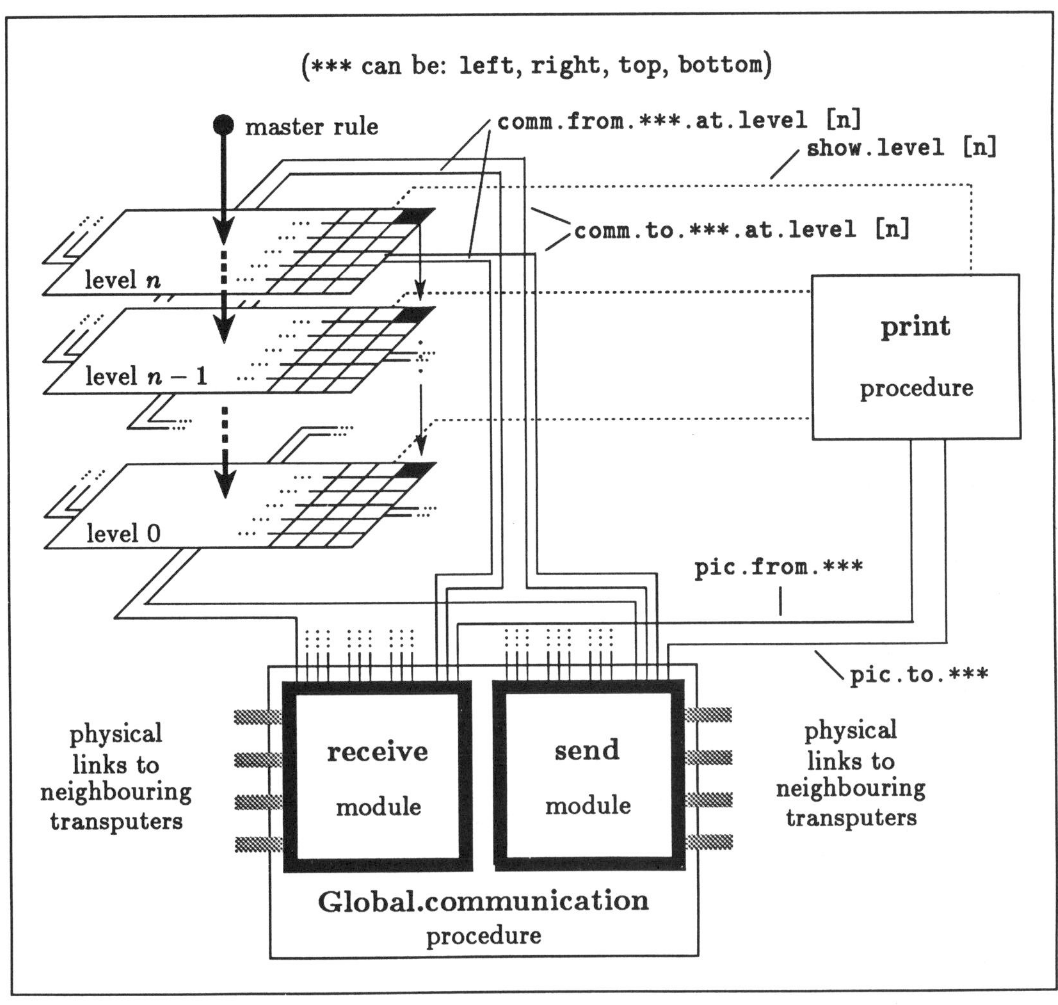

Figure 13.9: Global structure of generator process

to do the simulation, the procedure needs to know what the content of the edges of neighbouring transputers is. For this it uses a parallel procedure called *global.communication* which is responsible for every kind of communication between transputers. This process is also responsible for synchronising the transputers. When the next life of the automaton is generated, the automaton generator process sends its information to the screen. To accomplish this, it uses the third parallel procedure, called *print*. As already mentioned in 3, the aim of *print* is to expand the length of the grid if need be, and transport it to the right-hand neighbour. *Print* is also responsible for transporting the screen information received from its bottom neighbour, but this functionality be elaborated in the presentation.

Possible extension

In the current implementation there is a master rule (this is also represented in figure 13.9 as a dot), above level n. This means that the same rule is used in each cell at the top level. A possible extension to this would be to connect the data-level to the top-rule-level. In this way, a circle would be created, in which the output of one level indirectly influences itself. This extension is very easy to implement and may be interesting to examine. The connection is indicated by the dotted line in figure 13.9.

13.3 Experiments

Using the environment described in this paper, we have made some experiments to illustrate the use and the power of the system. One of the classical examples in the world of cellular automata is the Game Of Life. We have implemented this example using a history of three lives. Pictures of the simulation will be shown in the presentation.

In a second experiment we simulated the construction of ice cristals. The master rule in this example is a random generator that generates a direction to move a particle in. Every cell in the grid can take up to eight different states[17]. The generation of the next visual state of the process needs two simulation cycles. In cycle one, the particles are pushed in a random direction. In cycle two, they actually move to a new cell[18]. A cell will generate an ice particle (when a particle moves into it), whenever one of the neighbouring cells of that cell contains an ice particle.

The simulation starts with three ice particles in a medium of water. During the evolution the cristal patterns become visible. Also from this experiment some pictures will be shown.

13.4 References

- Tomasso, Toffoli and Norman, Margolus: Cellular automata machines. MIT press : 1987.

- Rumelhart, D. and McClelland: Parallel distributed processing. Volume 1: Foundations Bradford books: 1986.

- Minsky, M.: The society of mind. Simon and Schuster: 1985.

[17]Four states (one for each direction) to represent that a particle is being pushed in a certain direction. Two states to know whether there is or isn't a particle in a cell. One additional state to represent that the cell contains a particle not being pushed yet. One state representing a cell that contains an ice particle.

[18]only when there are no collisions between particles. If collision occurs, only one particle moves.

- Physica D. in: Cellular automata. Volume 10D nr. 1-2. North-Holland Amsterdam: 1984.

- Complex Dynamics: Volume 1 number 2. April 1987: p. 245-256.

- Complex Dynamics: Volume 1 number 5. October 1987: p. 967-993.

- Steels, Luc: Steps toward common sense. AI-memo nr. 88-3: 1988.

- Steels, Luc: Artificial intelligence and complex dynamics. AI-memo nr. 88-2: 1988.

Chapter 14

Self-organizing systems and their transputer implementation

D.A. Linkens and S.B. Hasnain
Department Of Control Engineering,
University Of Sheffield

Abstract In this paper three AI-related self-organizing structures are considered, these being relevant to the areas of system identification and control, and pattern recognition. Self-organizing systems tend to be complex and computing intensive, and hence should be candidates for possible transputer parallelism implementation. The Group Method Of Data Handling (GMDH) technique is a multi-layer self-organizing algorithm based on a non-linear mathematical model of data. Although known for some time, its use has been limited because of very heavy computing power required for realisation. It is, however, ideally suited to parallelism, and has been successfully coded in Occam and tested as a diagnostic tool on medical data. A comparison between the GMDH and a multi-layer perceptron neural network applied to this data will be presented. The second structure described is the self-organizing controller (SOC) due to Barron. Again, this is a complex system and has been coded in Occam. The resulting SOC system had been applied to a medical application involving anaesthesia, and is currently being evaluated for aircraft flight control. The third structure is fuzzy logic control. To perform this work, linking an alien language to Occam was necessary. The knowledge base for the rules are best coded in an AI language such as Lisp. The available Lisp was written in C language and operates in an interpretive mode. Parallel C was used to compile the C code and then linked to the Occam program having the final control algorithm and also the process simulation. Results are presented for the case of fuzzy control of muscle relaxation.

14.1 Introduction

In systems engineering there has been much interest in recent years in the concepts of self-adaption and self-tuning. Many practical applications of self-adaptive control have been investigated covering disciplines as wide apart as industrial processes, aerospace and biomedicine. The emphasis has been mainly on strongly algorithmic approaches to given limited structures with well defined, and usually linear, models.

The work described in this paper follows an alternative approach which considers the possibility of systems which have a self-organizing capability. Such systems do not have a rigidly fixed structure chosen a priori, but rather allow for on-line modifications to structures as well as to parameters. A further feature is that the self-organizing concepts may include heuristics for decision making, and hence mixed arithmetic and symbolic computational aspects must be considered. Clearly, this means that such techniques are closely related to AI principles and developments. In fact, the GMDH technique described in section 14.2 has structural similarities with neural networks and comparative studies are being undertaken using both approaches.

Not surprisingly, all of the three self-organizing methods described in the following sections are computationally very intensive. Thus, transputer power and parallelism is an attractive proposition for such systems, which require fast processing if they are to be used for on-line control purposes. The methods are very different in style, with the GMDH being heavily algorithmic and intended for the production of a detailed mathematical model of a process. In contrast, the other two methods are intended to provide control strategies which give adequate performance even in the absence of a detailed mathematical model of the plant being controlled.

14.2 Group method of data handling (GMDH)

The design of a successful control system depends on the ability to predict its response during the given operating conditions. This information can be either extracted from the differential equation describing the dynamics of the system or be extrapolated from its measured input-output response map. A comprehensive mathematical description is generally not available, so the approach based on system identification is relied upon.

The classical approach in the design of detection and classification has been to determine explicitly all the relevant characteristics of the process being observed and to use these measurements with a simplifying assumption in the design synthesis. Often the mathematical structure of the classifier is assumed and its design consists of calculating the best or even the appropriate structure and its coefficients from a representative data base.

The deterministic approach to complex plant modelling and control often fails because the dynamics of the sub-components and their inter-connection are not easily understood. The information available is not enough to construct differential equations for the system, so a different approach based on predictive polynomials is tried. The prediction polynomial is a regression equation which connects future values of all input and output variables. Regression analysis allows us to evaluate the coefficients of the polynomial by the criterion of mean square error. The polynomial description of a system determines its ability, performance and invariance, and can be used for synthesis of an optimal control system.

Polynomial description is determined in two ways.

1. From differential equations, by replacing the time derivatives by finite differences.

2. By performing regression analysis on the sampled input and output observation of the system.

The Group Method of Data Handling(GMDH) based on the principle of heuristic self-organization belongs to the second group. GMDH is intended for the solution of diverse interpolation problems of engineering cybernetics, such as identification of the static and dynamic characteristics of plants, pattern recognition, prediction of random processes and events, optimal control and storage of information etc. It was first presented by the Russian scientist A.G. IVAKHNENKO, since then a great deal of attention has been given to this method in and outside the U.S.S.R. A survey of its development and use can be found in Farlow(1980). It has found use in ecological modelling (Ivakhnenko and Koppa, 1971), real time estimation and control(Ikeda, 1976), materials modelling(Kokot and Patareu, 1980), wheat productivity(Khomovnenko and Kolomiets, 1980), and long range planning(Pokrass and Golubeva, 1980). Its utilisation has, however, been impeded by the heavy computational burden imposed, in spite of the simplification from the Kolmogorov-Gabor polynomial. It is considered a powerful approach to the identification of non-linear systems because it avoids the increasing computational load for determining the order and parameters in the identified models.

To make the ideas clear, suppose that the input consists of N observables X_1, X_2, X_3, ... X_N. Also suppose that the output may be considered as the estimate of some property of the input process. In general, Y will be some non-linear function of the X as follows,

$$Y(t) = f(x_1\ x_2\ , \ldots\ldots\ x_N)$$

The problem is to determine the unknown structure f(X_1, X_2, ... X_N) from the available past data. For a practical use the prediction algorithm should have simplicity, need a small amount of computation time, be well suited for real-time operation and be applicable to a small amount of available data. Let us assume that f(X_1, X_2, ... X_N) is represented by a polynomial of a certain order with respect to X_i. The Kolmogorov-Gabor polynomial for the stationary stochastic process provides a conceptual basis for (1).

$$Y = a_0 + \sum_{i=1}^{N} a_i \times x_i + \sum_{i=1}^{N}\sum_{j=1}^{N} a_ij \times x_i \times x_j + \sum_{i=1}^{N}\sum_{j=1}^{N}\sum_{k=1}^{N} a_{ijk} \times x_i \times x_j \times x_k$$

The Kolmogorov-Gabor polynomial requires a large amount of data together with computation of high-dimensional matrices to determine the large number of coefficients in (2). The GMDH provides us with an alternative to deal with matrices of large dimension, and makes it possible to solve complex problems when the data sequence is relatively small.

The GMDH can be realized by many algorithms which differ with respect to the construction of the complete description. The most commonly used is the multi-layered perceptron type structure shown in Figure 14.1. It uses partial polynomials of second order and self-sampling thresholds.

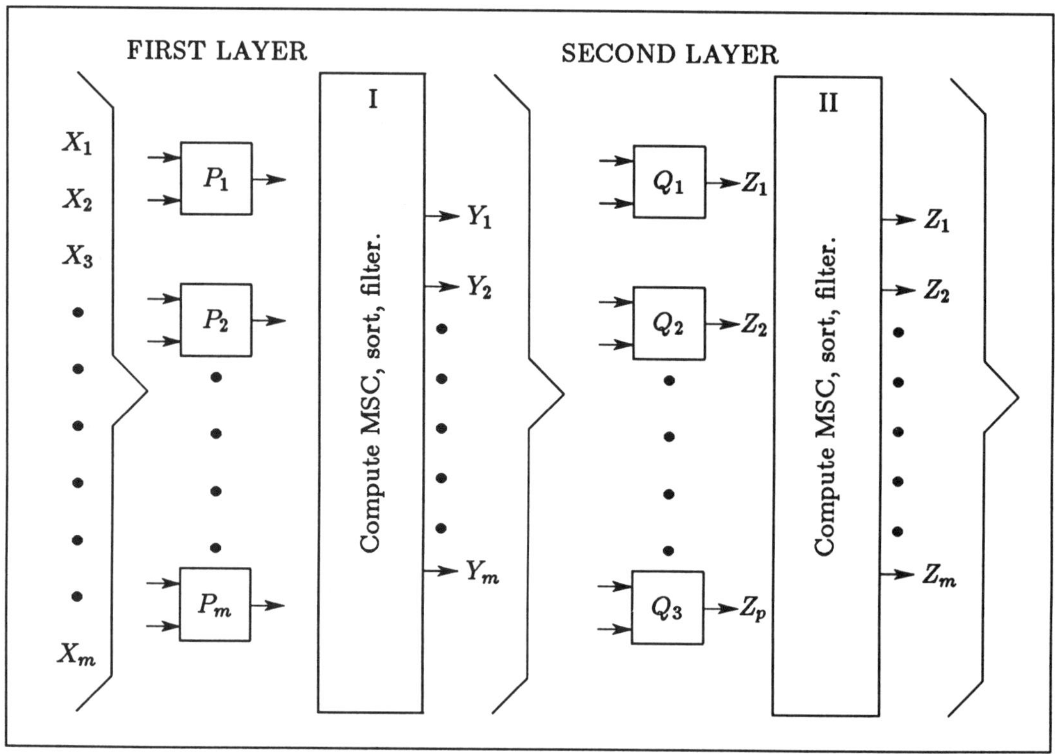

Figure 14.1: GMDH schematic

The basic steps in constructing a GMDH description of a process are as follows.

1. The original data is divided into training and checking sequences, the separation

rule being a very heuristic one. Usually the training and the checking sequences are taken alternately or on the basis of the magnitude of the variance from the mean value.

2. Quadratic polynomials are formed for all possible combinations of X_i variables taking two at a time.

EX: for 3 variables X_1, X_2, X_3, the following set of polynomials is formed

$$Y_1 = P1(x_1, x_2) = a_{10} + a_{11} \times x_1 + a_{12} \times x_2 + a_{13} \times x_1 \times x_1 + a_{14} \times x_2 \times x_2 + a_{15} \times x_1 \times x_2$$

$$Y_2 = P1(x_1, x_3) = a_{20} + a_{21} \times x_1 + a_{22} \times x_3 + a_{23} \times x_1 \times x_1 + a_{24} \times x_3 \times x_3 + a_{25} \times x_1 \times x_3$$

$$Y_3 = P1(x_2, x_3) = a_{30} + a_{31} \times x_2 + a_{32} \times x_3 + a_{33} \times x_2 \times x_2 + a_{34} \times x_3 \times x_3 + a_{35} \times x_2 \times x_3$$

3. For each polynomial a system of Normal Gaussian equations is constructed using all the data points in the training set. By solving these equations, the values of the intermediate variables Y_i are determined.

4. The models are used to predict the system response in the training set data region. The predictions are passed through some form of selection criteria, the most widely used being the mean square error(MSE).

$$MSE = \frac{1}{NC} \sum_{i=1}^{NC} [Y(t) - \hat{Y}(t)]^2$$

where $\hat{Y}(t)$ denotes the predicted value, and NC are the number of data points in the checking set.

5. The models Y_1, Y_2, Y_3, are ordered with respect to the smallest MSE. The models with MSE less then a specified threshold are allowed to pass to the next level of GMDH. The number of functions selected at this level is arbitrary.

6. At the next level the independent variables for the new training and checking sets are found by mapping the original training and checking sets through the single layer which has been formed.

7. New polynomials are formed according to step 2, and for each layer, steps 2 to 6 are repeated. As each new layer is formed, the smallest MSE is stored, and plotted

as a function of layer number. The procedure is terminated when the smallest overall MSE is reached at any level. The global minimum is the point of optimum complexity for this choice of network heuristics. The Ivakhnenko Polynomial is formed at this point by choosing the best element in the layer of optimum complexity.

14.2.1 Selection criteria

Since two different selection methods will rarely select the same group of functions, selection of variables is of prime importance in GMDH. The criteria should be able to take forward the best model in a manner so as not to lose any significant information. The mean square error has a significant weakness since it selects models which sometimes duplicate the information at the expense of discarding useful information. Some other criteria of interest are:

1. Regularity criteria

2. Minimum bias criteria

3. Balance of variable criteria

4. Residual criteria

14.2.2 GMDH and parallel processing

Different system identification methods with specific ranges of applicability have been invented but a common feature of all such methods is the fact that they are realized in the form of series computer programs which significantly increases the computer running time. GMDH offers wide possibilities of parallelism for the information processing operations required in the construction of its models.

In constructing the multilayer GMDH, all independent variables in one layer are combined, two at a time, to predict the local polynomial. These combinations can be considered as separate independent blocks performing the same task on different inputs. GMDH is ideally suited for an SIMD machine, but this approach requires design of specific hardware for the particular job. Therefore the transputer, which is a MIMD machine, was used, and in the authors opinion is capable of emulating the SIMD architecture without loss of any speed or efficiency. In a hardware realization it is important to isolate blocks, and to organize communication between these blocks in such a way that it is independent of the specific realization of these blocks. The transputer is a high performance single chip computer whose architecture facilitates the implementation of these blocks in the construction of a parallel processing system.

The GMDH algorithm could be made more efficient if an array of transputers is used, where each block is calculated by a different transputer, thus reducing the computer running time very significantly.

14.2.3 GMDH on transputers

In order to code the GMDH algorithm in Occam, the main algorithm is divided into a number of small processes. Each process is independent in itself and communicates with other processes by channels. If we have three independent variables in the first layer, three combinations result in estimating three local polynomials as shown in Figure 14.2, which are then processed further by the given selection criteria. In the second layer, another set of local polynomials is determined in a similar manner. In order to make the algorithm more efficient, an array of three transputers has been used as shown in Figure 14.3. The process to calculate the Ivakhnenko Polynomial, from the combination of two independent variables, is transmitted from the host to the three slave transputers and each one is provided with a different input. The three transputers perform their work simultaneously and calculate the required polynomials. These calculated values are transmitted back to the host and further calculations regarding the MSE are performed, prior to moving to the next layer of the GMDH algorithm. The flow diagram of the GMDH algorithm for four transputers is shown in Figure 14.4.

In each layer combinations of independent variables are used to form partial polynomials.

Example: For 3 variables

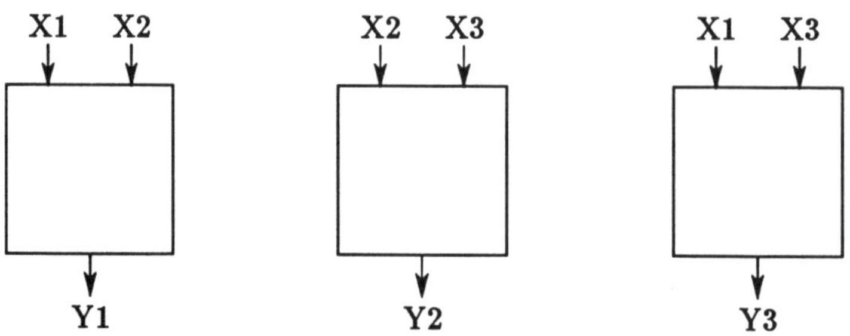

All combinations are independent and can be executed in parallel.

With an increase in the number of variables the time is reduced by (1/no. of combinations) as compared to sequential computing.

Figure 14.2: GMDH and parallelism

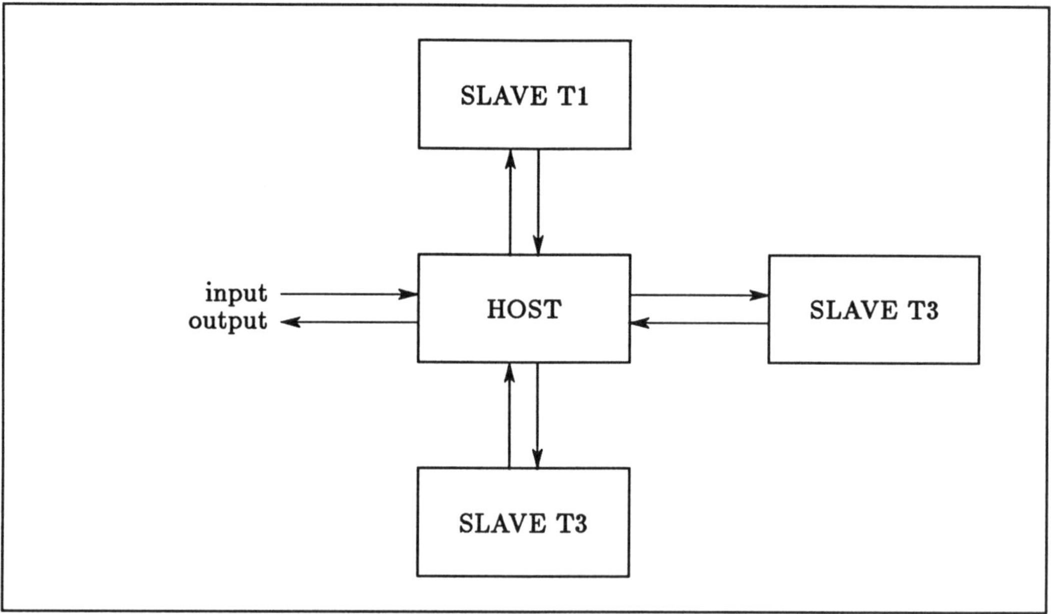

Figure 14.3: Transputer arrangement for 3 variables

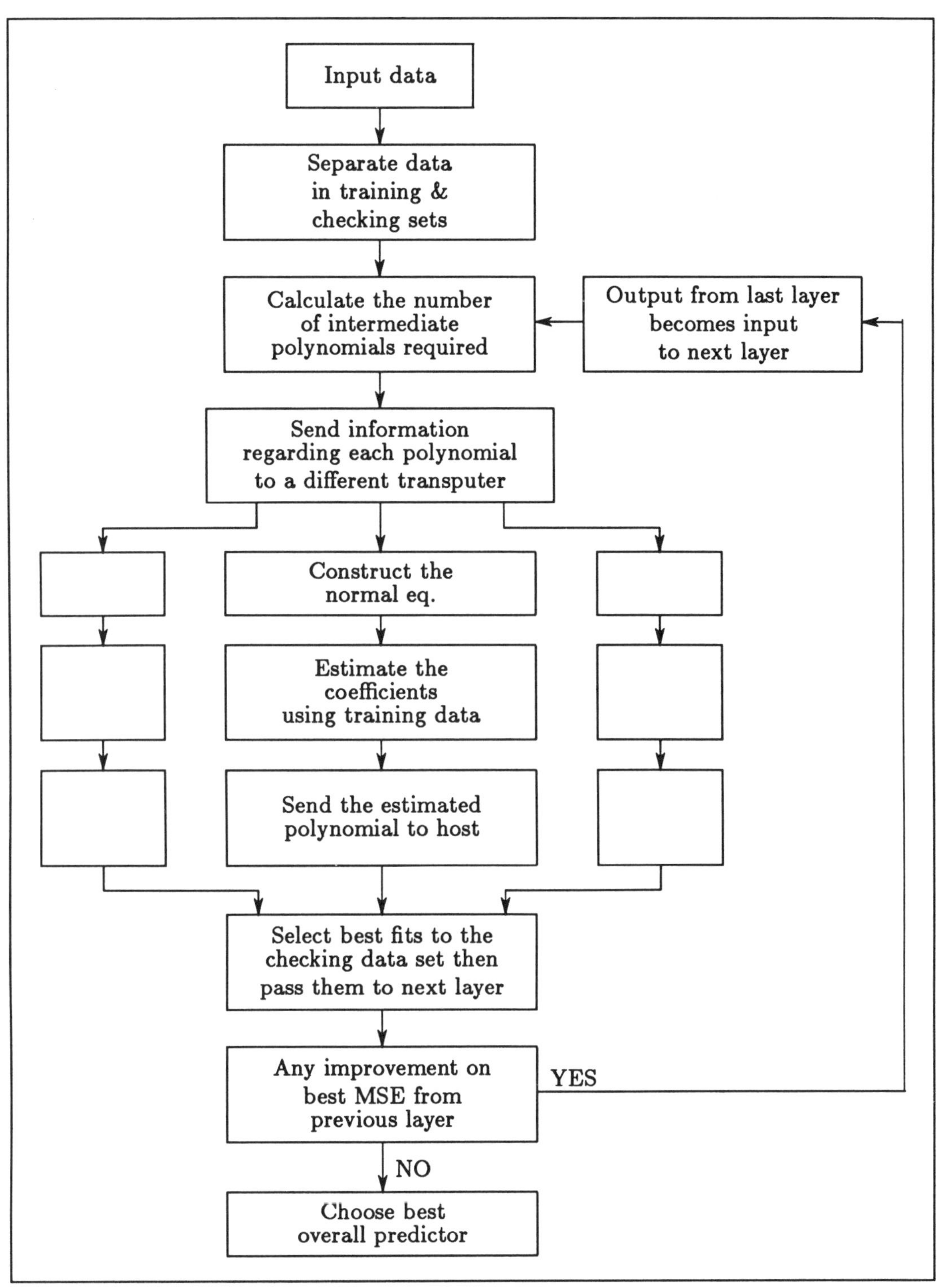

Figure 14.4: Flow diagram of GMDH algorithm on transputers

A benchmark data set was used to validate the technique. It consists of three independent variables, (X_1) radiation in relative gram calories, (X_2) average soil moisture tension and (X_3) air temperature in deg. The dependent variable is milligrams of vitamins B2 in turnip green. This data was first used to predict the Ivakhnenko Polynomial on one transputer and then on four transputers. It was noted that the time required by four transputers was about half the time required by one transputer. This difference in time increases with an increase in the number of independent variables.

This idea can be extended to any number of transputers depending upon the independent variables present in the data. For example four independent variables require six partial polynomials to be predicted and need seven transputers, similarly for five independent variables eleven transputers are required.

The technique has also been applied to the area of decision-making in medicine. This involves a decision rule applied to a patient's measurement vector to decide between possible diseases in a differential diagnosis leading to possible treatments. Two case studies have been undertaken using published data, one being concerned with the detection of the cardiac abnormality in patients with diabetes (Zola et al, 1986). The other study considered the effects of human growth hormones on the level of blood glucose, also in diabetic patients (Fatourechi, 1969). In both cases the number of points in the data sets were small, but the GMDH method was able to give good model fitting. Also, it was successful when used in a predictive mode, the full details being given in Hasnain and Linkens (1988).

The GMDH has a multi-layer structure and is self-organizing in style, and therefore has some similarities with neural networks. Recently, a comparison has been made between the performance of GMDH and the multi-layer perceptron neural network with a back-propagation algorithm, using the medical data sets referred to above. Both techniques have also been applied to a climatological problem involving the need for frost protection via predictive methods. The initially encouraging results will be described in the verbal presentation.

14.3 Self-organizing control

When the parameters and characteristics of a controlled plant are variable and depend on the magnitude of disturbances or other operating conditions in ways which are unknown or difficult to predict, the overall control system must be designed to have very low sensitivity to changes in operating conditions. A control system can be called "adaptive" if it achieves invariant control response throughout the operational envelope of the controlled vehicle. In common usage, however, the term "adaptive" is used for those systems which adjust themselves on-line to improve their behavior in terms of computed control performance indices.

The Bionics approach to adaptive control has emphasized development of self-organizing control (SOC) structures. The SOC can re-adapt many times within the closed-loop response period of the plant by modification of its internal signal pathways. The adaptive controller obtains information while the plant is operating and uses this acquired knowledge to improve system performance. This technique places minimum dependence on a priori modelling, requires no pretraining and possesses unique capabilities for control of plants having multiple response variables with strong interactions among the variables, especially the actuators.

The self-organizing controller (SOC), invented by BARRON (1968), is an evolutionary form of adaptive controller in which guided random search results are used to achieve flexibility and speed of adaption.

14.3.1 Elementary SOC and principle of operation

The key to SOC lies in the modification of internal signal paths by on-line changes in controller Probability State Variables (PSV). The SOC employing the PSV principle is shown in Figure 14.5 in its most elementary form. The controller portion consists of two elements, a Performance Assessment (PA) module and a PSV module. In essence, a PA module evaluates system performance on the basis of the error signal (e) and informs the PSV module through the binary reward/punishment (rp) signal of the results of the evaluation. The (rp) signal may be thought of as a "good/bad" comment of the PA module on the last incremental change (Δu) made by the PSV module in its output signal (U). The PSV module performs a self-evaluation by comparing the most recent Δu with (rp). As a result of this self-evaluation it either incrementally increases or decreases (as appropriate) the probability that the next Δu will have the same sense as the last one.

Through this iterative process of system performance measurement and self-evaluation, the SOC controls the plant in a manner which is ideally suited to plant dynamics characteristics. Although SOC systems cannot have an explicit "teacher" and must rely on self assessment of performance, empirical modelling can usually be guided by an explicit, stored data base with gauging of performance by means of a goodness-of-fit criterion.

14.3.2 High speed SOC for multiple goal/multiple actuator control

Plants having multiple-goals and multiple-actuators often exhibit an interdependence among goals. Thus, the operation of one of the actuators for control of one of the goals will result in a significant change in the remaining plant variables thereby requiring that

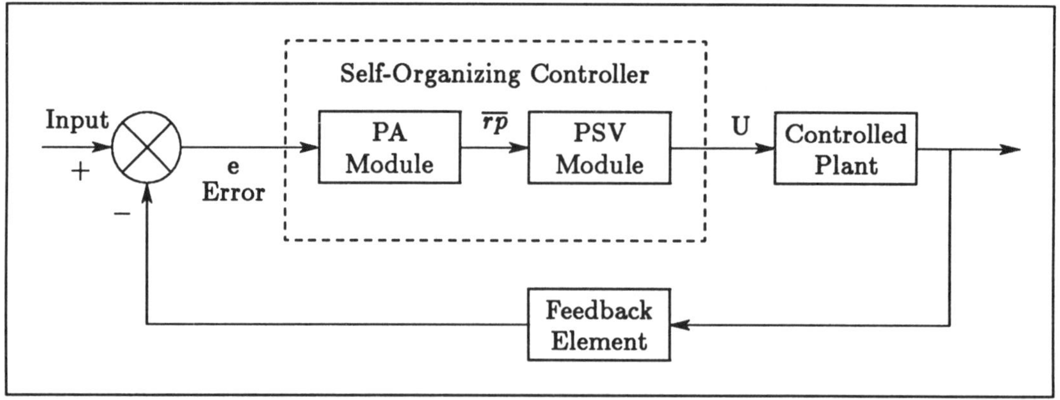

Figure 14.5: Elementary SOC

the system be capable of control despite the interdependence of the several goals and actuators in the plant. High speed SOC provides simultaneous, multiple-goal multiple-actuator control in which the instantaneous influence of each actuator or error signal is identified and a self-organizing controller compensates for changing the polarities of actuator, direct and cross-coupled effects (Barron, 1967).

A schematic diagram of the entire system using SOC is shown in Figure 14.6 where multiple command inputs X_{c1} ... X_{ck} from an external source, such as the stick of an aircraft, are all simultaneously fed to a summing point with measured response variables X_{mi} ... X_{mk} which are provided by the sensors, there normally being one sensor for testing the response of each of the variables or goals of the plant. The summing point provides a plurality of error signals e_1 ... e_k to a SOC system which provides the actuator excitation signals U_1 ... U_k based upon the evaluation of the system performance.

A SOC for a multiple-actuator system is shown in Figure 14.7. The controller includes a combination of performance assessment units PA_1 ... PA_k, there being one PA unit for each goal of the system and all working in parallel. All PA units synchronise to evaluate the performance relating to the variable with which each is associated. The output from each PA unit is fed into a combination of logic circuits AL_{ii} ... AL_{ji} ... AL_{ki}, each actuation logic circuit being composed of a coupling unit, a clock, and a PSV unit. For each PA unit the number of actuation logic units is equal to the number of actuators. All these actuation logic units work in parallel and the output signals U_i ... U_k are fed to the goal weighting logic (GWL) circuits GWL_1 .. GWL_k, there being one GWL unit for each actuator. The GWL circuits provides actuator excitation signals U_i ... U_k in response to signals applied, and thereby alter plant operation.

The complex arrangement of SOC with the large amount of logic presents a problem for sequential computing and simulation. The parallel arrangement inside the SOC, especially for multiple-goal multiple-actuator control can be realised via transputers, thereby

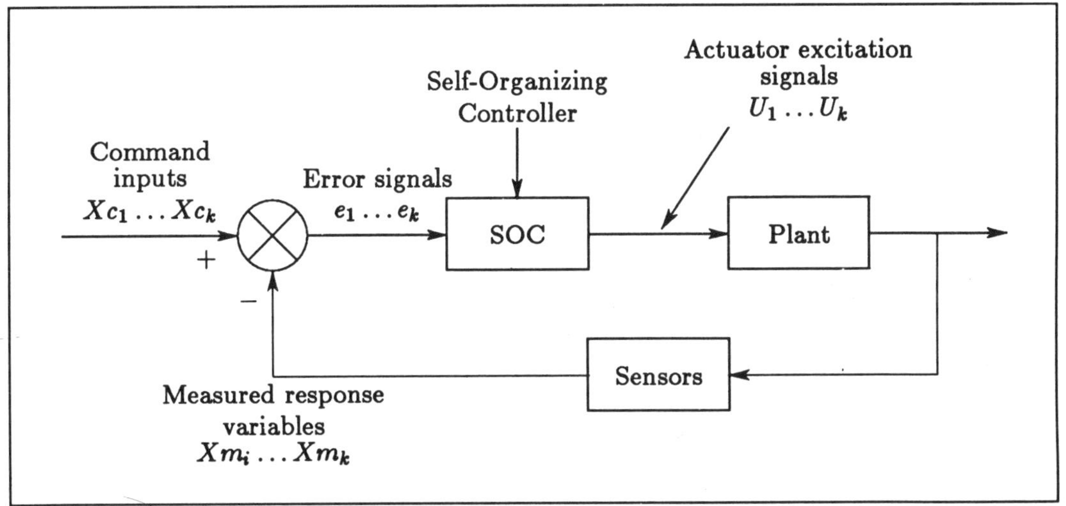

Figure 14.6: Multi-sensor SOC

enhancing the power and speed of control. The SOC is not suitable for a SIMD machine as the process to be controlled needs a separate processor for its simulation if efficiency is kept in mind. The algorithms were first developed and validated using Fortran on a main-frame computer. The process used for investigation was that of drug administration for muscle relaxation in operating theatres, for which a well-developed non-linear model was available. Figure 14.8a shows the response of the total system to a series of step commands, which is considered to be an adequate response in terms of speed and overshoot. The algorithms were recorded into Occam, as were the model equations, and the equivalent results are shown in Figure 14.8b, again representing good performance.

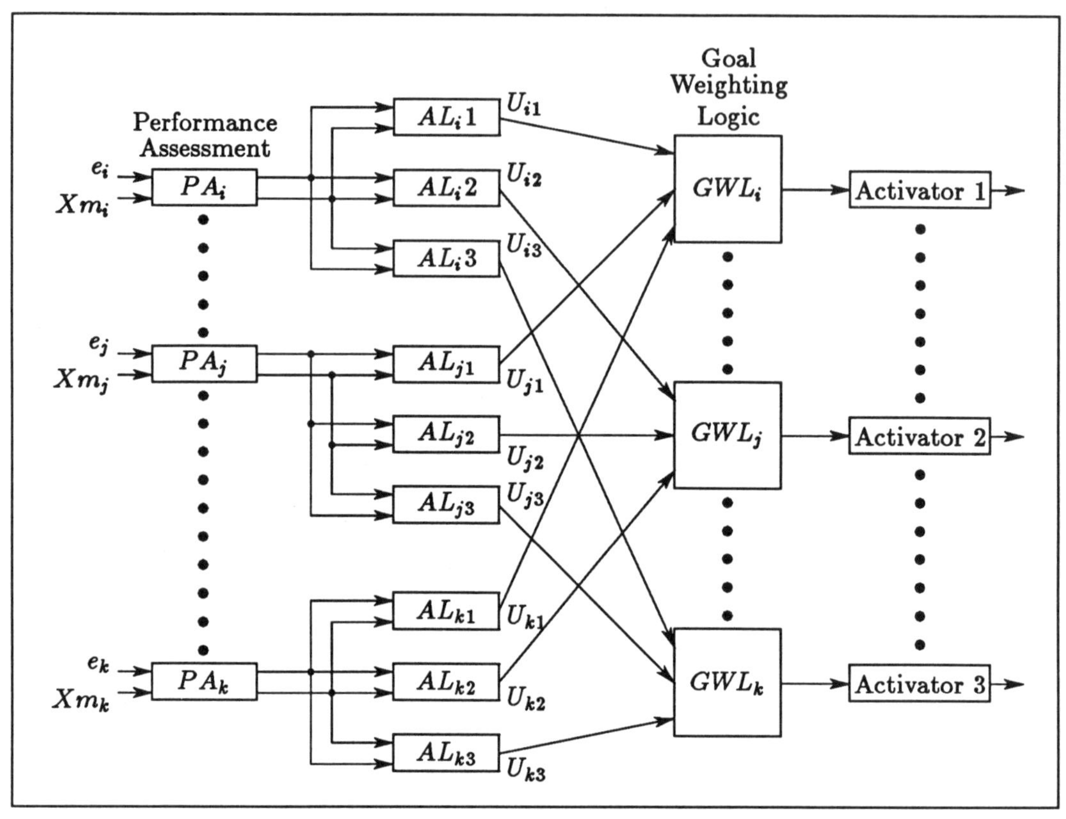

Figure 14.7: Multiple actuator ALU

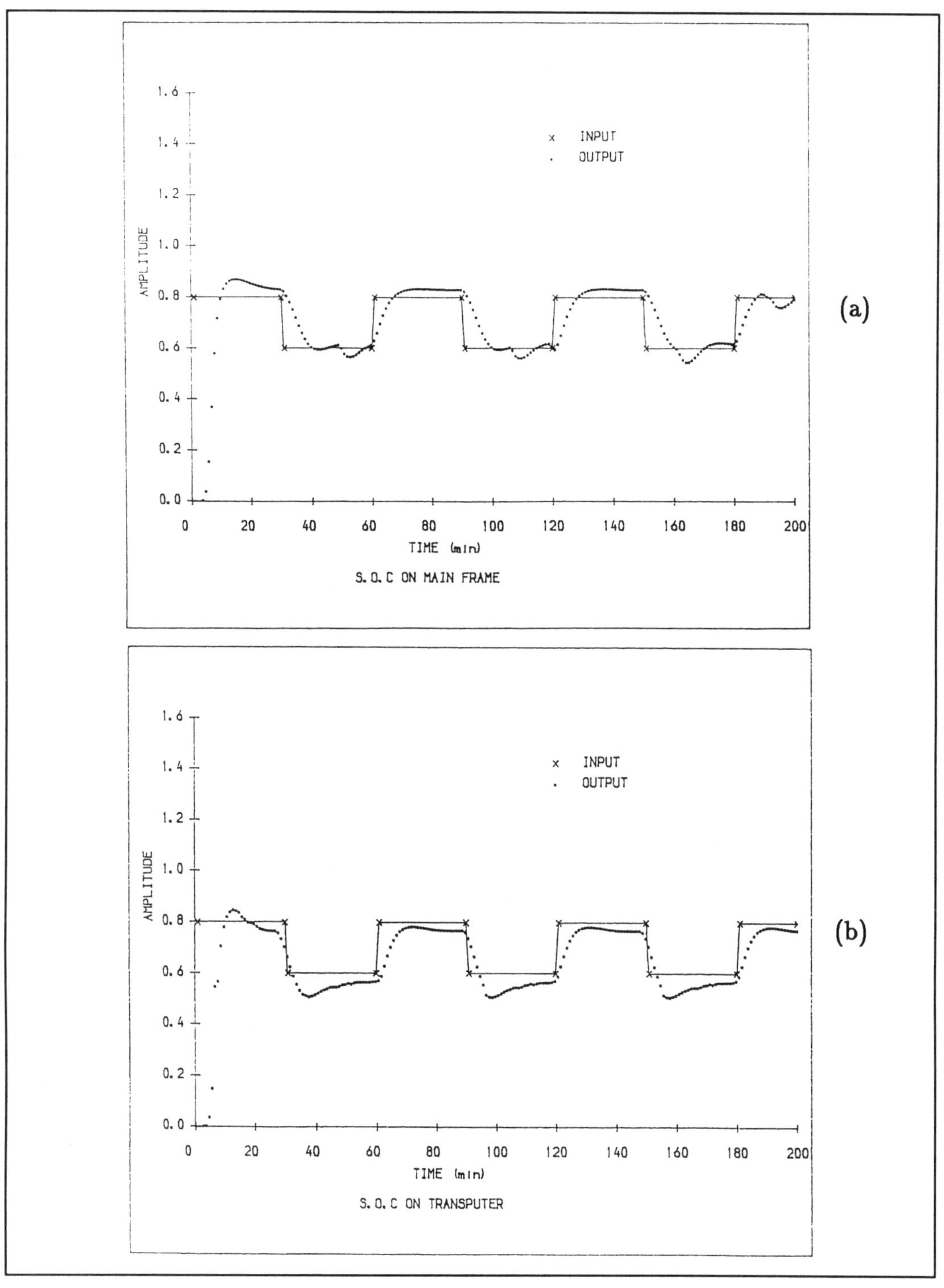

1.6
1.4
1.2
1.0
0.8
0.6
0.4
0.2
0.0
AMPLITUDE
x INPUT
. OUTPUT
0
20
40
60
80
100
120
140
160
180
200
TIME (min)
S.O.C ON MAIN FRAME
(a)
1.6
1.4
1.2
1.0
0.8
0.6
0.4
0.2
0.0
AMPLITUDE
x INPUT
. OUTPUT
0
20
40
60
80
100
120
140
160
180
200
TIME (min)
S.O.C ON TRANSPUTER
(b)

Figure 14.8:

14.3.3 Adaptive learning control

The Adaptive Learning Controller(ALC) is another form of SOC, being a very promising learning network that demonstrates problem solving capability. ALC consists of two neuron-like adaptive elements: Associative Search Element (ASE) and Adaptive Critic Element (ACE) (Barto et al, 1983). The most attractive features of the system are:

1. Knowledge of system dynamics, i.e. a mathematical model of the system, is not necessary in order to develop a control law. The controller learns to develop by association of input and output signals.

2. The system to be controlled can be time-varying and/or non-linear.

3. A wide class of measures of performance can be optimized.

4. A non-uniform sampling rate can be used.

5. The algorithms are naturally adaptive. They can be used to directly control the system or to optimize the performance of an existing control system.

The ASE operates by generating an output pattern, by receiving an evaluation from its environment in the form of scalar payoff or reinforcement, updating the contents of its memory, and then repeating this generate-and-test procedure. As this kind of learning proceeds, each input causes the retrieval of better choices for the pattern to be associated to that of the input. In order to discover what response lead to improvement in performance, ASE employs a trial and error, or generate-and-test search process. As shown in Figure 14.9, the state vector of the system is sampled and fed into a decoder, which transforms each state vector into a n-component binary vector, whose components are all zero except for a single one in the position corresponding to the state of system at that instant. This vector is provided as an input to the ASE, the adaptive element receives the signal through the reinforcement pathway and this information is used in the ASE.

The learning action needs to be more distinctive to ensure convergence that lead to least punishment in cases in which only punishment is available. An Adaptive Critic Element (ACE) is introduced to overcome this problem. Among other functions the ACE constructs predictions of reinforcement so that if punishment is less then its expected level then it acts as a reward. As shown in Figure 14.10 the ACE receives the externally supplied signal which it uses on the basis of the current vector, to compute an improved reinforced signal that it sends to the ACE. The central idea behind the ACE algorithm is that predictions are formed that predict not only reinforcement but also future predictions of reinforcement.

Considering a system such as an inverted pendulum the four-state vectors are divided

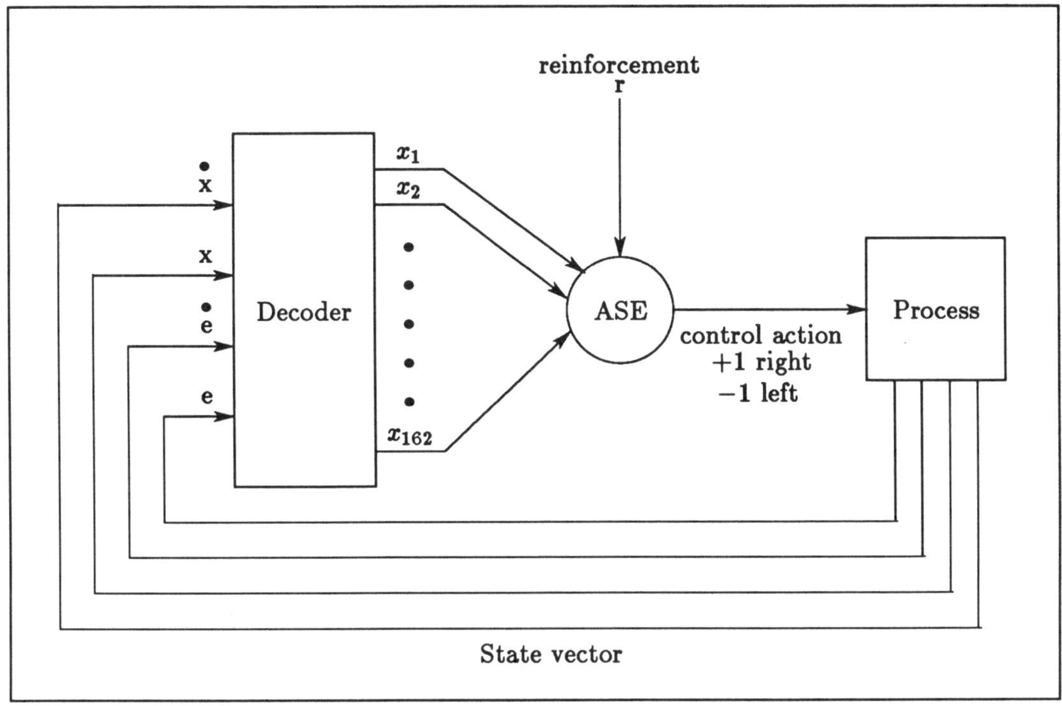

Figure 14.9: Block diagram for ASE

into 162-component binary vectors. As depicted from Figure 14.10 the ALC is quite complex and the computing time involved is enormous. In order to use the ALC for a control application, it must be fast enough to deal with the changing variables. Parallel computing seems a good solution to overcome the problems of logic operations and handling the number of component binary vectors which result at every sampling interval.

14.4 Fuzzy control

Many systems involving man-machine interaction are characterized by a high degree of performance but they cannot be analysed to a comparable degree of accuracy. The human involved is often an adequate controller because he is able to construct in his mind a model of the process which is just accurate enough to carry out the task in hand. This model includes all the essential features of the process required by him to do the job. The control engineer does not have the ability to extract the bare essentials from a process when he is replacing the human by an automatic controller. Considerable insight into such systems can be gained by modelling the method of human decision-making in these situations. The human is also capable of learning through experience which makes him less dependent on an accurate knowledge of his environment before he carries out a task.

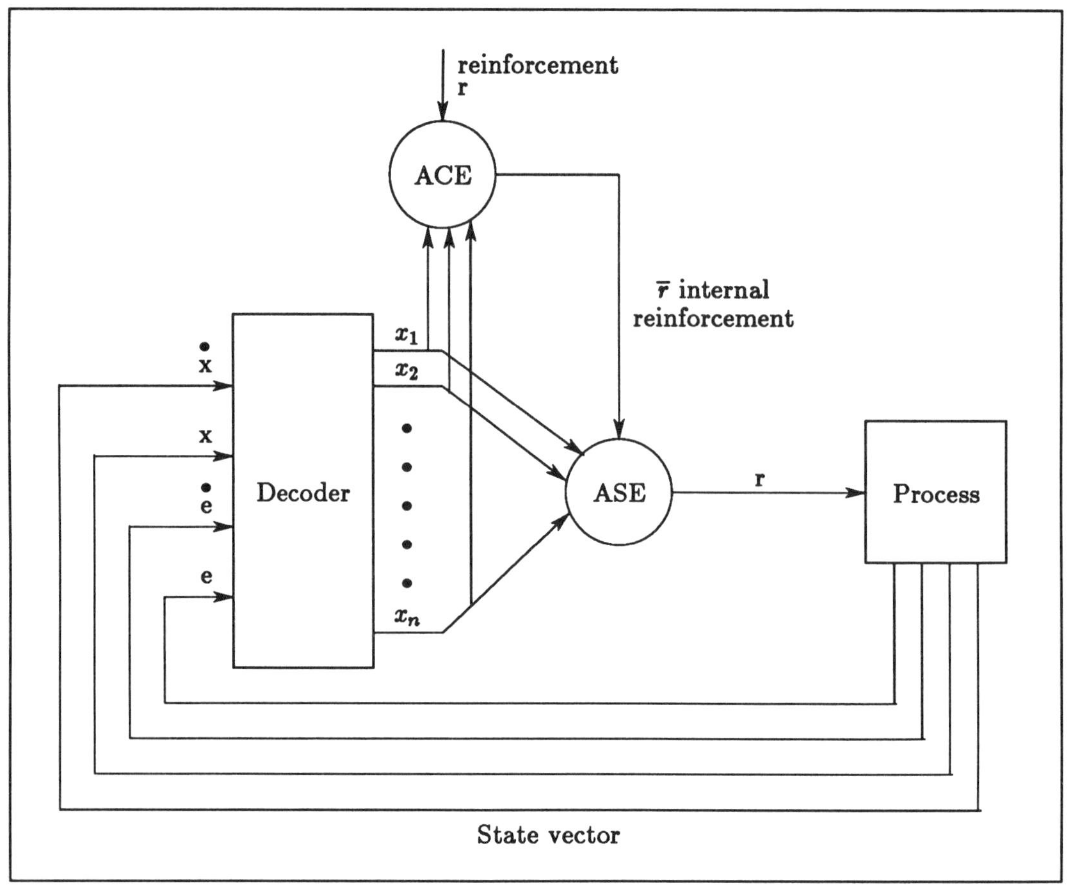

Figure 14.10: Block diagram for ALC

So, any attempt to automate the role of human being must, to some extent, model his powers of expression and reasoning as well as learning capabilities.

Zadeh's theory of Approximate Reasoning (AR) which models the human decision-making process is important when designing such controllers. The basis of the AR theory by Zadeh (1973, 1976) forms the theoretical starting point of fuzzy adaptive control.

14.4.1 A simple controller

A simple fuzzy controller described here is designed to regulate the output of a process around a given set-point. The output at regular intervals is sampled and sent to the controller. The controller Figure 14.11 shows the configuration in relation to a single-input/output process. In general there are two inputs and one output to the controller.

One of the inputs is the process error E, the other input CE is the change in error, obtained by subtracting the error at the last sampling instant from the present one. Movements toward the set point are positive changes in error, and movements away are negative change in error. The control action U is the change in input to be applied to the process.

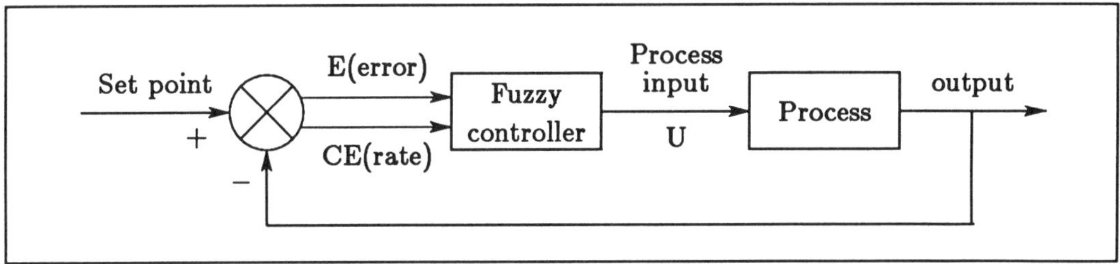

Figure 14.11: General configuration of fuzzy controller

The linguistic synthesis of the fuzzy controller relates the state variables, E and CE to the action variable U, by means of the linguistic protocol. This linguistic protocol consists of a set of fuzzy rules which define individual control situations to form a fuzzy conditional sentence or algorithm. A section of such an algorithm might be

If Error is ...

then If Change in Error is ...

then Output is...

Else

If Error is ...

then If Change in Error is ...

then Output is...

Each rule is a fuzzy conditional statement connecting the output to the input.

In the fuzzy controller the universe of discourse are discrete, thus membership vectors rather than membership functions are considered.

The variables are therefore defined by Fuzzy subsets in the following manner.

$$\begin{array}{llll} \textit{Error} & E & = (e,\ \mu_E(e)) & ,\ e \in E \\ \textit{Change in Error} & CE & = (c,\ \mu_{CE}(c)) & ,\ c \in CE \\ \textit{Change in Input} & U & = (u,\ \mu_U(u)) & ,\ u \in U \end{array}$$

Figure 14.12 shows the main components involved in the fuzzy control system. Error and its rate of change are first calculated and then converted into fuzzy variables after being scaled. Zadeh's rule of inference is used to infer the fuzzy output. The deterministic input is then calculated by defuzzifying the input.

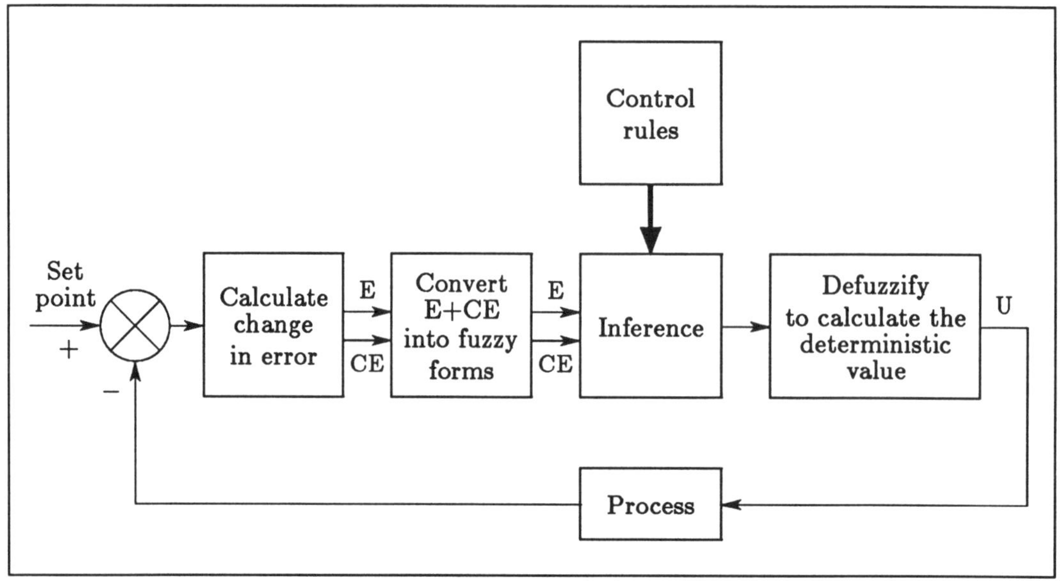

Figure 14.12: Block diagram of rule-based fuzzy controller

14.4.2 Fuzzy control in parallel

The fuzzy control of a process is quite complex as indicated by Figure 14.12. Fuzzification, defuzzification and scanning of the control rules to find the appropriate one makes the system very slow. Parallel processing presents a possible solution. In order to experiment with the transputer, an experimental process(muscle-relaxant drug model), the fuzzy control logic and the control rules were all coded in Occam and run on a single transputer. The results were encouraging, with considerable gain in speed. Trials showed that since the control rules are linguistic and Occam is not suitable for handling linguistic problems some alternative language should be used.

There are many problem-solving systems that are based on matching simple rules to given problems. They are often called rule-based expert systems, and sometimes they are called If-Then systems or situation-action systems or production-rule systems. Lisp is a powerful language to implement rule-based systems with great potential to handle linguistic rules and commands.

The available transputer Lisp system was originally written in 'C' language and capable of running on a single transputer. In order to implement it as an interactive system which can advise the control algorithm on other transputers it has to be linked with Occam.

The 'C' run-time library for the Transputer contains some extra functions to allow 'C' programs to send and receive messages across Occam channels. This allows 'C' programs to communicate with other concurrently executing processes. Some of the functions used are as follows, with only the arguments required by the functions being described here:

```
outword (w,chanp)
int w, * chanp;
```

(Output word w to channel pointed to by chanp)

```
outbyte (b,chanp)
char b;
int * chanp;
```

(Output byte b to channel pointed to by chanp)

```
inmess (chanp,buf,n bytes)
int * chanp, n bytes;
char buf [ ];
```

(Reads n bytes from channel pointed to by chanp into buf)

```
outmess (chanp,buf,n bytes)
int * chanp, n bytes;
char buf [ ];
```

(Write n bytes from buf to channel pointed to by chanp)

Inside the 'C' program, functions are called with the following parameters:

```
typedef int CHAN;
main(argc,argv,envp,in,inlen,out,outlen)
int argc,inlen,outlen;
char * argv [ ], * exp [ ] ;
char * in [ ], * out [ ] ;
```

Two different techniques are available to link 'C' language with Occam.

OPTION1: Using the alien filer Inside the TDS(Transputer Development System) 'C' is considered as an alien language. A facility is provided to compile and run the 'C' programs by using an Alien filer. 'C'programs are complied outside the TDS system and the Hex code is brought into the TDS environment by using the filing utilities. The Hex code is compiled in association with the other Occam processes. The main problem encountered using this technique was that all communication of any kind including the data files required by the Lisp, had to go through the communication functions between C and Occam and then outside the TDS enviornment. Another problem was that the Alien Compiler being a Beta1 release of INMOS had very limited library functions and other facilities as compared to the final release thus restricting its proper usage.

OPTION2: Using the 3L C A more recent and practical approach to link 'C' with Occam, or to run parallel 'C' programs on Transputers was presented by 3L Ltd. The following steps are required to achieve this objective:

1. The Occam program having all the communication functions is compiled using a stand alone compiler. The object file produced is then linked with the standard libraries used, to produce an executable file with an extention of (B4).

2. The 'C' program is compiled using the 3L compiler to produce an object file. In our case the Lisp interpreter consists of 23, 'C' modules, so each one had to be compiled separately to produce a (.BIN) object file.

3. Once a 'C' program is successfully compiled it must be linked with external functions like printf from the 'C' run time library. All the object codes are combined and linked to produce an executable file. The normal choice of extention for the executable file is(.B4).

4. The configurer is driven by a user-written configuration file which describes the system to be built. This file lists all the physical processors in the system, the wires connecting them, the tasks to be loaded into the system and their interconnections.

5. The Output from the configurer can be directly run using the afserver. The actual configuration of the transputer network attached to the PC must match the declaration of the configuration file.

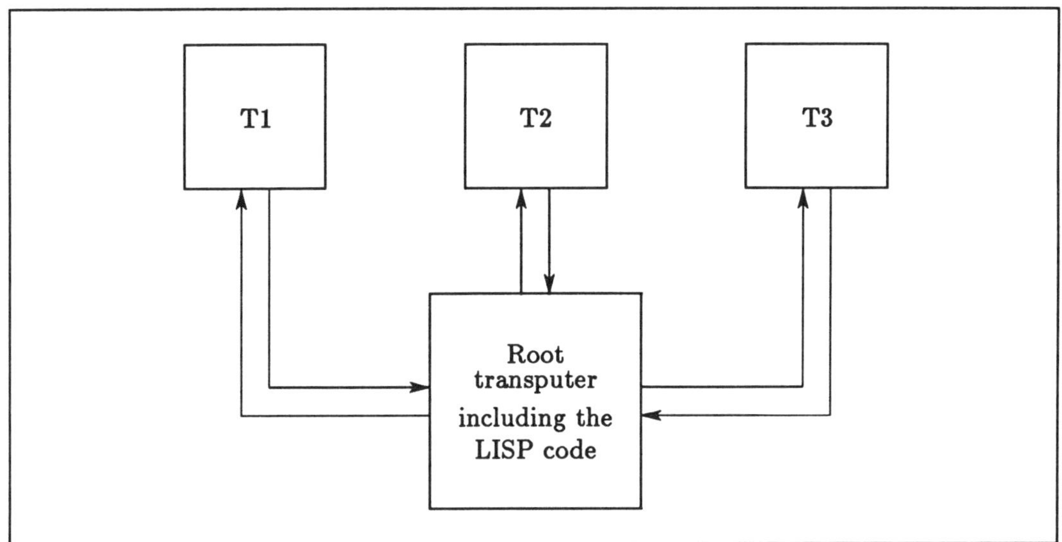

Figure 14.13: Transputer arrangement for fuzzy control

The major advantage of this second method using the 3L compiler is that external data files used by Lisp can be accessed directly, and no TDS is required in the whole operation. The configuration of the Lisp system when implemented is shown in Figure 14.13. The Lisp code containing the rules(knowledge) is loaded on the root transputer, and the process which is the muscle relaxant model(in this case) along with the fuzzy control algorithms is loaded on the slave transputers. Whenever a decision point is reached by any slave transputer it can gain advice from the Lisp system by communicating over the channels. An example of the Lisp-based fuzzy control applied to the muscle relaxant model is shown in Figure 14.14. The output response to a step command shows an adequate rise-time, but with some steady state offset which could be detrimental in certain cases.

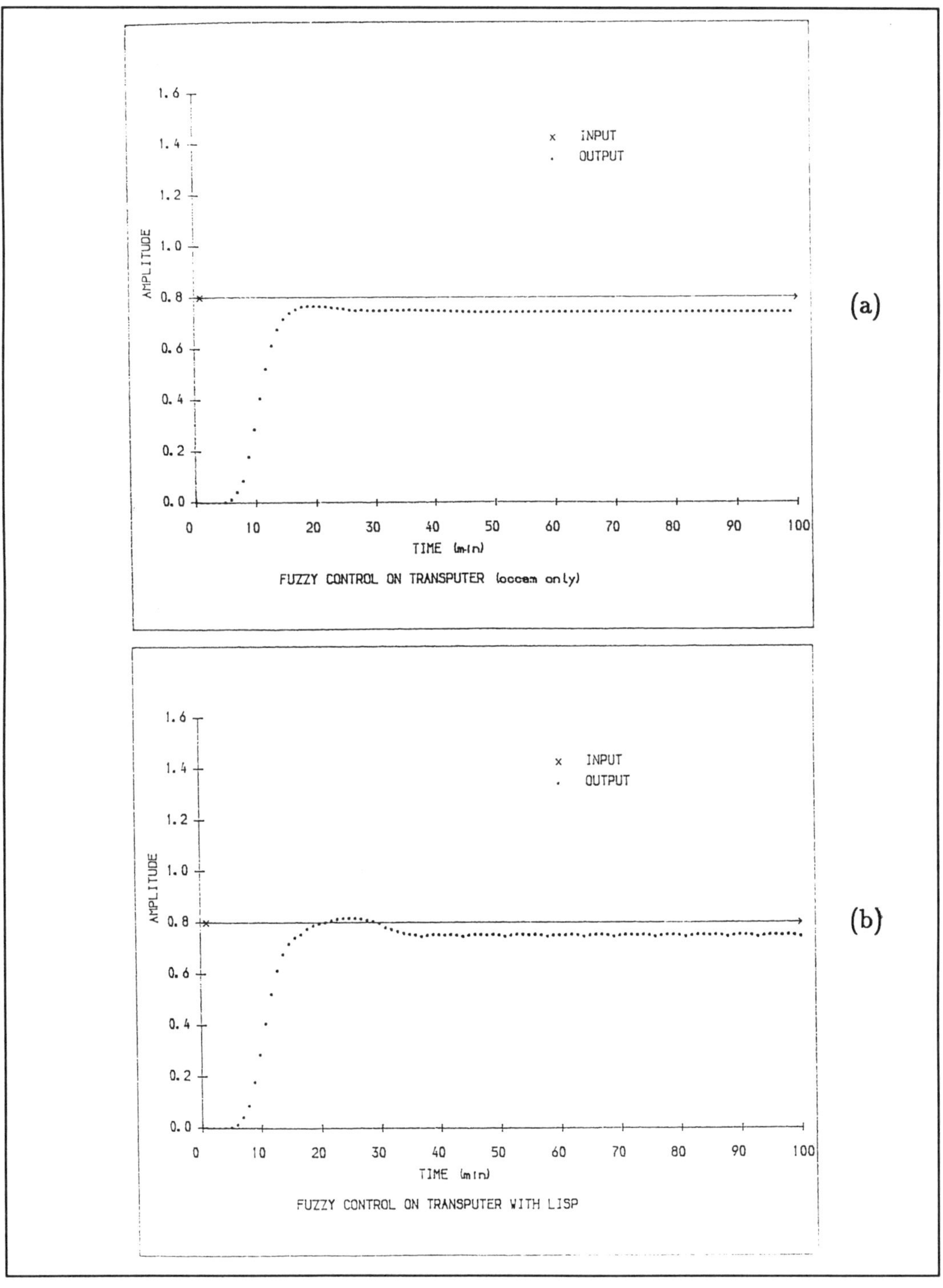
1.6
1.4
1.2
1.0
0.8
0.6
0.4
0.2
0.0
AMPLITUDE
x INPUT
. OUTPUT
0
10
20
30
40
50
60
70
80
90
100
TIME (min)
FUZZY CONTROL ON TRANSPUTER (occam only)
(a)
1.6
1.4
1.2
1.0
0.8
0.6
0.4
0.2
0.0
AMPLITUDE
x INPUT
. OUTPUT
0
10
20
30
40
50
60
70
80
90
100
TIME (min)
FUZZY CONTROL ON TRANSPUTER WITH LISP
(b)

Figure 14.14:

It is now possible to explore the concepts of self-organization to the fuzzy rule set used for control purposes. This is currently being investigated following the early work of Mamdani & Procyk, and the more recent research on satellite control by Gill and Daley.

14.5 Conclusions

Several methods of self-organizing control relating to system design have been described, and a common feature is that they are all very intensive computationally. To provide an acceptable speed of response for such algorithms the exploitation of inherent parallelism via transputer networks is possible. This has been implemented for each of the three self-organizing methods covered in this paper. The AI concepts involved in these approaches require both algorithmic and heuristic components. Thus, for the GMDH technique the heavy burden of arithmetic processing can easily be coded via Occam. Similarly, the multi-layer decision making is also easily accommodated. This is not, however, true when self-organizing fuzzy control is considered. In this case the heuristics necessary for automatic rule selection and rule modification are better coded in an AI language such as Lisp. The two types of approach have been implemented for transputers and results obtained for practical applications. Work is proceeding on linguistic self-learning and comparisons with neural network results.

14.6 References

Barron, R.L, 1967, 'Self-Organizing Control Systems for providing multiple-goal, multiple actuator control', US patent No. 3519, 998, Sept 29 1967.

Barron, R.L, 1968, 'Self-Organizing Control', Control Eng, Jan.

Barto, A.G, Sutton, R.S and Anderson, C.W, 1983, 'Neuron like adaptive elements that can solve difficult learning control problems', IEEE Trans on Systems, Man and Cybernetics, Vol SMC-13, No 5.

Draper, N.R, and Smith, H., 1966, 'Applied regression analysis', Wiley, NewYork.

Farlow, S.J., 1980, 'Self-organizing methods in modelling, GMDH type algorithms', Marcel Dekker Inc.

Fatourechi, V, Molner, G.D, Ackerman, E, Rosevear, J.W, Moxness, K.E, and Taylor, W.F., 1969, 'Growth hormone and glucose interrelationships in Diabetes :Studies with insulation infusion during continuous blood glucose analysis', Journal of Clinical Endocrinology and Metabolism, Vol.29, Pt.1.

Hasnain, S.B, Linkens, D.A., 1988, 'The use of transputer parallelism for the Group Method Of Data Handling (GMDH) self-organizing identification algorithm', in

'Parallel processing in control – the Transputers and other architectures', P. Peregrinus Ltd.

Ikeda S, Mikiko O., 1976, 'Sequential GMDH algorithm and its application to river flow prediction', IEEE Trans Systems, Man and Cybernetics, Vol. SMC-6.

Ivakhnenko, A, G, 1968, 'The group method of data handling – a rival of stochastic approximation', Soviet Automatic Control, Vol.13, No.3.

Ivakhnenko, A, G, and Koppa, Y.V., 1971, 'Mathematical simulation of complex ecological systems', Soviet Automatic Control, Vol 4.

Khomovnenko, M.G, and Kolomiets, N.G, 1980, 'Self-organization of a system of single partial models for predicting the wheat harvest', Soviet Automatic Control, Vol 13.

Kokot, V.S, Patareu, S.G., 1980, 'Processing of experimentally measured densities of metals Using GMDH', Soviet Automatic Control, Vol 13.

Pokrass, V.L, and Golubeva, L.V., 1980, 'Self-organization of a mathematical model for long range planning of the cost of coal mining', Soviet Automatic Control, Vol 13.

Zadeh, L.A, 1973, 'Outline of a new approach to the analysis of complex systems and decision processes', IEEE Trans Systems, Man and Cybernetics, SMC-1.

Zadeh, L.A, 1976, 'A fuzzy algorithmic approach to the definition of complex or imprecise concepts', Int Journal of Man-machine Studies, vol 8.

Zola, B, Khan, J.K, Juni, J.E, and Vinik, A.I., 1986, 'Abnormal Cardiac function in diabetic patients with autonomic neuropathy in the absence of ischemic heart disease'. Journal Of Clinical Endocrinology and Metabolism .Vol 63, No1.

Chapter 15

The suitability of transputer networks for various classes of algorithms

M. Korsloot
A.J. Klaassen
J.M. Mulder
Delft University of Technology
Dept. of Electrical Engineering
Section Computer Architecture
P.O.Box 5031, 2600 GA Delft, The Netherlands
duteca!mark@uunet.uu.net

Abstract A model predicting the speedup of applications with a certain order of computation and communication complexity has been developed. In this model it is assumed that the communication locality of an application is inverse proportional to the number of processors on which it is executed. A processor is modeled as consisting of a CPU, a fast memory, a slow memory, a communication memory, and 4 buses connecting these components. A set of four equations describes the traffic over these buses. Using these equations, it is possible to predict speedups and bus utilizations for different configurations and applications.

When applying this model to transputer networks, two network configurations are evaluated, one with a shared memory and with a distributed memory. In the shared memory configuration, the links are not used and the external memory is shared between the transputers. Then only a very modest number of transputers (typically 1 or 2) can be used for a maximum performance. In the distributed memory configuration the transputers are connected via their links. Then somewhere about linear speedup can be achieved as the applications become more complex, assuming they can be parallelized easily. An implementation of the Hopfield neural network supports this claim.

Although the model is far from realistic, as it lacks notions such as network topology and routing, it seems a good first order approximation of the behavior of communicating processor architectures.

15.1 Introduction

The development of a large number of different multiprocessor systems has led to a situation where it is hard to predict anything about the performance of those systems. Each system has its own architecture with its own peculiarities, and it is normally only optimally suited for a specific class of applications. Therefore the need has risen to evaluate the performance of the combination of a specific application and a specific multiprocessor system. In this paper, applications are classified according to their computational complexity. This complexity is expressed in terms of memory and I/O traffic, and thus related to memory bandwidth available. The advantage of this is that no measures of processor performance, such as instructions per second (MIPS) is required, which makes a quantitative comparison of different architectures possible. The computational complexity can therefore be referred to as bandwidth complexity. This classification of applications is more general than, for example, the model of Marsan and Gerla [2], which is based on statistical methods, or the model of Vrsalovic et al. [7], which is centered on iterative algorithms.

Using the classification of applications, it is possible to predict the performance of a specific class of applications, when the maximum bandwidth of a system is known or can be computed. In this paper, a computational model is developed for communicating process architectures. Then this model is applied to a transputer network, showing the performance of several configurations. Finally, using the computational model, an example application, a neural network implementation, is described in more detail, together with an evaluation of its performance.

15.2 Computational model

To find out whether or not processors are suitable for AI-applications (or any application at all), we have developed an abstract computational model. In this model, all quantities are translated to an amount of data (in this case bytes) and afterwards related to bandwidth (i.e. to bytes per second) by normalizing the amount of data for a given time period. This makes a quantitative comparison possible.

Furthermore, algorithms are divided according to their complexity. We discern four classes of algorithms: linear, $O(x)$, logarithmic, $O(x.log_2(x))$, quadratic, $O(x^2)$ and exponential, $O(2^x)$. To explain this better, refer to Figure 15.1. Assume that a process has b_{io}

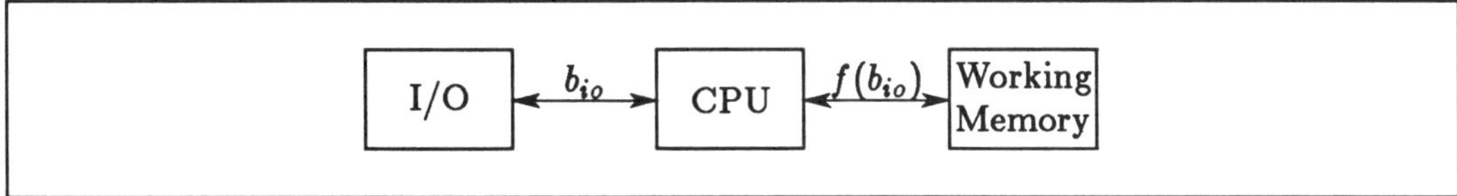

Figure 15.1: Abstract computational model.

bytes of input and output. These b_{io} bytes generate an amount of $f(b_{io})$ bytes of traffic between the processor and the working memory, where f is defined by the complexity of the algorithm. As an example, consider a simple sorting algorithm, where the sorting of x bytes takes in the order of $O(x^2)$ memory references. The exact function, of course, depends on the implementation, as both $4.x^2 + 3.x + 2$ and $x^2 - 8.x$ are of quadratic order.

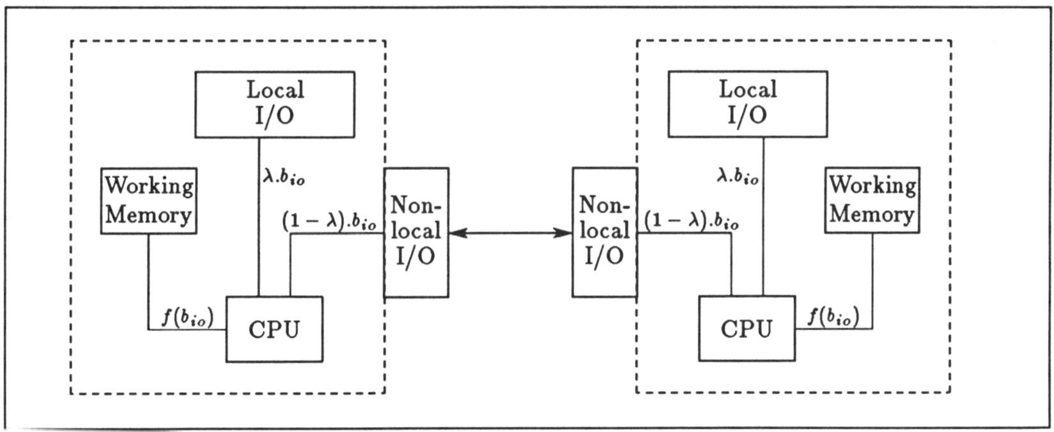

Figure 15.2: Abstract communicating process architecture.

$f(x)$	the process complexity function.
b_{io}	The amount of bytes processed.
b_{io}^N	The amount of bytes processed by each transputer in a N transputer network.
λ	The locality of I/O (ratio of local I/O references to the total number of I/O references).
h	Ratio of internal memory references to the total number of memory references.
N	The number of processors in the system.
L	The number of links of a transputer.
B_i	The bandwidth of bus i ($i = int$, ext or $link$).
B_i^{max}	The maximum bandwidth of bus i.
b_i	The amount of bytes transferred over bus i.
b_i^{max}	The maximum amount of bytes which can be transferred over bus i.
γ_i	Maximum utilization of memory i.
ρ_i	Effective utilization of bus i.
α^N	Speedup.

Table 15.1: Parameters of the model.

Now consider the more detailed version of the abstract computational model of Figure 15.2. This figure assumes two processors. Each processor consists of a CPU and working memory (as already shown in Figure 15.1). The I/O from Figure 15.1 is divided into local I/O and non-local I/O. Local I/O can be considered as I/O between multiple processes which are located on a single processor or references to that part of b_{io} that is located in the local memory. The quantity λ gives the fraction local I/O, compared to the total amount of I/O. Hence, the fraction of non-local I/O is (1-λ). For reasons of scalability and consistency, we assume that $\lambda.b_{io}$ bytes are transferred via local I/O to the working memory in all cases; however, this affects the situation for a single processor configuration adversely. For a single processor, the working memory can hold most or all data, comprising the local I/O, without the need for the extra traffic $\lambda.b_{io}$. It is important to remember this deviation from the optimum situation, as it will account for an anomaly in the model, as described later in this paper.

The local I/O only consumes local memory bandwidth of the processor. The local memory is usually a memory hierarchy, consisting of fast and slow memory. The ratio of fast memory references compared to the total number of references to local memory is defined to be h. Table 15.1 shows a list of all the model parameters.

Next, Figure 15.3 elaborates on the processor model of Figure 15.2. Four potential bottlenecks can be distinguished (the bus from the CPU to the internal bus is left out as it is not important for this model). The traffic on each of these buses can now be derived. bus I transfers $b_{io} + f(b_{io})$ bytes (the abstract computational model of Figure 15.1 imposes this). The amount $f(b_{io})$ always remains local, with a fraction $h.f(b_{io})$ over bus II and a fraction $(1 - h).f(b_{io})$ over bus III. The amount b_{io} is split into two parts. $\lambda.b_{io}$ remains local and $(1 - \lambda).b_{io}$ uses bus IV. The local traffic $\lambda.b_{io}$ is again split over buses II and III, according to the same ratio h. Together, this produces the following equations for the traffic on the buses:

I	$b_{io} + f(b_{io})$	(15.1)
II	$h.(\lambda.b_{io} + f(b_{io}))$	(15.2)
III	$(1 - h).(\lambda.b_{io} + f(b_{io}))$	(15.3)
IV	$(1 - \lambda).b_{io}$	(15.4)

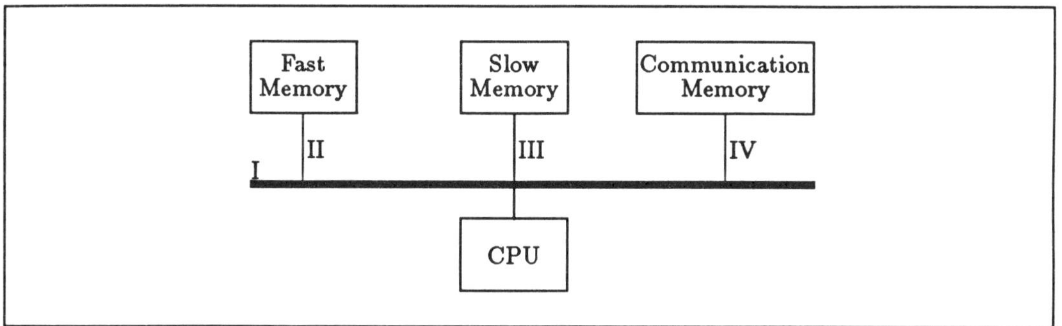

Figure 15.3: Abstract processor model.

15.3 Application of the computational model to transputers

Using the computational model of Section 15.2, it is possible to predict the performance of a transputer network. It is, however, important to note that the abstract processor model of Figure 15.3 does not completely match the transputer.

Table 15.2 shows the basic capacity measures of a transputer. For the prediction of the performance of transputer networks, mostly the maximum capacity measures are used in the computational model. A basic and important assumption is that each problem is perfectly scalable and that it is sufficiently large to keep all processors in an N-transputer

Transputer	T414-20	T800-30
Speed	10 MIPS	15 MIPS
Internal Mem.	2K bytes	4K bytes
	80 Mbytes/sec	80 Mbytes/sec
External Mem.	25 Mbytes/sec	25 Mbytes/sec
Links peak	20 Mbits/sec	20 Mbits/sec
sustained	0.8 Mbytes/sec	2.4 Mbytes/sec

Table 15.2: Basic figures of transputers.

network busy. When a problem is perfectly distributed over all nodes, we assume a uniform distribution of the chance of referencing an arbitrary node. From this it follows that $\lambda = 1/N$.

It is important for the mathematical soundness of the model to stress again the difference between bandwidth and number of bytes. If the memory bandwidth is B bytes/sec, then the number of bytes processed in a normalized time period equals b bytes.

The transputer contains three different forms of memory, each with a different bandwidth; the internal memory, the external memory and the communication memory. The term communication memory is used to be consistent with the other forms of memory. Of course there is no real "communication" memory, but the speed of the communication links can be expressed in bandwidth and thus also in bytes (again by normalizing for a given time period).

B_{int} is the bandwidth of the internal memory, B_{ext} of the external memory and B_{link} of the link memory. Their respective maxima (see Table 15.2) are $B_{int}^{max} = 80$M bytes/sec, $B_{ext}^{max} = 25$M bytes/sec and $B_{link}^{max} = 9.6$M bytes/sec (this is the bandwidth of all 4 links together). As it is not always desirable to use the maximum obtainable bandwidth of a bus (for example, to avoid queueing or bus congestion), we introduce a utilization factor for each bus, i.e. γ_{int}, γ_{ext}, and γ_{link}. Combining the bandwidth maxima with their respective utilizations gives the corresponding quantities, normalized for a given time period: b_{int}, b_{int}^{max}, b_{ext}, b_{ext}^{max}, b_{link}, and b_{link}^{max}. For example, the quantity b_{int}^{max} can be computed by normalizing the product $\gamma_{int}.B_{int}^{max}$ for a given time period.

In this paper, we treat two configurations. First the performance of a shared memory configuration is evaluated. As the links are not used, it is to be expected that this configuration is not ideal for transputer networks, as the design of transputers almost forces them to use their links. For completeness, however, this configuration will be evaluated though.

The second analyzed configuration is a distributed memory configuration, where each transputer has its own private memory, and communicates with other transputers over its links.

Shared memory configuration

Mapping the abstract model to a transputer network with a shared memory yields the following results. In fact this configuration is more an example of the model and its usage than a realistic application. In this configuration, the links are not used, the internal memory of the transputer serves as fast memory, and the external memory has the function of both slow memory and communication memory. Referring to Figure 15.3, this means that the external memory bus transfers the traffic of both buses III and IV.

To make it possible to use memory efficiently, without the use of extra buffers or the occurrence of queueing, a maximum utilization of $\gamma_{ext} = 0.6$ of the maximum memory bandwidth will be assumed.[1] For a configuration of N transputers, each transputer has only $1/N$-th of the external bandwidth available, compared to the situation where it is the only processor accessing the shared, external memory. This is, of course, a worst-case memory assumption, as a simple 4-way or 8-way (or even higher) interleaved memory will already increase the memory bandwidth considerably. Thus:

$$b^{max} = \frac{\gamma_{ext}.b_{ext}^{max}}{N} \tag{15.5}$$

Combining this with Equations 15.3 and 15.4 gives:

$$(1-h).f(b_{io}) + (1-\lambda.h).b_{io} = \frac{\gamma_{ext}.b_{ext}^{max}}{N} \tag{15.6}$$

For a transputer, the buses I and II of Figure 15.3 have an equal physical bandwidth. Therefore, the traffic on bus I is always the limiting factor, as the traffic on bus II is never higher than the traffic on bus I (h and $\lambda$are always ≤ 1). The maximum traffic on bus I (see Equation 15.1) is equal to b_{int}^{max}. Thus:

$$b_{int}^{max} = b_{io} + f(b_{io}) \tag{15.7}$$

Substituting the assumption $\lambda = 1/N$ and solving Equations 15.6 and 15.7 gives the optimum number of transputers which can efficiently use a shared memory.

Two cases have been investigated. In the first case, the maximum internal memory utilization of $\gamma_{int} = 1$ has been assumed, while the second case assumes $\gamma_{int} = 0.6$. This last value is a realistic value for a stack architecture, when only the data traffic is taken into account in relation to the total instruction and data traffic [3]. Table 15.3 shows the results for both cases, for several values of h. Within parentheses, the first decimal

[1] 0.6 is a typical γ used by memory system designers, assuming a Poisson arrival of memory requests.

of the computed optimum number is given. However, the optimum discrete number of transputers is always the integer part of the computed number. For $h = 0.75$ and $\gamma_{int} = 1$, the computed number was less than 1, which is, of course, impossible. From these results it is obvious that a shared memory configuration for a network of transputers is not very efficient, as was to be expected from the design of the transputer, which is centered on communication via its links.

	$\gamma_{int} = 1$				$\gamma_{int} = 0.6$		
$f(x)$	$h = 1.0$	$h = 0.9$	$h = 0.75$	$f(x)$	$h = 1.0$	$h = 0.9$	$h = 0.75$
x	1.(4)	1.(2)	1	x	1.(6)	1.(4)	1.(1)
$x.log_2(x)$	1.(9)	1.(3)	1	$x.log_2(x)$	2.(4)	1.(6)	1.(2)
x^2	2.(8)	1.(5)	1	x^2	3.(3)	1.(9)	1.(2)
2^x	3.(4)	1.(5)	1	2^x	3.(8)	2.(1)	1.(2)

Table 15.3: Optimum number of nodes for shared memory system.

Distributed memory configuration

Now another configuration is examined, where the links are used to interconnect the transputers. The internal memory serves as fast memory, the external memory serves as slow memory, and the links have the function of communication memory. Again, the traffic on buses I and II is equal, so only Equation 15.1 is taken into consideration. The maximum traffic on bus I is equal to the maximum internal memory traffic for a shared memory configuration. Thus:

$$\gamma_{int}.b_{int}^{max} = b_{io} + f(b_{io}) \tag{15.8}$$

The traffic on bus III is equal to the maximum external memory traffic (see Equation 15.3), which gives:

$$\gamma_{ext}.b_{ext}^{max} = (1 - h).(\lambda.b_{io} + f(b_{io})) \tag{15.9}$$

Using Equation 15.4 for the traffic over the links (bus IV) gives:

$$\gamma_{link}.b_{link}^{max} = (1 - \lambda).b_{io} \tag{15.10}$$

Because we strive for a maximum performance, the amount of bytes transferred b_{io} must be maximized. This will cause one bus to become the bottleneck (i.e. one will become saturated first). The process is then said to be ***bound*** by the saturated bus. For example, when the internal bus is the bottleneck, the process is called ***internal-bus bound***.

When one bus is saturated, the effective usage percentage of the other buses can be computed. These utilizations are called ρ_{int}, ρ_{ext}, and ρ_{link}, respectively. Note the difference with the utilizations γ, which define the maximum possible utilization of the memories, while the utilizations ρ define the effective bus utilizations. Again assuming that $\lambda = 1/N$ and that $\gamma_{int} = \gamma_{ext} = \gamma_{link} = 1$; and solving Equations 15.8, 15.9, and 15.10, the effective utilizations ρ can be computed. These values for γ assume that the maximum bandwidth is used for all buses. For γ_{link}, a more realistic value would be 0.6, due to synchronization overhead and the fact that the links are not used all of the time; for γ_{int} a value of 0.6 would be reasonable as well (to avoid queueing) and for external memory references, there is no limiting factor, so $\gamma_{ext} = 1$ is realistic (there will never occur any queueing at the external memory as it serves as local memory for a single transputer). However, the results for $\gamma_{int} = \gamma_{ext} = \gamma_{link} = 1$ are almost equal to the results for $\gamma_{int} = \gamma_{link} = 0.6$ and $\gamma_{ext} = 1$, so these latter results are not shown here. Given $h = 0.75$, it appears that the external bus will never be the bottleneck (i.e. ρ_{ext} is always ≤ 1). Table 15.4 shows the resulting utilizations, which shows that an increase in the process complexity will change a link-bound process (i.e. $\rho_{link} = 1$) to become an internal-bus-bound process (i.e. $\rho_{int} = 1$), which was to be expected.

ρ_{int}

N	1	2	3	4	5	6	7	8
x	1	0.48	0.36	0.32	0.30	0.29	0.28	0.27
$x.log_2(x)$	1	1	0.87	0.75	0.69	0.65	0.63	0.61
x^2	1	1	1	1	1	1	1	1
2^x	1	1	1	1	1	1	1	1

ρ_{ext}

N	1	2	3	4	5	6	7	8
x	0.80	0.29	0.19	0.16	0.14	0.13	0.13	0.12
$x.log_2(x)$	0.80	0.83	0.60	0.50	0.45	0.43	0.41	0.39
x^2	0.80	0.76	0.74	0.74	0.73	0.73	0.73	0.73
2^x	0.80	0.77	0.76	0.75	0.75	0.75	0.75	0.75

ρ_{link}

N	1	2	3	4	5	6	7	8
x	0.00	1	1	1	1	1	1	1
$x.log_2(x)$	0.00	0.83	1	1	1	1	1	1
x^2	0.00	0.44	0.59	0.66	0.70	0.73	0.76	0.77
2^x	0.00	0.32	0.43	0.48	0.52	0.54	0.55	0.57

Table 15.4: Bus utilizations for $h = 0.75$.

To compute the speedup, the basic notion b_{io} is not adequate, as it is dependent on the number of transputers. Therefore the new notion b_{io}^N is introduced, with N denoting the number of transputers. Suppose x bytes have to be processed. On one transputer, this takes x/b^1_{io} seconds. Given that a problem is perfectly scalable, each transputer has only x/N bytes to process. The time this takes, is $\frac{x/N}{b^N_{io}}$ seconds. The speedup α^N is then equal to:

$$\alpha^N = \frac{N.b^N_{io}}{b^1_{io}} \tag{15.11}$$

Table 15.5 gives the results for α^N, given $h = 0.75$ and $\lambda = 1/N$. This shows that for complex applications, a linear speedup can be expected, when the application can easily be parallelized, and the problem is of course sufficiently large (when implementing a 2×2 matrix multiplication on a network of 16 transputers, it is not realistic to expect a speedup of 16).

N	1	2	3	4	5	6	7	8
x	1	0.96	1.08	1.28	1.50	1.73	1.96	2.19
$x.log_2(x)$	1	2	2.70	3.20	3.75	4.32	4.90	5.49
x^2	1	2	3	4	5	6	7	8
2^x	1	2	3	4	5	6	7	8

Table 15.5: The speedup α^N for $h = 0.75$.

However, the assumption that $f(x) = x$ for a $O(x)$ process may be too simple a generalization. A somewhat more realistic assumption is $f(x) = C.x$. Table 15.6 shows the influence of the parameter C on the obtainable speedup for a linear complexity process. From these results, it appears that the assumption $C = 1$ is sufficient to get meaningful results. For more complex algorithms the internal bus already is saturated for a small value of C (look at the last two rows of Table 15.5), so the influence of C on such processes is negligible. Introducing the constant value C has only some influence for processes with a low complexity.

C	1	2	3	4	5	6	7	8
$N = 4$	1.28	1.92	2.56	3.20	3.84	4	4	4
$N = 8$	2.19	3.29	4.39	5.49	6.58	7.68	8	8

Table 15.6: The speedup α^N as a function of C, for $f(x) = C.x$ and $h = 0.75$.

Next the influence of various parameters on the speedup can be shown. Since it is to be expected that transputers with more than 4 links will become available soon,[2] a new parameter L is introduced, indicating the number of links. Two cases will be treated.

[2]The new T810 is said to have 6 links and an increased on-chip memory.

The first case demonstrates the influence of h, γ_{int}, γ_{ext}, and γ_{link}. The second case demonstrates the influence of the number of links L on the speedup obtainable for the least complex function $f(x) = C.x$.

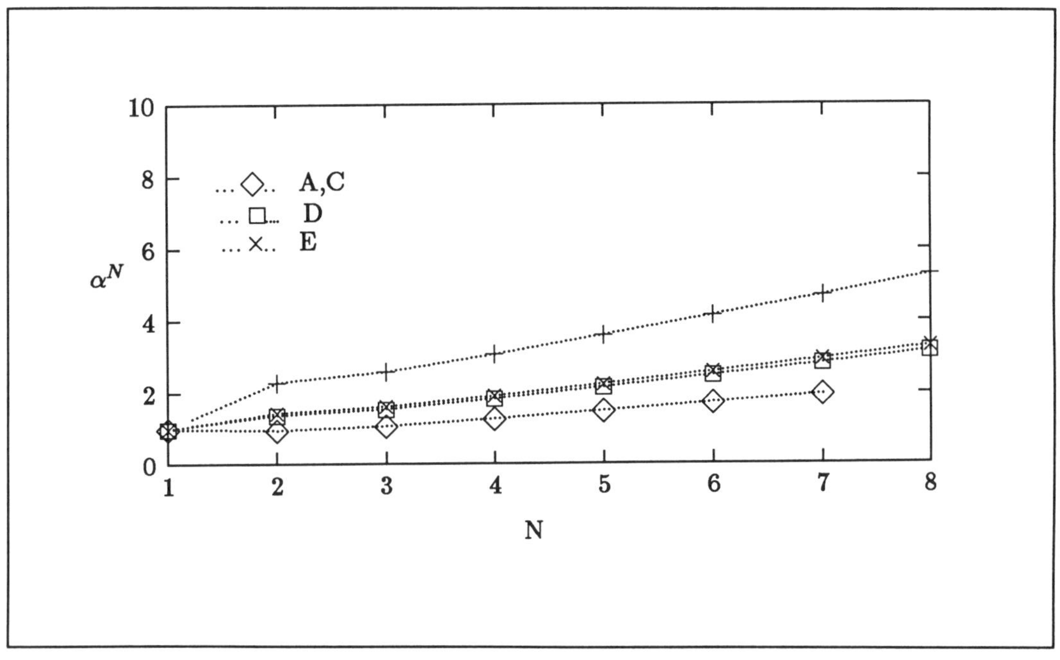

Figure 15.4: α^N as function of N for $f(x) = x$.

Figures 15.4 and 15.5 show the influence of h, γ_{int}, γ_{ext}, and γ_{link}. Figure 15.4 shows the situation for $f(x) = x$ and Figure 15.5 for $f(x) = x.log_2(x)$. They show α^N as function of N for the following 5 situations (γ_{ext} is always 1):

	h	γ_{int}	γ_{link}	L
A	0.75	1	1	4
B	0.25	1	1	4
C	0.75	0.6	0.6	4
D	0.25	0.6	0.6	4
E	0.75	0.6	0.6	6

The influence of the various parameters on the speedup is rather small. Special attention must be paid to the situation where h decreases, since then the model sometimes predicts a superlinear speedup. For example, when h decreases from 0.75 to 0.25 (say from situation A to B), then the external memory bus becomes saturated first, instead of the internal memory bus. Given that $\lambda = 1/N$ and that $\gamma_{ext}.b_{ext}^{max}$ = constant, Equation 15.9

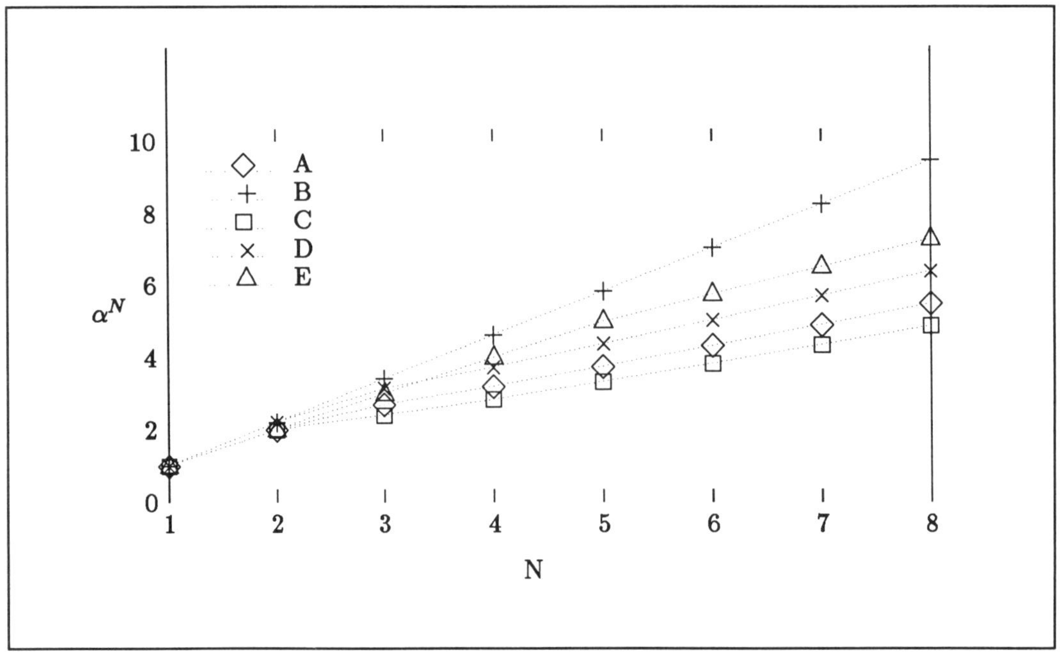

Figure 15.5: α^N as function of N for $f(x) = x.log_2(x)$.

becomes:

$$(1-h)(\frac{b_{io}^N}{N} + f(b_{io}^N)) = constant \tag{15.12}$$

This implies that $b_{io}^N > b_{io}^1$. Together with Equation 15.11, this means a superlinear speedup. In Figure 15.6 one can see the influence of L on the speedup for linear processes ($f(x) = x$). In this figure the speedup α^N is shown as function of C, with L and N as parameters. Increasing L causes a larger speedup when the same complexity remain constant.

15.4 Implementation of neural networks

Neural networks are mathematical models which inherently possess a large degree of parallelism and can be implemented in parallel easily. They are based on the hardware of the human brain which is massively parallel by nature. It however remains doubtful whether or not transputers are a good means for parallel neural network implementations. The processing bandwidth of processing elements of a neural network (which are called neurons) is modest compared to the communication bandwidth required. On the other hand, the processing power of a transputer is high, compared to its communication bandwidth. It is therefore questionable if the communication system of the transputer is

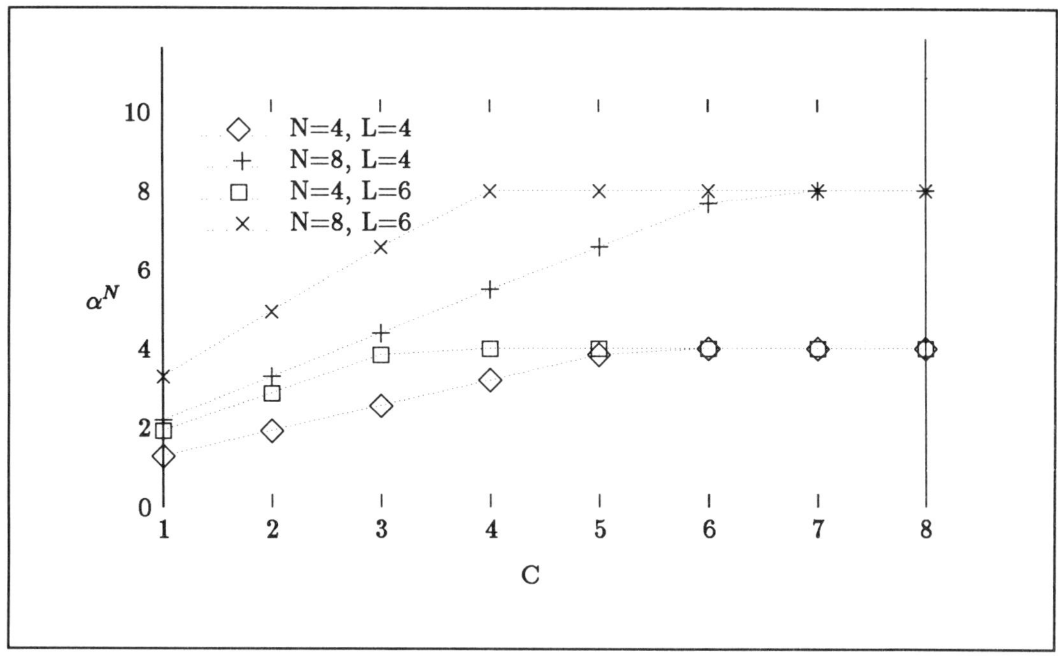

Figure 15.6: α^N as function of C, for various L and N.

always fast enough to keep the processor going. Furthermore, when the weights have to be updated synchronously, communication takes more time and thus further limits the obtainable speedup.[3] The way of implementation is of importance as well: parallel implementation of a Hopfield net at London University [5] only caused slowdown, compared to a single transputer implementation, whereas a parallel implementation at Delft University causes an almost linear speedup up to 4 transputers[4] [6]. This implementation was performed on a PC plug-in board, containing 4 transputers (each with 1M bytes of memory) and a crossbar switch [1]. On this board, which is designed at Delft University, a parallel dialect of C is being used [4]. This language is an extension of ANSI-C and contains several constructions that support explicit parallelism. Its main features are the inclusion of a *channel* data type, and the keywords *par* and *alt* for the creation and selection of parallel processes.

To determine the complexity of this application, the basic algorithm must be analyzed. The implementation of the Hopfield net is centered round a matrix-vector multiplication, where the matrix contains all the weights and the vector contains the states of all the neurons. On a parallel implementation with N transputers, each transputer has to perform $1/N$-th of the multiplication.

[3]Our implementation uses asynchronous updates.

[4]At the moment only 4 transputers are available. Therefore results are only measured up to $N = 4$.

```
for  (i = 0; i < x; i++)
   { for (j = sum = 0; j < x; j++)
       sum += weight_ji * vector_j;
     if (sum > 0) vector_i = 1;
     else vector_i = -1;
   }
```

Figure 15.7: Pseudo-code for Hopfield net implementation.

Suppose the Hopfield net consists of x neurons, the states of which are contained in the elements $vector_i$ of a vector, then each multiplication is of the form:

$$vector_i = f\left(\sum_{j=1}^{x} weight_{ij}.vector_j \right) \tag{15.13}$$

with $$f(x) = \begin{cases} 1 & \text{if } x > 0 \\ -1 & \text{otherwise} \end{cases}$$

Translating this formula to pseudo-code produces the program as given in Figure 15.7. In this program the variables i, j, x and sum can always be held in internal memory, together with the vector elements.[5] Since only the x neuron states belong to the I/O-stream, b_{io} equals x.

[5] A vector of length x implies a matrix of x^2 elements (of 4 bytes each). As the external memories of the transputer used can only contain 1M bytes each, x can never exceed 500. The vector, containing 500 elements of 4 bytes, can be put into the internal memory of 2K bytes.

	predicted speedup	measured speedup
N	α	α
2	2.00	1.88
3	2.99	2.69
4	3.53	3.59

Table 15.7: Predicted and measured speedups.

Now an estimation of $f(b_{io})$ can be deduced, using Figure 15.7. Both loop-variables i and j are loaded and stored once for both the inner and the outer loop. The variable x is only loaded once for both the inner and the outer loop. This sums up to $(2.2+2.1).x = 6.x$ references. The variable *sum* is loaded and stored once during the inner loop, giving $2x^2$ references. *Sum* is also loaded once per outer loop, giving x references. Furthermore, the matrix elements are all loaded once per inner loop, summing up to x^2 references and stored once in the outer loop, giving x references. Finally, the vector elements are loaded once during the inner loop, summing up to x^2 refences, and stored once in the outer loop, giving x references. This gives for $f(b_{io})$:

$$f(b_{io}) = 6x + 2x^2 + x + x^2 + x^2 + x = 4x^2 + 8x \tag{15.14}$$

Also a value for h can be estimated. Since only the x^2 references to the matrix elements are references to external memory the following formula holds:

$$h = \frac{3x^2 + 8x}{4x^2 + 8x} \approx 0.75 \tag{15.15}$$

With these values for $f(x)$ and h the values for the obtainable speedup α^N can be predicted. When $\gamma_{int} = \gamma_{ext} = \gamma_{link} = 1$, the process is of such complexity that the speedup is always linear. When $\gamma_{int} = \gamma_{link} = 0.6$ and $\gamma_{ext} = 1$, the speedup remains linear for $N = 2$, then it becomes external bus bound for $N = 3$ (i.e. $\rho_{ext} = 1$) and finally it becomes link bound for $N = 4$ (i.e. $\rho_{link} = 1$). The predicted speedups α^N can be seen in Table 15.7. It appears that they are in accordance with measured values for α^N.

15.5 Conclusions

It appears that the idea to translate all quantities into bandwidth makes a quantitative comparison possible. This idea provides a good insight in the ratio between the communication bandwidth and the processing bandwidth, required for efficient implementation of different classes of parallel algorithms.

For problems with a relatively low complexity, the communication bandwidth of a transputer is not high enough, so this class of problems is link bound and will achieve less than a linear speedup. For more complex functions, the situation is better. A solution is to increase the number of links to 6 or 8, and/or to choose those kind of algorithms which have a high complexity and a high locality (i.e. λ high). Increasing the number of links to 6 gives for simple, linear algorithms an increased speedup, compared to the situation for 4 links. The increase in speedup is a factor 1.5, unless the process becomes internal bus bound ($\rho_{int} = 1$), in which case the speedup becomes linear.

Although a superlinear speedup can be achieved for a low value of h, this is not a realistic situation. It is caused by the fact that the performance for a single transputer system with a low value of h is rather poor. By introducing more transputers, the total performance is, of course, increased, but it is still at a much lower level than for higher values of h.

Future research

The model as presented in this paper is, of course, only an approximation of reality. At the moment, several effects are not included in the model. One of them is the topology of the network. Another one is the process-switch latency, which is caused by the fact that several processes exist on a single transputer.

The model assumes a full connectivity between all transputers. This assumption, however, only holds for networks of up to four transputers (each transputer has only four links). Therefore several of the earlier derived results are, in fact, only accurate up to four transputers.

When more than four transputers are used, overhead will arise, because virtually, the full interconnectivity is still assumed. The overhead can be divided into two parts, hop packets and routing activity. Hop packets are packets which are transported between connected transputers but which are not intended for the receiving transputer. This transputer then has to transport the hop packet to another transputer, eventually reaching its destination. The extra link traffic which is introduced by these hop packets can be modeled via γ_{link}. When hop packets are transported over the links, the effective link bandwidth for each transputer decreases. The exact decrease of this bandwidth, of course, depends on the number of hop packets, which in turn is dependent on the topology of the interconnection network, the number of transputers and the locality λ of each process. At the moment, we are developing a model for different topologies which takes the overhead of these hop packets into account.

The routing of hop packets has its effect on the internal bandwidth. Packets have to be transferred from and to the links over the internal bus, while the CPU has to determine which link to use to reach the eventual destination. Thus the effective internal bandwidth decreases, which can be modeled by decreasing γ_{int}. Again, the exact decrease depends on the number of hop packets (and the complexity of the routing algorithm).

The overhead, caused by process switches, can be modeled with γ_{int} as well. When a process switch takes place, the process context has to be saved, and retrieved later, thus consuming part of the internal bandwidth. Also, the CPU is busy part of the time, determining which process to schedule next, so it cannot execute a user process in the meantime. In the transputer, however, this scheduling is done in microcode, which is much more efficient than if the scheduling would be performed by an operating system. How much the internal bandwidth is affected depends on the rate of the process switches.

Concluding, this abstract computational model is valuable in evaluating the performance of different processor configurations. However, it is yet only an approximation to reality and further work is being undertaken to produce still better comparisons.

15.6 References

[1] P. Knoppers et al. Transputer network with flexible topology. *Microprocessing and Microprogramming*, 24:275–280, September 1988.

[2] M.A. Marsan and M. Gerla. Markov models for multiple bus multiprocessor systems. *IEEE Transactions on Computers*, C-31(3):239–248, March 1982.

[3] C.L. Mitchell. *Processor Architecture and Cache Performance.* PhD thesis, Computer Systems Laboratory, Department of Electrical Engineering and Computer Science, Stanford University, Stanford, July 1986.

[4] Parsec Developments, Leiden, the Netherlands. *Par.C System Manual*, September 1988.

[5] A.B. Smith. A parallel PDP network simulator. In *Proc. of the IEEE Conference on Neural Networks*, pages 377–384, 1987. Vol.3.

[6] R. van Ni

[7] D.F. Vrsalovic, D.P. Siewiorek and others. Performance Prediction and Calibration for a Class of Multiprocessors. ieeetc, pages 1353–1365, November 1988. Vol. C-37.